Shojo Beat

DAYTIME SHOOTING STAR

Story & Art by
Mika Yamamori

CONTENTS

STORY THUS FAR

Suzume Yosano is a second-year in high school. Born in the country, she grew up living a free and easy life. Due to family circumstances, she was forced to transfer to a school in Tokyo. Lost on her first day in the city, she is found by a man who later turns out to be her homeroom teacher, Mr. Shishio. Suzume gradually develops feelings for him.

For a while, the pair appear to be inseparable, but their romance comes to a swift end when Shishio unexpectedly breaks up with Suzume. Shishio may have acted out of love, but his decision leaves Suzume heartbroken and hopeless—that is, until her friends help her get back on her feet. Finally able to put her days with Shishio behind her, Suzume finds the courage to move forward.

Throughout all of this, Suzume's friend Mamura has remained by her side—despite being shot down by Suzume when he confessed his love to her. Suzume believes there's no way Mamura is still interested in her. But Mamura proves her wrong, telling her, "That isn't true."

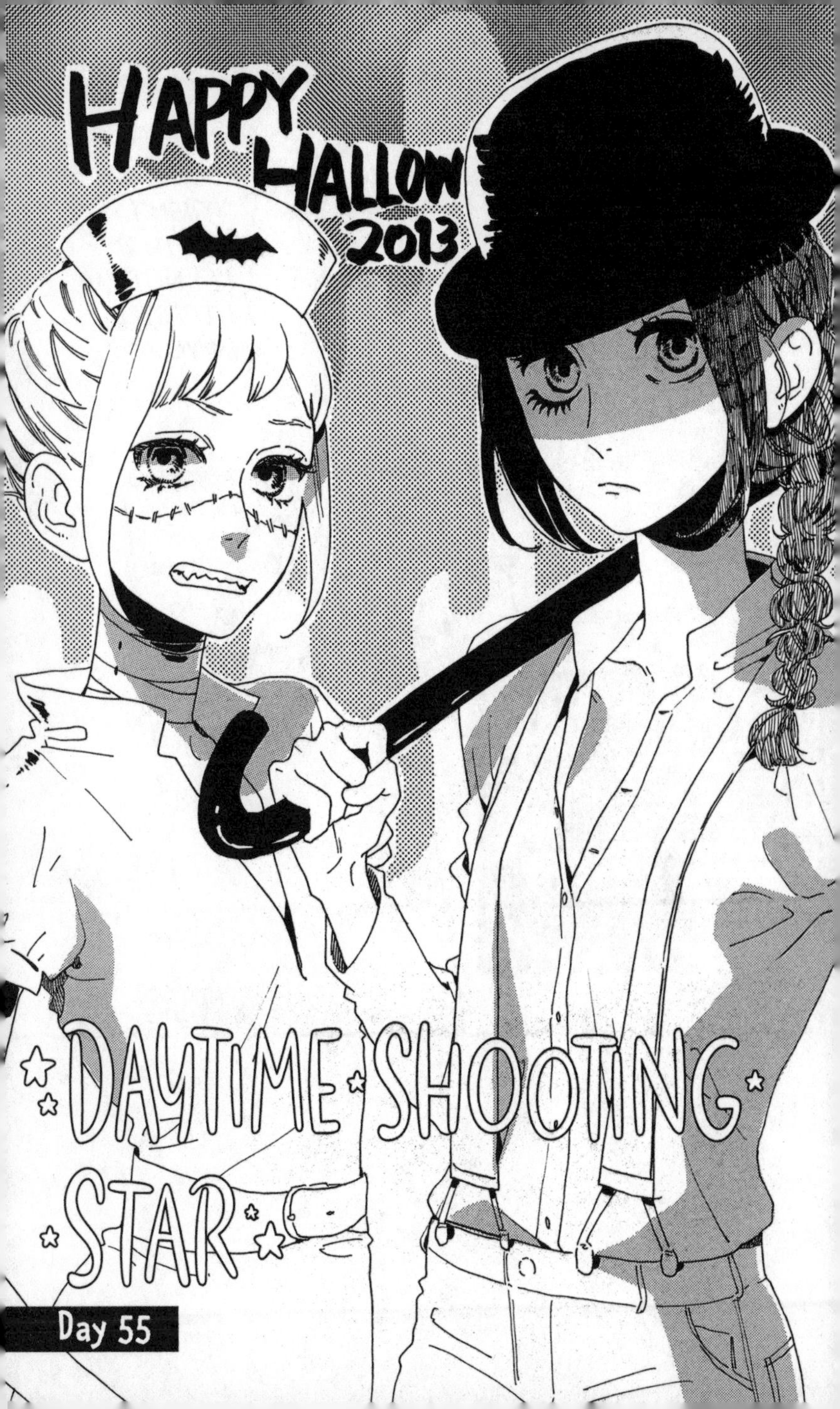
HAPPY HALLOW 2013
DAYTIME SHOOTING STAR
Day 55

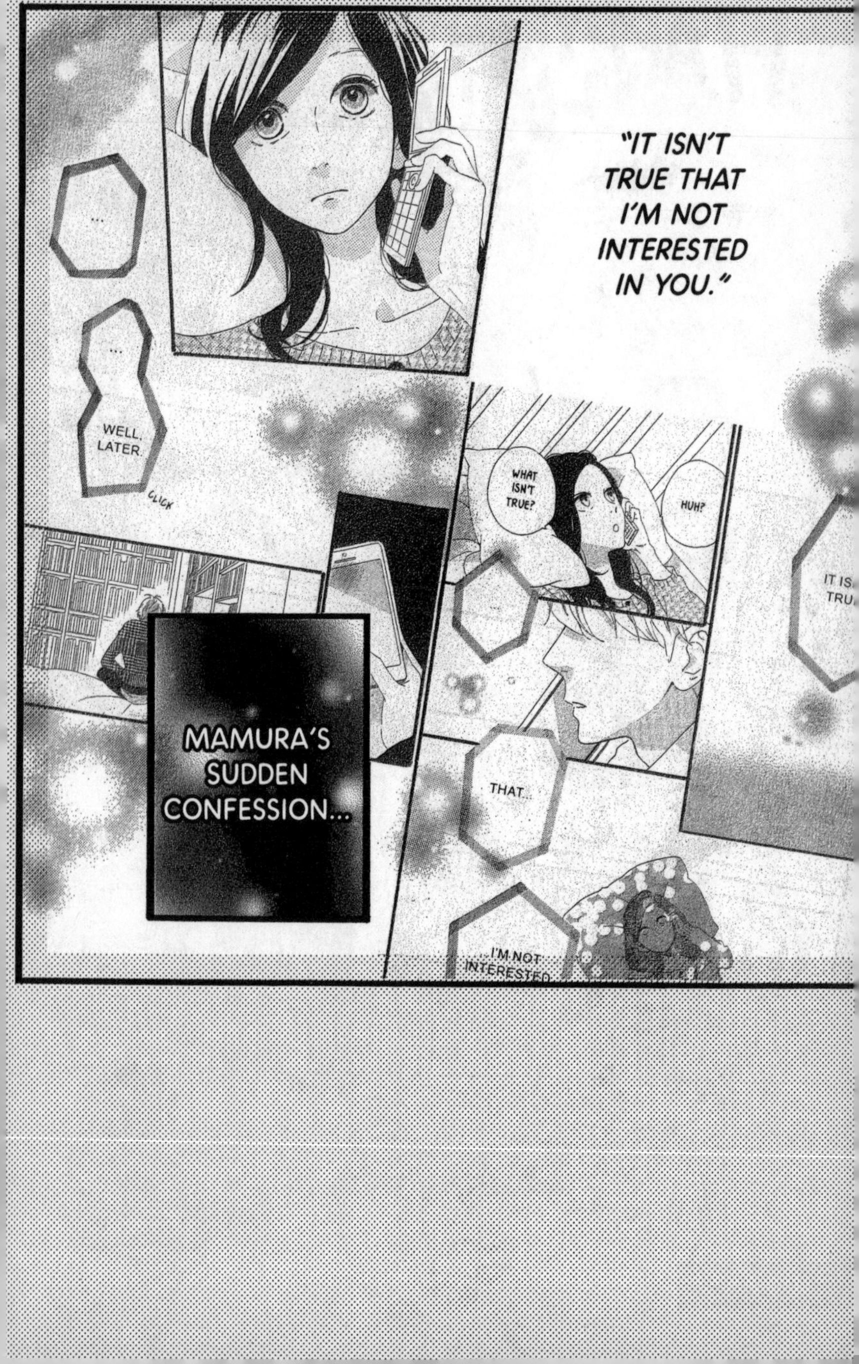

"IT ISN'T TRUE THAT I'M NOT INTERESTED IN YOU."
...
...
WELL, LATER.
CLICK
IT IS TRU
HUH?
WHAT ISN'T TRUE?
THAT...
I'M NOT INTERESTED
MAMURA'S SUDDEN CONFESSION...

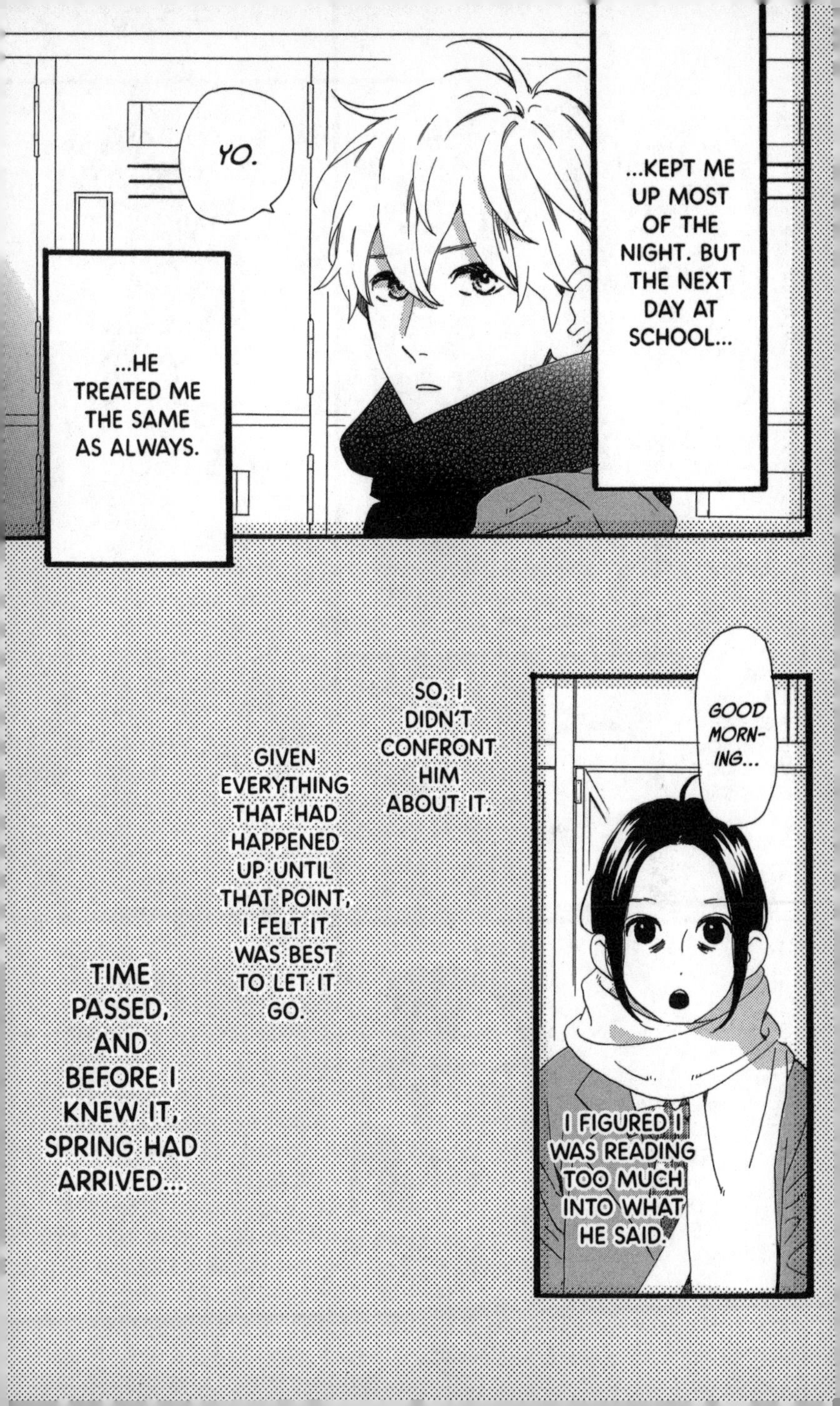
...KEPT ME UP MOST OF THE NIGHT. BUT THE NEXT DAY AT SCHOOL...
YO.
...HE TREATED ME THE SAME AS ALWAYS.
GOOD MORN-ING...
I FIGURED I WAS READING TOO MUCH INTO WHAT HE SAID.
SO, I DIDN'T CONFRONT HIM ABOUT IT.
GIVEN EVERYTHING THAT HAD HAPPENED UP UNTIL THAT POINT, I FELT IT WAS BEST TO LET IT GO.
TIME PASSED, AND BEFORE I KNEW IT, SPRING HAD ARRIVED...

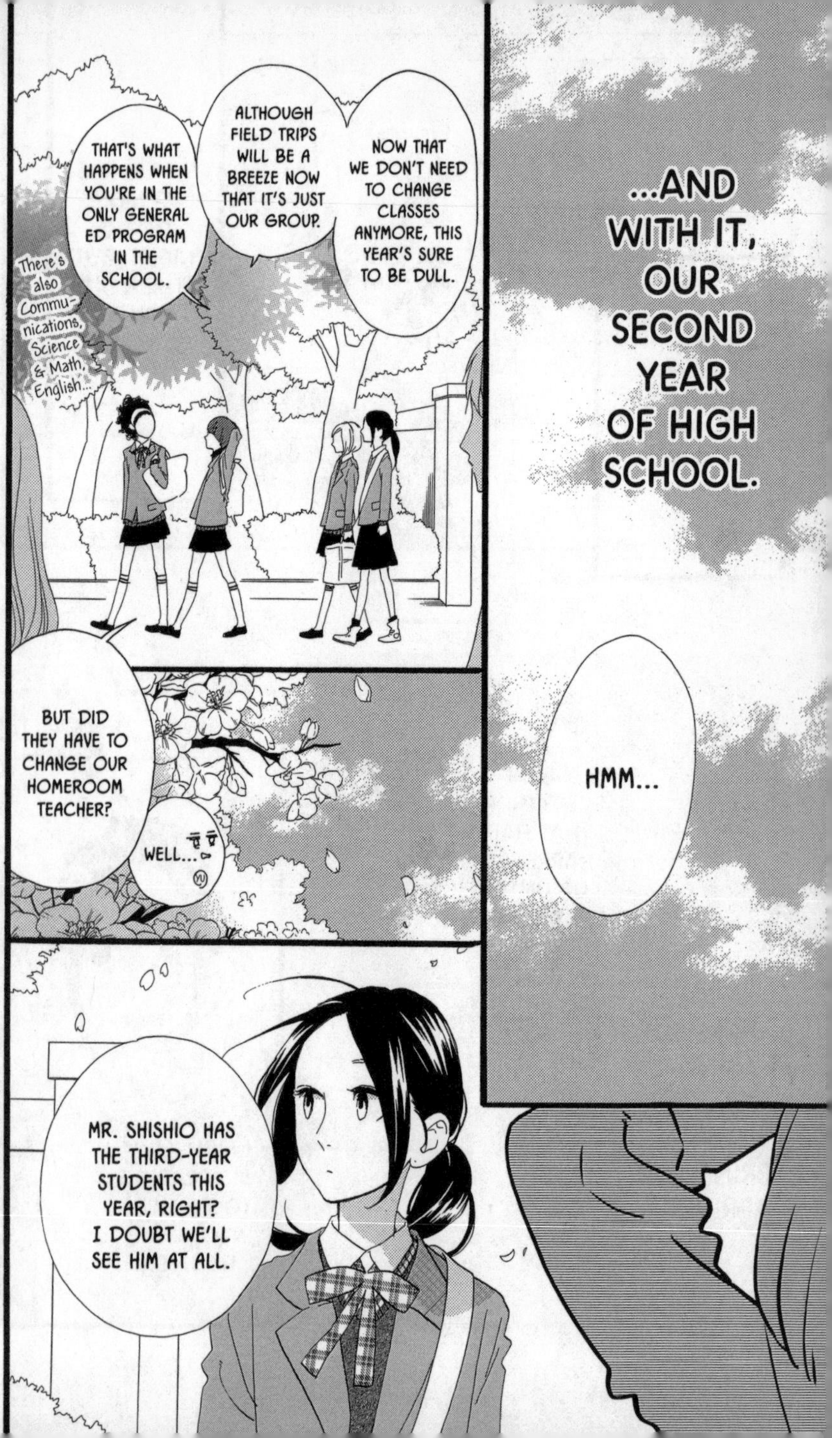
...AND WITH IT, OUR SECOND YEAR OF HIGH SCHOOL.
HMM...
NOW THAT WE DON'T NEED TO CHANGE CLASSES ANYMORE, THIS YEAR'S SURE TO BE DULL.
ALTHOUGH FIELD TRIPS WILL BE A BREEZE NOW THAT IT'S JUST OUR GROUP.
THAT'S WHAT HAPPENS WHEN YOU'RE IN THE ONLY GENERAL ED PROGRAM IN THE SCHOOL.
There's also Communications, Science & Math, English...
BUT DID THEY HAVE TO CHANGE OUR HOMEROOM TEACHER?
WELL...
MR. SHISHIO HAS THE THIRD-YEAR STUDENTS THIS YEAR, RIGHT? I DOUBT WE'LL SEE HIM AT ALL.

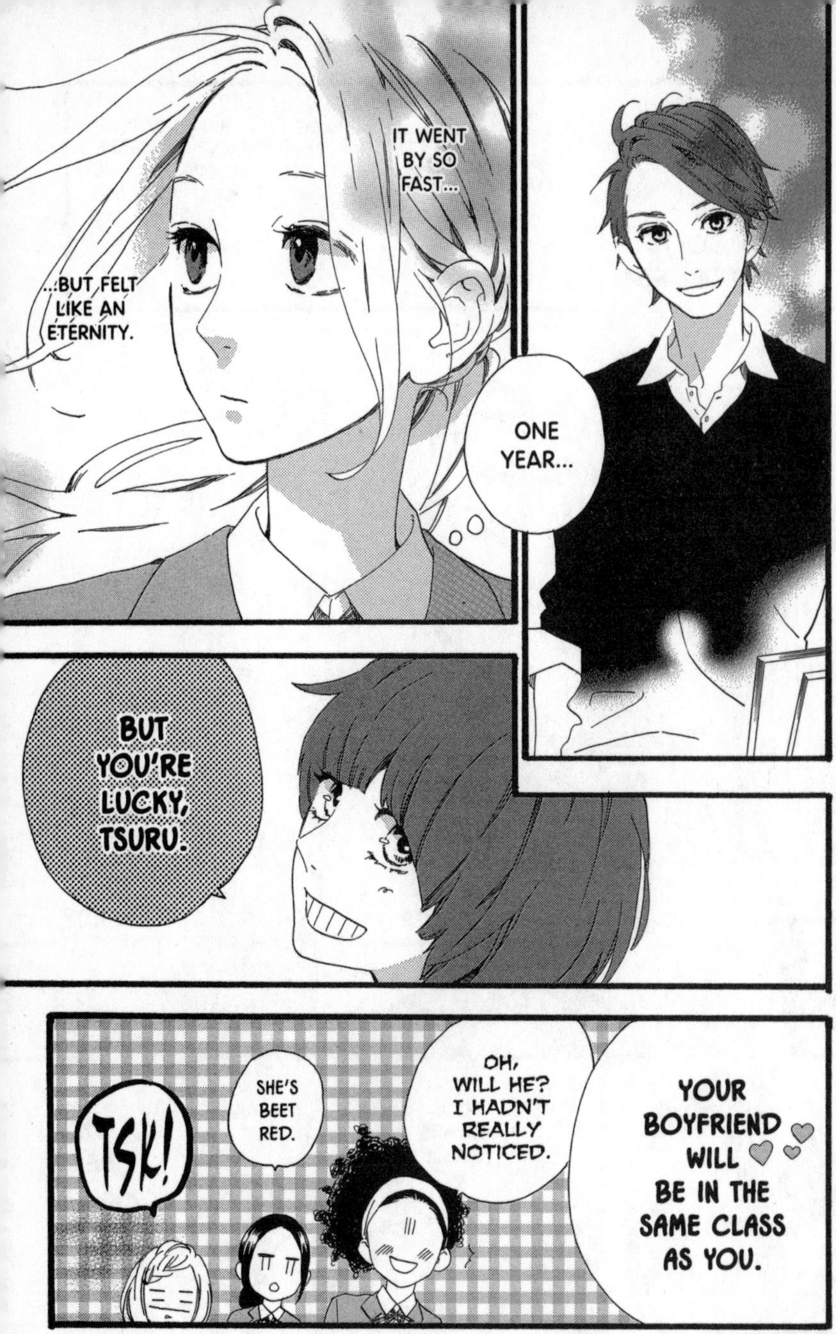
ONE YEAR...
IT WENT BY SO FAST...
...BUT FELT LIKE AN ETERNITY.
BUT YOU'RE LUCKY, TSURU.
YOUR BOYFRIEND WILL BE IN THE SAME CLASS AS YOU.
OH, WILL HE? I HADN'T REALLY NOTICED.
SHE'S BEET RED.
TSK!

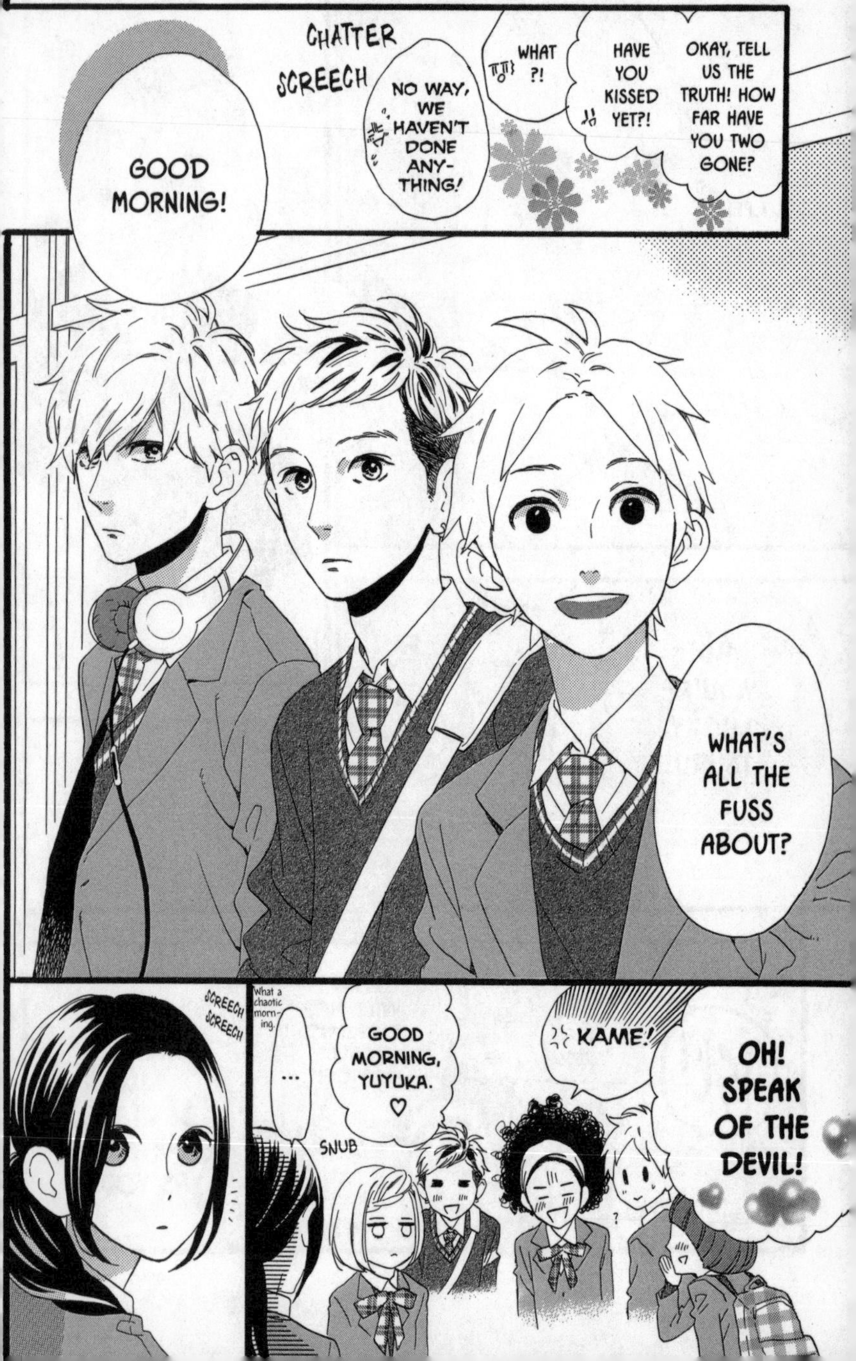
OKAY, TELL US THE TRUTH! HOW FAR HAVE YOU TWO GONE?
HAVE YOU KISSED YET?!
WHAT ?!
NO WAY, WE HAVEN'T DONE ANYTHING!
CHATTER
SCREECH
GOOD MORNING!
WHAT'S ALL THE FUSS ABOUT?
OH! SPEAK OF THE DEVIL!
KAME!
GOOD MORNING, YUYUKA. ♡
SNUB
...
What a chaotic morning.
SCREECH SCREECH

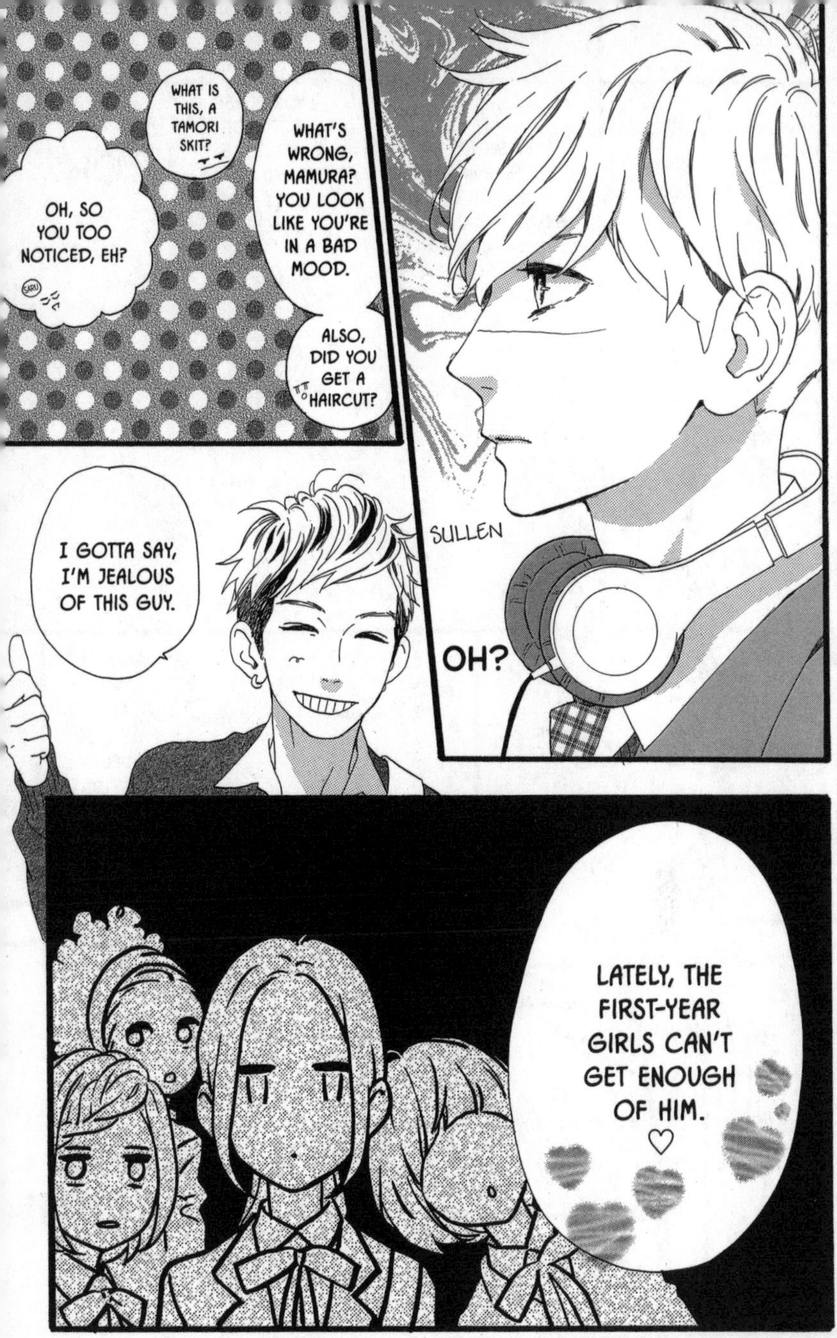
SULLEN
OH?
WHAT'S WRONG, MAMURA? YOU LOOK LIKE YOU'RE IN A BAD MOOD.
ALSO, DID YOU GET A HAIRCUT?
WHAT IS THIS, A TAMORI SKIT?
OH, SO YOU TOO NOTICED, EH?
I GOTTA SAY, I'M JEALOUS OF THIS GUY.
LATELY, THE FIRST-YEAR GIRLS CAN'T GET ENOUGH OF HIM. ♡

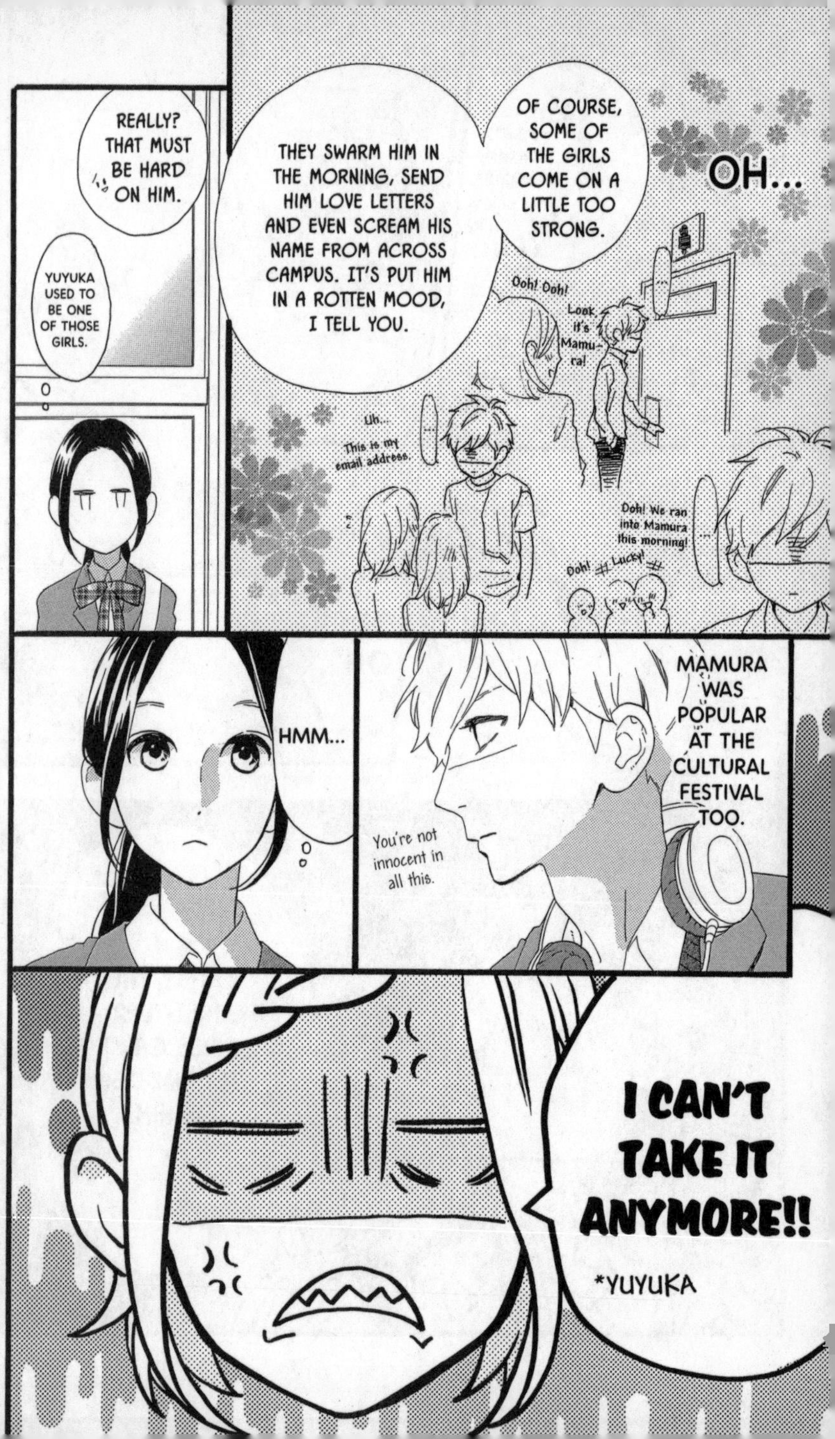
OH...
OF COURSE, SOME OF THE GIRLS COME ON A LITTLE TOO STRONG.
THEY SWARM HIM IN THE MORNING, SEND HIM LOVE LETTERS AND EVEN SCREAM HIS NAME FROM ACROSS CAMPUS. IT'S PUT HIM IN A ROTTEN MOOD, I TELL YOU.
Ooh! Ooh!
Look it's Mamura!
Uh...
This is my email address.
Ooh! We ran into Mamura this morning!
Ooh!
Lucky!
REALLY? THAT MUST BE HARD ON HIM.
YUYUKA USED TO BE ONE OF THOSE GIRLS.
MAMURA WAS POPULAR AT THE CULTURAL FESTIVAL TOO.
You're not innocent in all this.
HMM...
I CAN'T TAKE IT ANYMORE!!
*YUYUKA

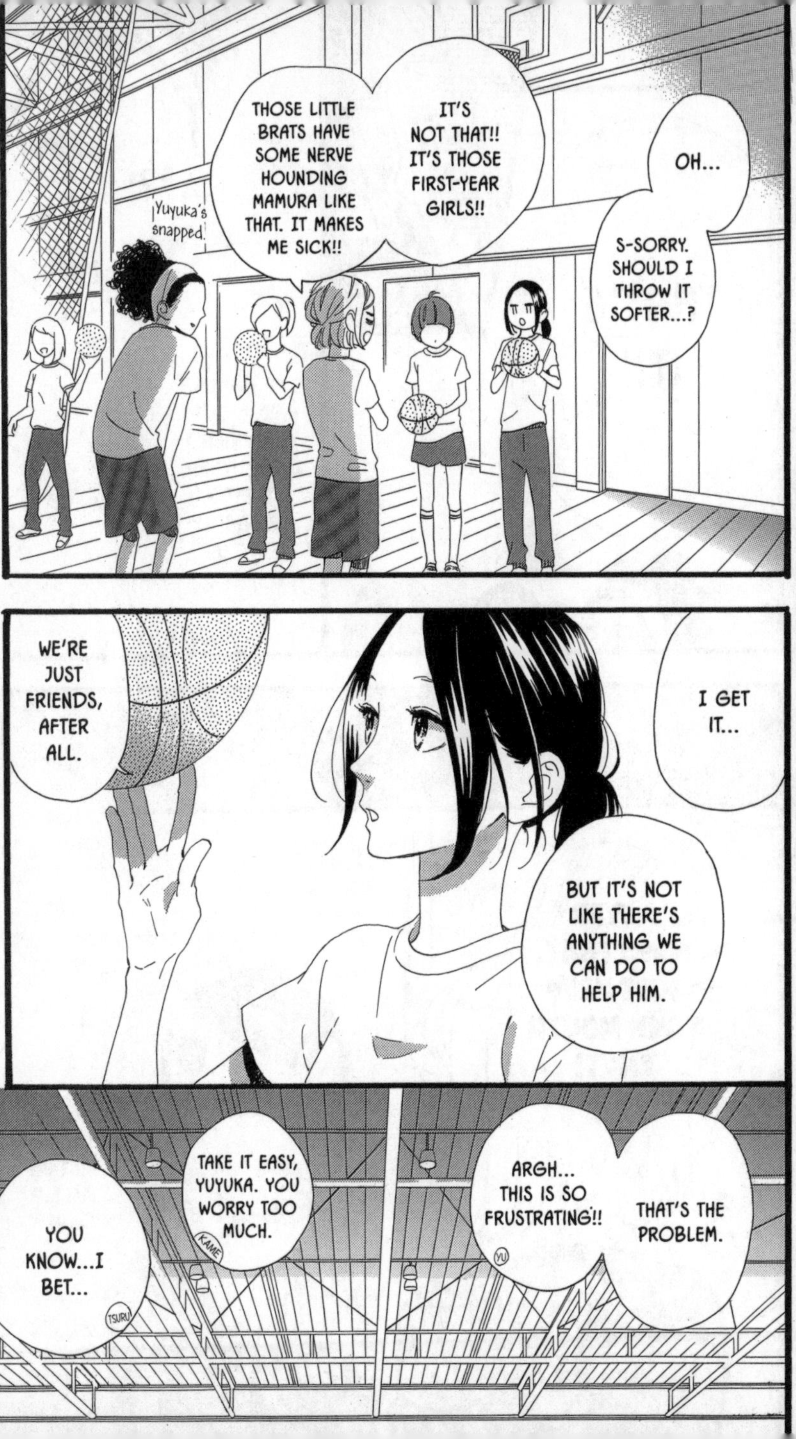
OH...
S-SORRY. SHOULD I THROW IT SOFTER...?
IT'S NOT THAT!! IT'S THOSE FIRST-YEAR GIRLS!!
THOSE LITTLE BRATS HAVE SOME NERVE HOUNDING MAMURA LIKE THAT. IT MAKES ME SICK!!
Yuyuka's snapped.
I GET IT...
BUT IT'S NOT LIKE THERE'S ANYTHING WE CAN DO TO HELP HIM.
WE'RE JUST FRIENDS, AFTER ALL.
THAT'S THE PROBLEM.
ARGH... THIS IS SO FRUSTRATING!!
YU
TAKE IT EASY, YUYUKA. YOU WORRY TOO MUCH.
KAME
YOU KNOW...I BET...
TSURU

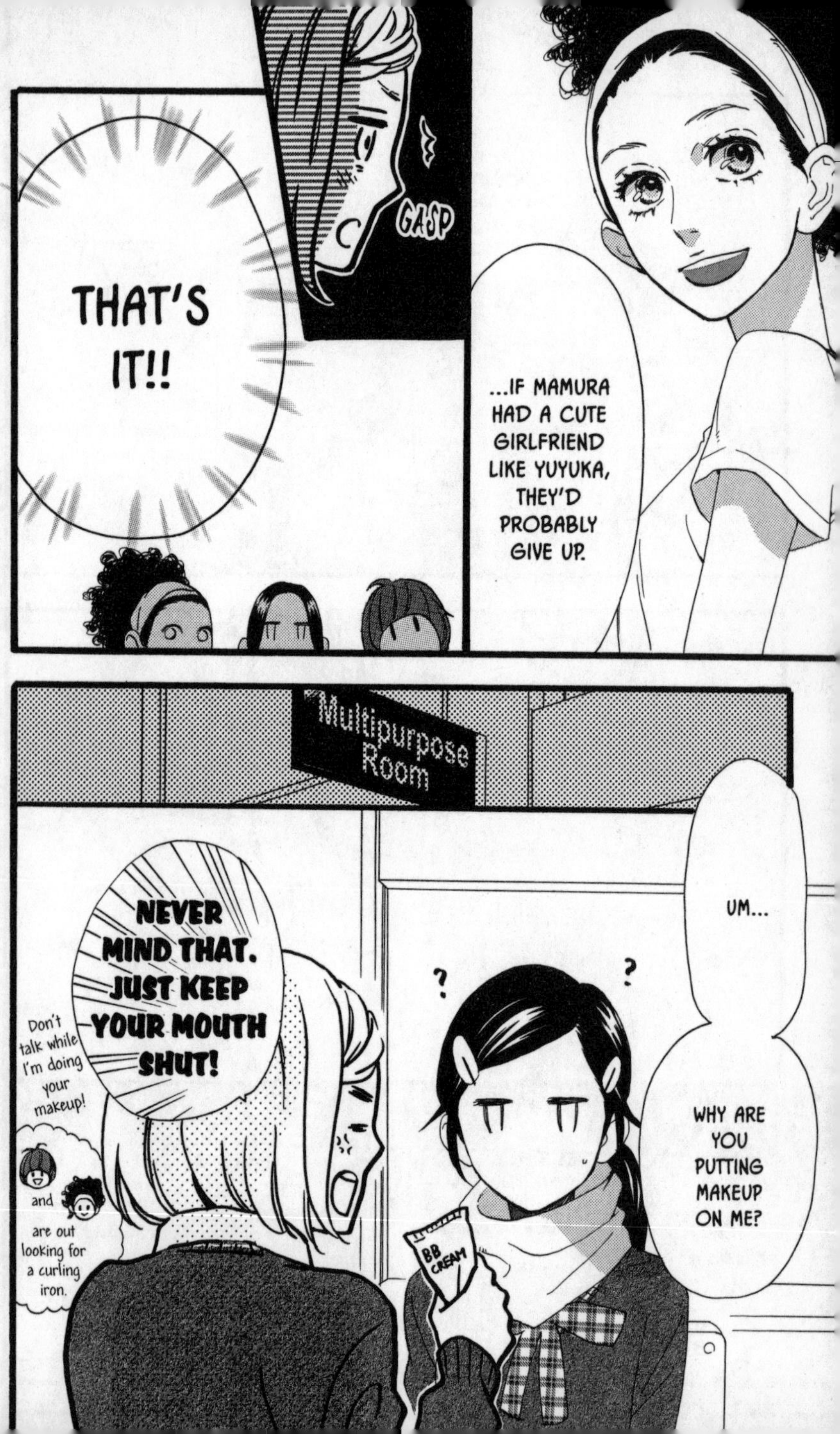
...IF MAMURA HAD A CUTE GIRLFRIEND LIKE YUYUKA, THEY'D PROBABLY GIVE UP.
GASP
THAT'S IT!!
Multipurpose Room
UM...
WHY ARE YOU PUTTING MAKEUP ON ME?
?
?
BB CREAM
NEVER MIND THAT. JUST KEEP YOUR MOUTH SHUT!
Don't talk while I'm doing your makeup!
and
are out looking for a curling iron.

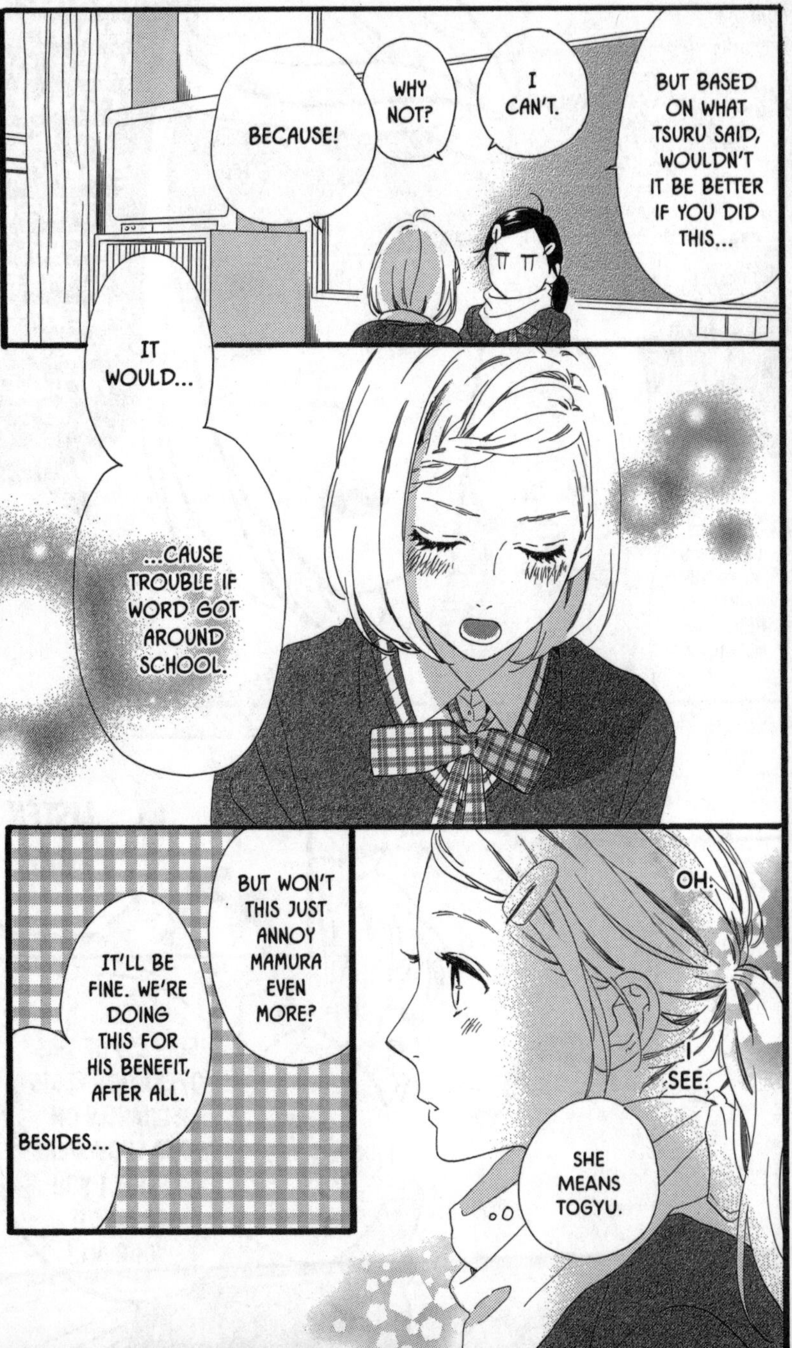
BUT BASED ON WHAT TSURU SAID, WOULDN'T IT BE BETTER IF YOU DID THIS...
I CAN'T.
WHY NOT?
BECAUSE!
IT WOULD...
...CAUSE TROUBLE IF WORD GOT AROUND SCHOOL.
OH.
I SEE.
SHE MEANS TOGYU.
BUT WON'T THIS JUST ANNOY MAMURA EVEN MORE?
IT'LL BE FINE. WE'RE DOING THIS FOR HIS BENEFIT, AFTER ALL.
BESIDES...

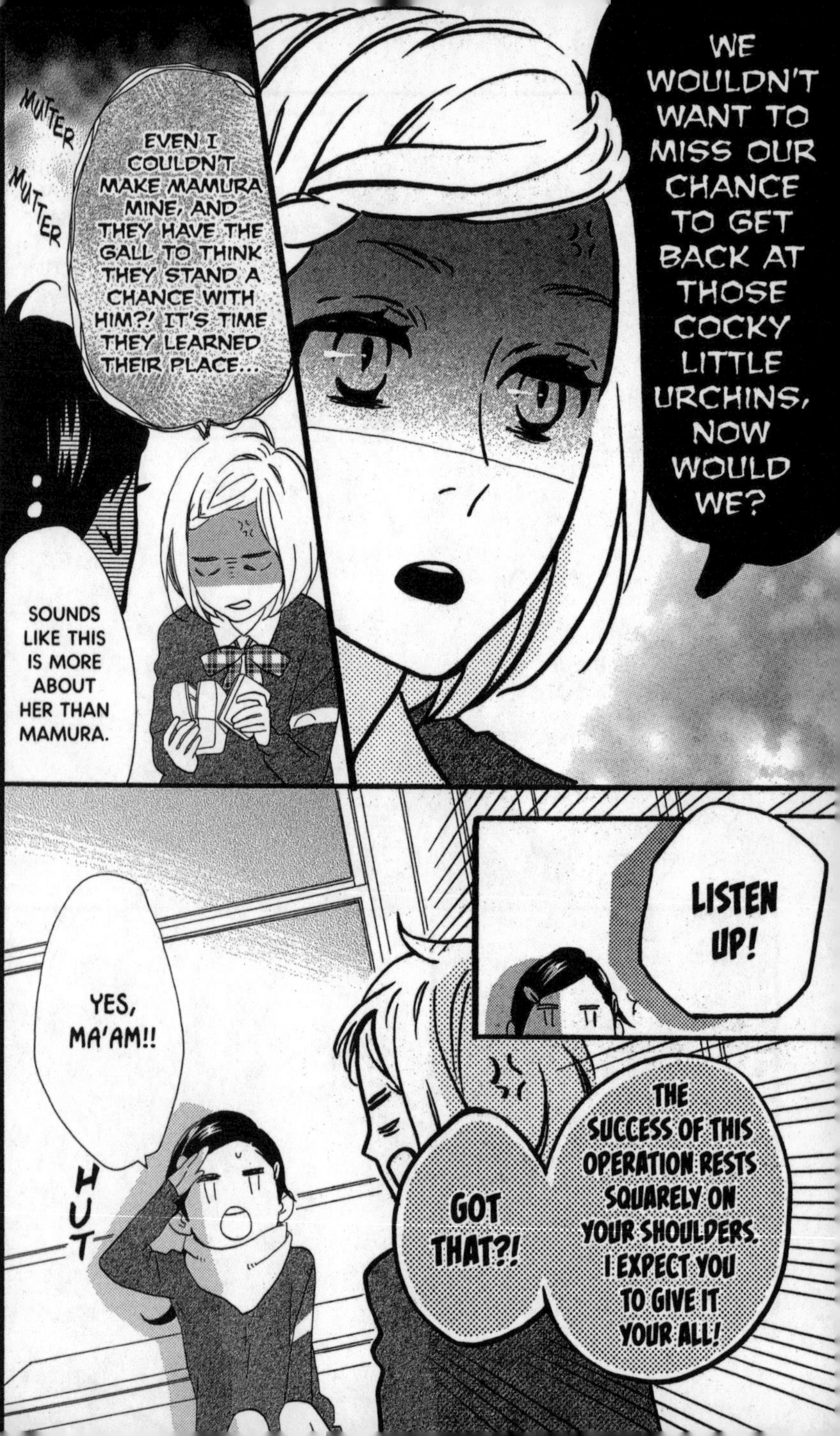
WE WOULDN'T WANT TO MISS OUR CHANCE TO GET BACK AT THOSE COCKY LITTLE URCHINS, NOW WOULD WE?
MUTTER
MUTTER
EVEN I COULDN'T MAKE MAMURA MINE, AND THEY HAVE THE GALL TO THINK THEY STAND A CHANCE WITH HIM?! IT'S TIME THEY LEARNED THEIR PLACE...
SOUNDS LIKE THIS IS MORE ABOUT HER THAN MAMURA.
LISTEN UP!
THE SUCCESS OF THIS OPERATION RESTS SQUARELY ON YOUR SHOULDERS. I EXPECT YOU TO GIVE IT YOUR ALL!
GOT THAT?!
YES, MA'AM!!
HUT

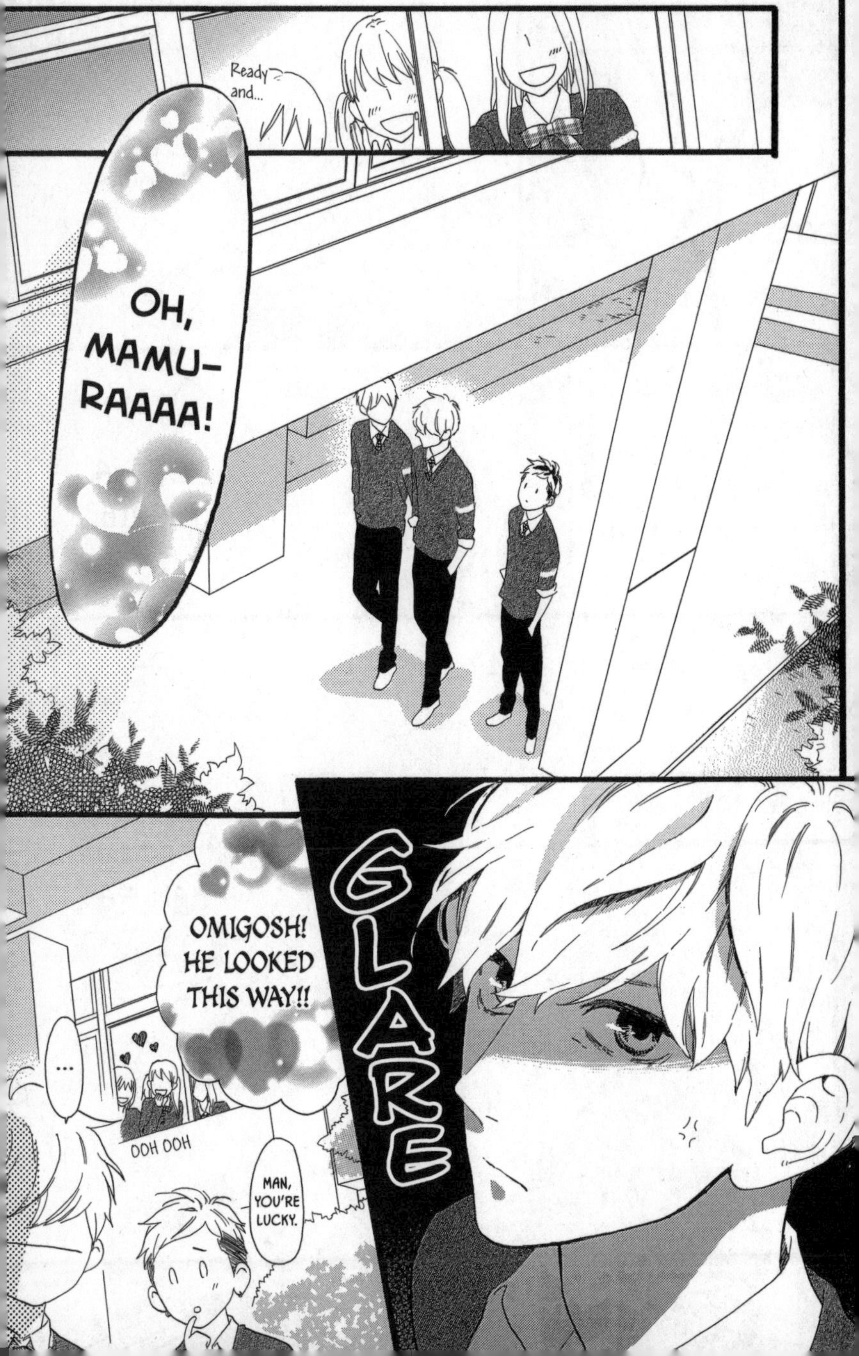
Ready and...
OH, MAMU-RAAAA!
GLARE
OMIGOSH! HE LOOKED THIS WAY!!
MAN, YOU'RE LUCKY.
...
DOOH DOOH

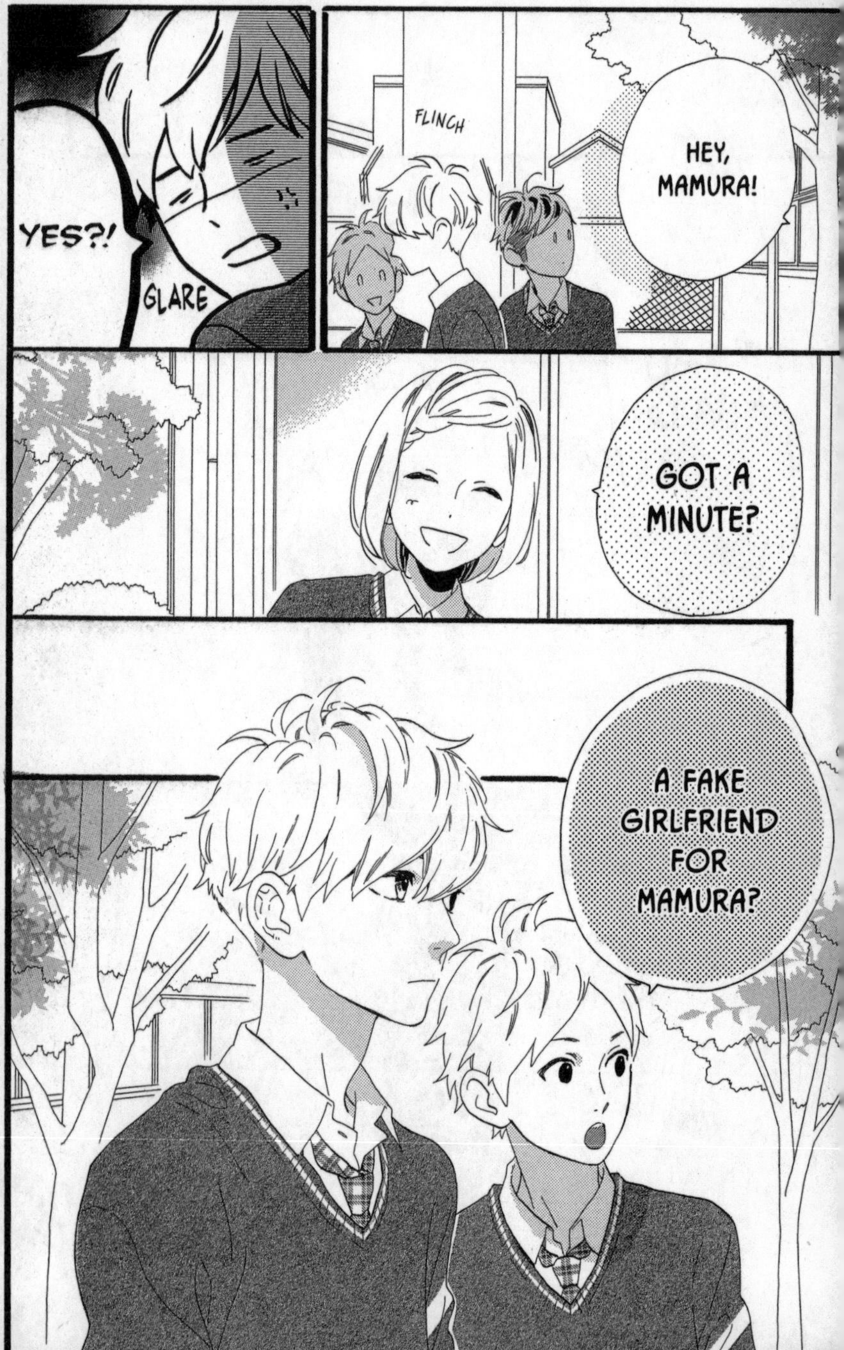
HEY, MAMURA!
FLINCH
YES?!
GLARE
GOT A MINUTE?
A FAKE GIRLFRIEND FOR MAMURA?

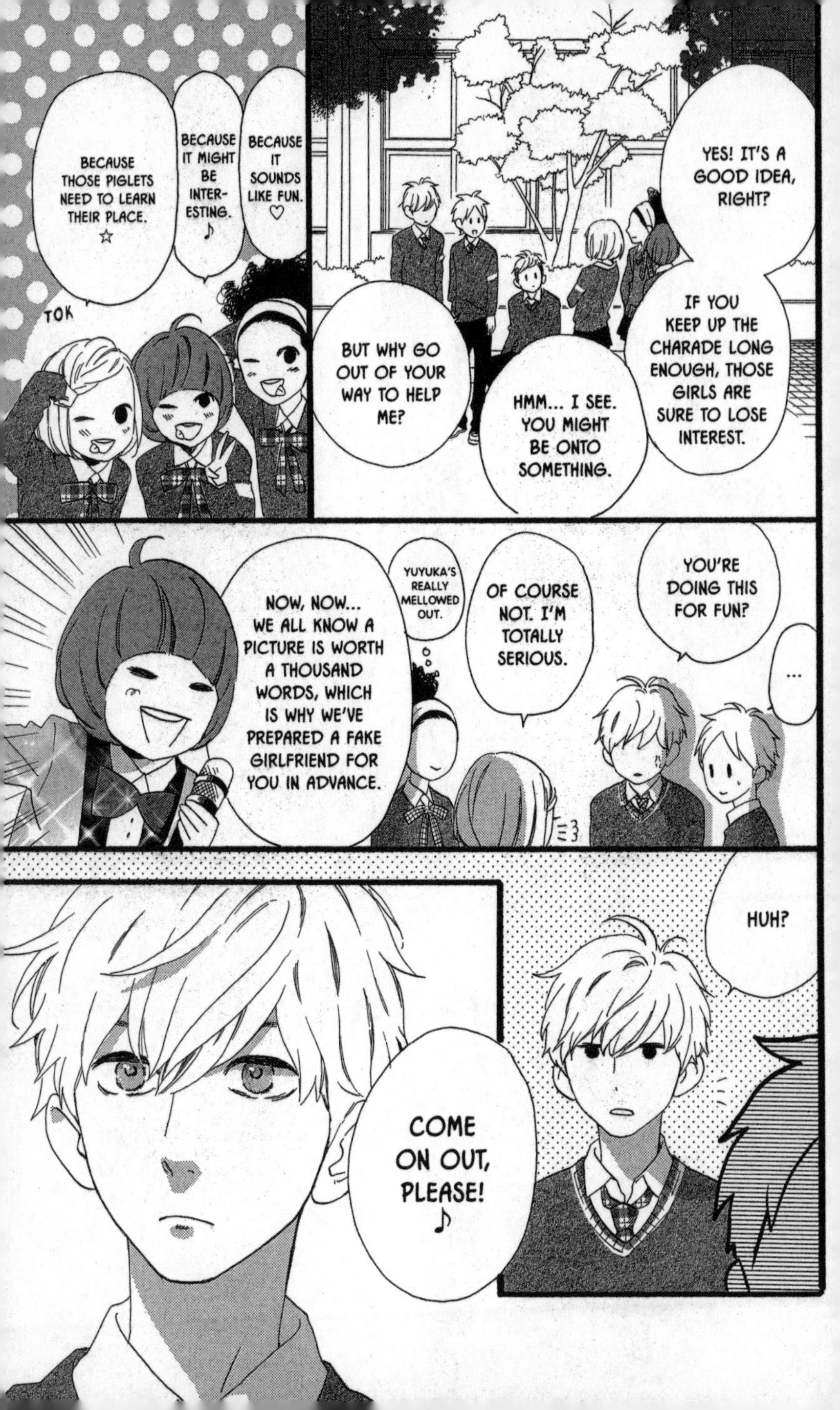
YES! IT'S A GOOD IDEA, RIGHT?
IF YOU KEEP UP THE CHARADE LONG ENOUGH, THOSE GIRLS ARE SURE TO LOSE INTEREST.
HMM... I SEE. YOU MIGHT BE ONTO SOMETHING.
BUT WHY GO OUT OF YOUR WAY TO HELP ME?
BECAUSE IT SOUNDS LIKE FUN. ♡
BECAUSE IT MIGHT BE INTERESTING. ♪
BECAUSE THOSE PIGLETS NEED TO LEARN THEIR PLACE. ☆
TOK
...
YOU'RE DOING THIS FOR FUN?
OF COURSE NOT. I'M TOTALLY SERIOUS.
YUYUKA'S REALLY MELLOWED OUT.
NOW, NOW... WE ALL KNOW A PICTURE IS WORTH A THOUSAND WORDS, WHICH IS WHY WE'VE PREPARED A FAKE GIRLFRIEND FOR YOU IN ADVANCE.
HUH?
COME ON OUT, PLEASE! ♪

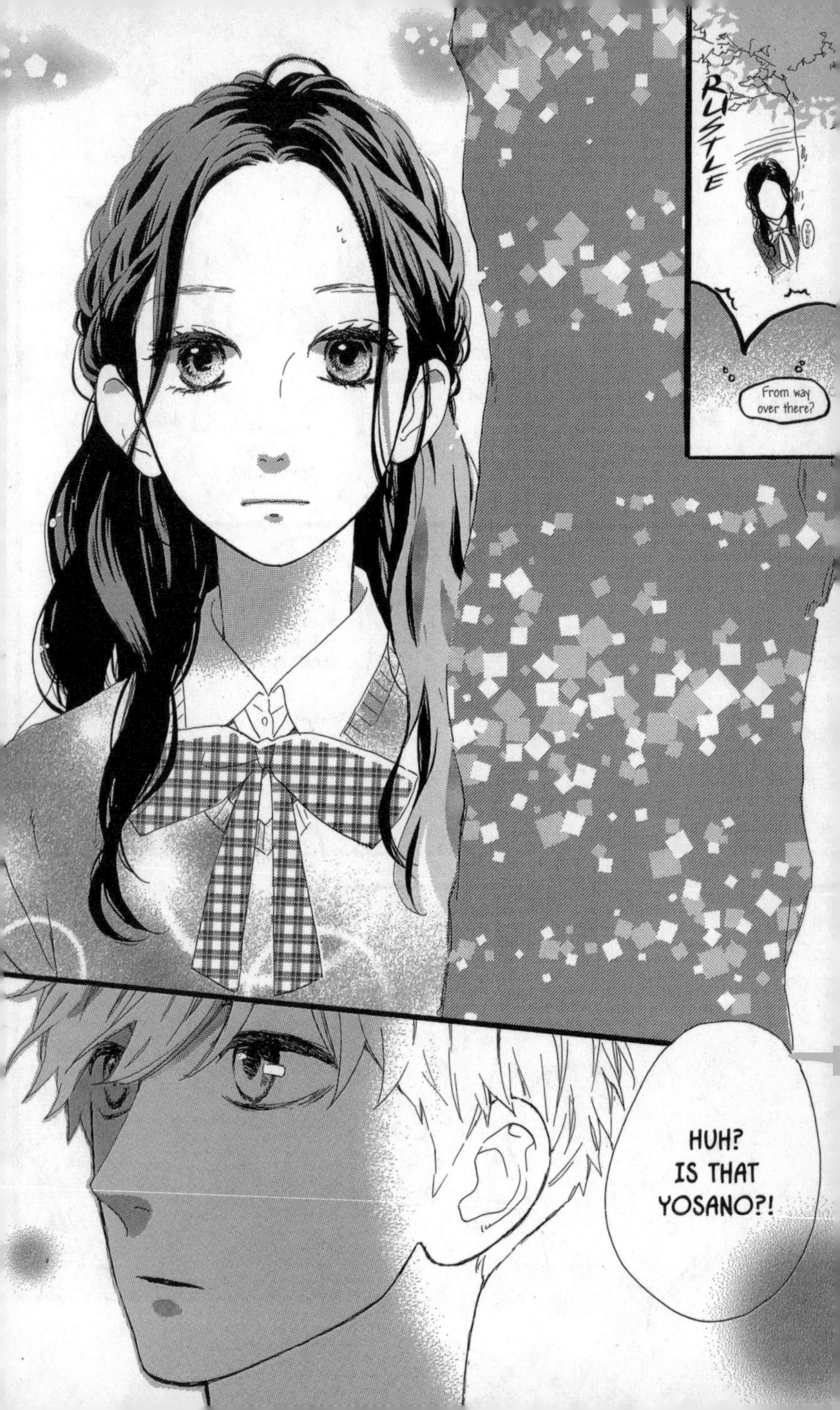
RUSTLE
TREE
From way over there?
HUH? IS THAT YOSANO?!

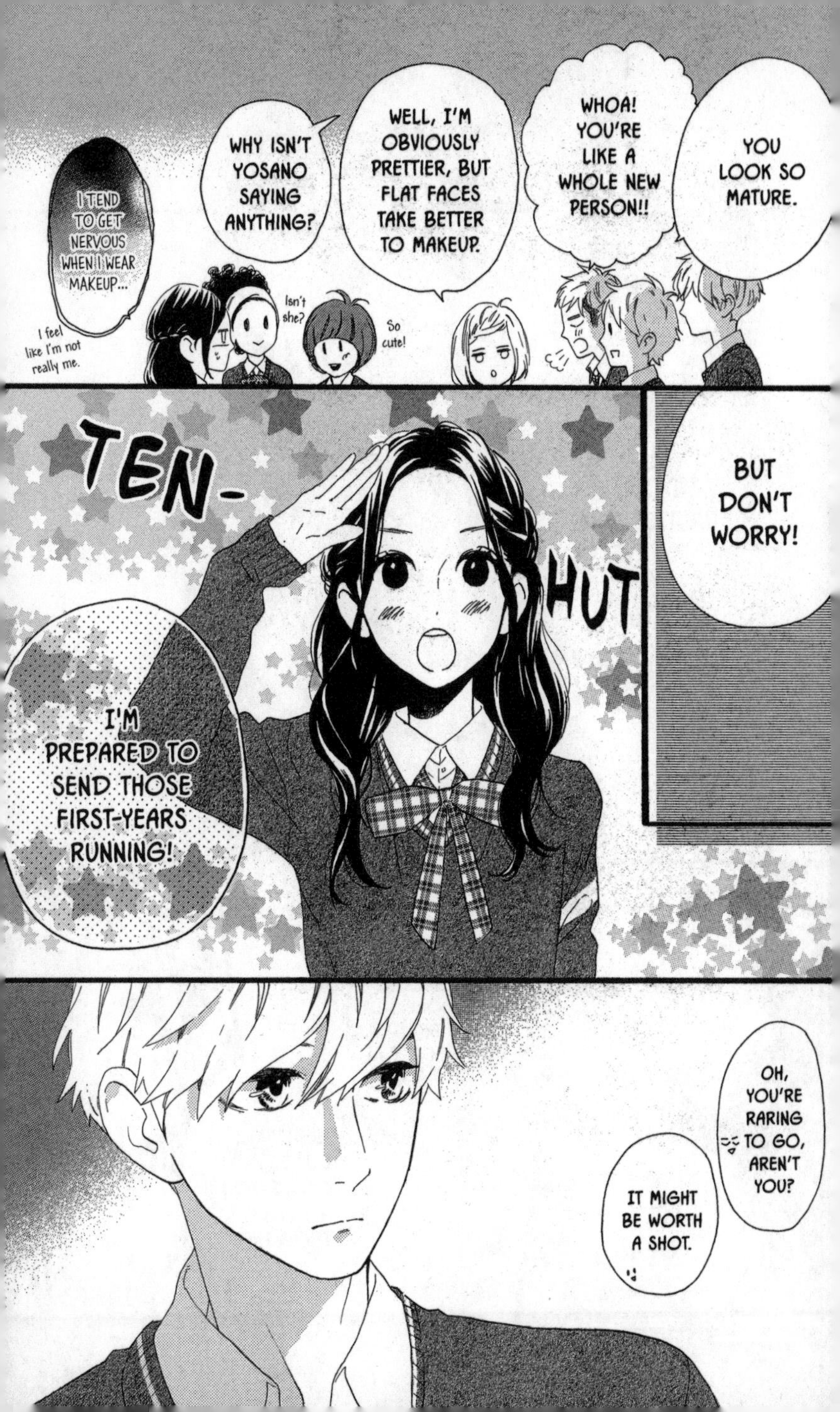
YOU LOOK SO MATURE.
WHOA! YOU'RE LIKE A WHOLE NEW PERSON!!
So cute!
WELL, I'M OBVIOUSLY PRETTIER, BUT FLAT FACES TAKE BETTER TO MAKEUP.
Isn't she?
WHY ISN'T YOSANO SAYING ANYTHING?
I TEND TO GET NERVOUS WHEN I WEAR MAKEUP...
I feel like I'm not really me.
BUT DON'T WORRY!
TEN-
HUT
I'M PREPARED TO SEND THOSE FIRST-YEARS RUNNING!
OH, YOU'RE RARING TO GO, AREN'T YOU?
IT MIGHT BE WORTH A SHOT.

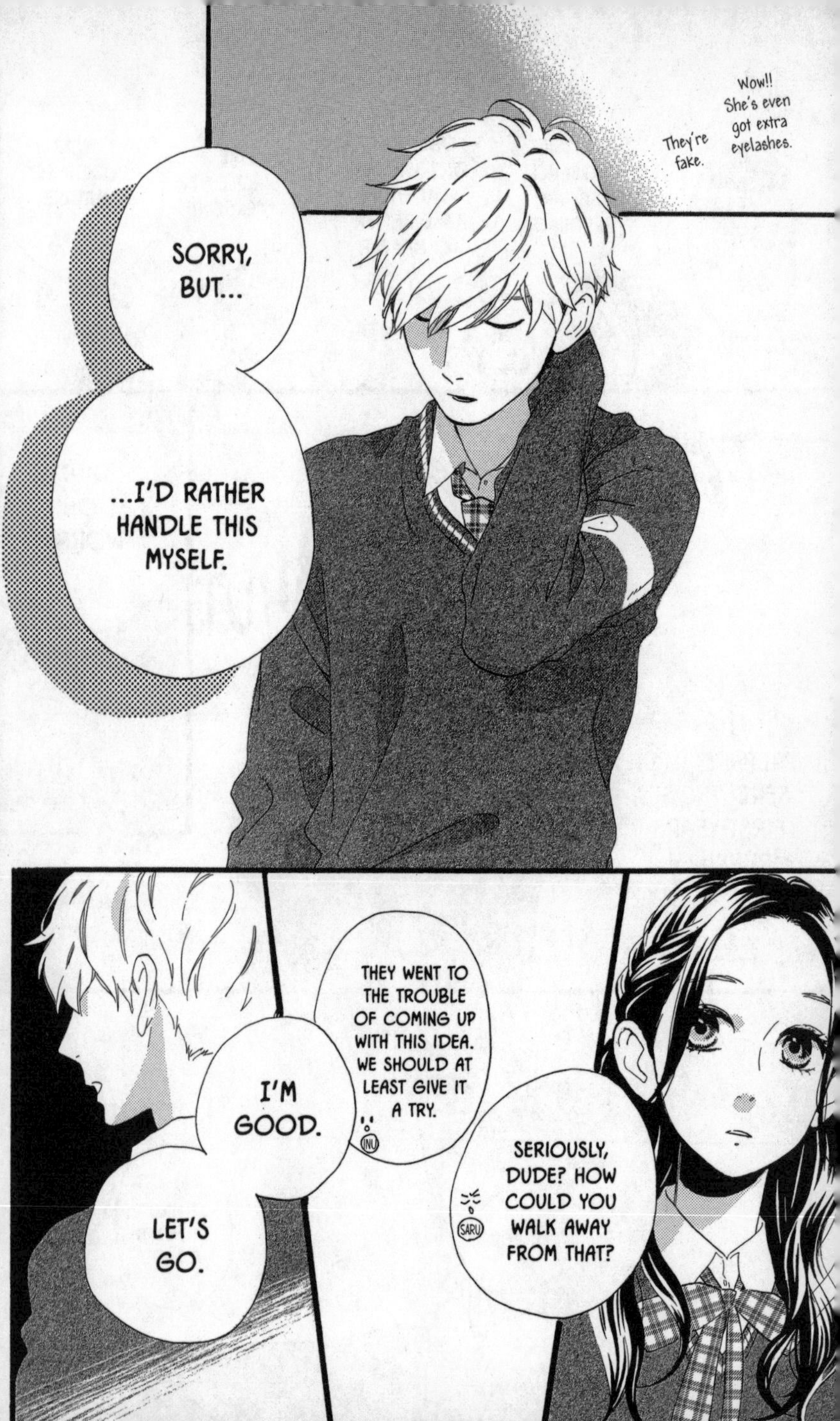
Wow!! She's even got extra eyelashes.
They're fake.
SORRY, BUT...
...I'D RATHER HANDLE THIS MYSELF.
SARU
SERIOUSLY, DUDE? HOW COULD YOU WALK AWAY FROM THAT?
INU
THEY WENT TO THE TROUBLE OF COMING UP WITH THIS IDEA. WE SHOULD AT LEAST GIVE IT A TRY.
I'M GOOD.
LET'S GO.

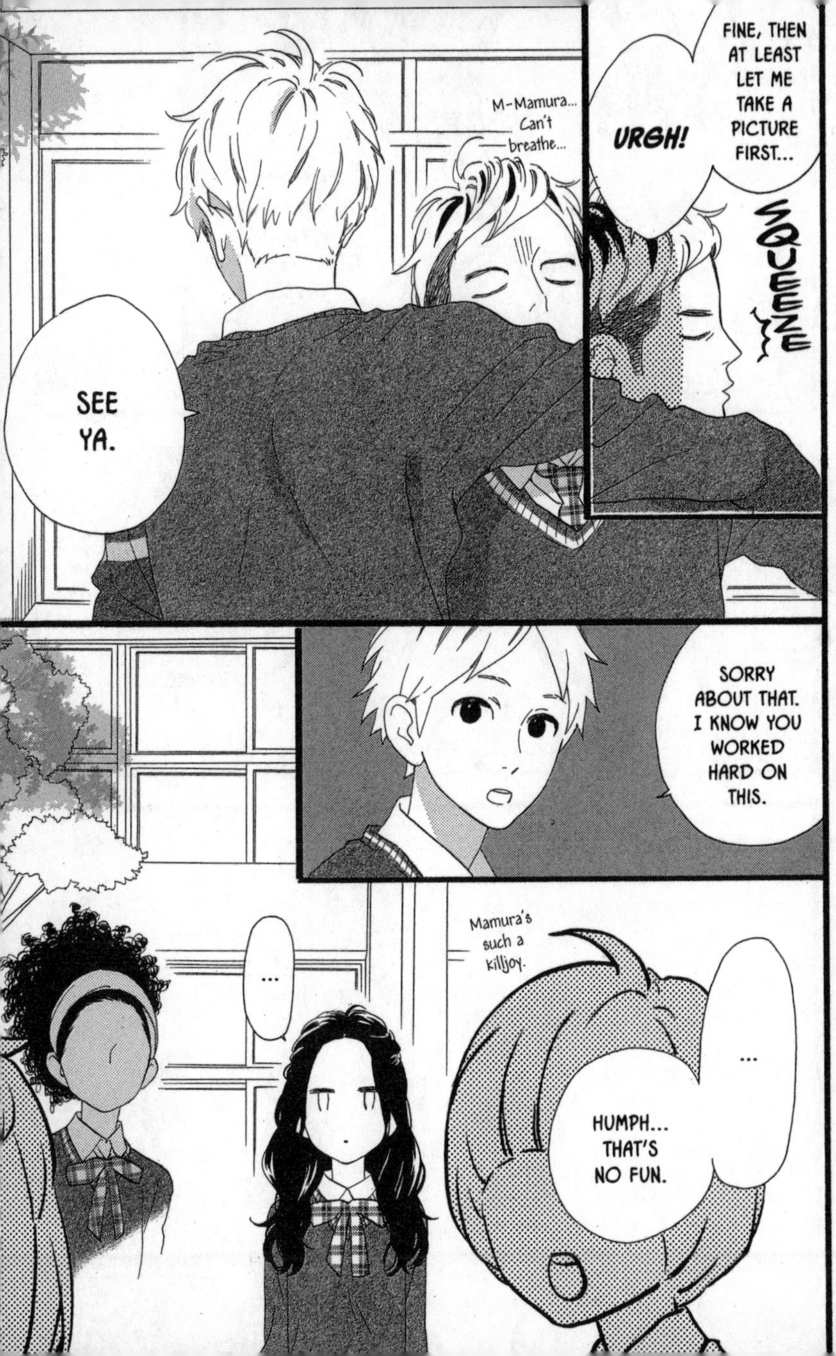
FINE, THEN AT LEAST LET ME TAKE A PICTURE FIRST...
URGH!
SQUEEZE
M-Mamura... Can't breathe...
SEE YA.
SORRY ABOUT THAT. I KNOW YOU WORKED HARD ON THIS.
...
HUMPH... THAT'S NO FUN.
Mamura's such a killjoy.
...

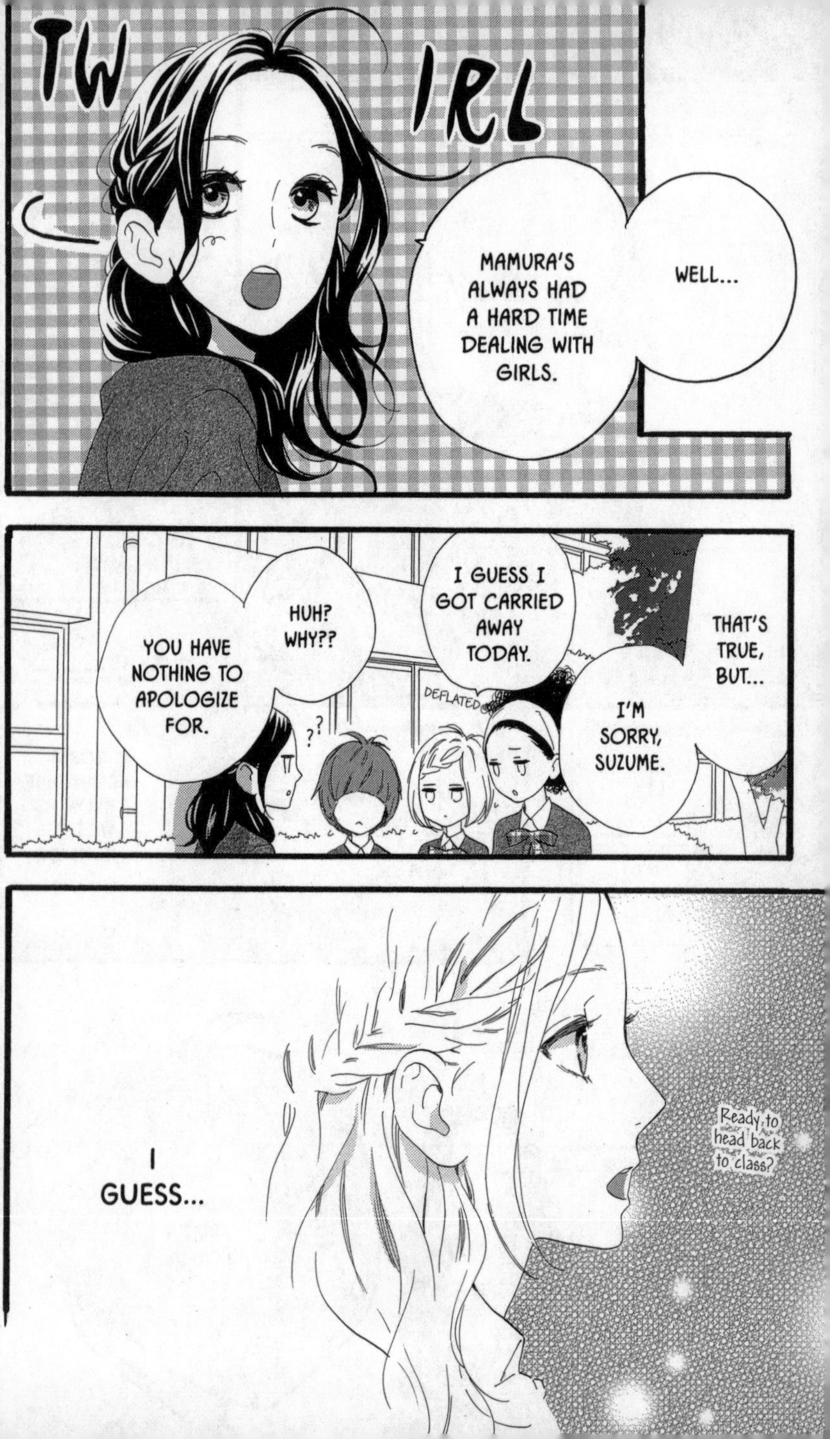
TWIRL
WELL...
MAMURA'S ALWAYS HAD A HARD TIME DEALING WITH GIRLS.
THAT'S TRUE, BUT...
I'M SORRY, SUZUME.
I GUESS I GOT CARRIED AWAY TODAY.
DEFLATED
HUH? WHY??
YOU HAVE NOTHING TO APOLOGIZE FOR.
Ready to head back to class?
I GUESS...

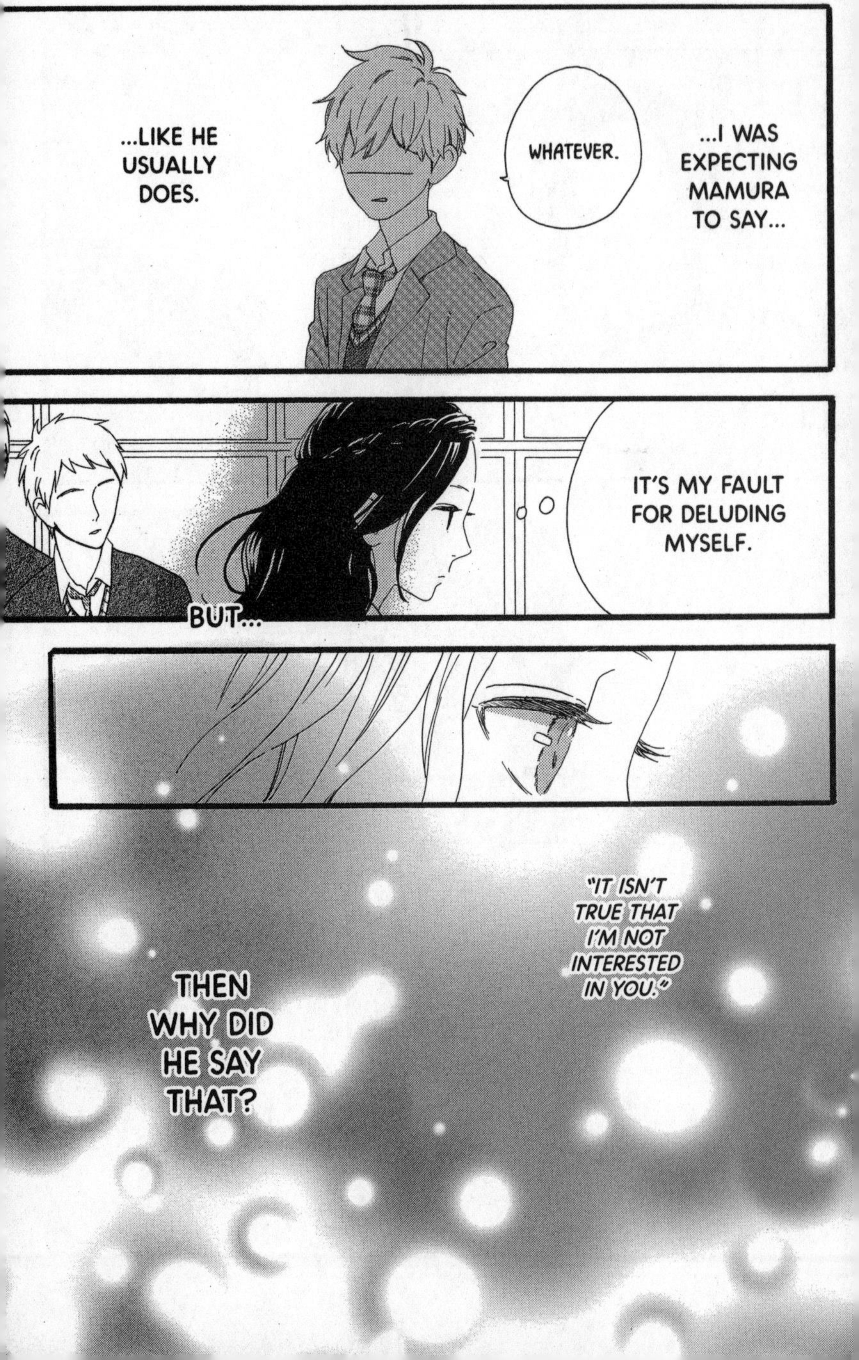
...I WAS EXPECTING MAMURA TO SAY...
WHATEVER.
...LIKE HE USUALLY DOES.
IT'S MY FAULT FOR DELUDING MYSELF.
BUT...
"IT ISN'T TRUE THAT I'M NOT INTERESTED IN YOU."
THEN WHY DID HE SAY THAT?

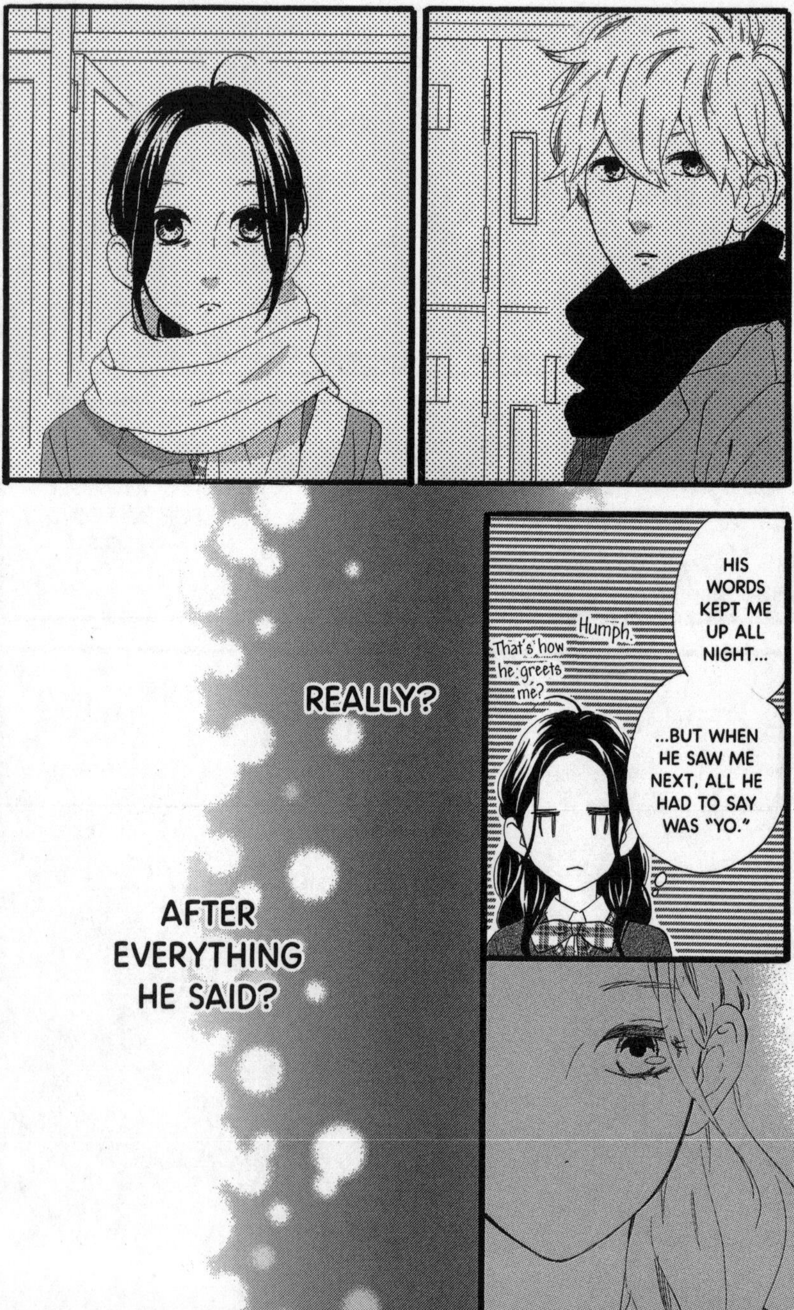
HIS WORDS KEPT ME UP ALL NIGHT...
...BUT WHEN HE SAW ME NEXT, ALL HE HAD TO SAY WAS "YO."
Humph.
That's how he greets me?
REALLY?
AFTER EVERYTHING HE SAID?

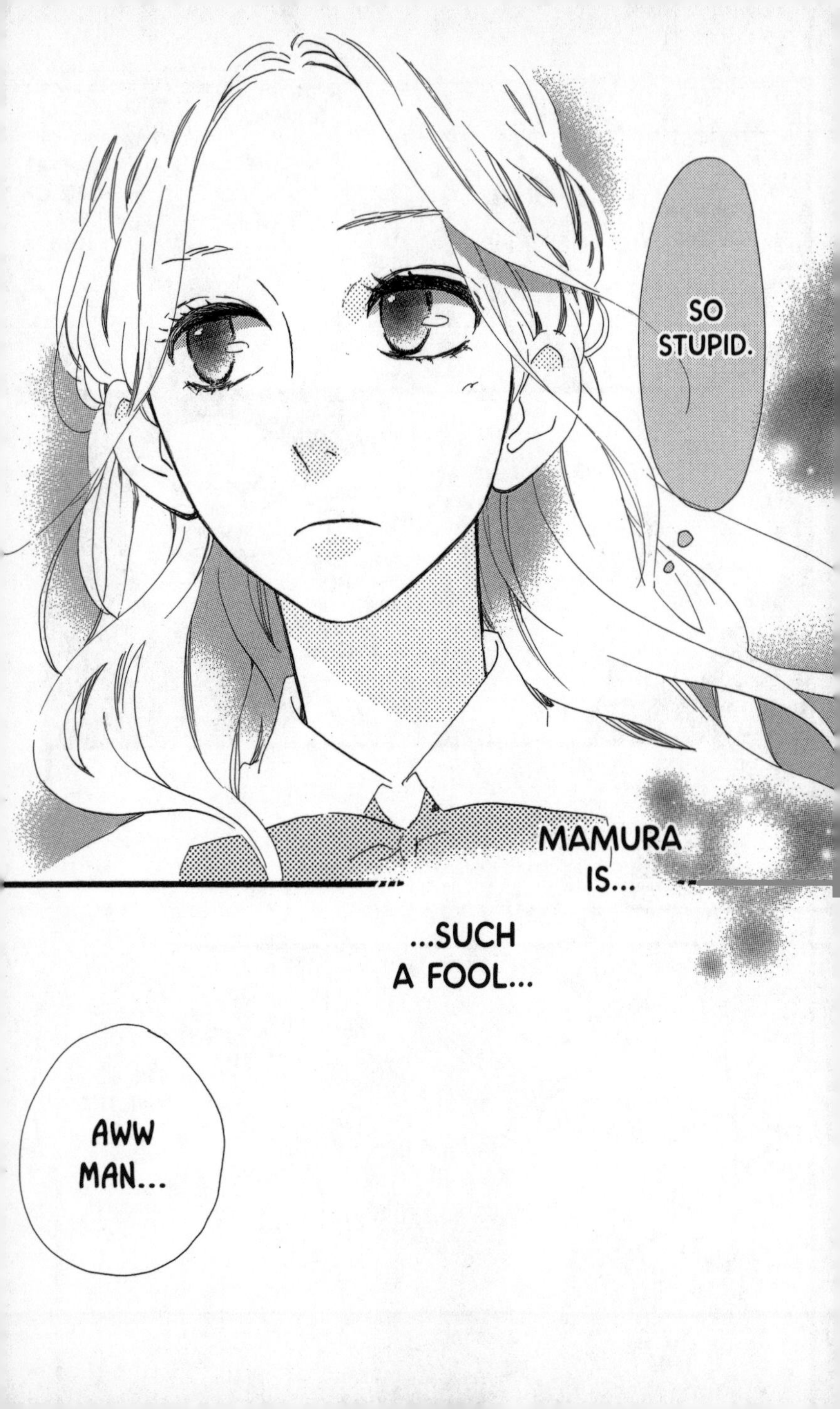
SO STUPID.
MAMURA IS...
...SUCH A FOOL...
AWW MAN...

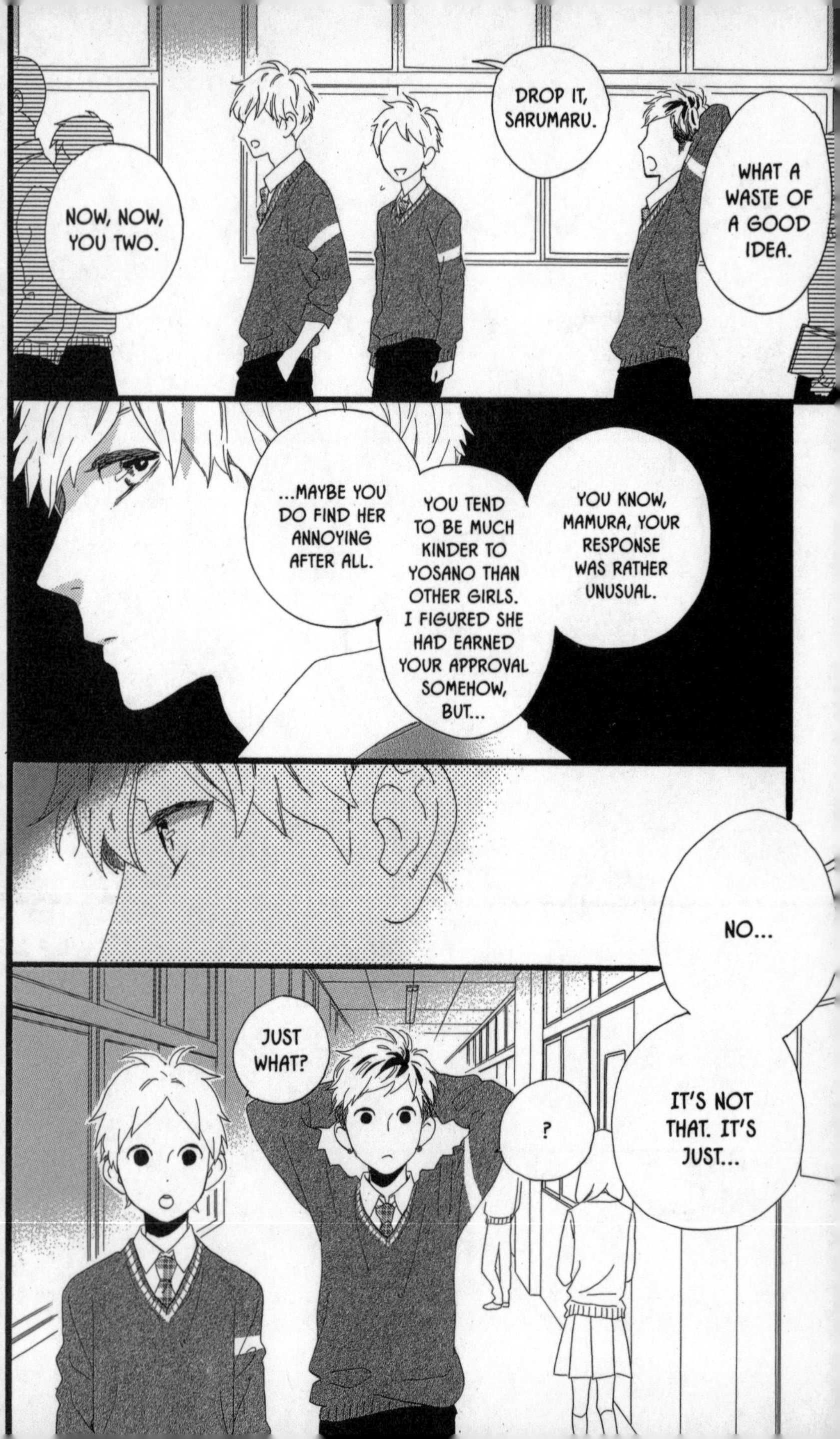
WHAT A WASTE OF A GOOD IDEA.
DROP IT, SARUMARU.
NOW, NOW, YOU TWO.
YOU KNOW, MAMURA, YOUR RESPONSE WAS RATHER UNUSUAL.
YOU TEND TO BE MUCH KINDER TO YOSANO THAN OTHER GIRLS. I FIGURED SHE HAD EARNED YOUR APPROVAL SOMEHOW, BUT...
...MAYBE YOU DO FIND HER ANNOYING AFTER ALL.
NO...
IT'S NOT THAT. IT'S JUST...
?
JUST WHAT?

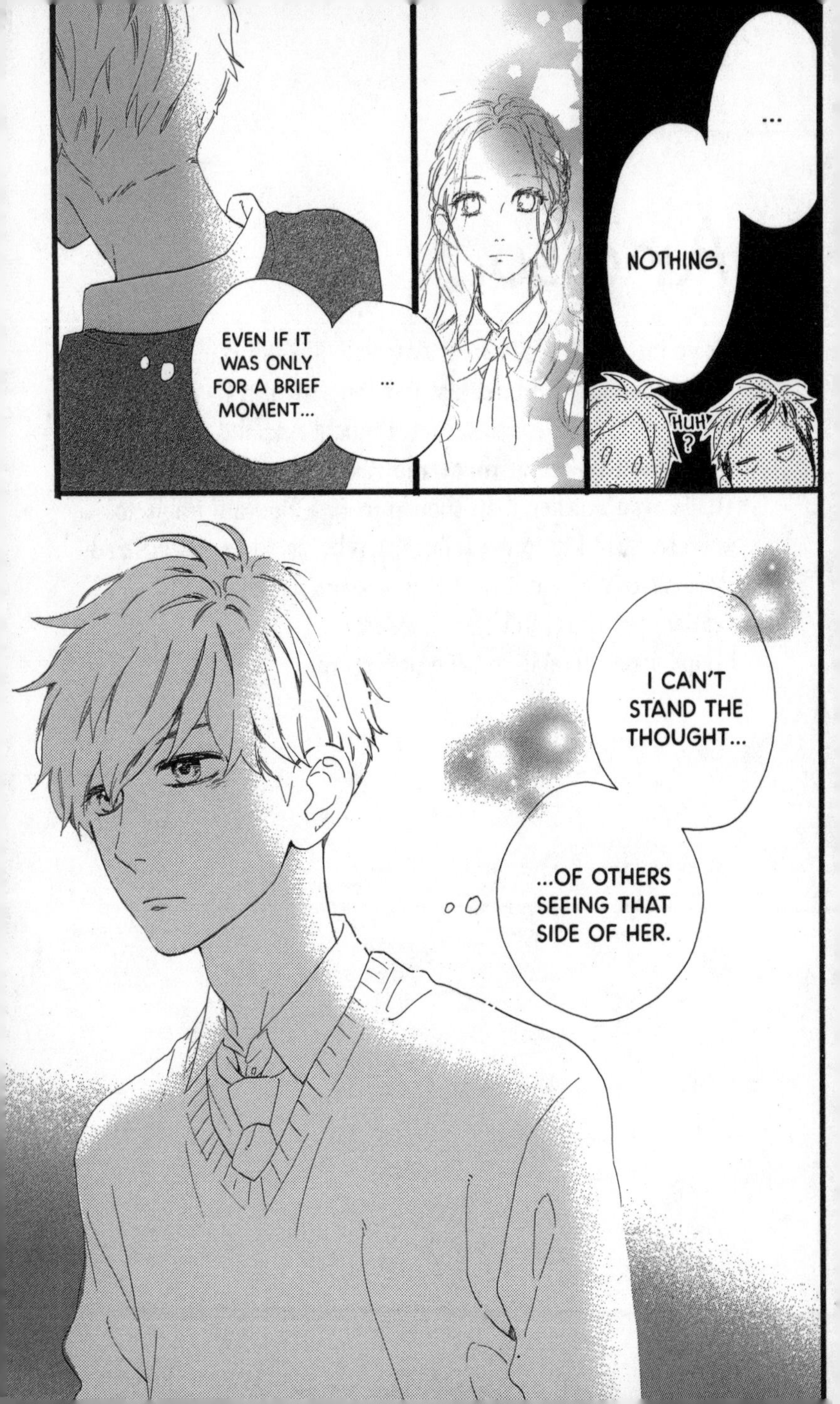
...
NOTHING.
HUH?
...
EVEN IF IT WAS ONLY FOR A BRIEF MOMENT...
I CAN'T STAND THE THOUGHT...
...OF OTHERS SEEING THAT SIDE OF HER.

And so...

We've hit *Daytime Shooting Star* vol. 9!! Clap clap clap!!
I never thought it would last this long... But it has, and I owe it all to you. Thank you very much! And the next volume will be out in **three months**!
That's even quicker than shonen manga. How am I able to work so fast? I keep my skills sharp by writing nonserialized stories!! That's right!! Last year, I wrote five of them!!
And so, I'm going full steam ahead!
I hope you'll be able to keep up with me.

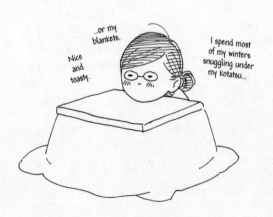

I spend most of my winters snuggling under my kotatsu...
...or my blankets.
Nice and toasty.

Daytime Shooting Star

Day 56

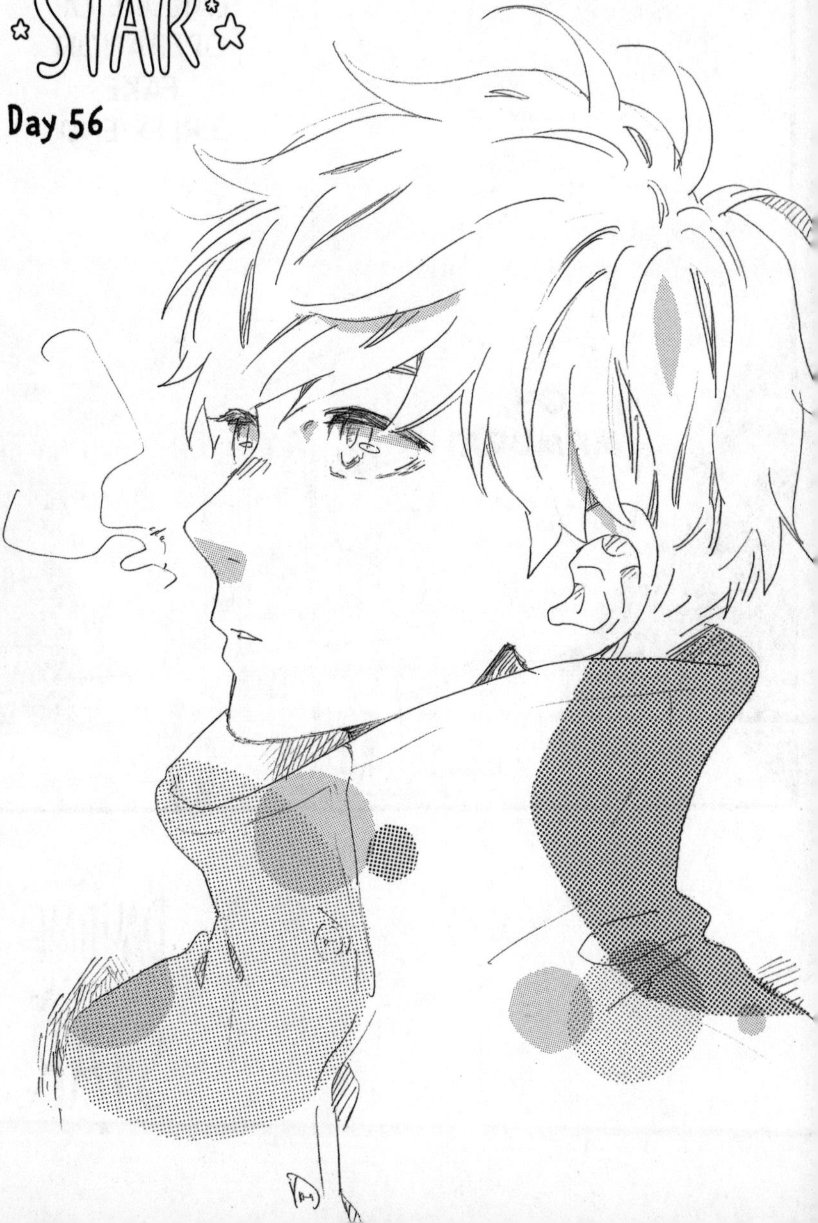

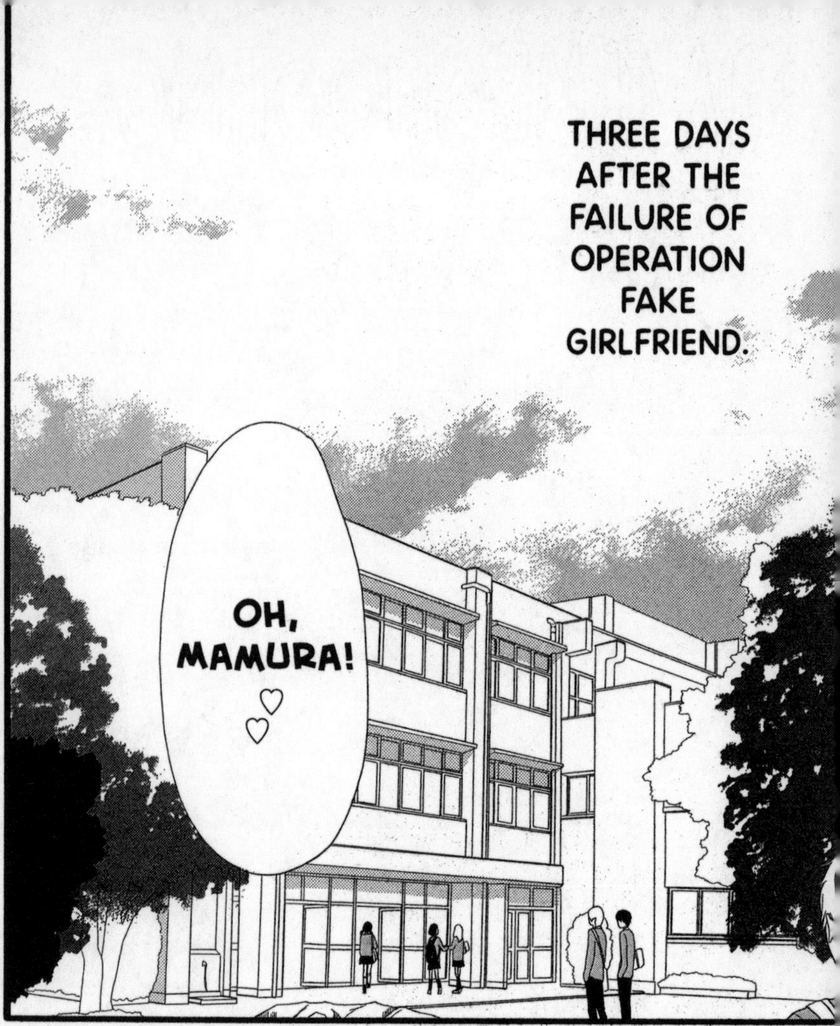
THREE DAYS AFTER THE FAILURE OF OPERATION FAKE GIRLFRIEND.
OH, MAMURA! ♡ ♡

DAYTIME SHOOTING STAR

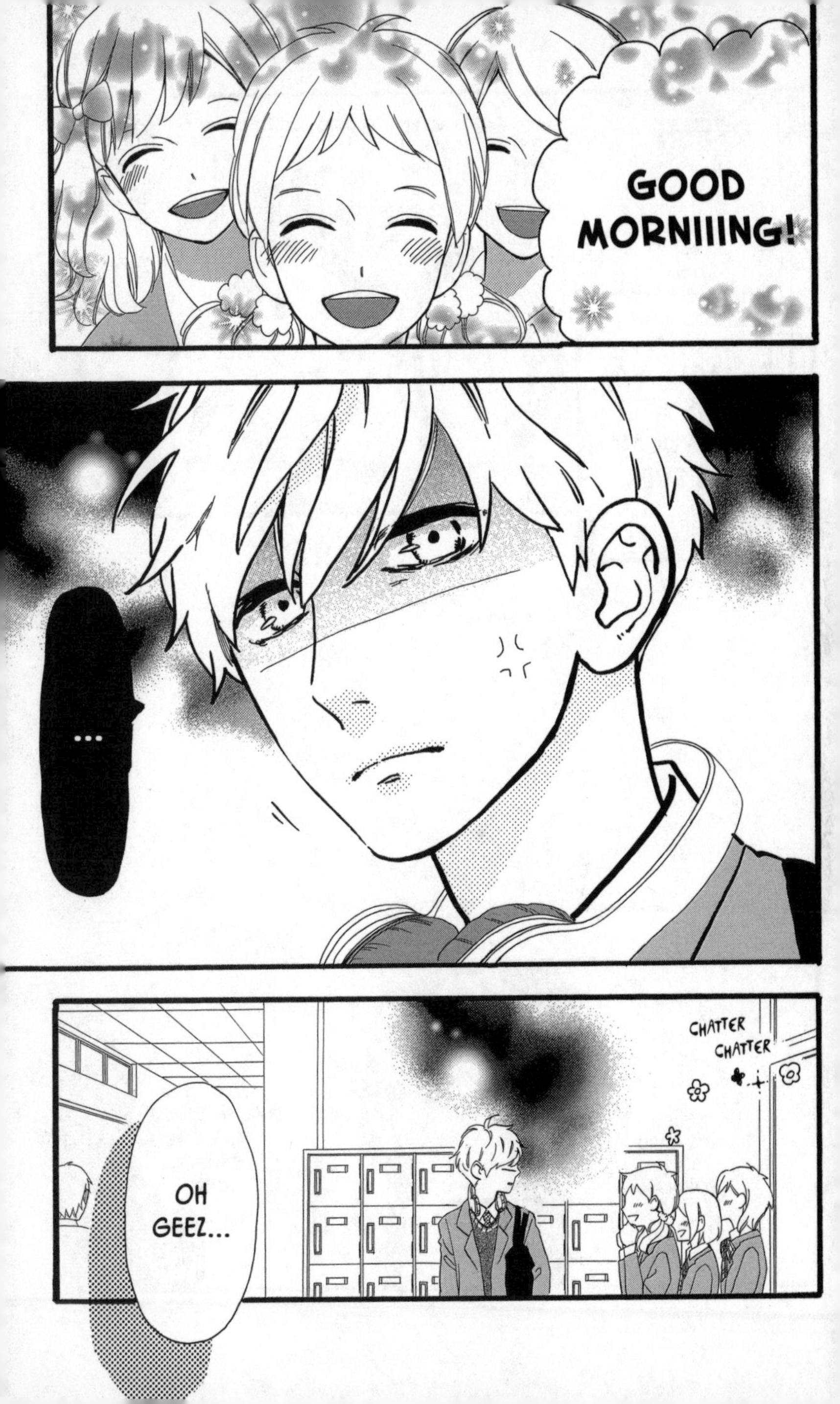
GOOD MORNIIIING!
...
CHATTER CHATTER
OH GEEZ...

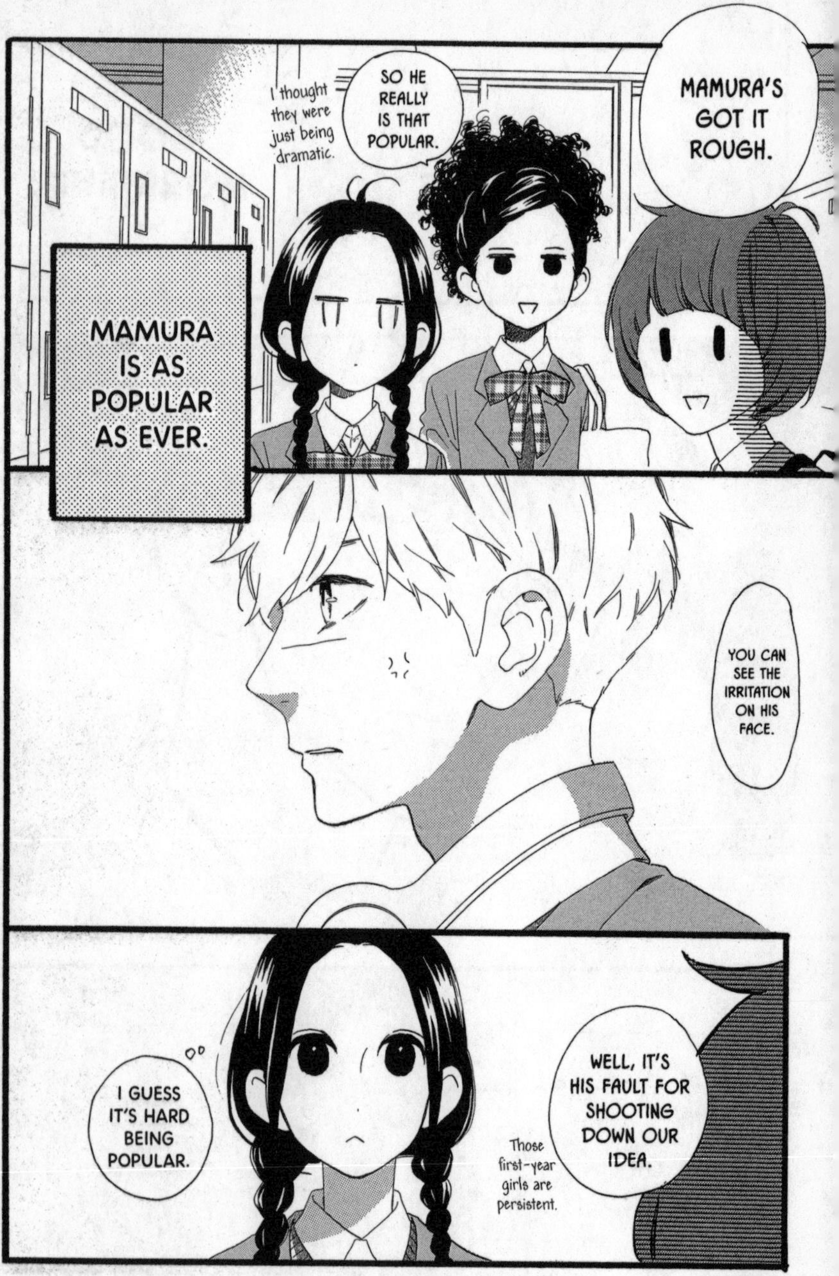
MAMURA'S GOT IT ROUGH.
SO HE REALLY IS THAT POPULAR.
I thought they were just being dramatic.
MAMURA IS AS POPULAR AS EVER.
YOU CAN SEE THE IRRITATION ON HIS FACE.
WELL, IT'S HIS FAULT FOR SHOOTING DOWN OUR IDEA.
Those first-year girls are persistent.
I GUESS IT'S HARD BEING POPULAR.

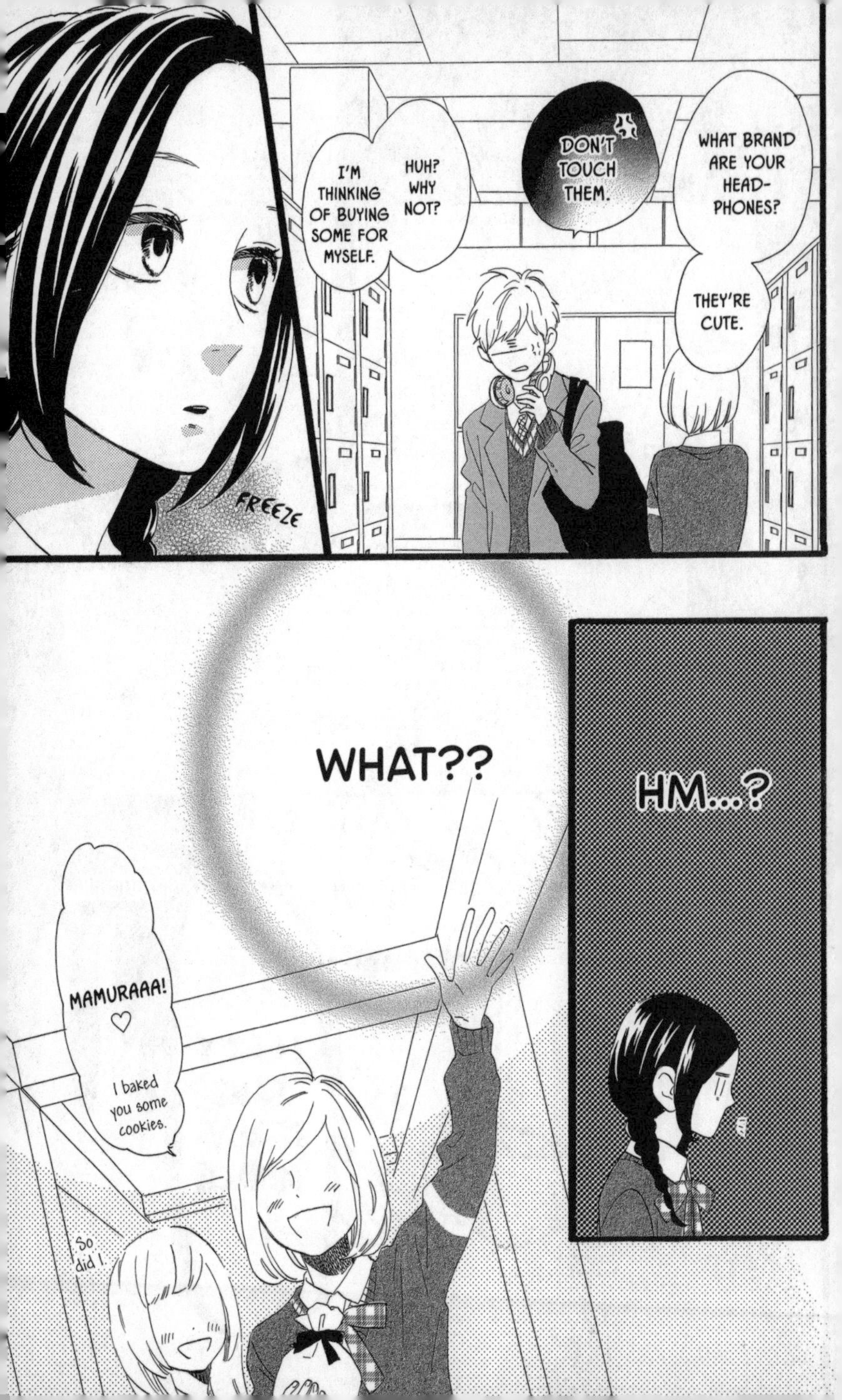

WHAT BRAND ARE YOUR HEAD-PHONES?
THEY'RE CUTE.
DON'T TOUCH THEM.
HUH? WHY NOT?
I'M THINKING OF BUYING SOME FOR MYSELF.
FREEZE
HM...?
WHAT??
MAMURAAA! ♡
I baked you some cookies.
So did I.

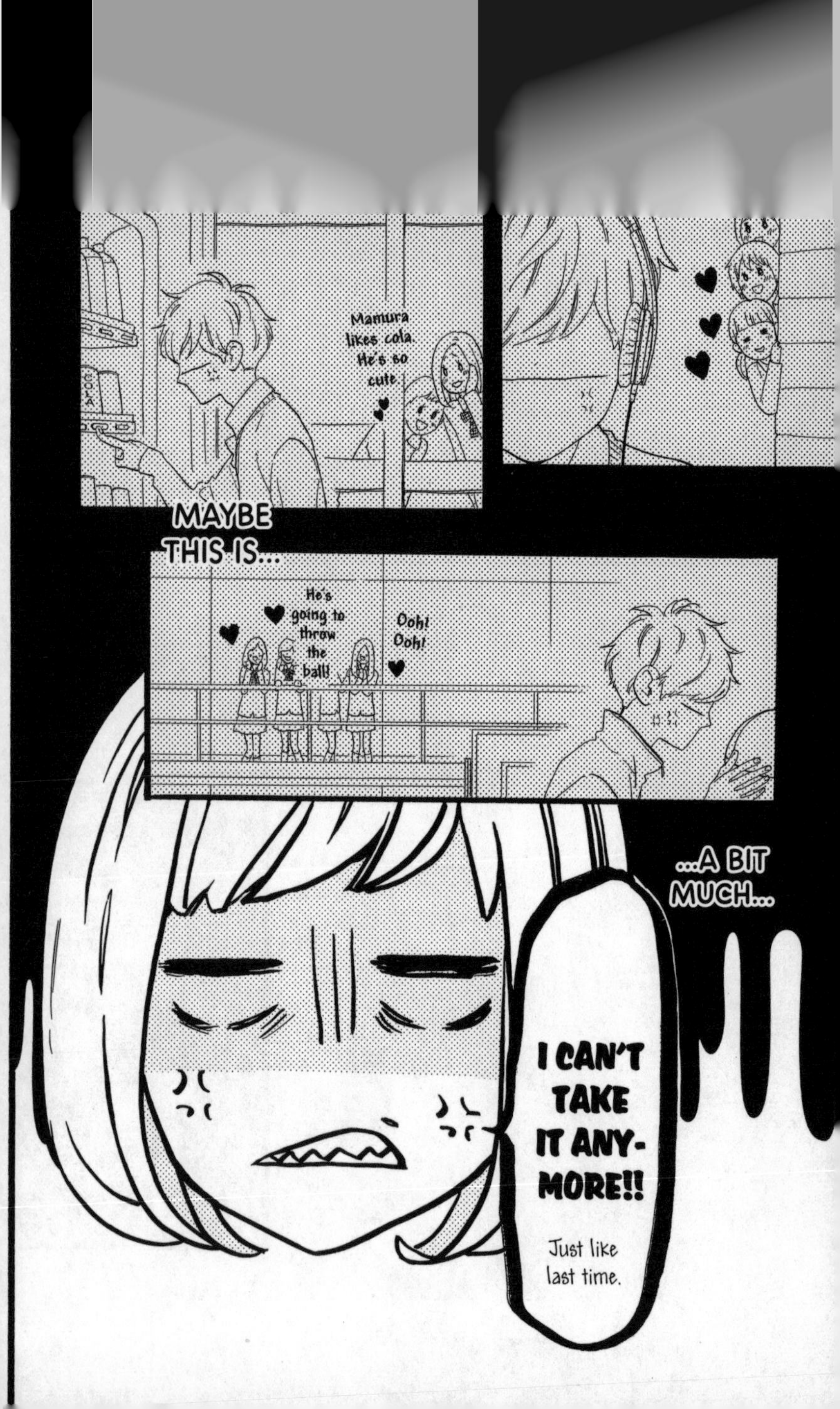

Mamura likes cola. He's so cute.
MAYBE THIS IS...
Ooh! Ooh!
He's going to throw the ball!
...A BIT MUCH...
I CAN'T TAKE IT ANY-MORE!!
Just like last time.

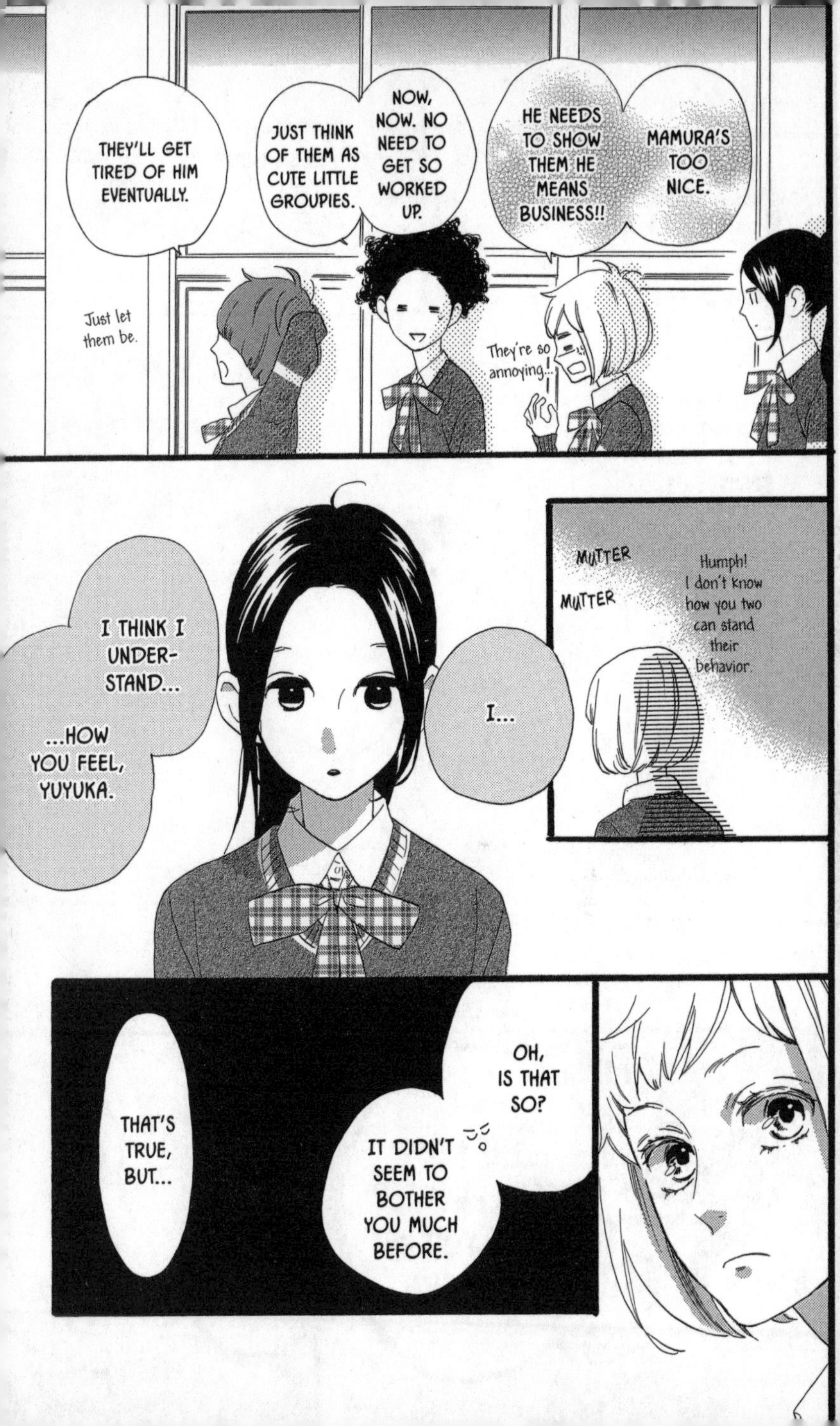
MAMURA'S TOO NICE.
HE NEEDS TO SHOW THEM HE MEANS BUSINESS!!
They're so annoying...
NOW, NOW. NO NEED TO GET SO WORKED UP.
JUST THINK OF THEM AS CUTE LITTLE GROUPIES.
THEY'LL GET TIRED OF HIM EVENTUALLY.
Just let them be.
Humph! I don't know how you two can stand their behavior.
MUTTER
MUTTER
I...
I THINK I UNDER-STAND...
...HOW YOU FEEL, YUYUKA.
OH, IS THAT SO?
IT DIDN'T SEEM TO BOTHER YOU MUCH BEFORE.
THAT'S TRUE, BUT...

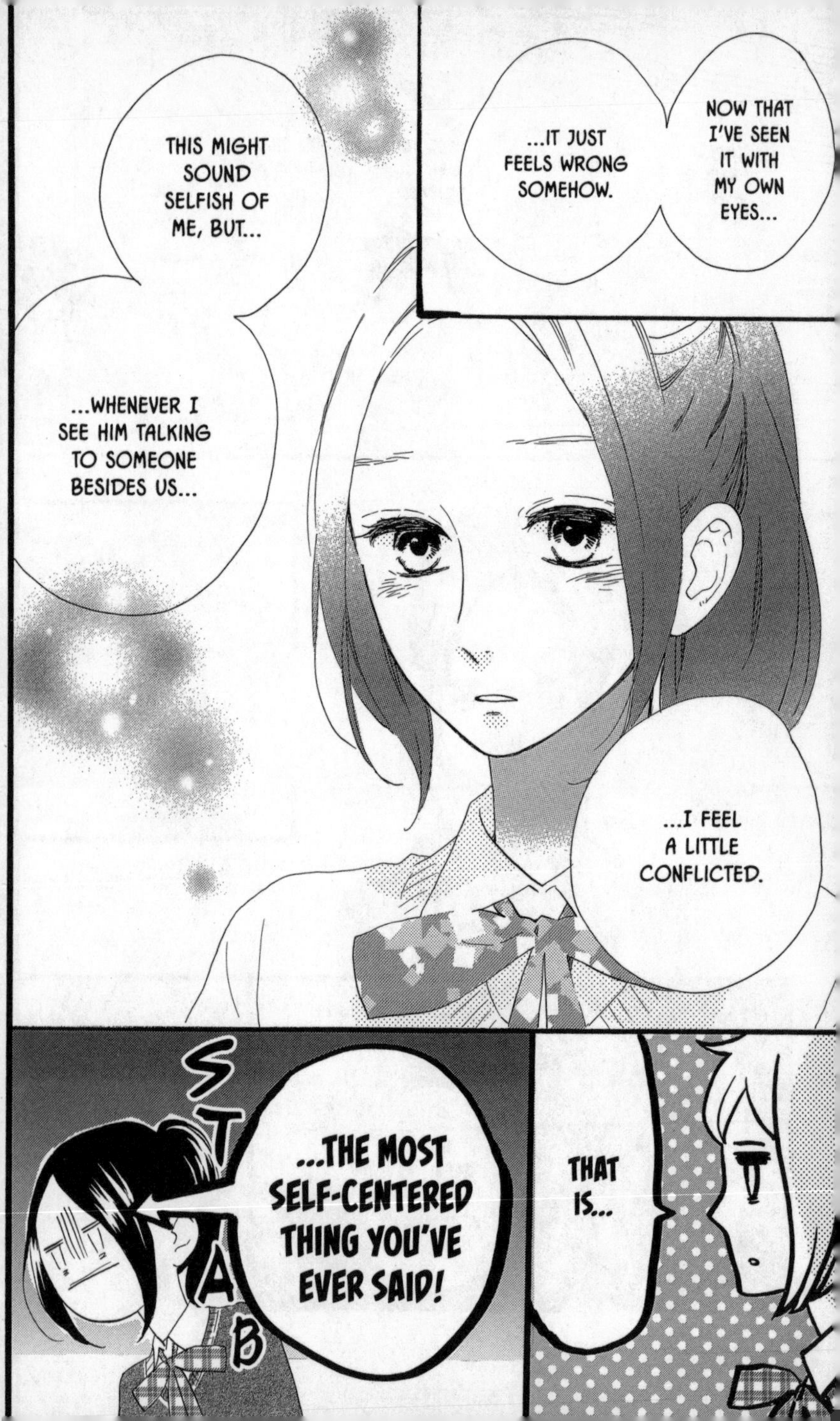
NOW THAT I'VE SEEN IT WITH MY OWN EYES...
...IT JUST FEELS WRONG SOMEHOW.
THIS MIGHT SOUND SELFISH OF ME, BUT...
...WHENEVER I SEE HIM TALKING TO SOMEONE BESIDES US...
...I FEEL A LITTLE CONFLICTED.
THAT IS...
...THE MOST SELF-CENTERED THING YOU'VE EVER SAID!
STAB

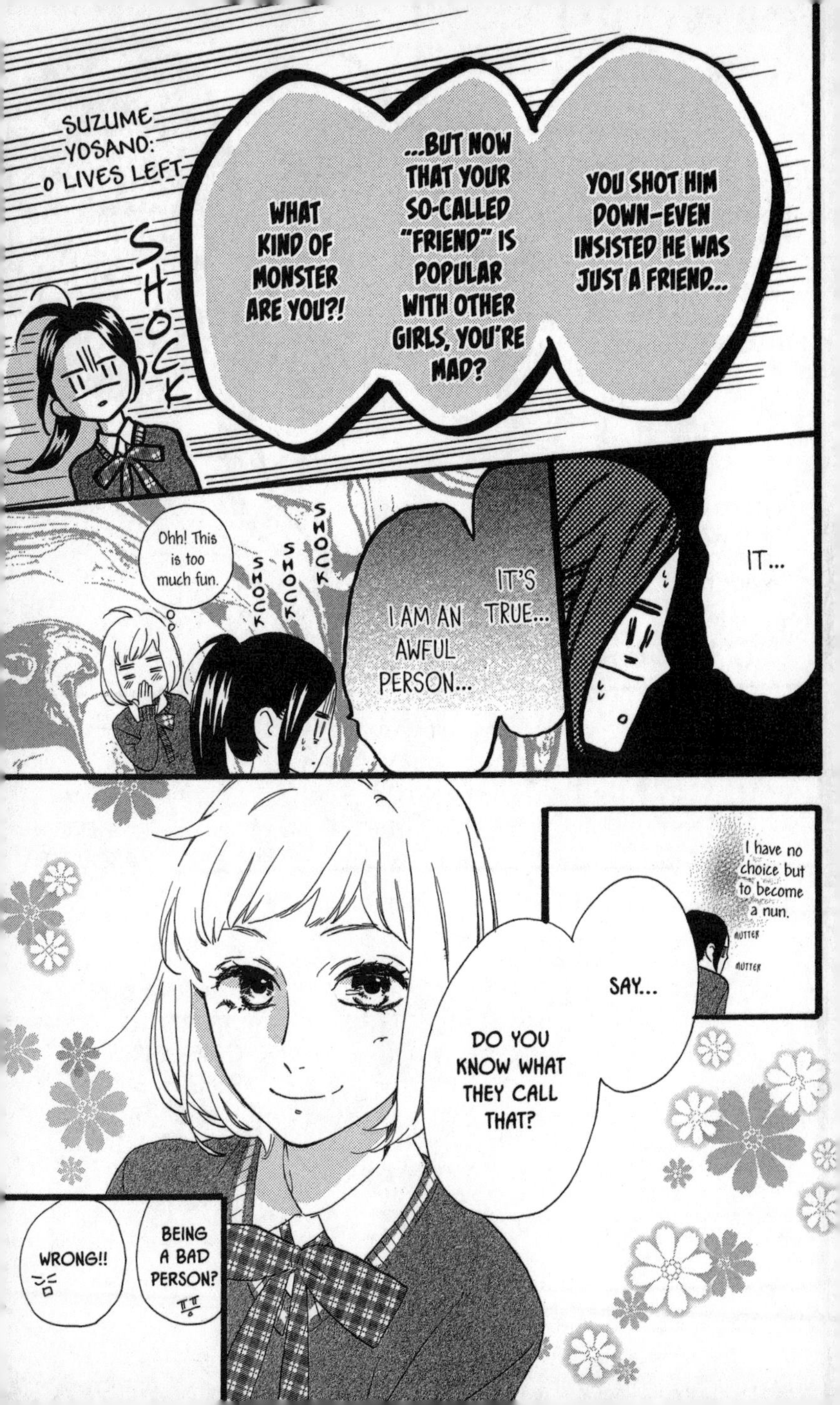
YOU SHOT HIM DOWN—EVEN INSISTED HE WAS JUST A FRIEND...
...BUT NOW THAT YOUR SO-CALLED "FRIEND" IS POPULAR WITH OTHER GIRLS, YOU'RE MAD?
WHAT KIND OF MONSTER ARE YOU?!
SUZUME YOSANO: 0 LIVES LEFT
SHOCK
IT...
IT'S TRUE...
I AM AN AWFUL PERSON...
SHOCK
SHOCK
SHOCK
Ohh! This is too much fun.
I have no choice but to become a nun.
MUTTER
MUTTER
SAY...
DO YOU KNOW WHAT THEY CALL THAT?
BEING A BAD PERSON?
WRONG!!

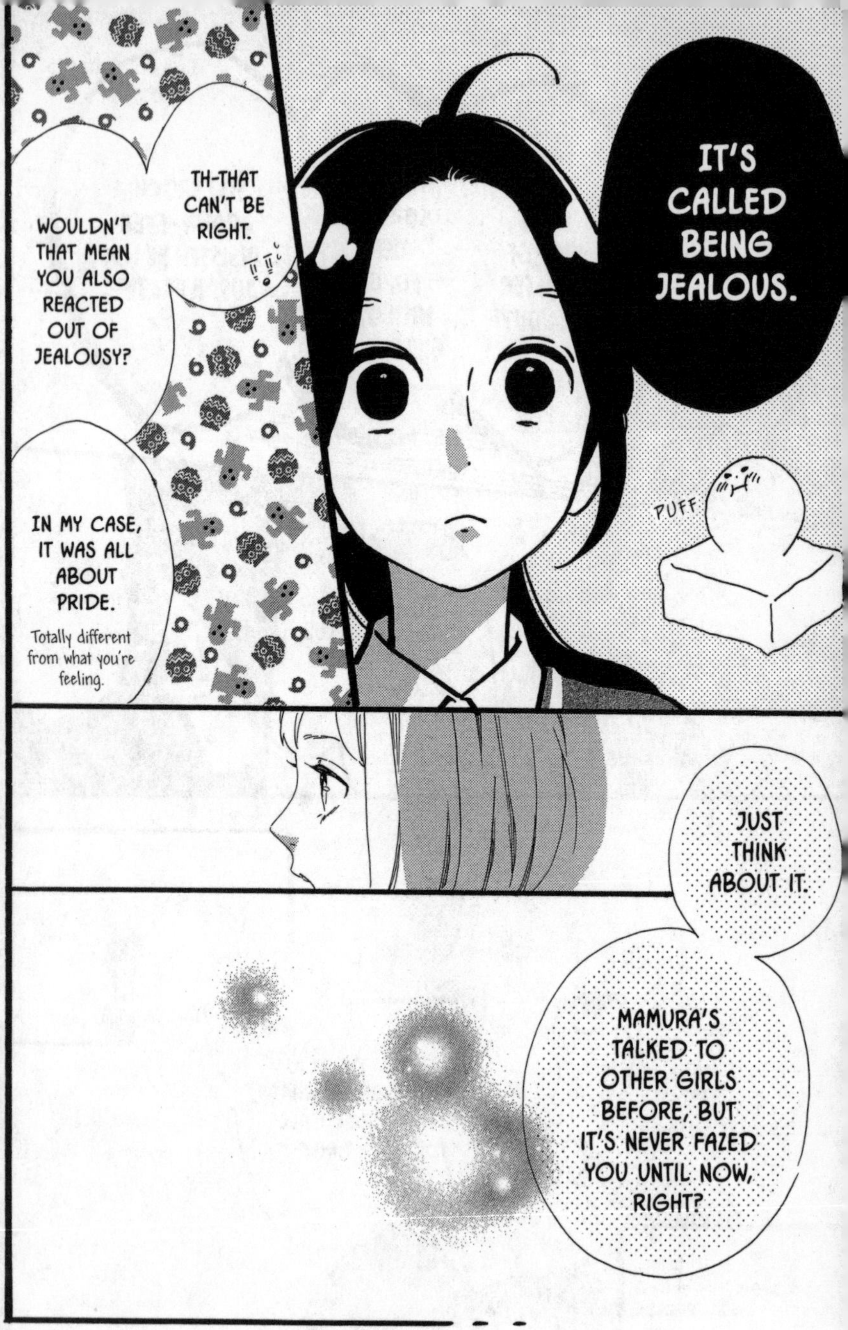
IT'S CALLED BEING JEALOUS.
PUFF
TH-THAT CAN'T BE RIGHT.
WOULDN'T THAT MEAN YOU ALSO REACTED OUT OF JEALOUSY?
IN MY CASE, IT WAS ALL ABOUT PRIDE.
Totally different from what you're feeling.
JUST THINK ABOUT IT.
MAMURA'S TALKED TO OTHER GIRLS BEFORE, BUT IT'S NEVER FAZED YOU UNTIL NOW, RIGHT?

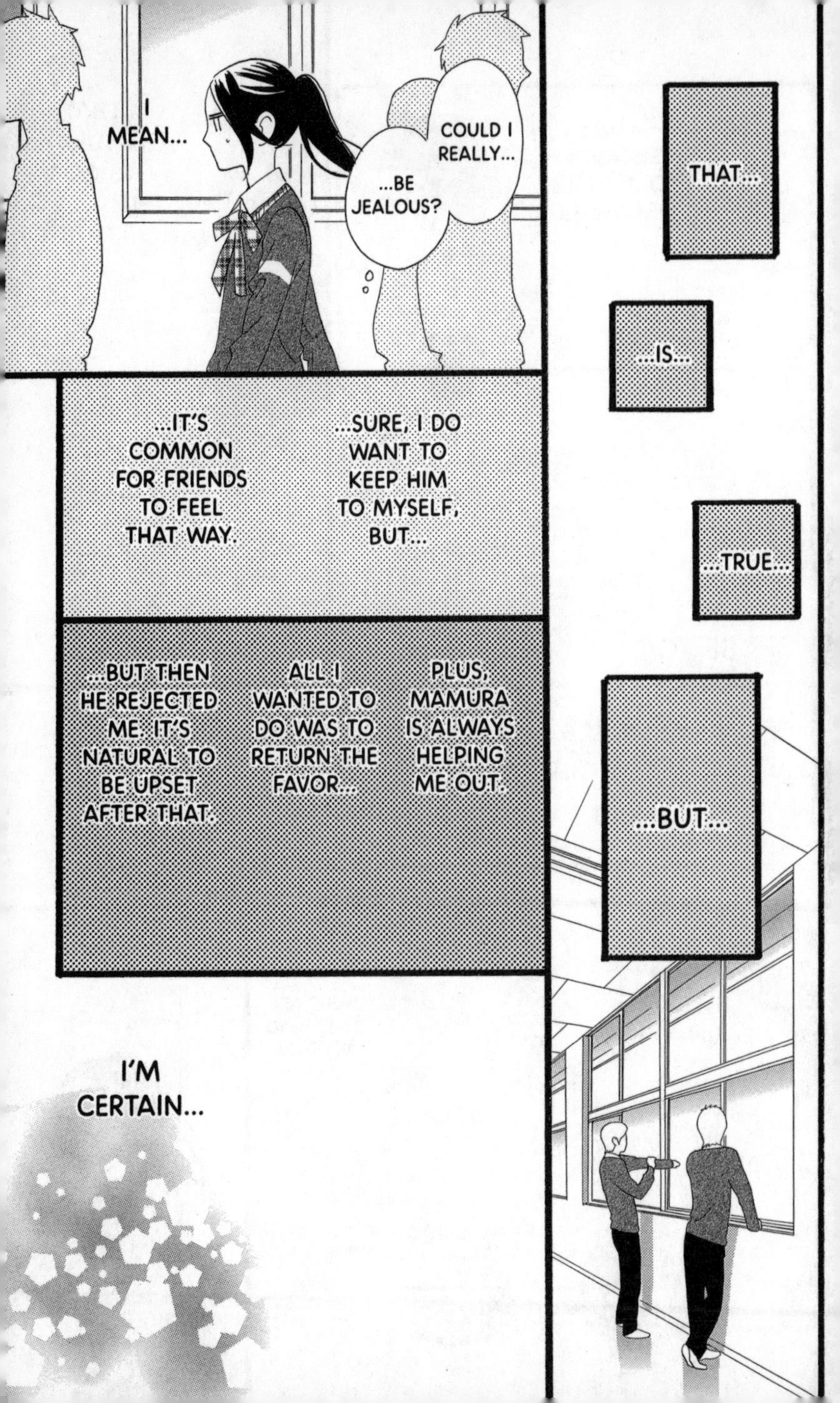
THAT...
...IS...
...TRUE...
...BUT...
COULD I REALLY...
...BE JEALOUS?
I MEAN...
...SURE, I DO WANT TO KEEP HIM TO MYSELF, BUT...
...IT'S COMMON FOR FRIENDS TO FEEL THAT WAY.
PLUS, MAMURA IS ALWAYS HELPING ME OUT.
ALL I WANTED TO DO WAS TO RETURN THE FAVOR...
...BUT THEN HE REJECTED ME. IT'S NATURAL TO BE UPSET AFTER THAT.
I'M CERTAIN...

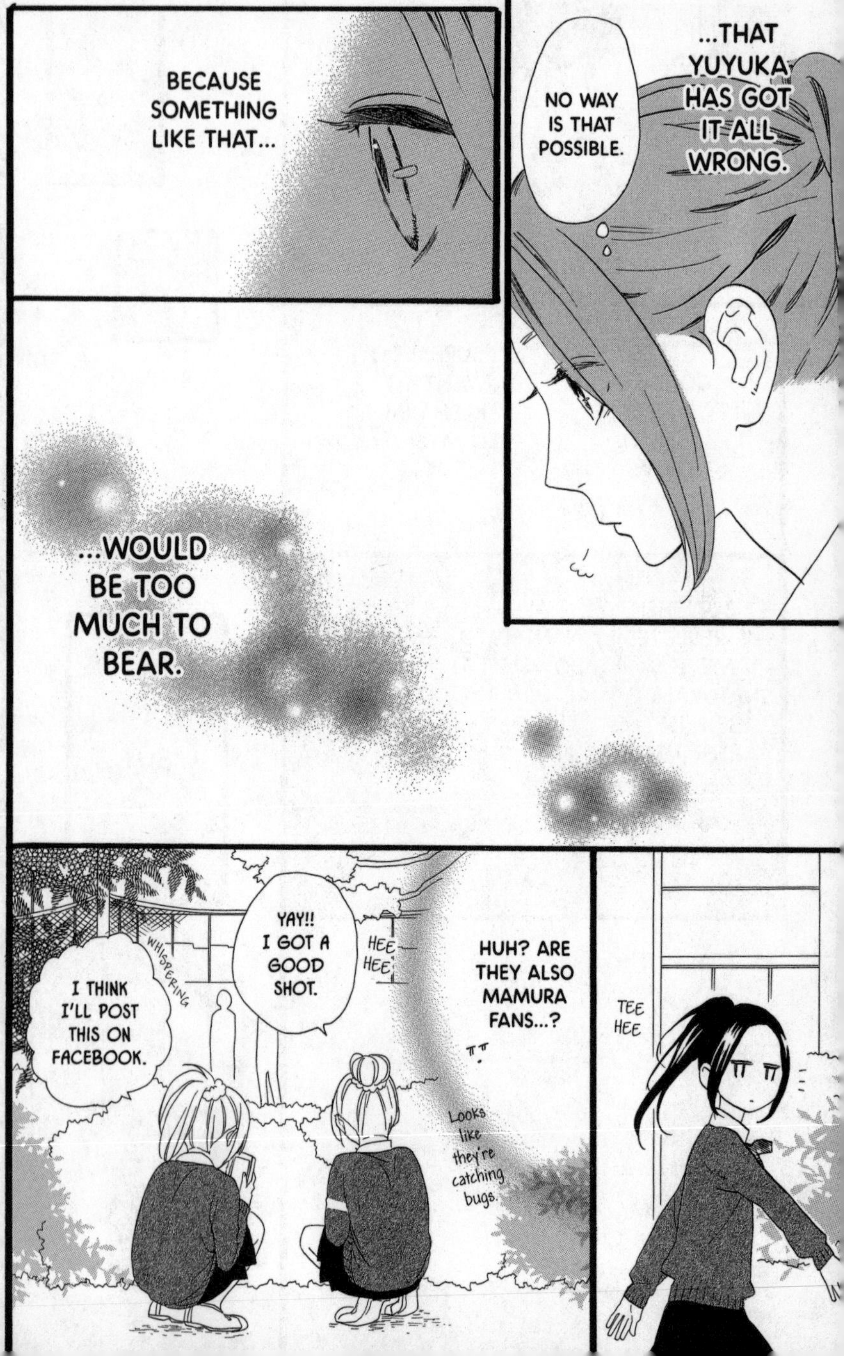
...THAT YUYUKA HAS GOT IT ALL WRONG.
NO WAY IS THAT POSSIBLE.
BECAUSE SOMETHING LIKE THAT...
...WOULD BE TOO MUCH TO BEAR.
TEE HEE
HUH? ARE THEY ALSO MAMURA FANS...?
Looks like they're catching bugs.
HEE HEE
YAY!! I GOT A GOOD SHOT.
WHISPERING
I THINK I'LL POST THIS ON FACEBOOK.

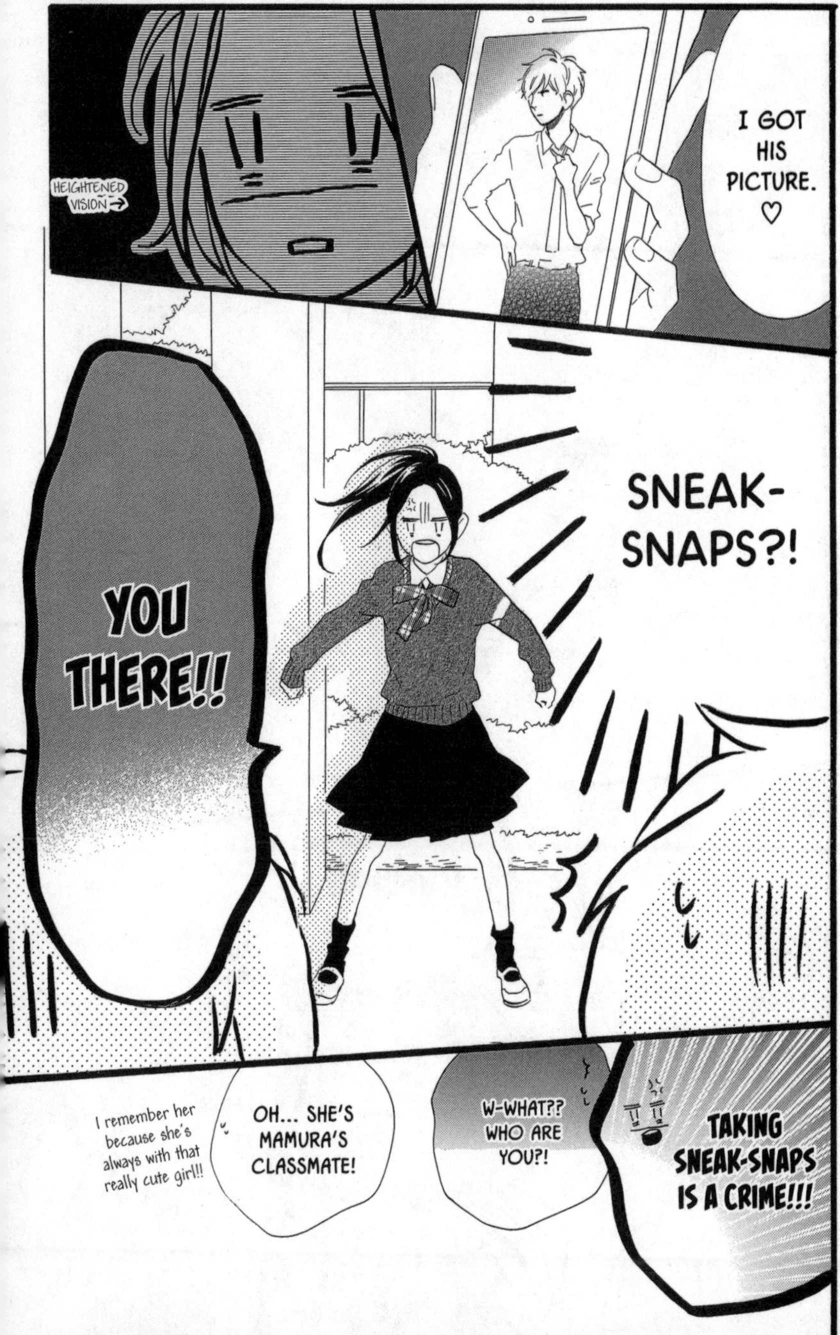
I GOT HIS PICTURE. ♡
HEIGHTENED VISION
SNEAK-SNAPS?!
YOU THERE!!
TAKING SNEAK-SNAPS IS A CRIME!!!
W-WHAT?? WHO ARE YOU?!
OH... SHE'S MAMURA'S CLASSMATE!
I remember her because she's always with that really cute girl!!

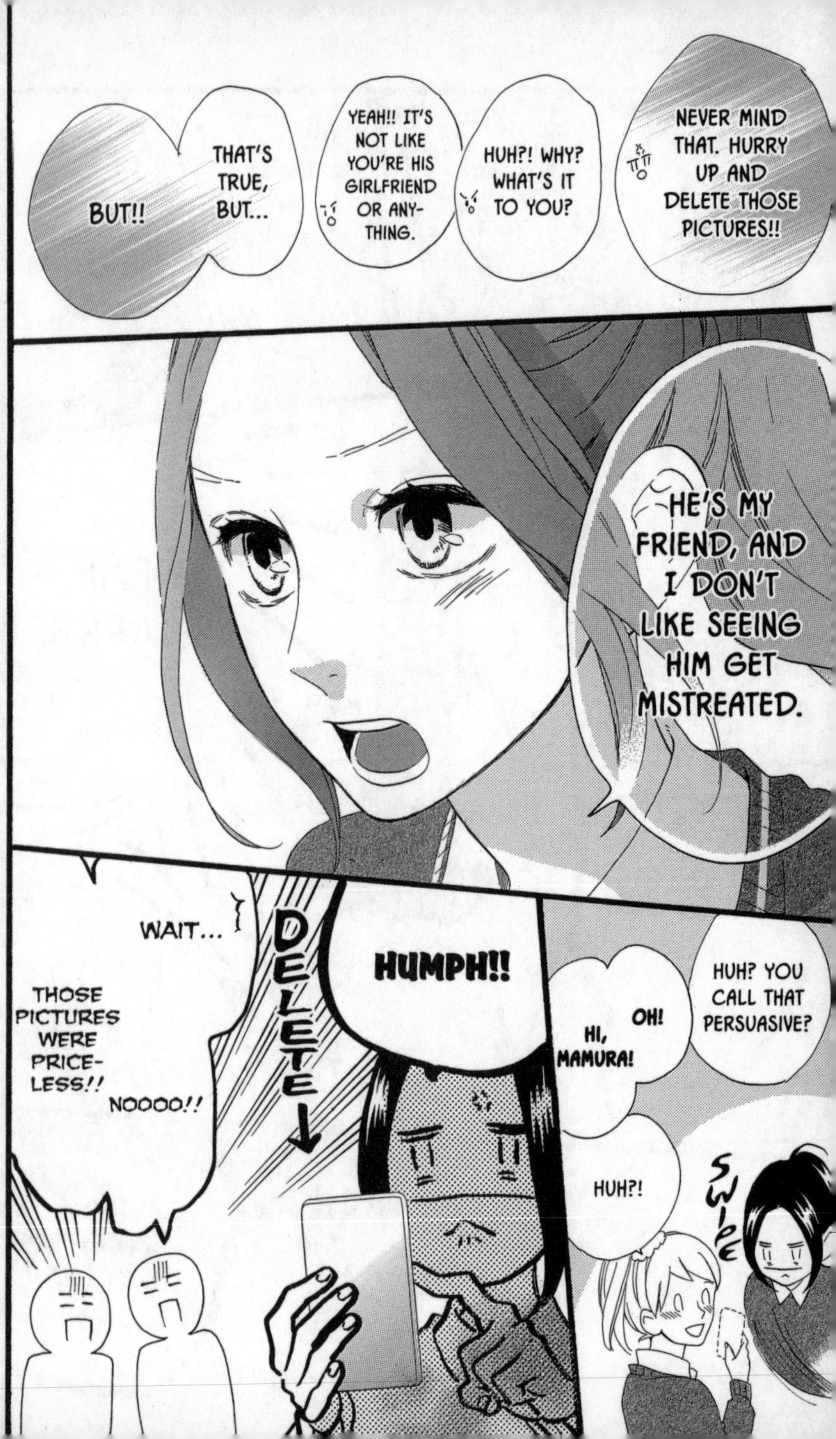
NEVER MIND THAT. HURRY UP AND DELETE THOSE PICTURES!!
HUH?! WHY? WHAT'S IT TO YOU?
YEAH!! IT'S NOT LIKE YOU'RE HIS GIRLFRIEND OR ANYTHING.
THAT'S TRUE, BUT...
BUT!!
HE'S MY FRIEND, AND I DON'T LIKE SEEING HIM GET MISTREATED.
HUH? YOU CALL THAT PERSUASIVE?
OH!
HI, MAMURA!
SWIPE
HUH?!
HUMPH!!
DELETE
WAIT...
THOSE PICTURES WERE PRICELESS!!
NOOOO!!

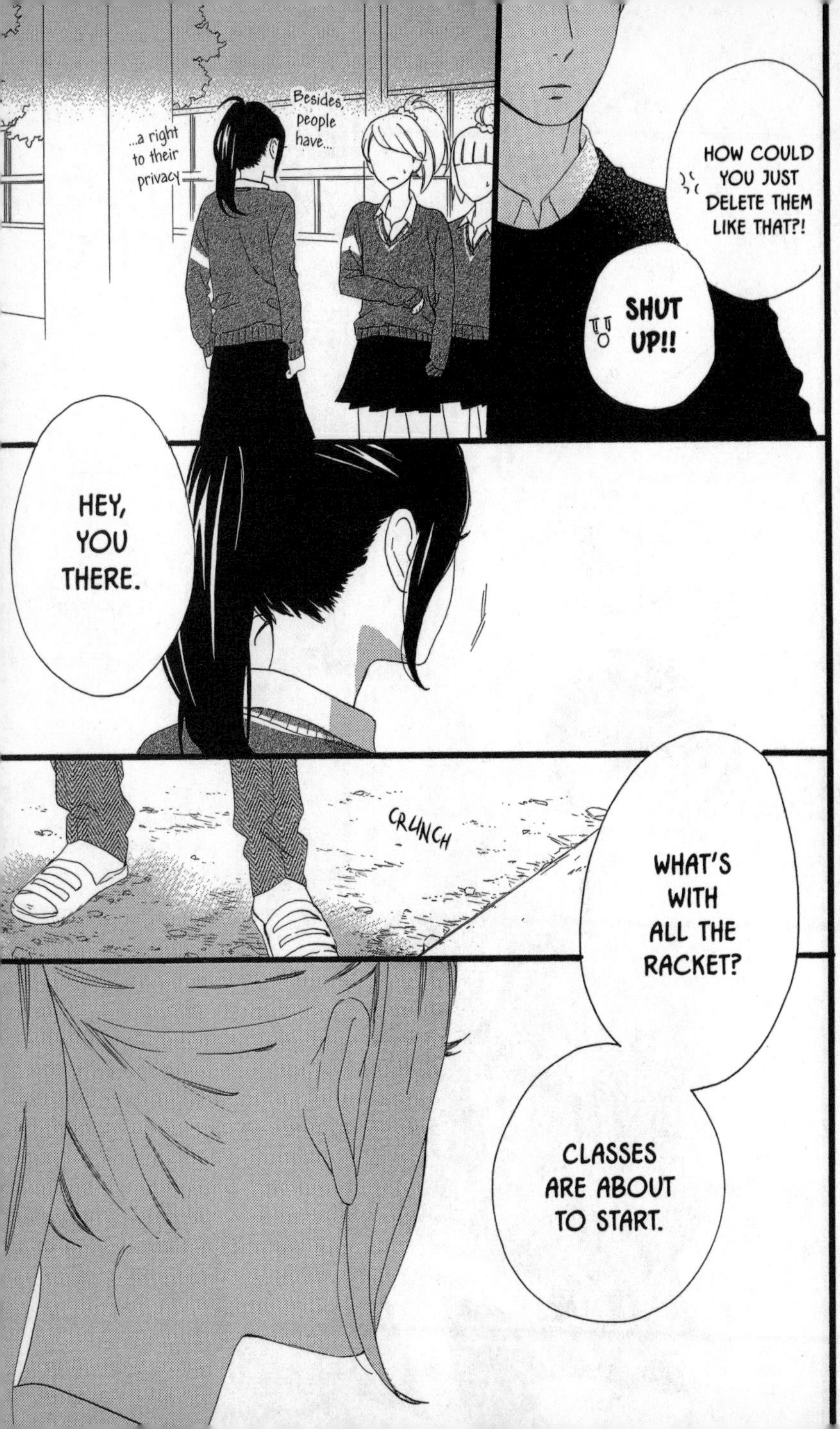
HOW COULD YOU JUST DELETE THEM LIKE THAT?!
SHUT UP!!
Besides, people have...
...a right to their privacy
HEY, YOU THERE.
WHAT'S WITH ALL THE RACKET?
CRUNCH
CLASSES ARE ABOUT TO START.

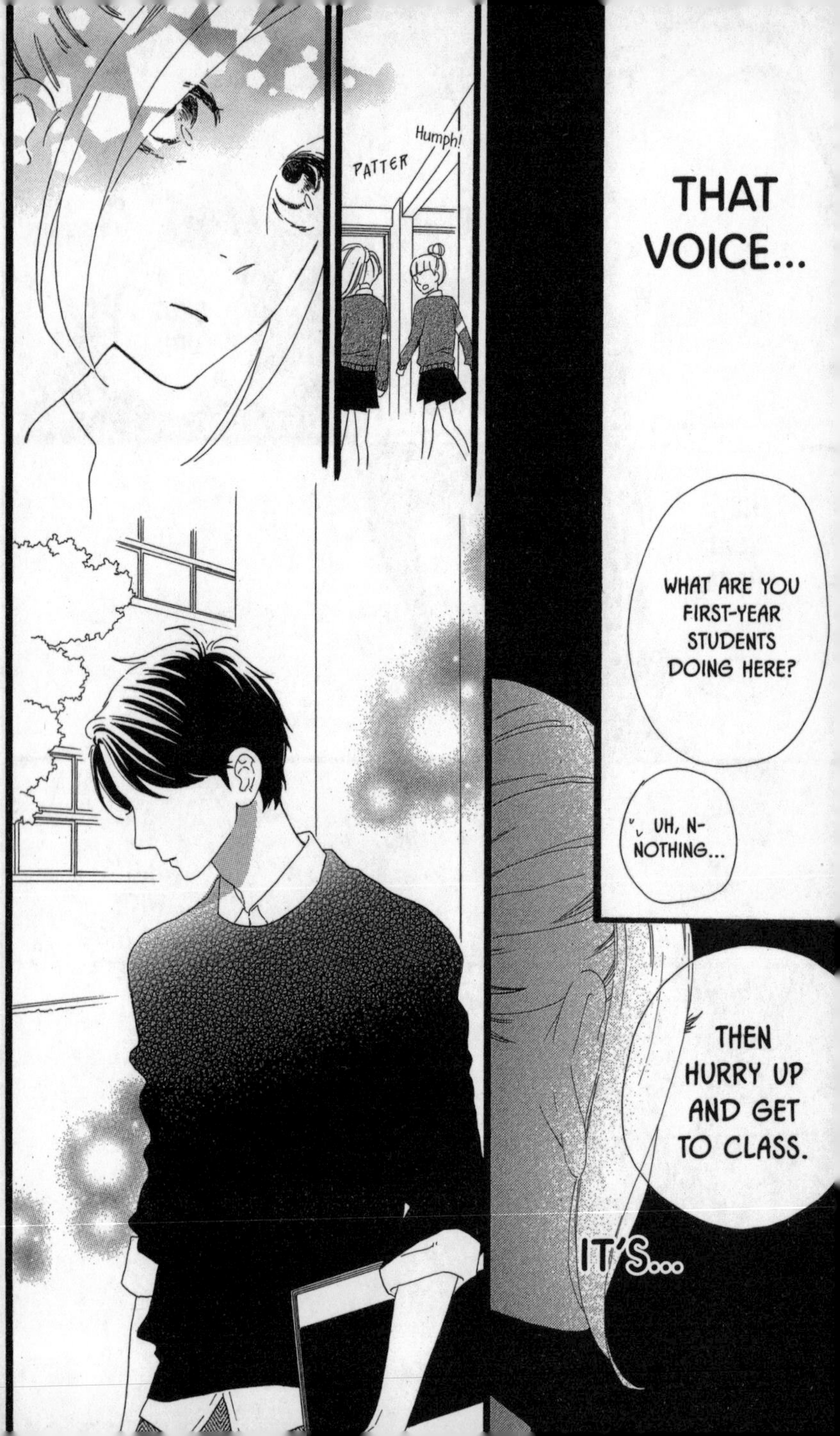
THAT VOICE...
WHAT ARE YOU FIRST-YEAR STUDENTS DOING HERE?
UH, N-NOTHING...
THEN HURRY UP AND GET TO CLASS.
IT'S...
Humph!
PATTER

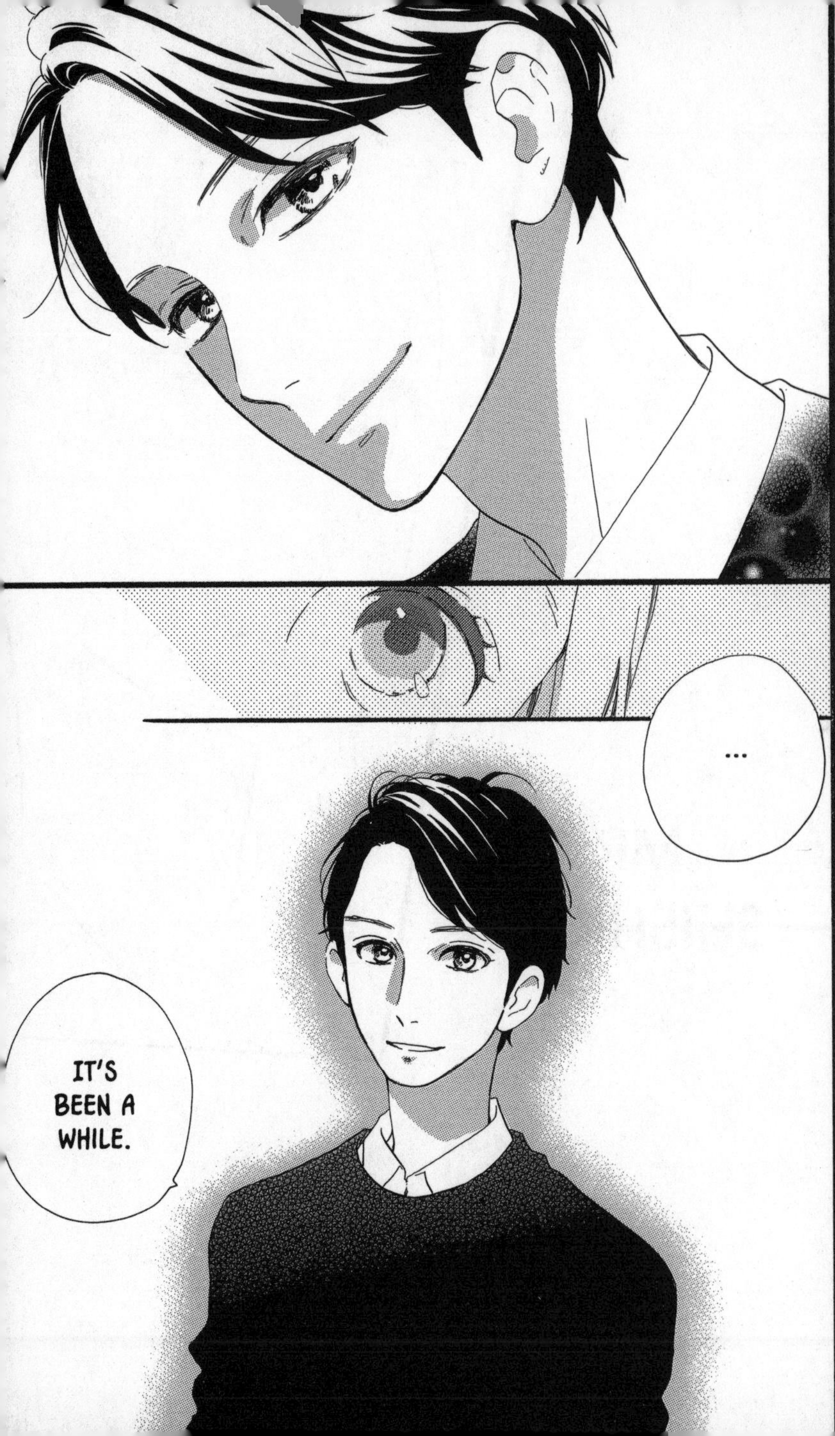
...
IT'S BEEN A WHILE.

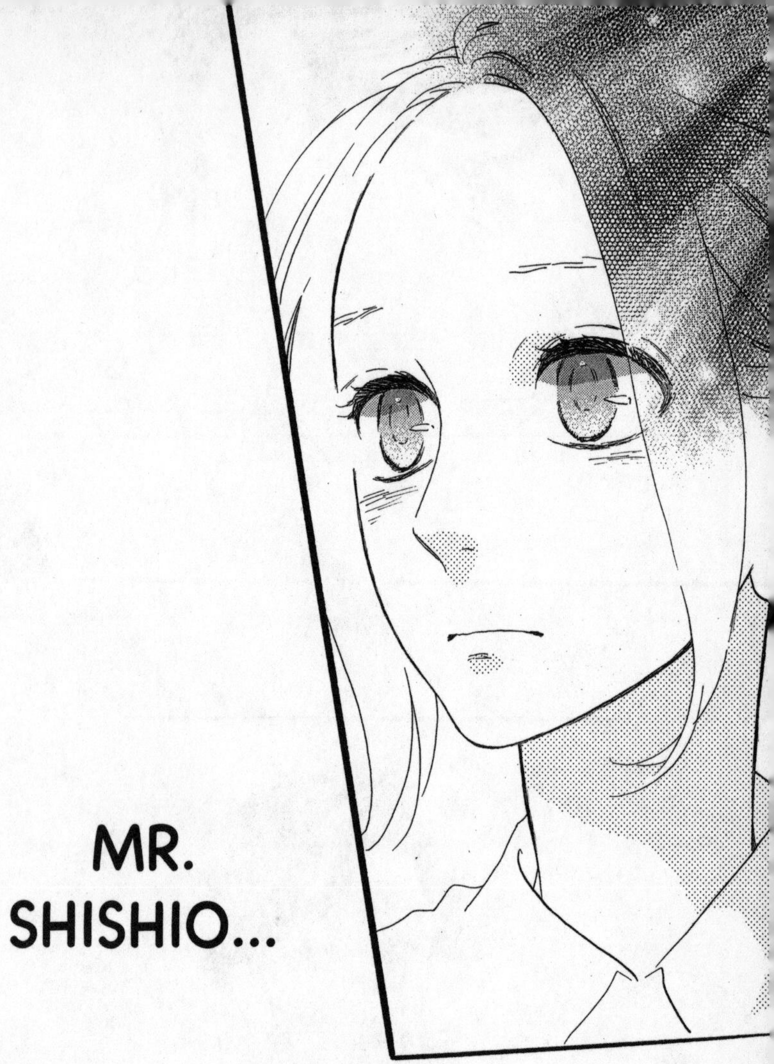
MR. SHISHIO...

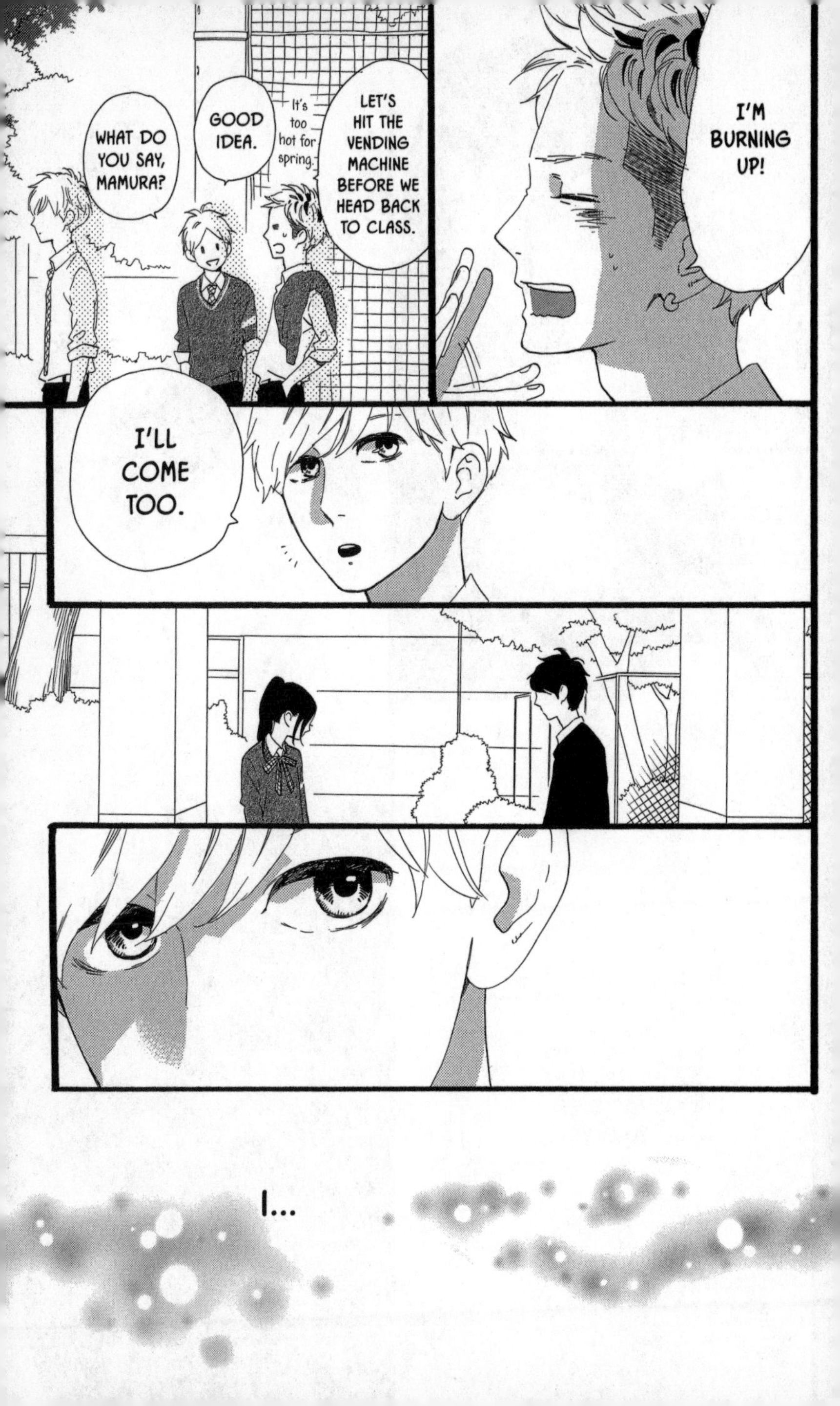
I'M BURNING UP!
LET'S HIT THE VENDING MACHINE BEFORE WE HEAD BACK TO CLASS.
It's too hot for spring.
GOOD IDEA.
WHAT DO YOU SAY, MAMURA?
I'LL COME TOO.
I...

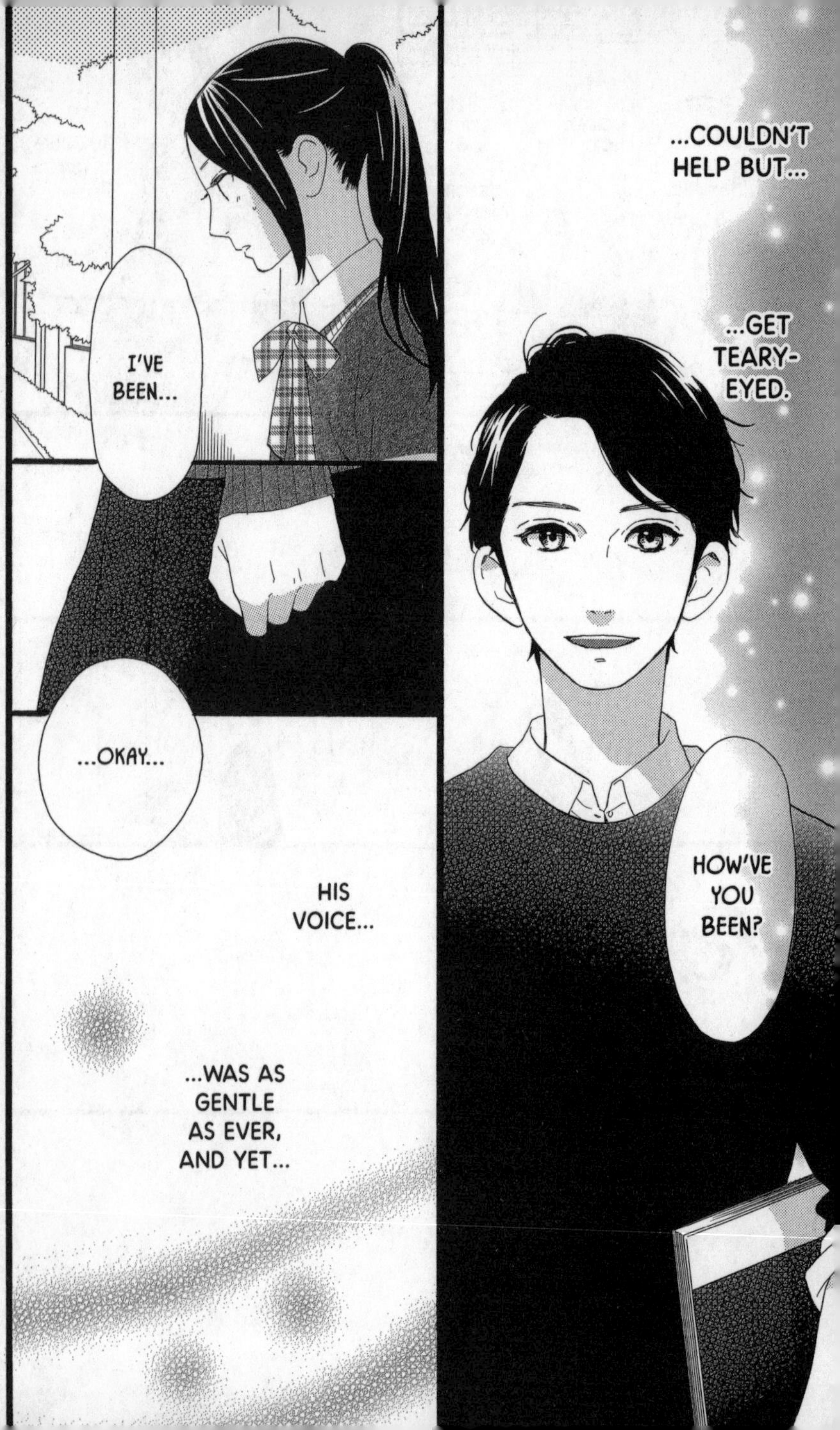
...COULDN'T HELP BUT...
...GET TEARY-EYED.
HOW'VE YOU BEEN?
I'VE BEEN...
...OKAY...
HIS VOICE...
...WAS AS GENTLE AS EVER, AND YET...

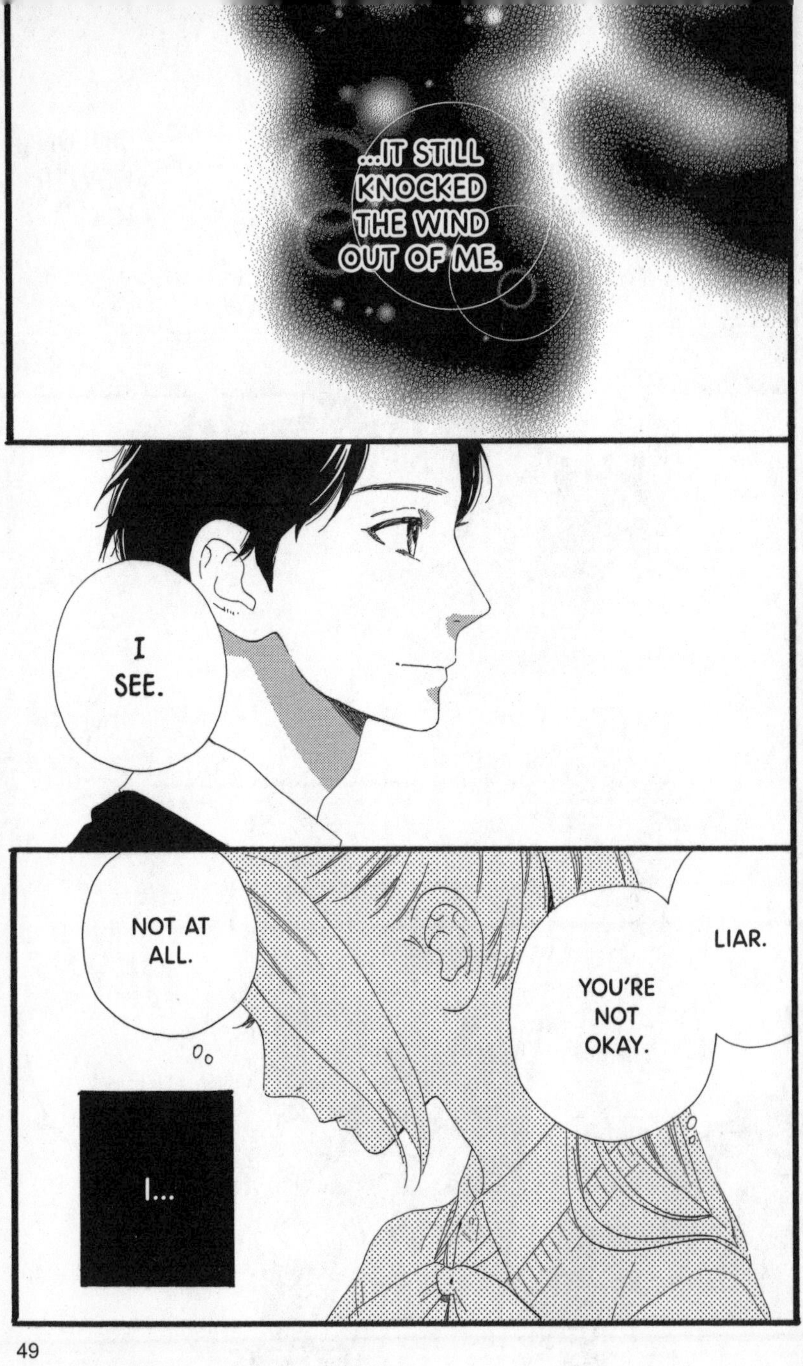

...IT STILL KNOCKED THE WIND OUT OF ME.
I SEE.
LIAR.
YOU'RE NOT OKAY.
NOT AT ALL.
I...

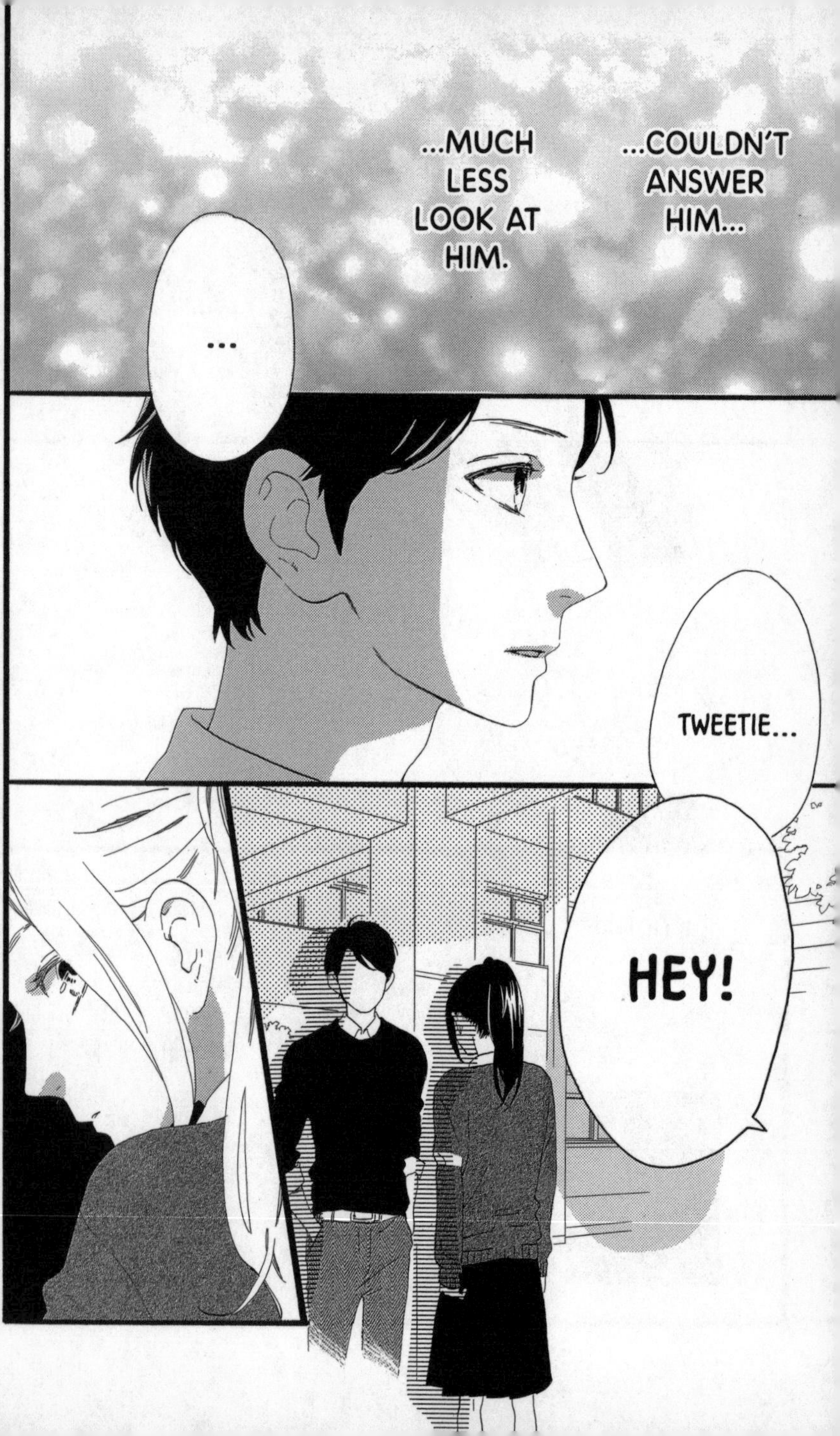
...COULDN'T ANSWER HIM...
...MUCH LESS LOOK AT HIM.
...
TWEETIE...
HEY!

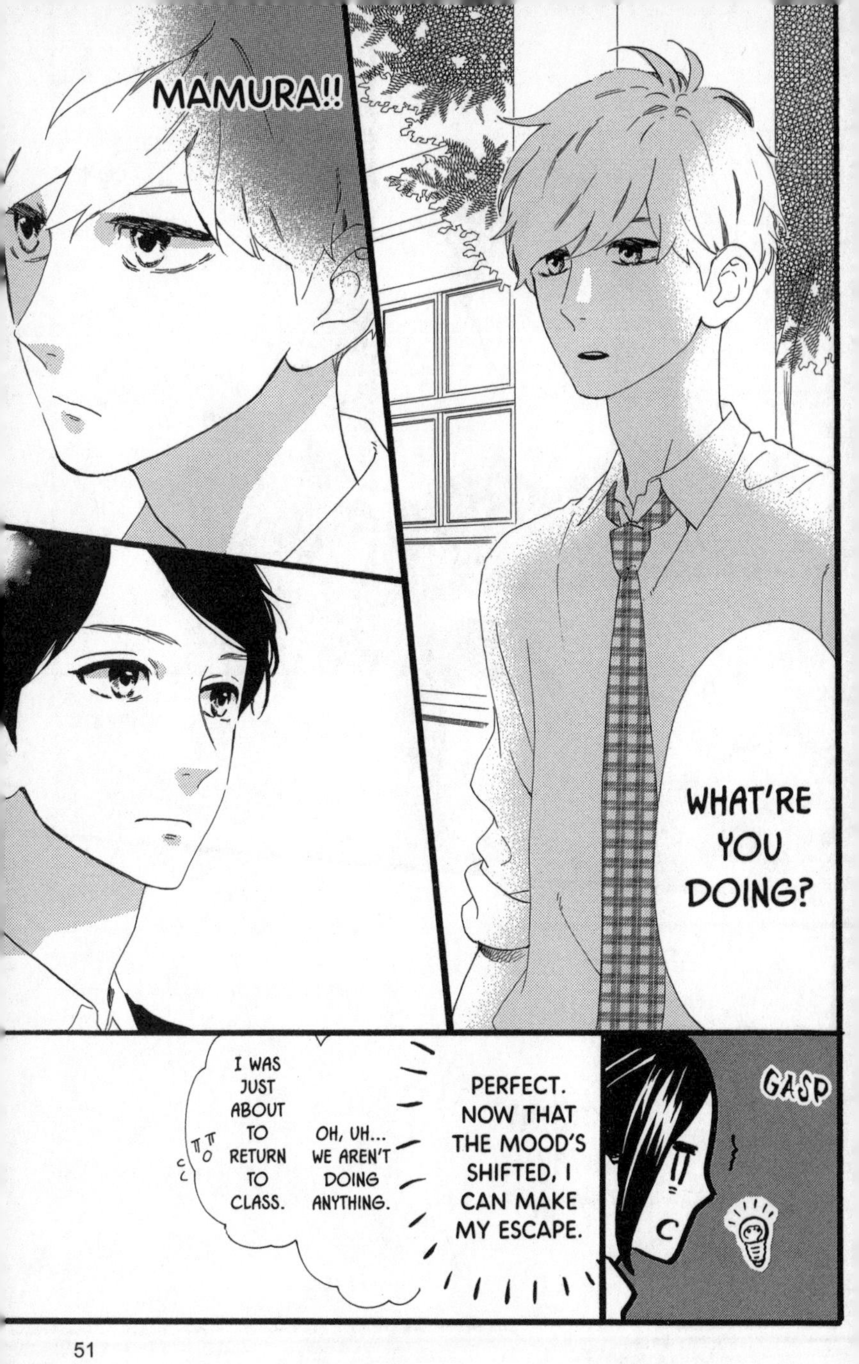
WHAT'RE YOU DOING?
MAMURA!!
GASP
PERFECT. NOW THAT THE MOOD'S SHIFTED, I CAN MAKE MY ESCAPE.
OH, UH... WE AREN'T DOING ANYTHING.
I WAS JUST ABOUT TO RETURN TO CLASS.

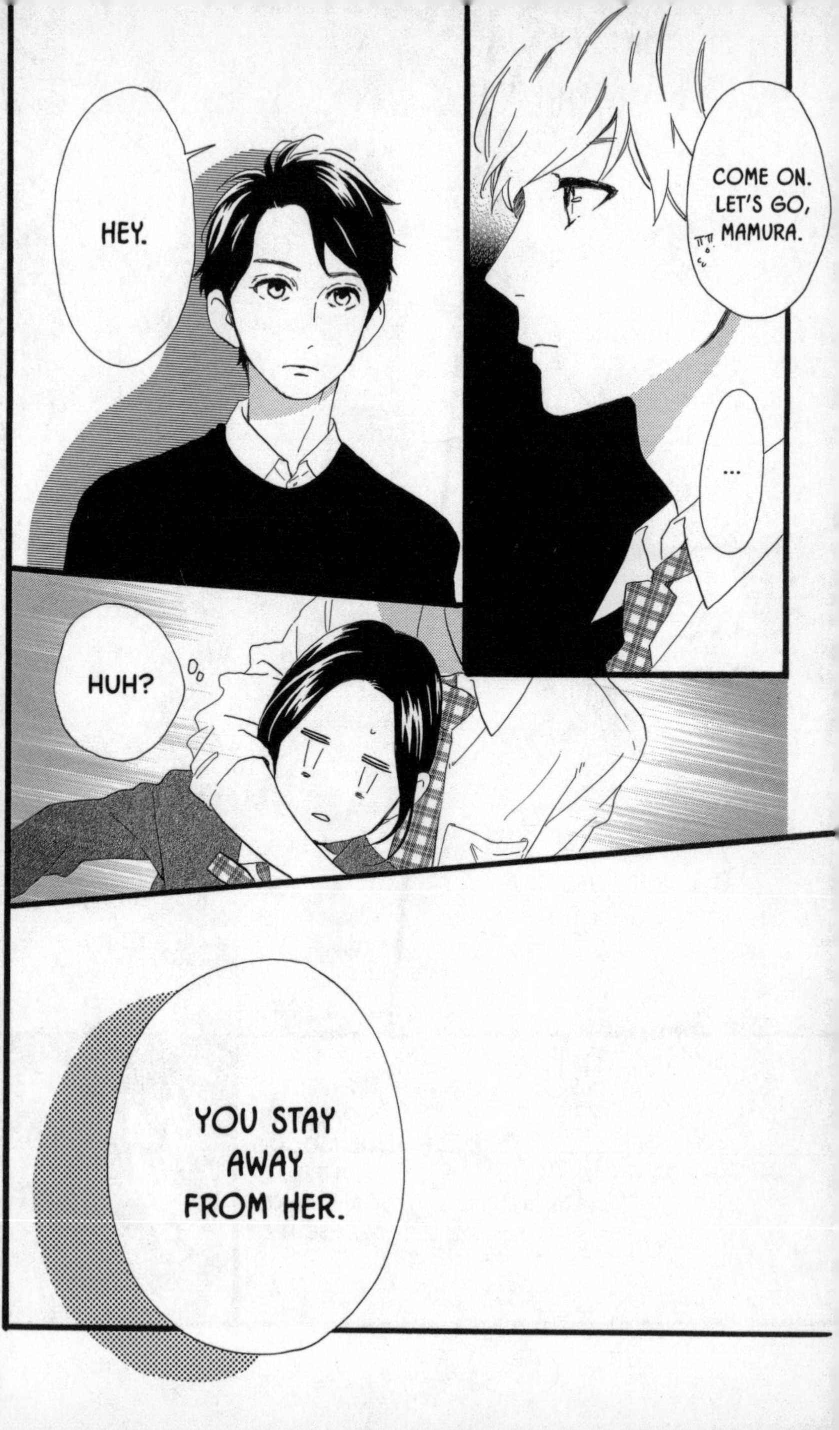
COME ON. LET'S GO, MAMURA.
...
HEY.
HUH?
YOU STAY AWAY FROM HER.

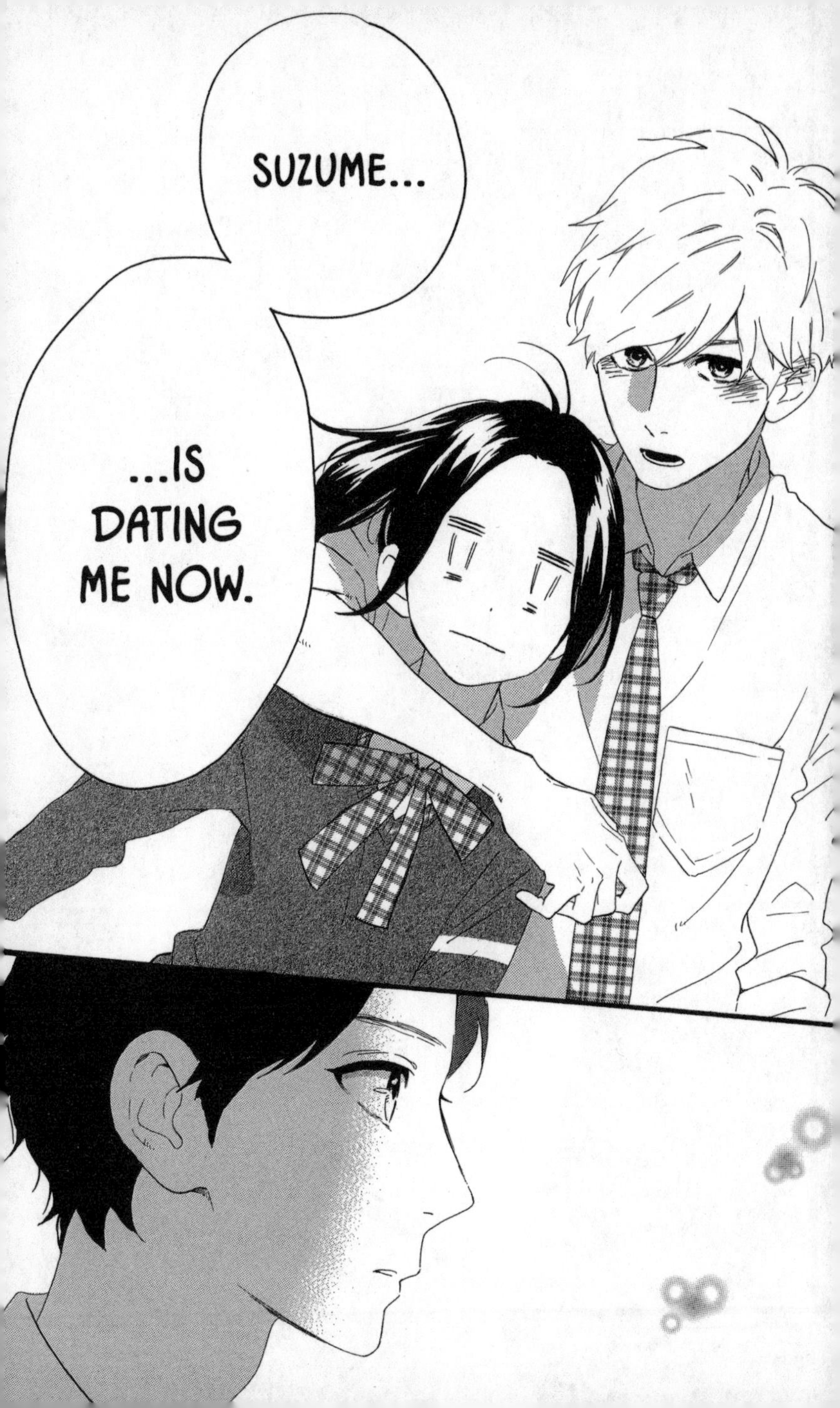
SUZUME...
...IS DATING ME NOW.

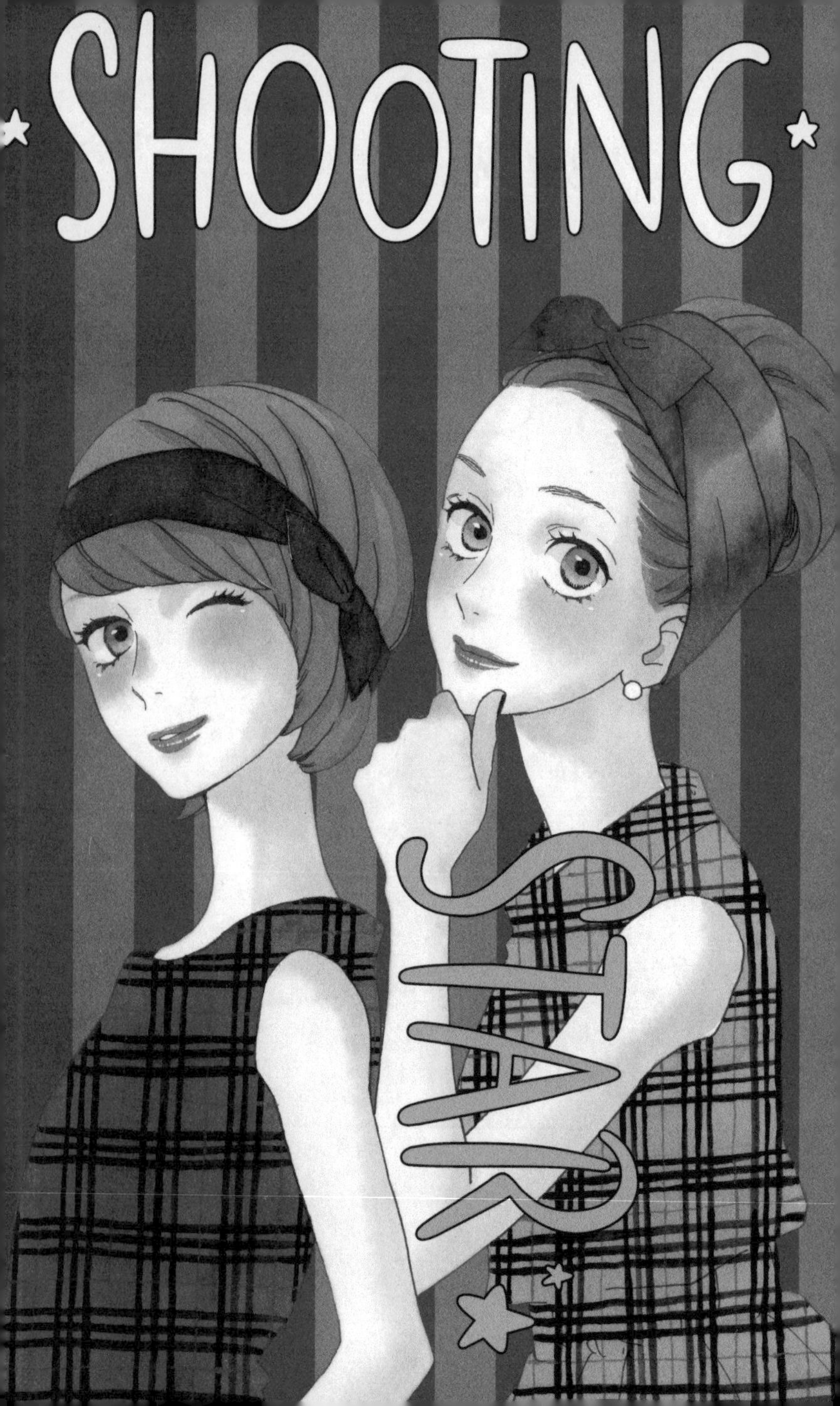
SHOOTING
STAR

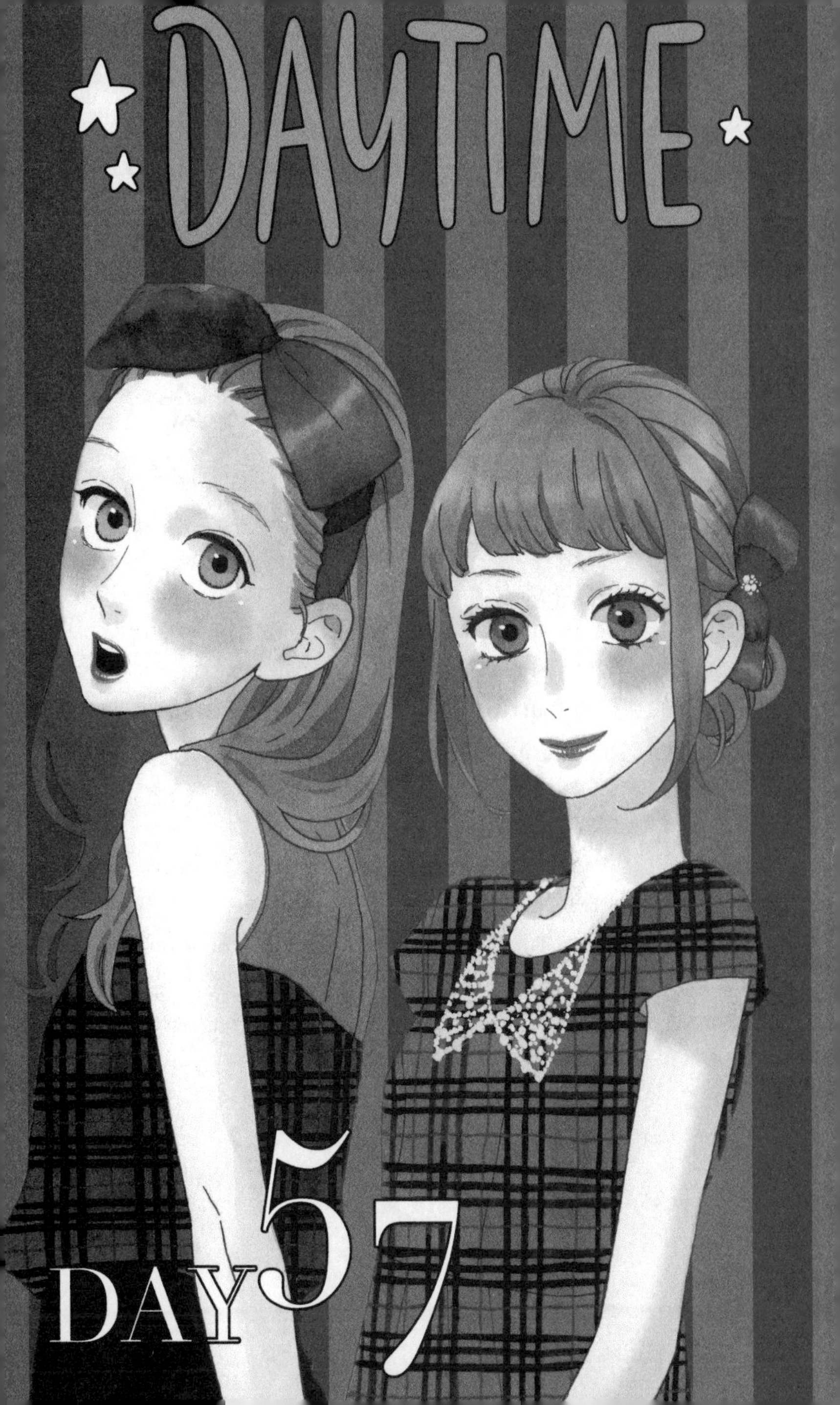
DAYTIME
DAY 57

earth music & ecology

Japan Label

Clothing collaboration! ⭐⭐

There is a project in the works called "*Margaret* Dream Tour," in which I will work with the winners of a lottery comprised entirely of *Daytime Shooting Star* readers to design dresses inspired by Suzume and Yuyuka! *Margaret* is still working out the details, so I don't have much more information than that. But to have the chance to design clothing inspired by my characters with your help—and put them up for sale—it's just...! This is truly a dream come true! I am very grateful!!

I believe further details will be revealed in a future issue of *Margaret* magazine, so be sure to keep an eye out!! And look out for posts from earth Japan Label's Twitter account also!!

I believe the items will go on sale this May. Maybe there'll be some sort of campaign.

I hope to have your support when it launches! ♫

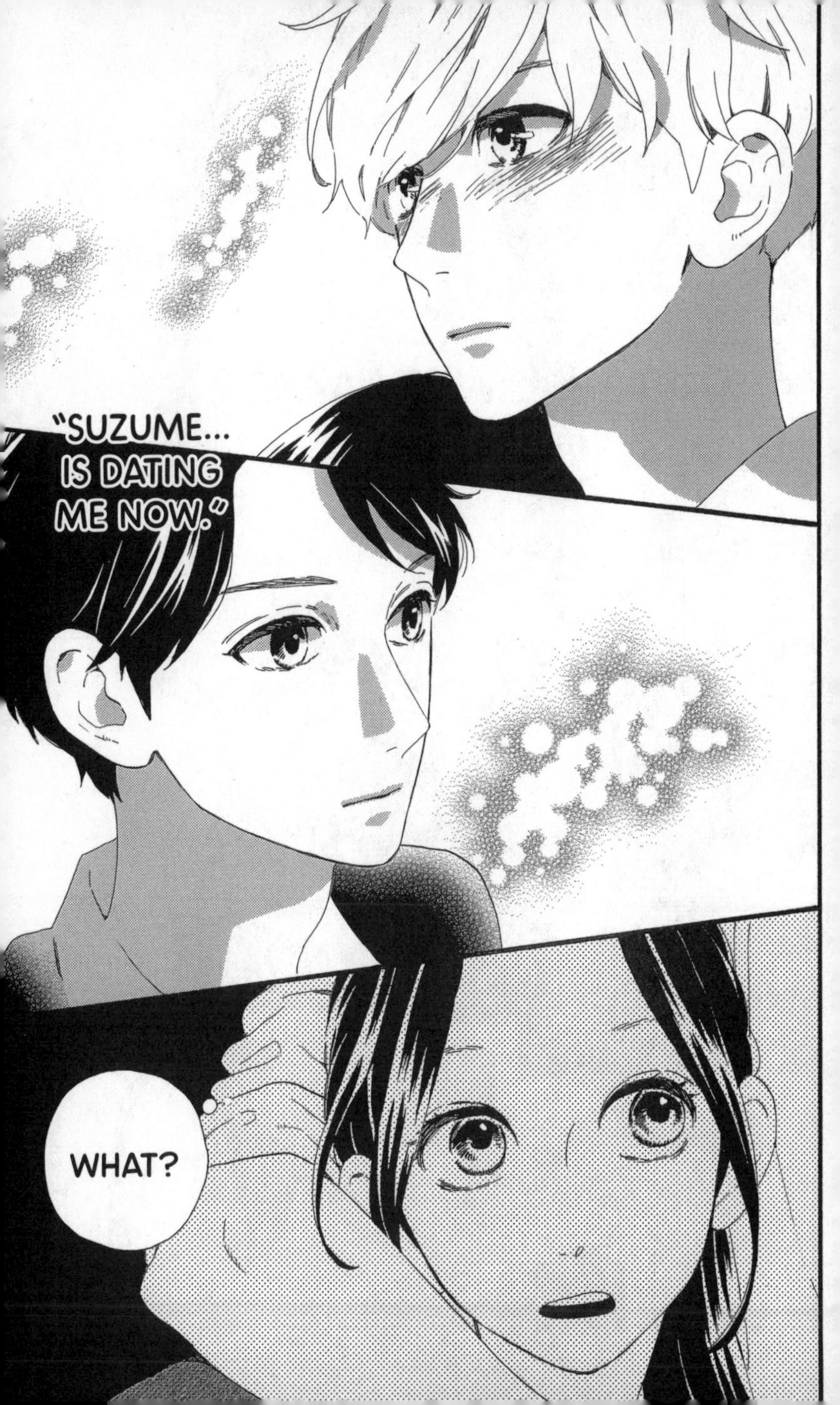
"SUZUME... IS DATING ME NOW."
WHAT?

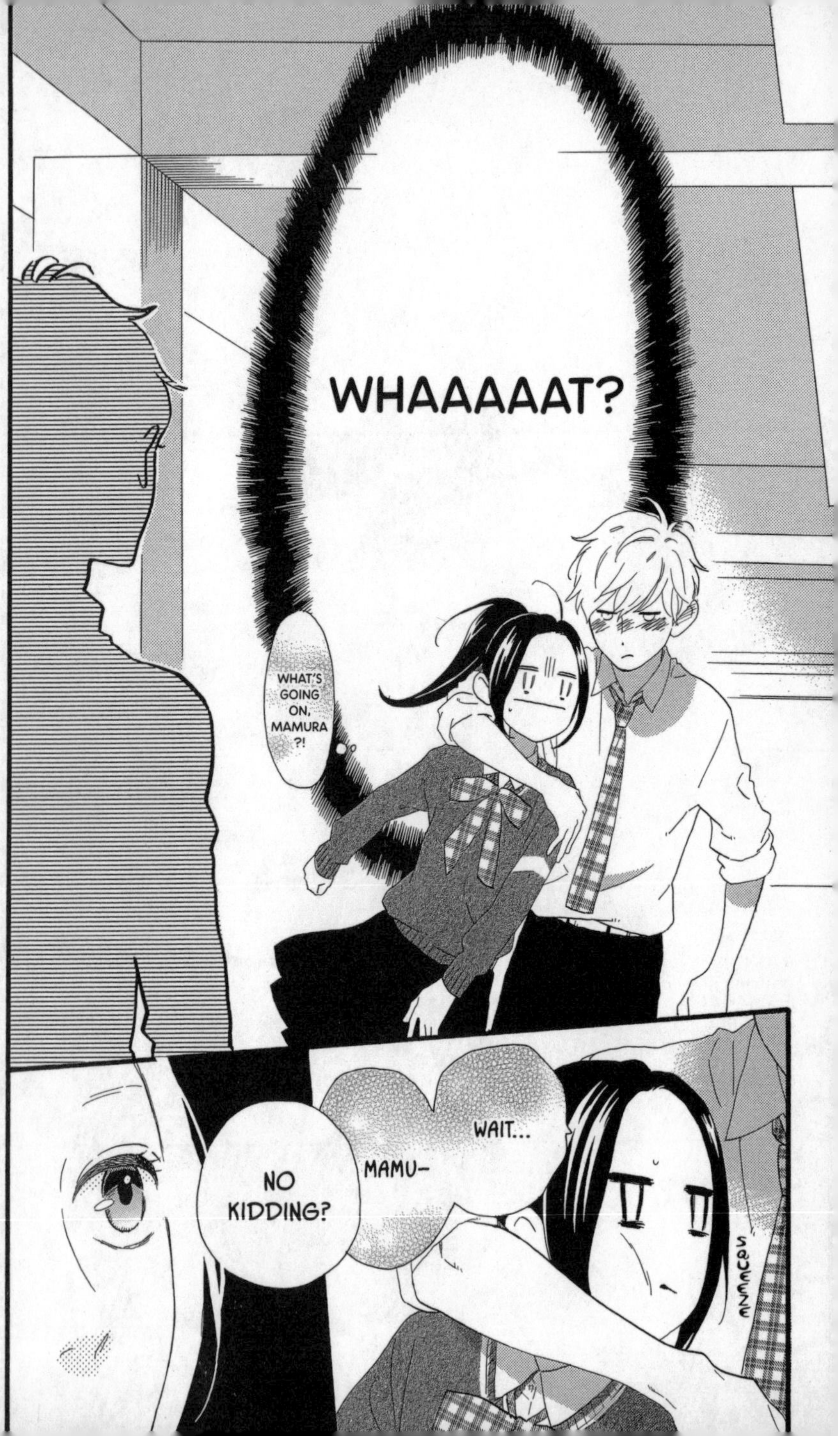
WHAAAAAT?
WHAT'S GOING ON, MAMURA ?!
WAIT...
MAMU-
SQUEEZE
NO KIDDING?

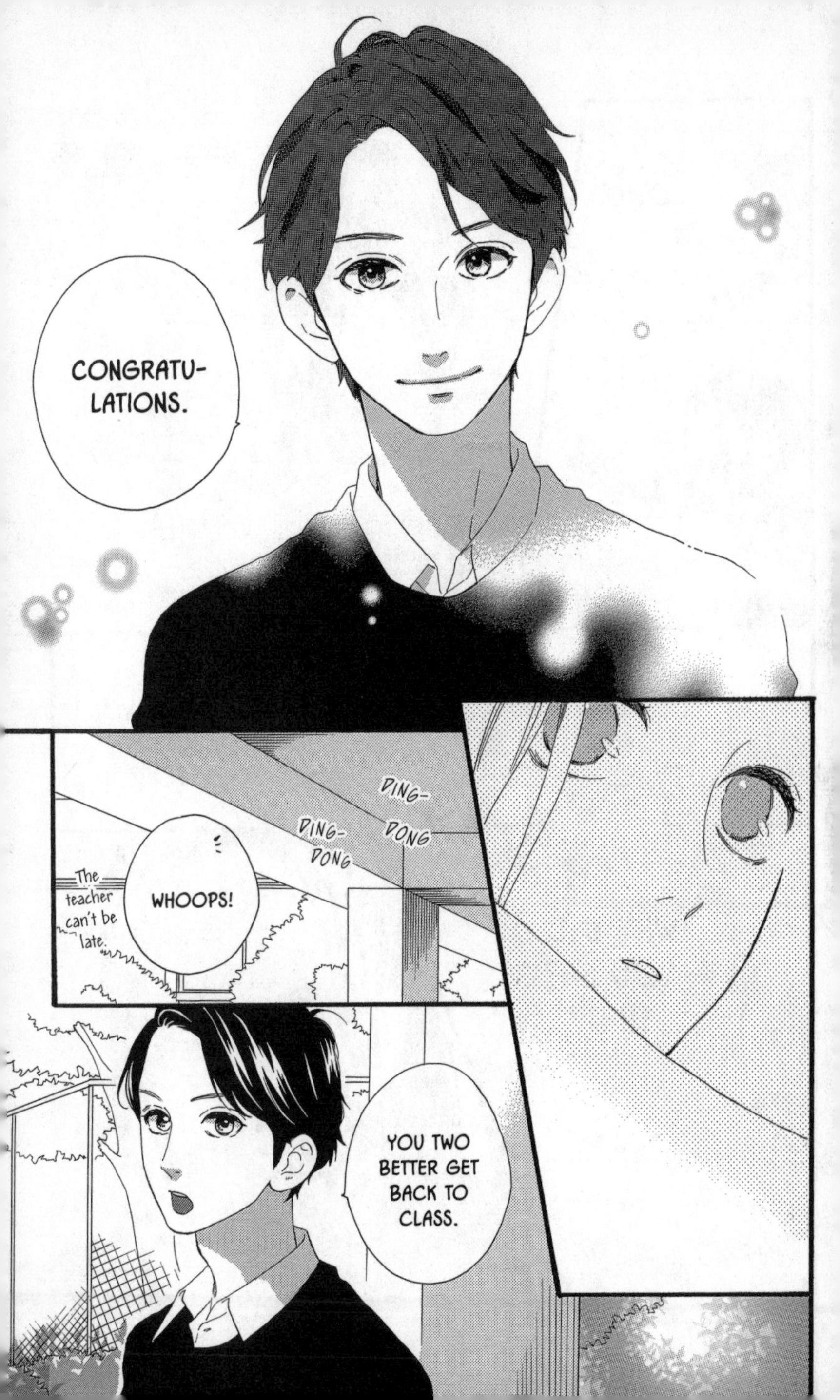
CONGRATU-
LATIONS.
DING-DONG
DING-DONG
WHOOPS!
The teacher can't be late.
YOU TWO BETTER GET BACK TO CLASS.

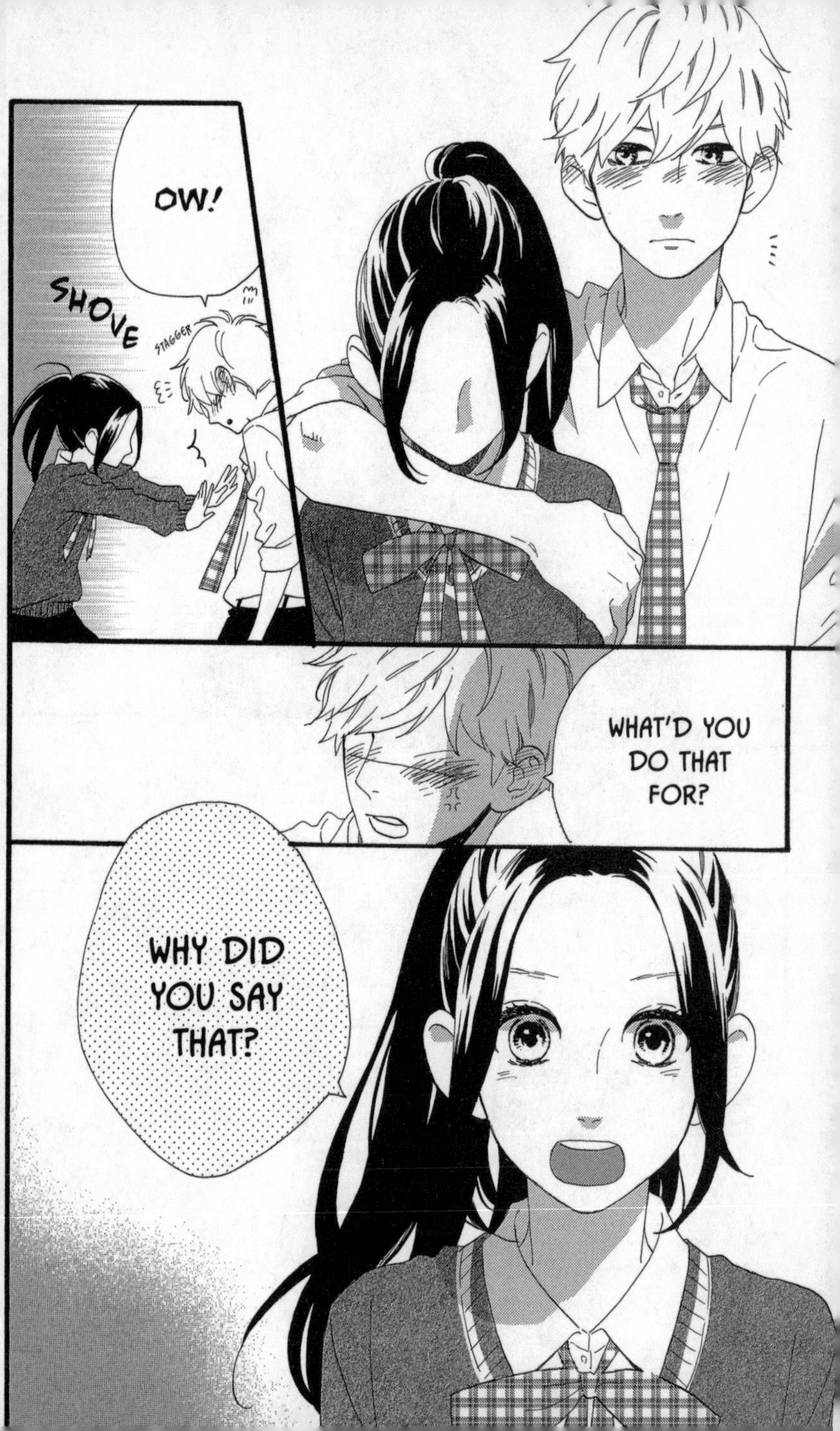
OW!
SHOVE
STAGGER
WHAT'D YOU DO THAT FOR?
WHY DID YOU SAY THAT?

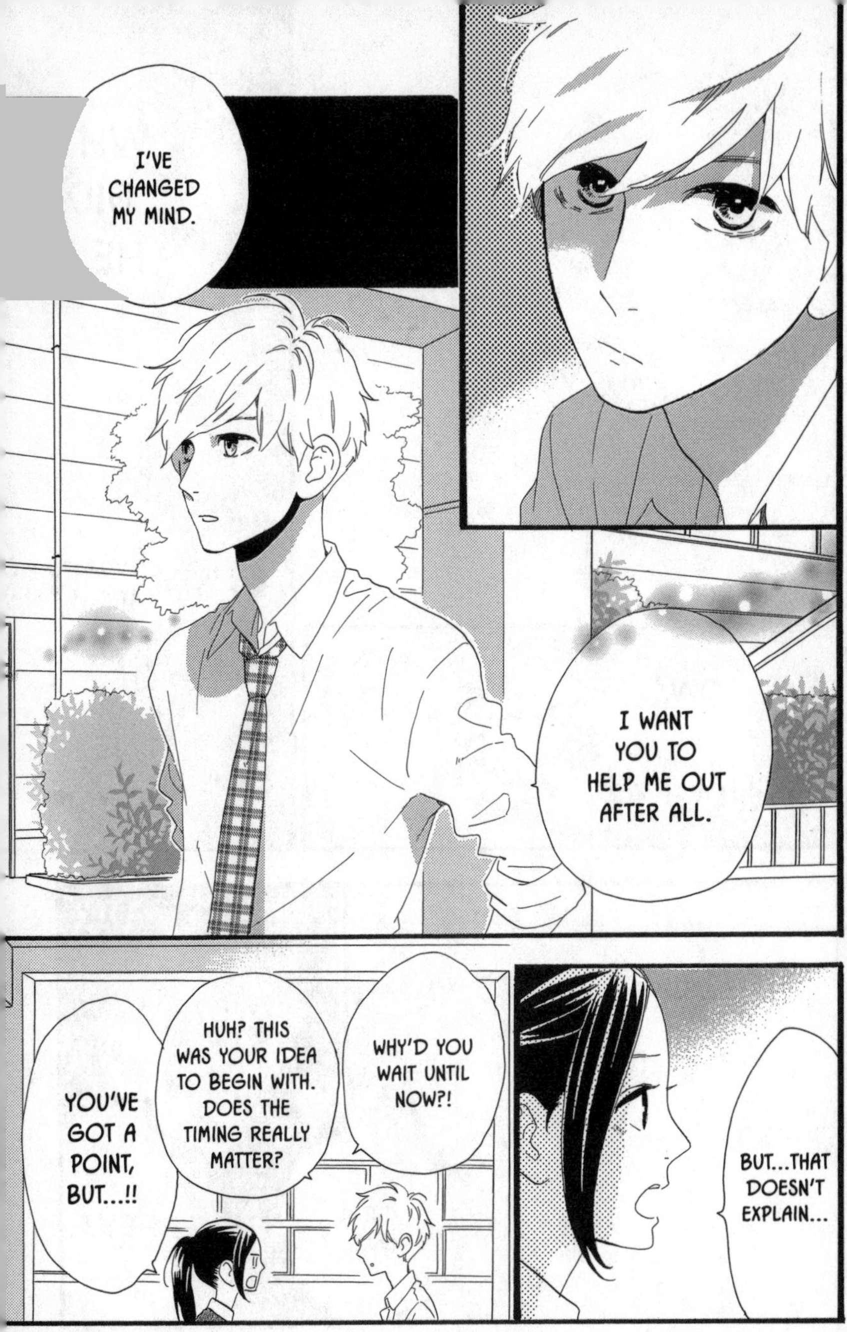
I'VE CHANGED MY MIND.
I WANT YOU TO HELP ME OUT AFTER ALL.
BUT...THAT DOESN'T EXPLAIN...
WHY'D YOU WAIT UNTIL NOW?!
HUH? THIS WAS YOUR IDEA TO BEGIN WITH. DOES THE TIMING REALLY MATTER?
YOU'VE GOT A POINT, BUT...!!

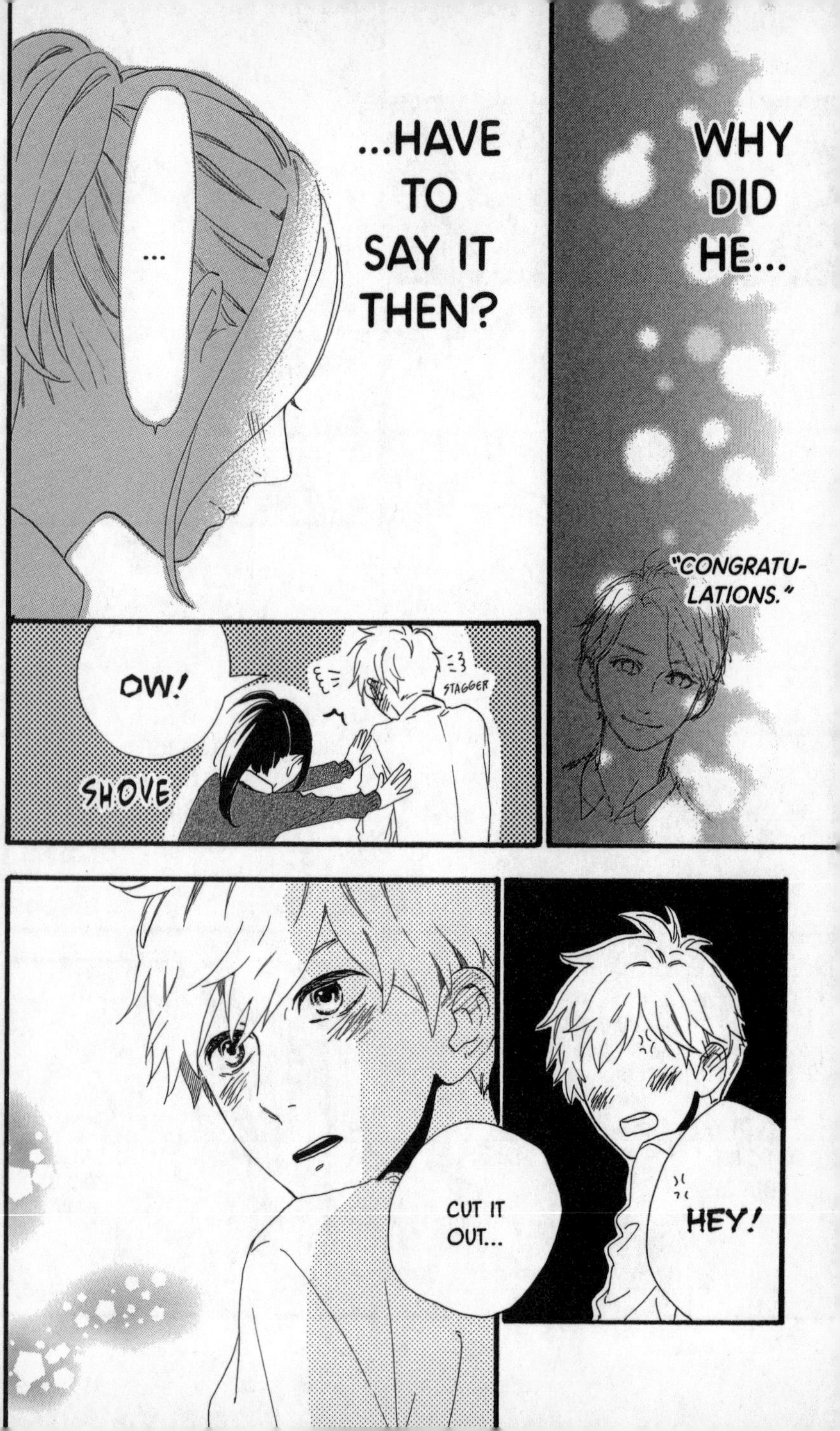

WHY DID HE...
"CONGRATULATIONS."
...HAVE TO SAY IT THEN?
...
STAGGER
OW!
SHOVE
HEY!
CUT IT OUT...

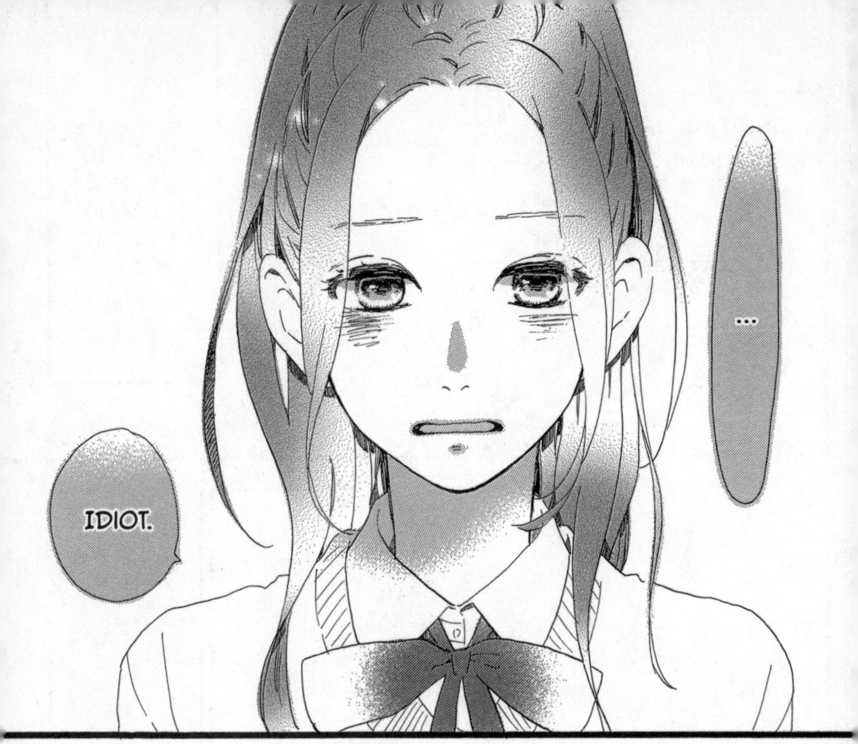
...
IDIOT.

HE HAS...

...THE WORST TIMING.

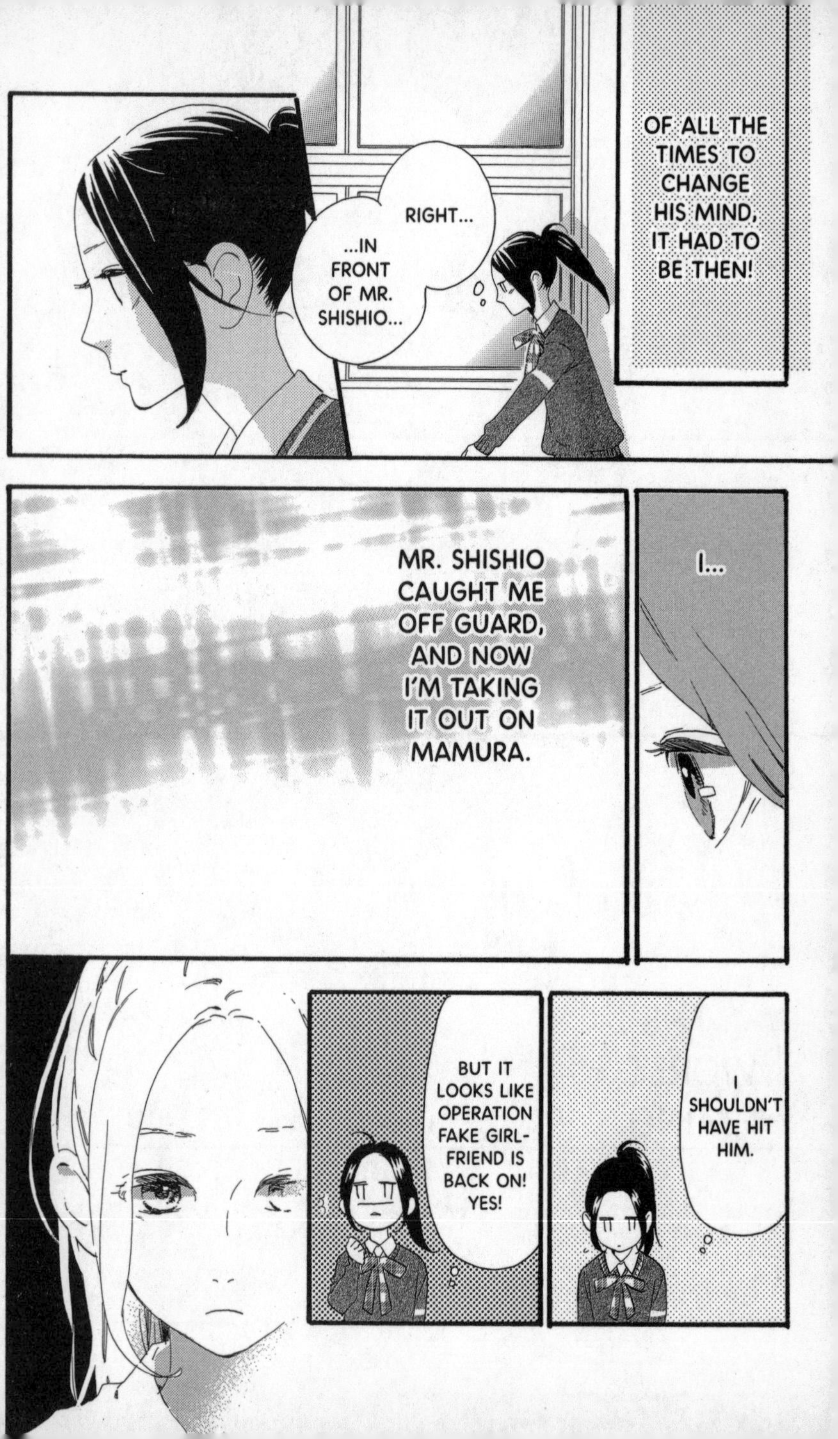
OF ALL THE TIMES TO CHANGE HIS MIND, IT HAD TO BE THEN!
RIGHT...
...IN FRONT OF MR. SHISHIO...
I...
MR. SHISHIO CAUGHT ME OFF GUARD, AND NOW I'M TAKING IT OUT ON MAMURA.
I SHOULDN'T HAVE HIT HIM.
BUT IT LOOKS LIKE OPERATION FAKE GIRL-FRIEND IS BACK ON! YES!

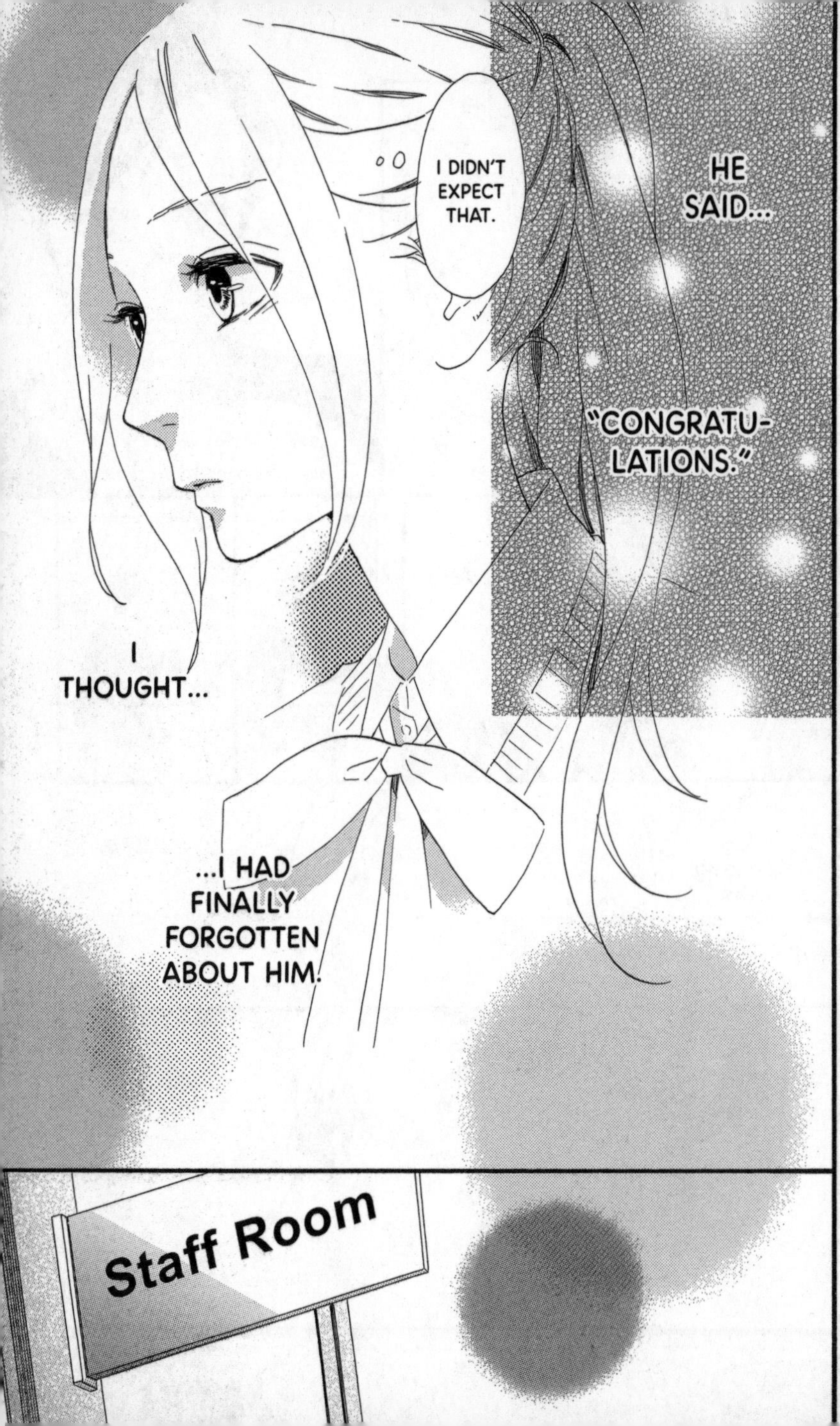
HE SAID...
"CONGRATULATIONS."
I DIDN'T EXPECT THAT.
I THOUGHT...
...I HAD FINALLY FORGOTTEN ABOUT HIM.
Staff Room

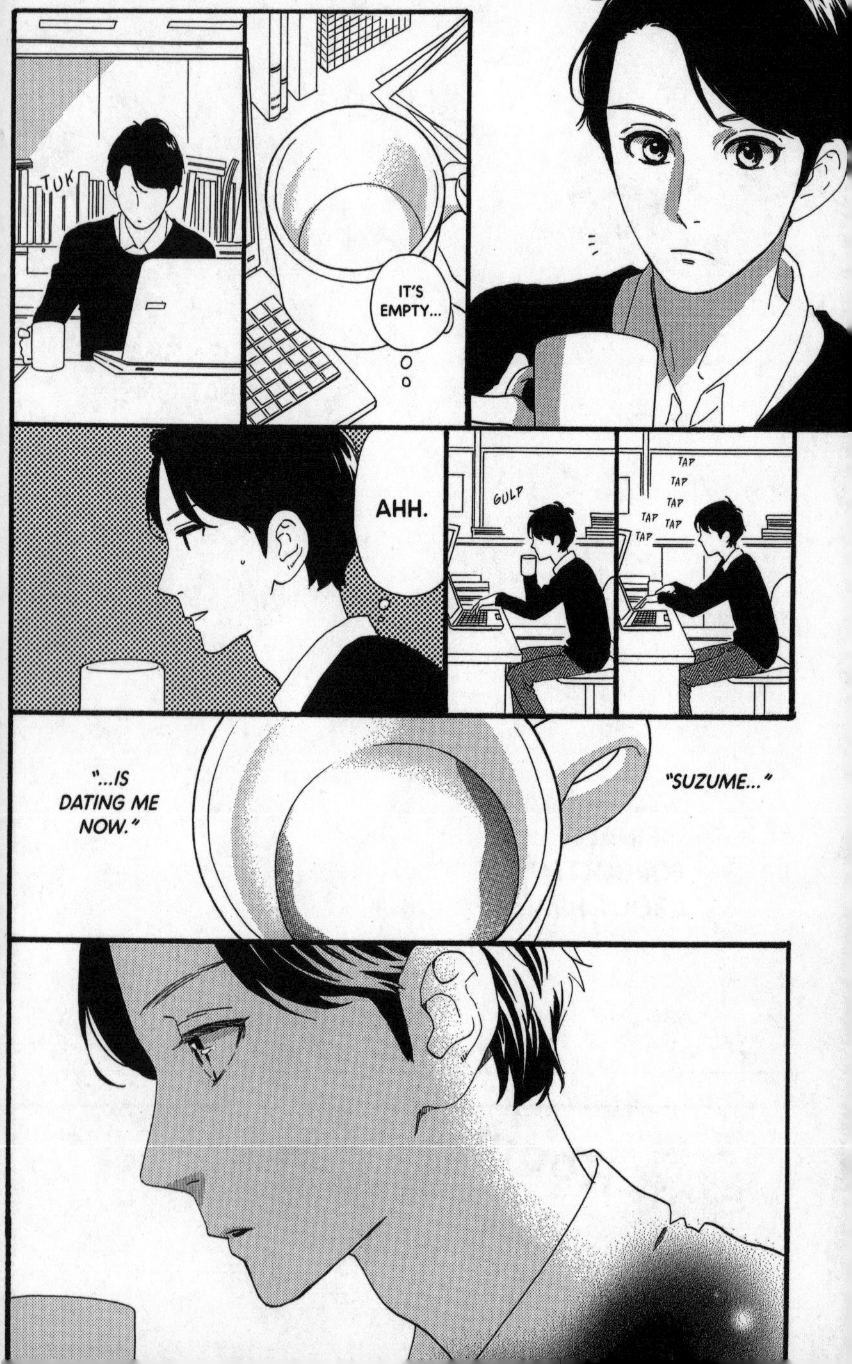
IT'S EMPTY...
TUK
TAP TAP TAP TAP TAP TAP
GULP
AHH.
"SUZUME..."
"...IS DATING ME NOW."

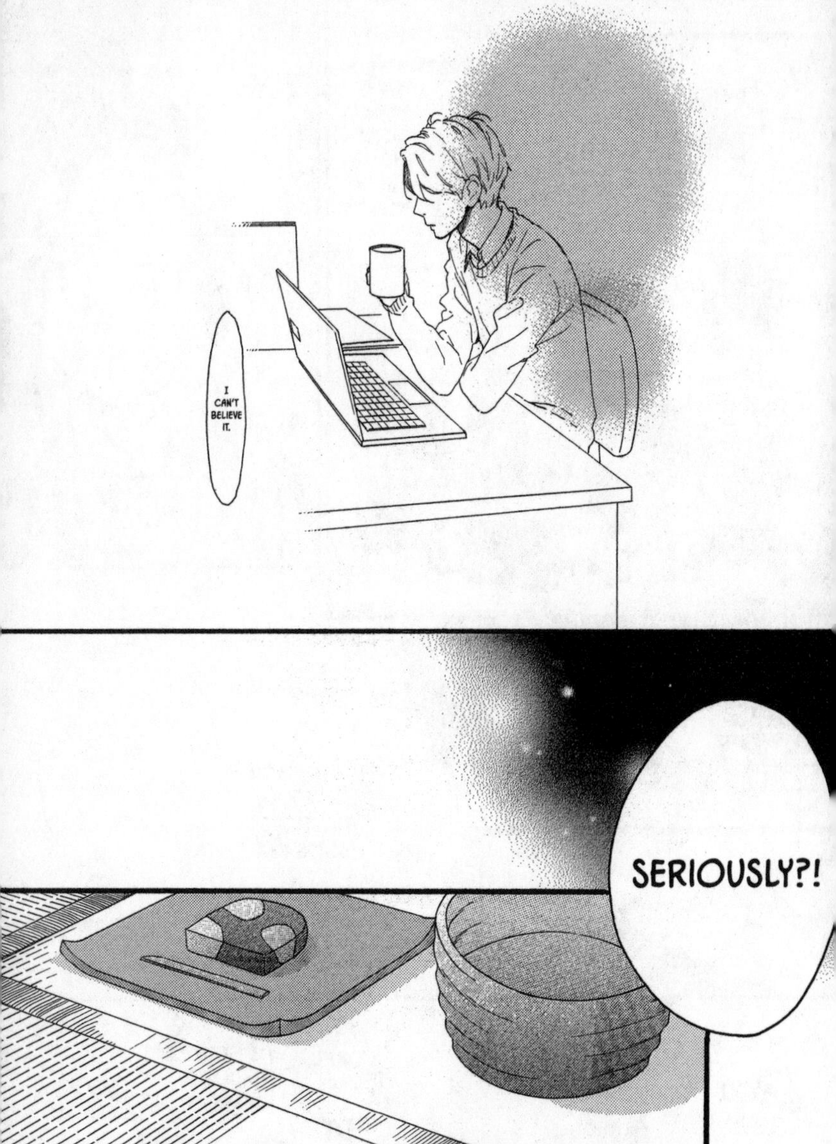
I CAN'T BELIEVE IT.
SERIOUSLY?!

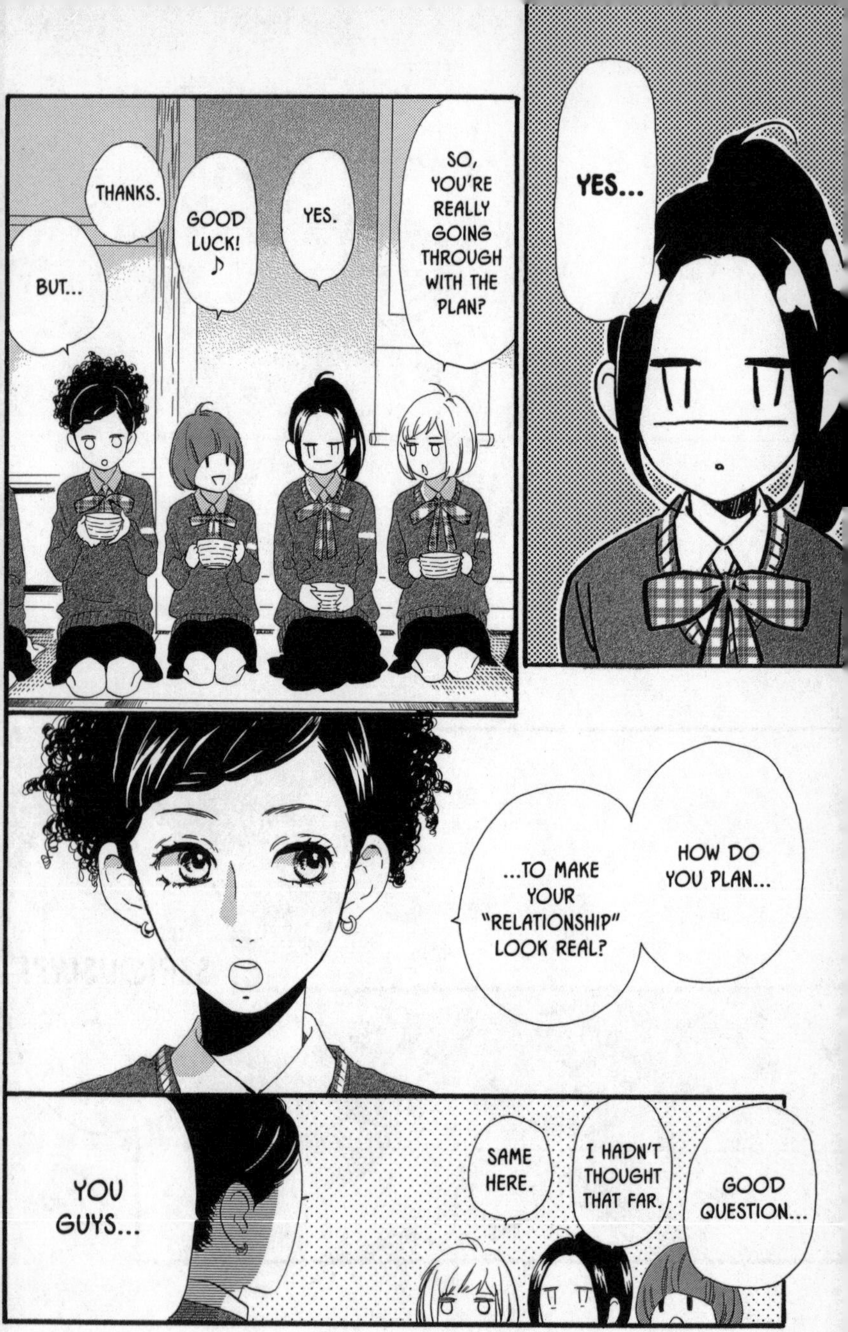
YES...
SO, YOU'RE REALLY GOING THROUGH WITH THE PLAN?
YES.
GOOD LUCK! ♪
THANKS.
BUT...
HOW DO YOU PLAN...
...TO MAKE YOUR "RELATIONSHIP" LOOK REAL?
GOOD QUESTION...
I HADN'T THOUGHT THAT FAR.
SAME HERE.
YOU GUYS...

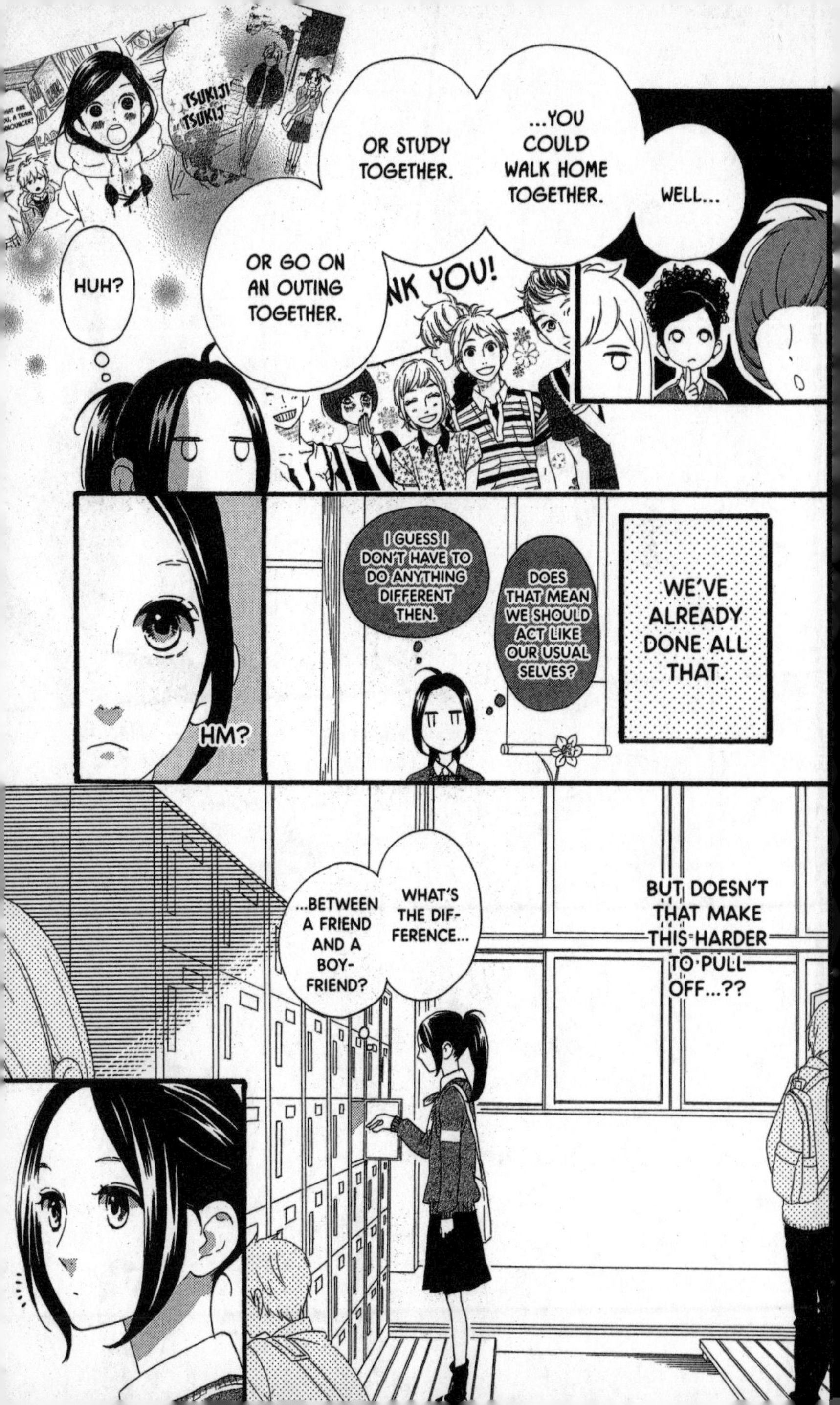
WELL...
...YOU COULD WALK HOME TOGETHER.
OR STUDY TOGETHER.
OR GO ON AN OUTING TOGETHER.
NK YOU!
TSUKIJI TSUKIJI
HUH?
WE'VE ALREADY DONE ALL THAT.
DOES THAT MEAN WE SHOULD ACT LIKE OUR USUAL SELVES?
I GUESS I DON'T HAVE TO DO ANYTHING DIFFERENT THEN.
HM?
BUT DOESN'T THAT MAKE THIS HARDER TO PULL OFF...??
WHAT'S THE DIF-FERENCE...
...BETWEEN A FRIEND AND A BOY-FRIEND?

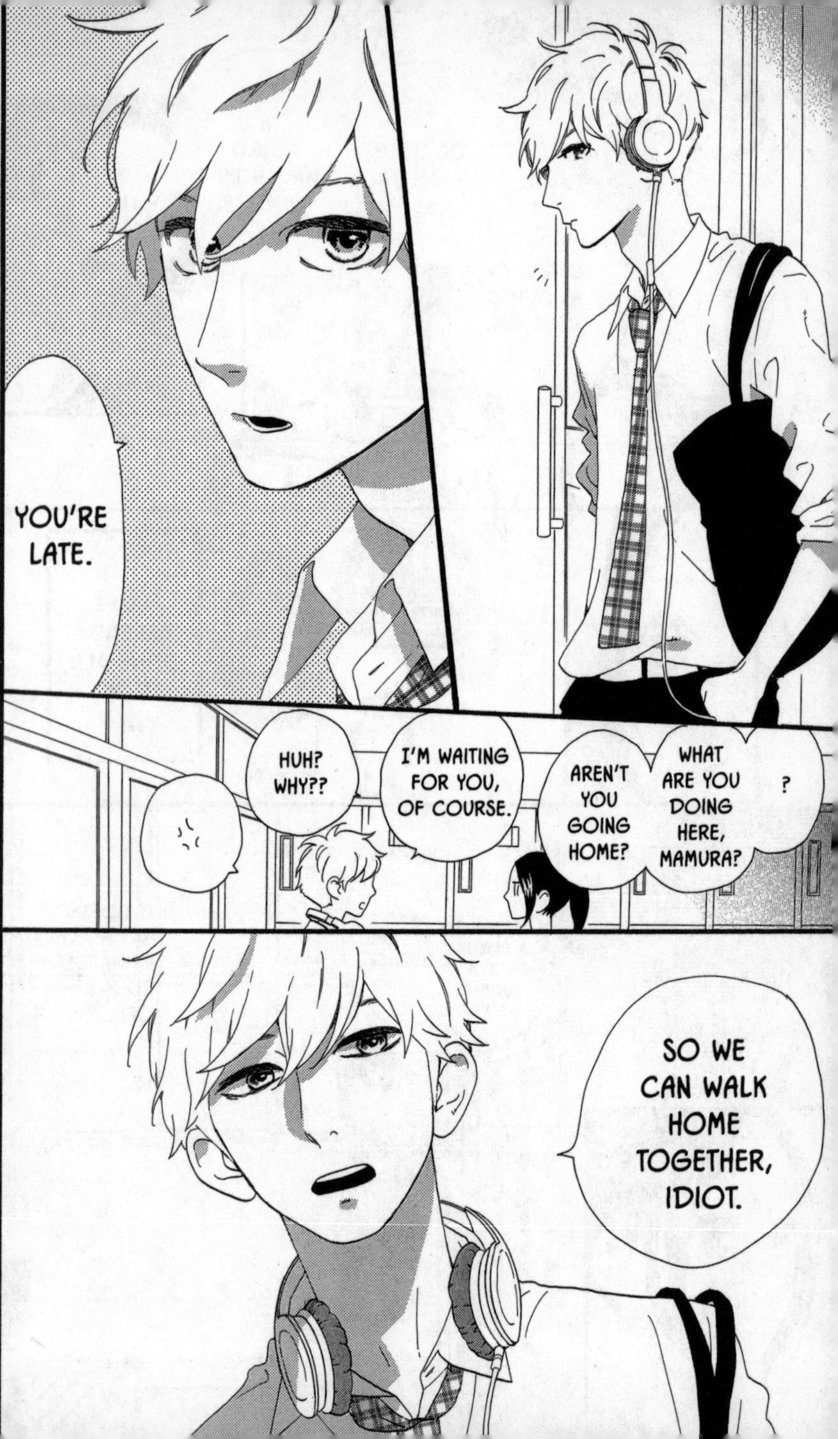
YOU'RE LATE.
?
WHAT ARE YOU DOING HERE, MAMURA?
AREN'T YOU GOING HOME?
I'M WAITING FOR YOU, OF COURSE.
HUH? WHY??
SO WE CAN WALK HOME TOGETHER, IDIOT.

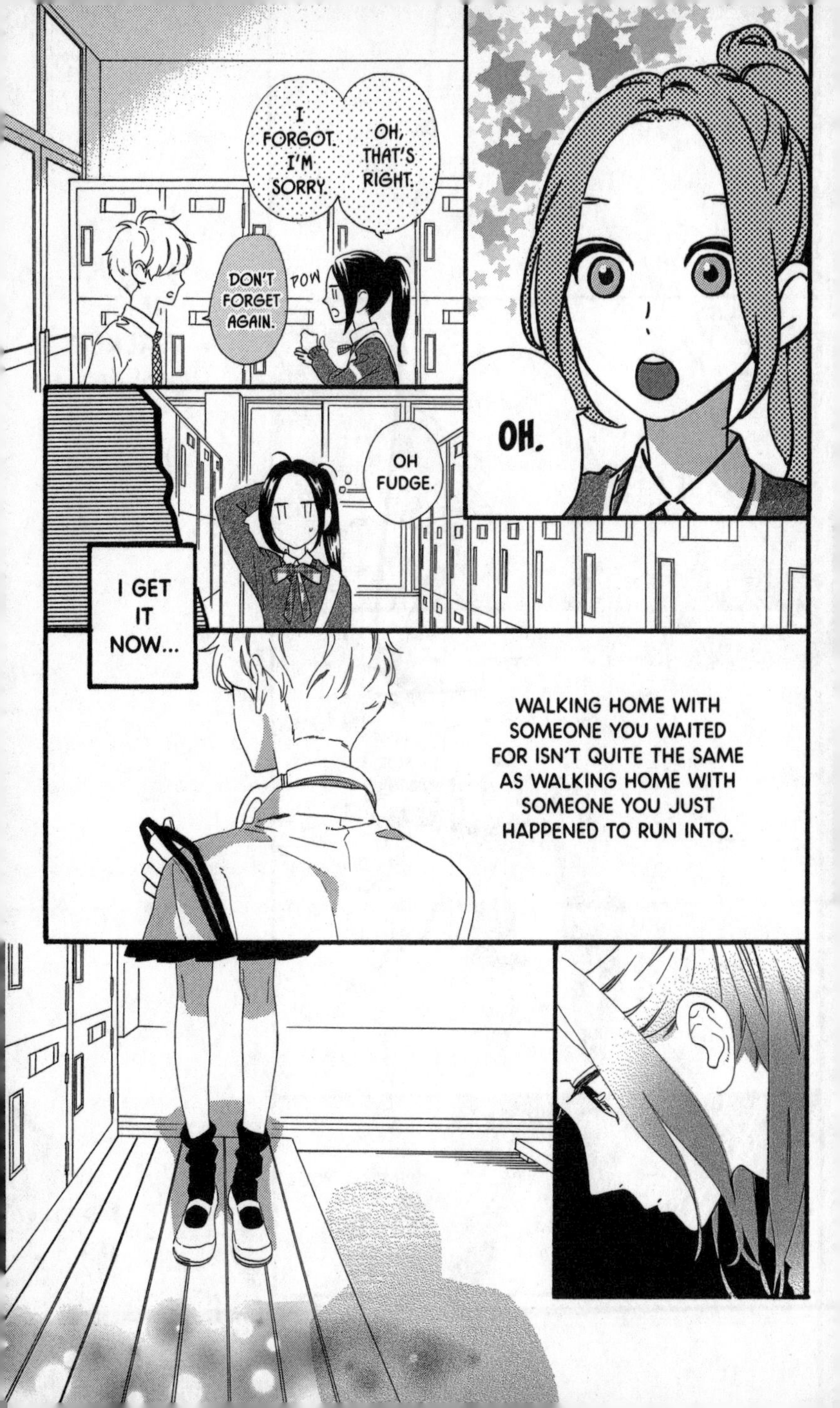
OH.
OH, THAT'S RIGHT.
I FORGOT. I'M SORRY.
POW
DON'T FORGET AGAIN.
OH FUDGE.
I GET IT NOW...
WALKING HOME WITH SOMEONE YOU WAITED FOR ISN'T QUITE THE SAME AS WALKING HOME WITH SOMEONE YOU JUST HAPPENED TO RUN INTO.

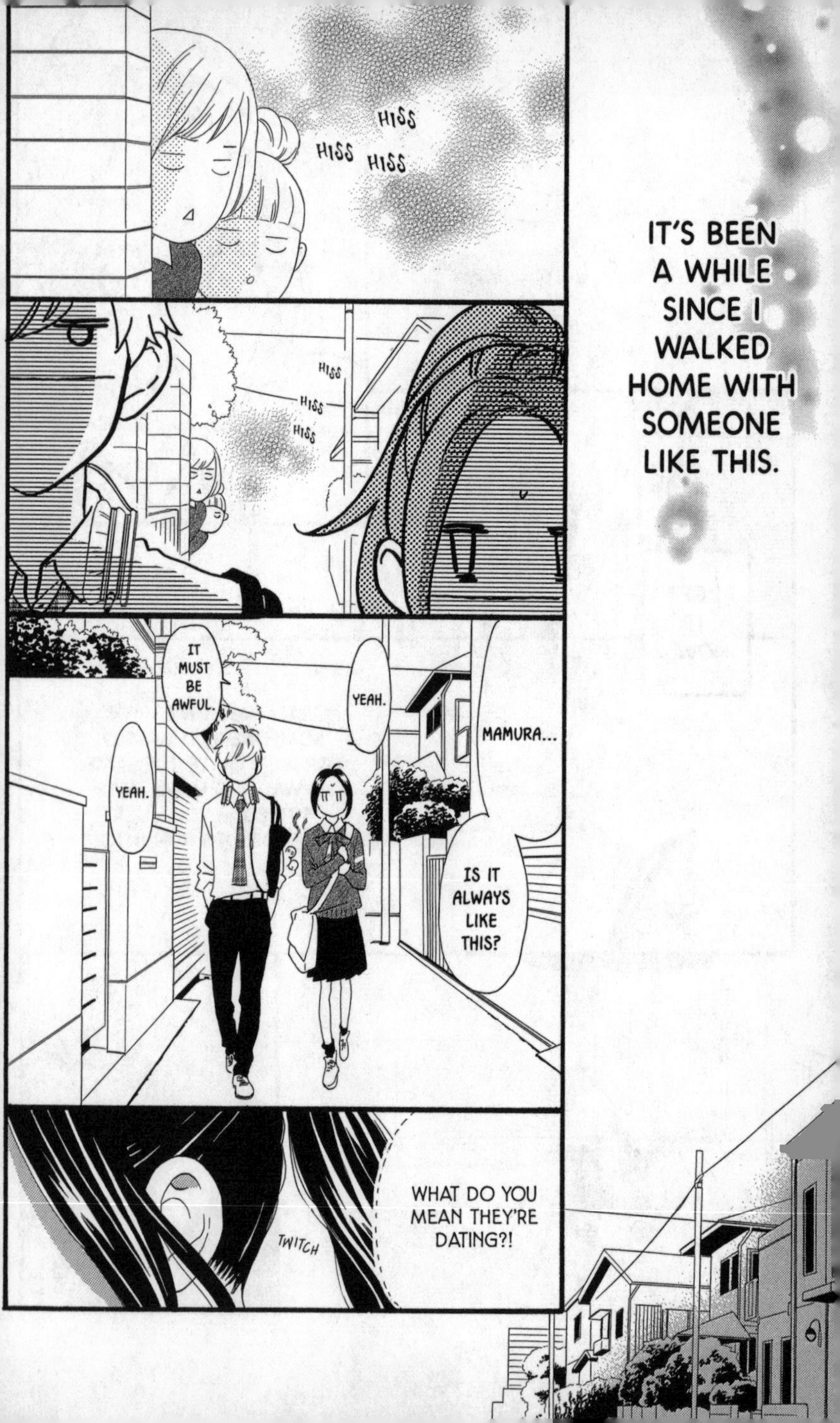
IT'S BEEN A WHILE SINCE I WALKED HOME WITH SOMEONE LIKE THIS.
HISS
HISS
HISS
HISS
HISS
HISS
MAMURA...
IS IT ALWAYS LIKE THIS?
YEAH.
IT MUST BE AWFUL.
YEAH.
WHAT DO YOU MEAN THEY'RE DATING?!
TWITCH

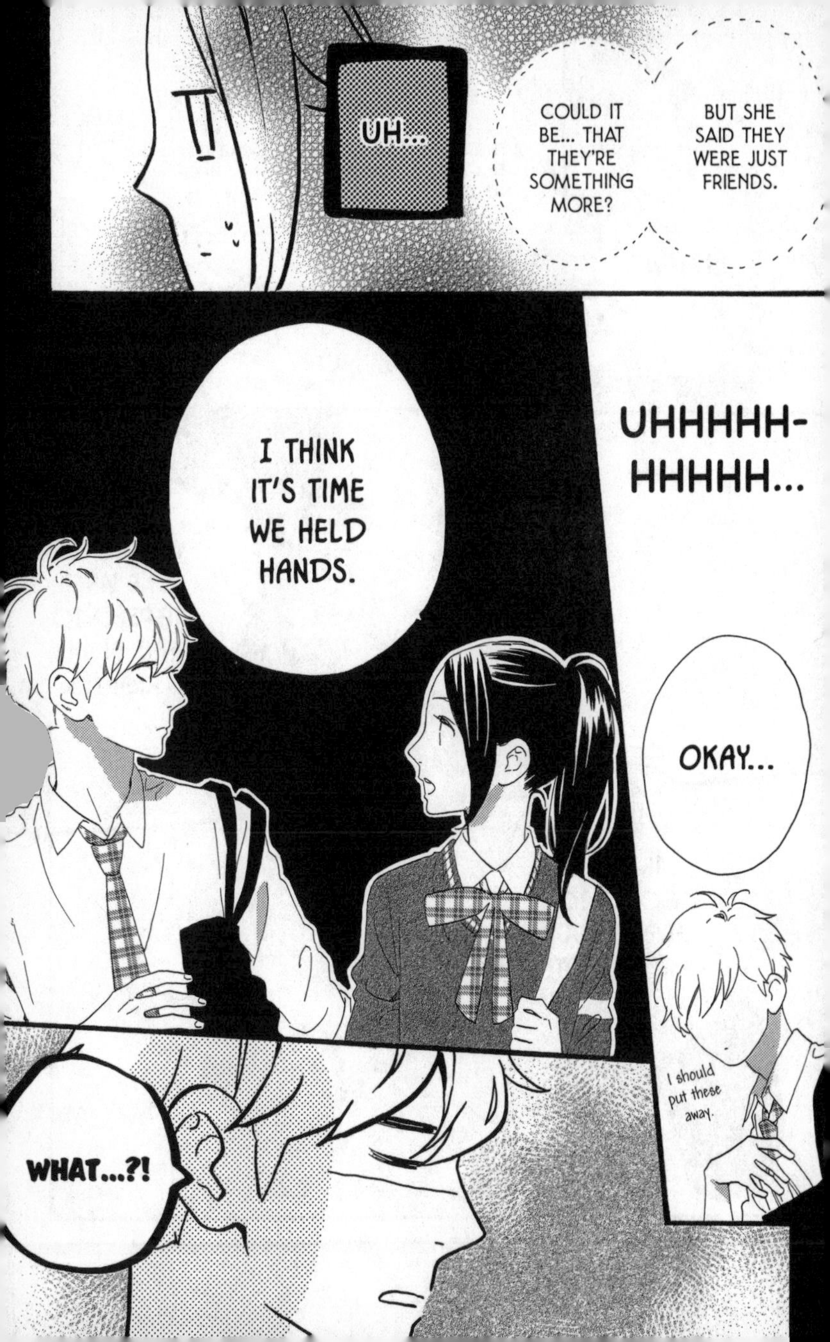
BUT SHE SAID THEY WERE JUST FRIENDS.
COULD IT BE... THAT THEY'RE SOMETHING MORE?
UH...
UHHHHH-HHHHH...
OKAY...
I should put these away.
I THINK IT'S TIME WE HELD HANDS.
WHAT...?!

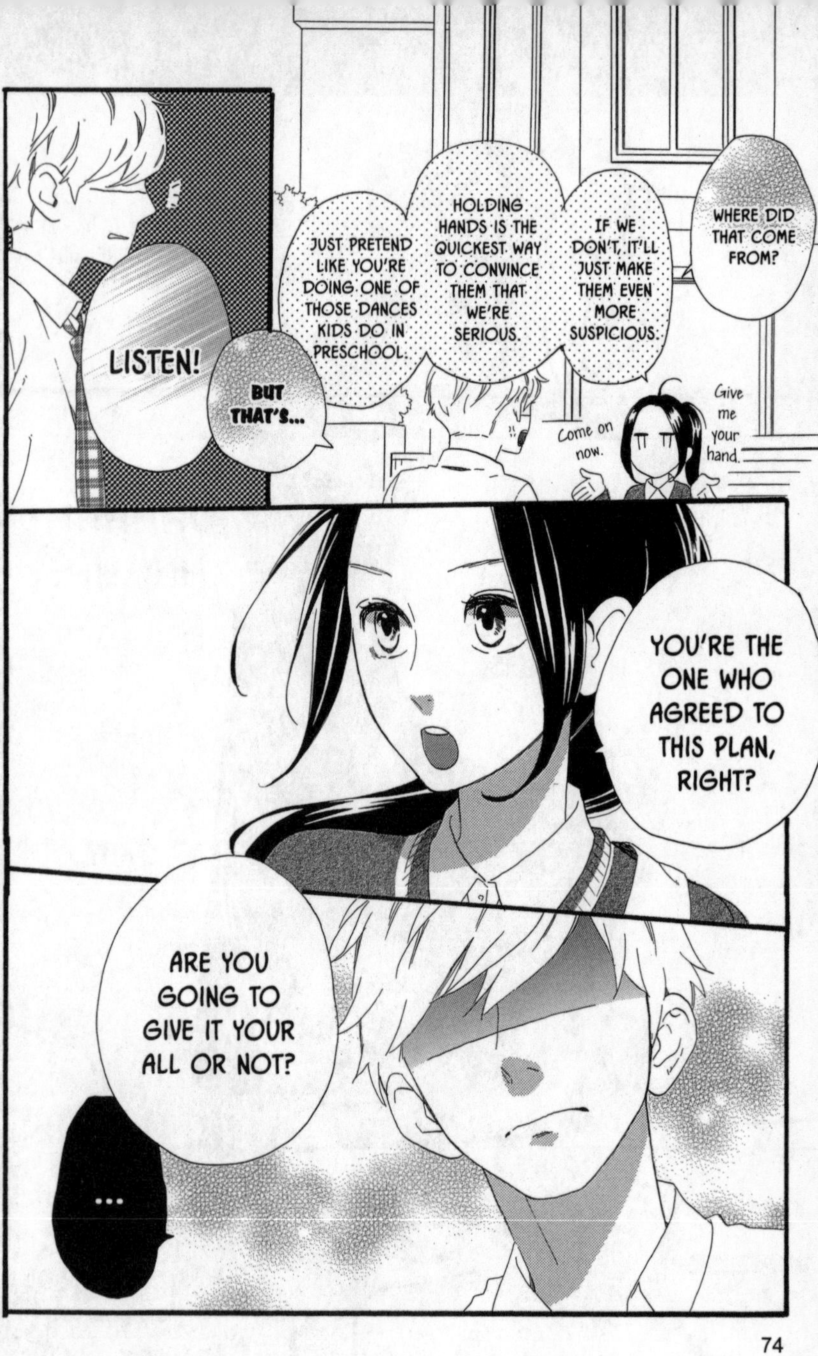
WHERE DID THAT COME FROM?
IF WE DON'T, IT'LL JUST MAKE THEM EVEN MORE SUSPICIOUS.
HOLDING HANDS IS THE QUICKEST WAY TO CONVINCE THEM THAT WE'RE SERIOUS.
JUST PRETEND LIKE YOU'RE DOING ONE OF THOSE DANCES KIDS DO IN PRESCHOOL.
Give me your hand.
Come on now.
BUT THAT'S...
LISTEN!
YOU'RE THE ONE WHO AGREED TO THIS PLAN, RIGHT?
ARE YOU GOING TO GIVE IT YOUR ALL OR NOT?
...

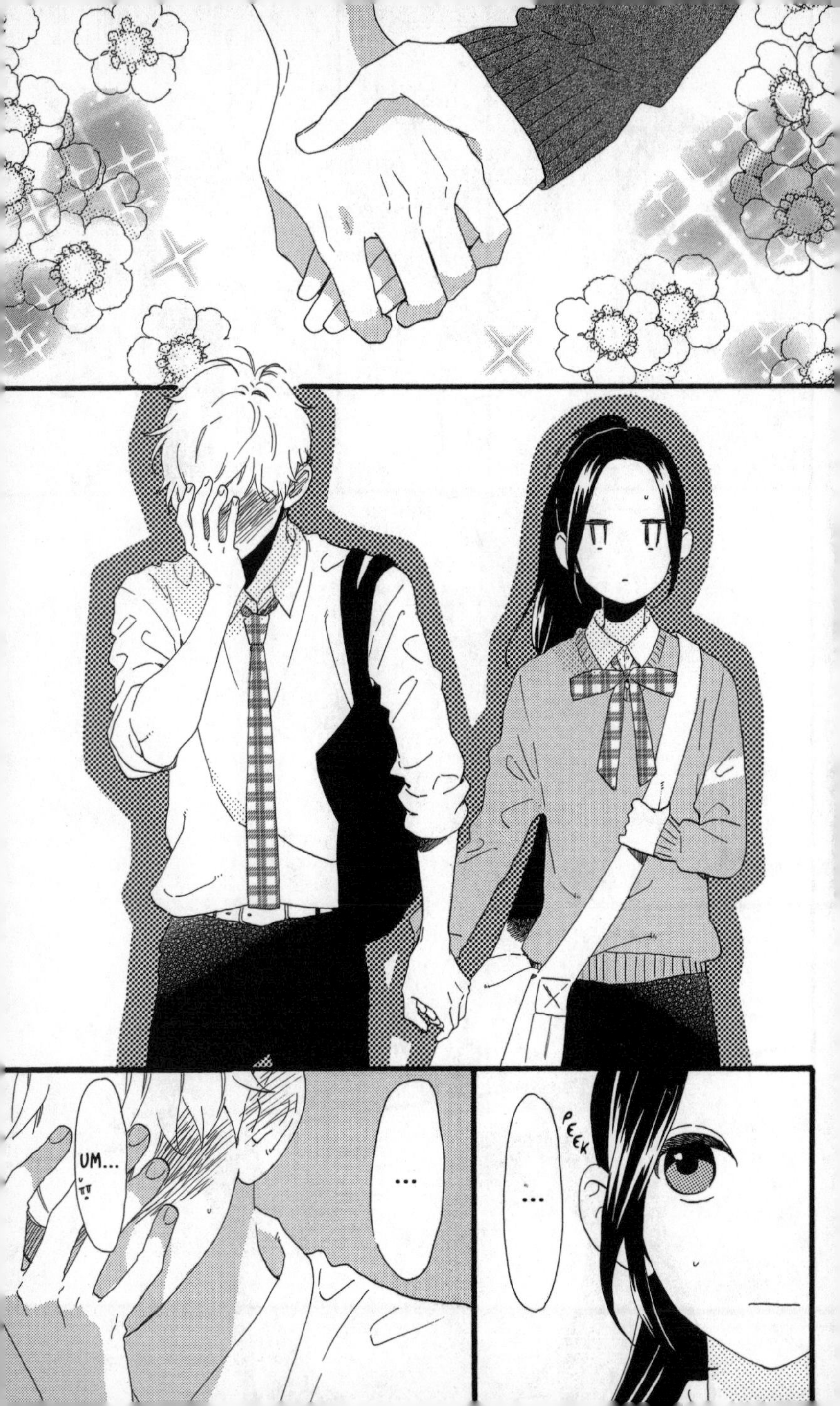

PEEK
...
...
UM...

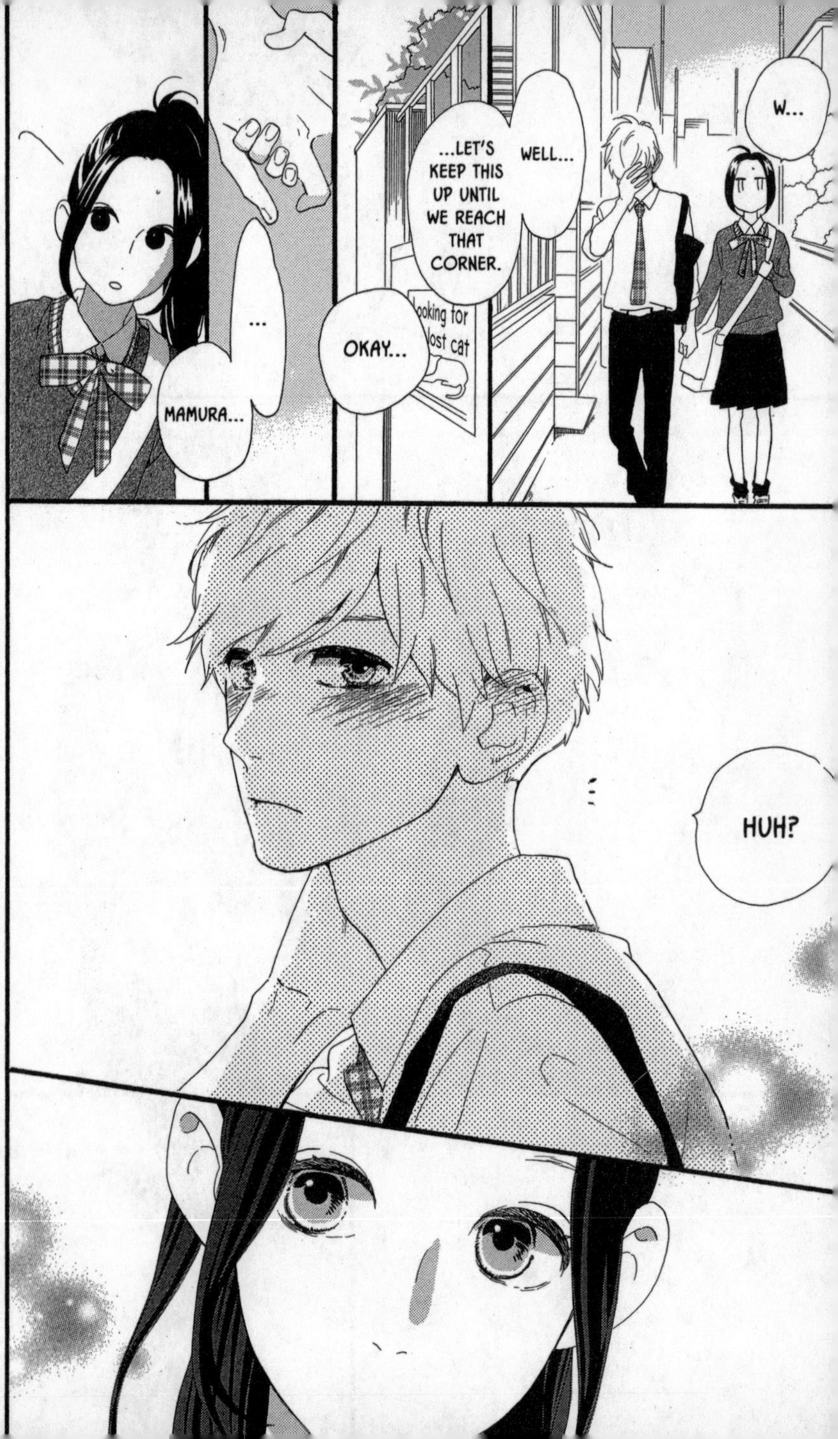
W...
WELL...
...LET'S KEEP THIS UP UNTIL WE REACH THAT CORNER.
OKAY...
ooking for
lost cat
...
MAMURA...
HUH?

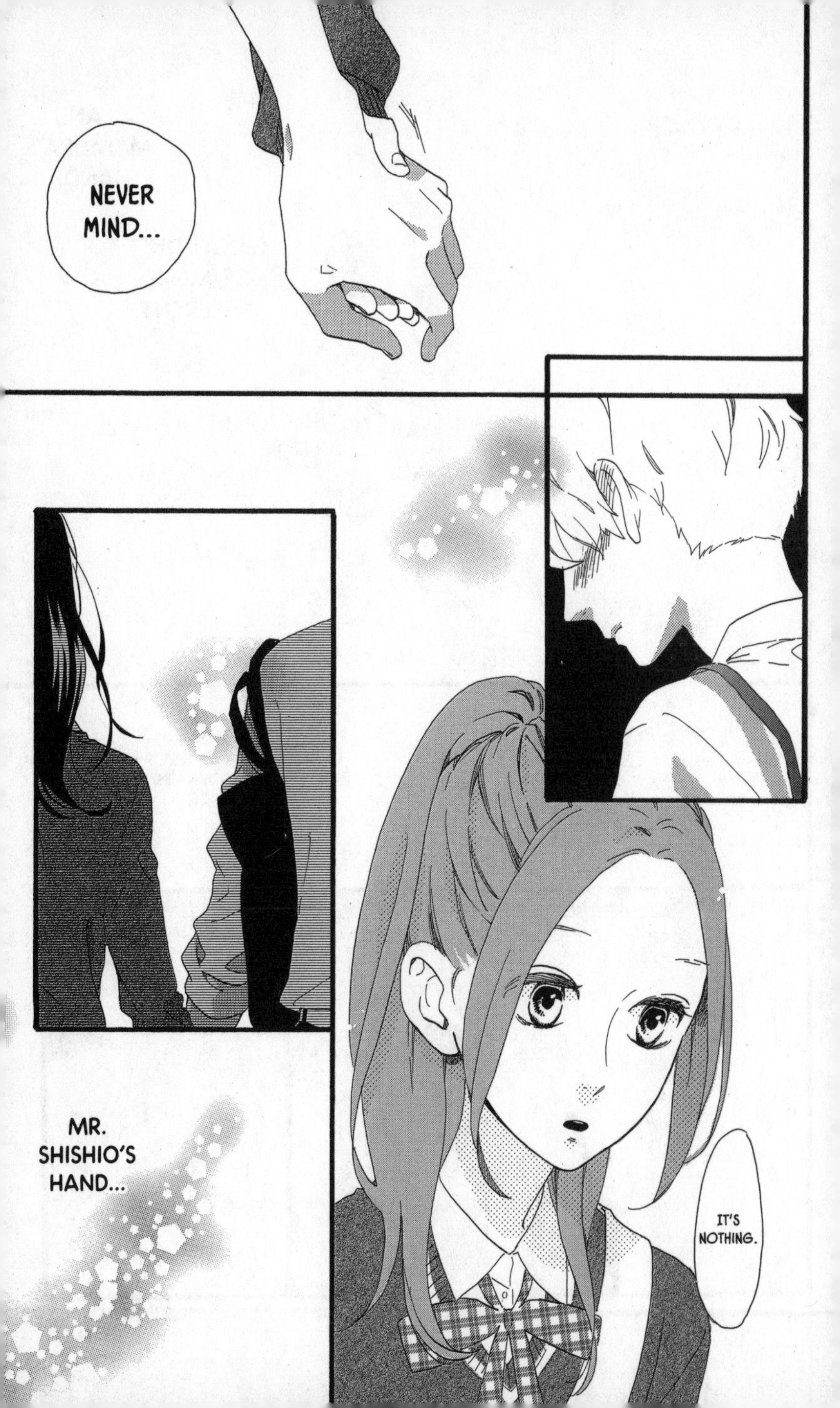
NEVER MIND...
IT'S NOTHING.
MR. SHISHIO'S HAND...

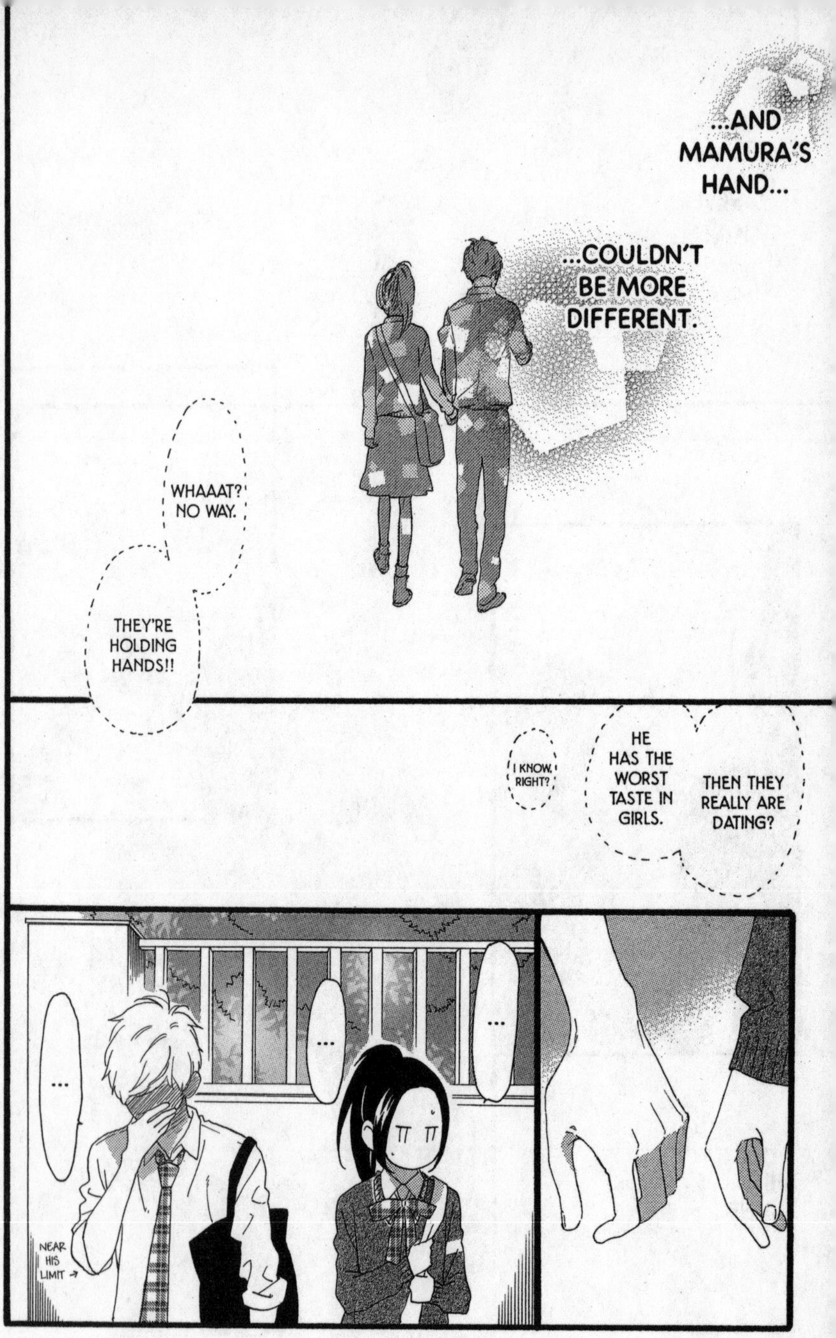
...AND MAMURA'S HAND...
...COULDN'T BE MORE DIFFERENT.
WHAAAT? NO WAY.
THEY'RE HOLDING HANDS!!
THEN THEY REALLY ARE DATING?
HE HAS THE WORST TASTE IN GIRLS.
I KNOW, RIGHT?
...
...
...
NEAR HIS LIMIT

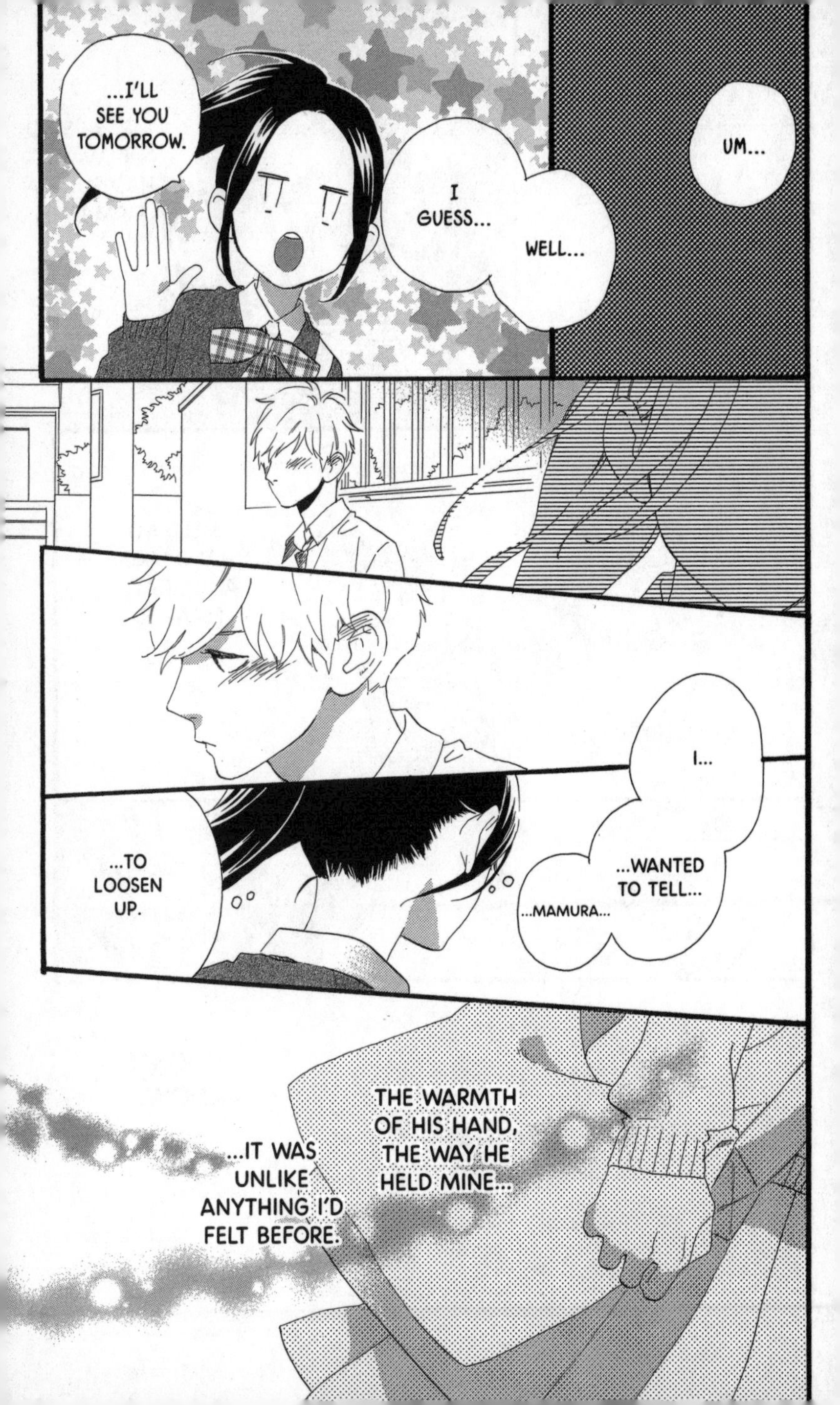
UM...
I GUESS... WELL...
...I'LL SEE YOU TOMORROW.
I...
...WANTED TO TELL...
...MAMURA...
...TO LOOSEN UP.
THE WARMTH OF HIS HAND, THE WAY HE HELD MINE...
...IT WAS UNLIKE ANYTHING I'D FELT BEFORE.

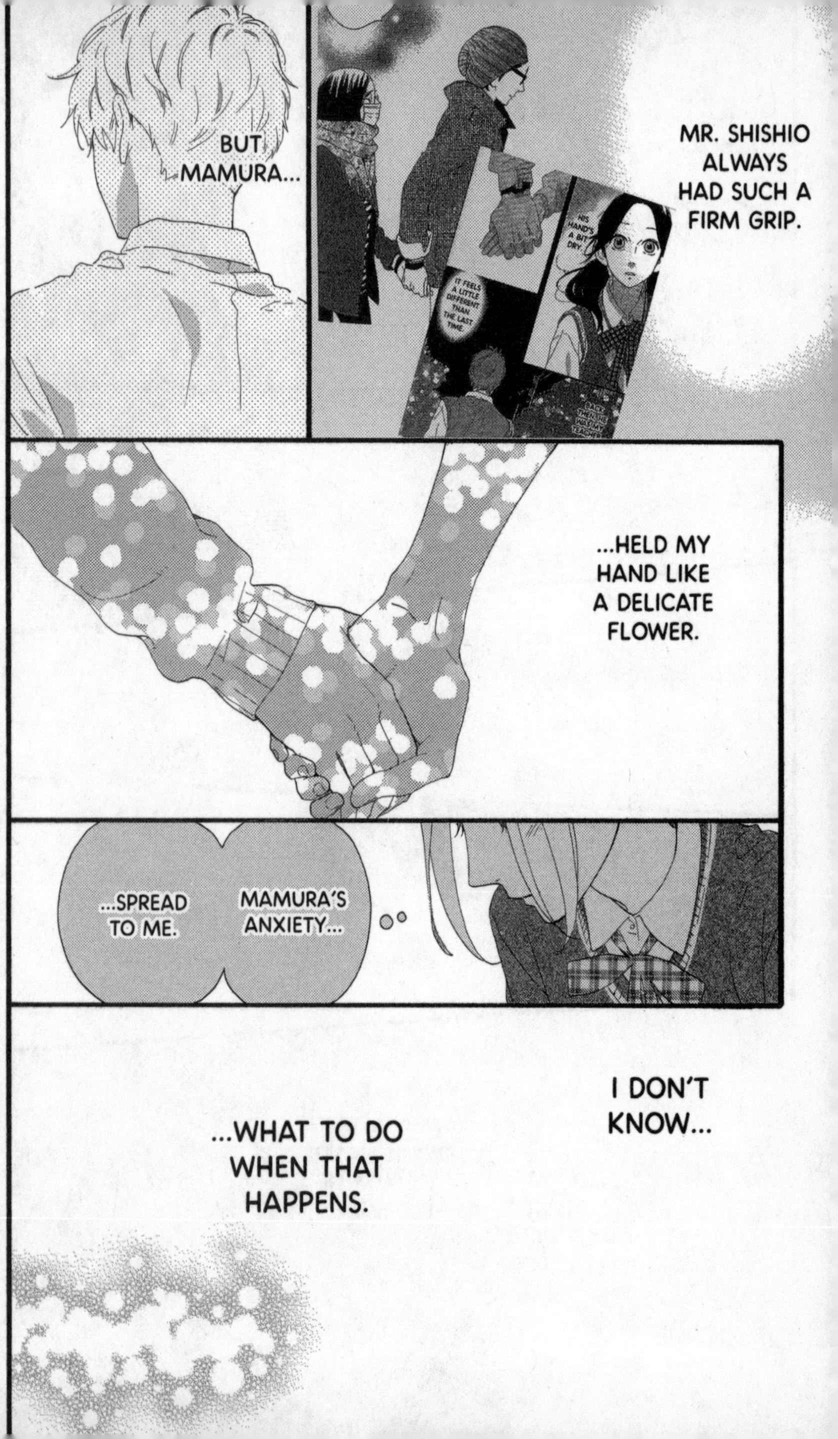

MR. SHISHIO ALWAYS HAD SUCH A FIRM GRIP.
HIS HAND'S A BIT DRY.
IT FEELS A LITTLE DIFFERENT THAN THE LAST TIME.
BUT MAMURA...
...HELD MY HAND LIKE A DELICATE FLOWER.
MAMURA'S ANXIETY...
...SPREAD TO ME.
I DON'T KNOW...
...WHAT TO DO WHEN THAT HAPPENS.

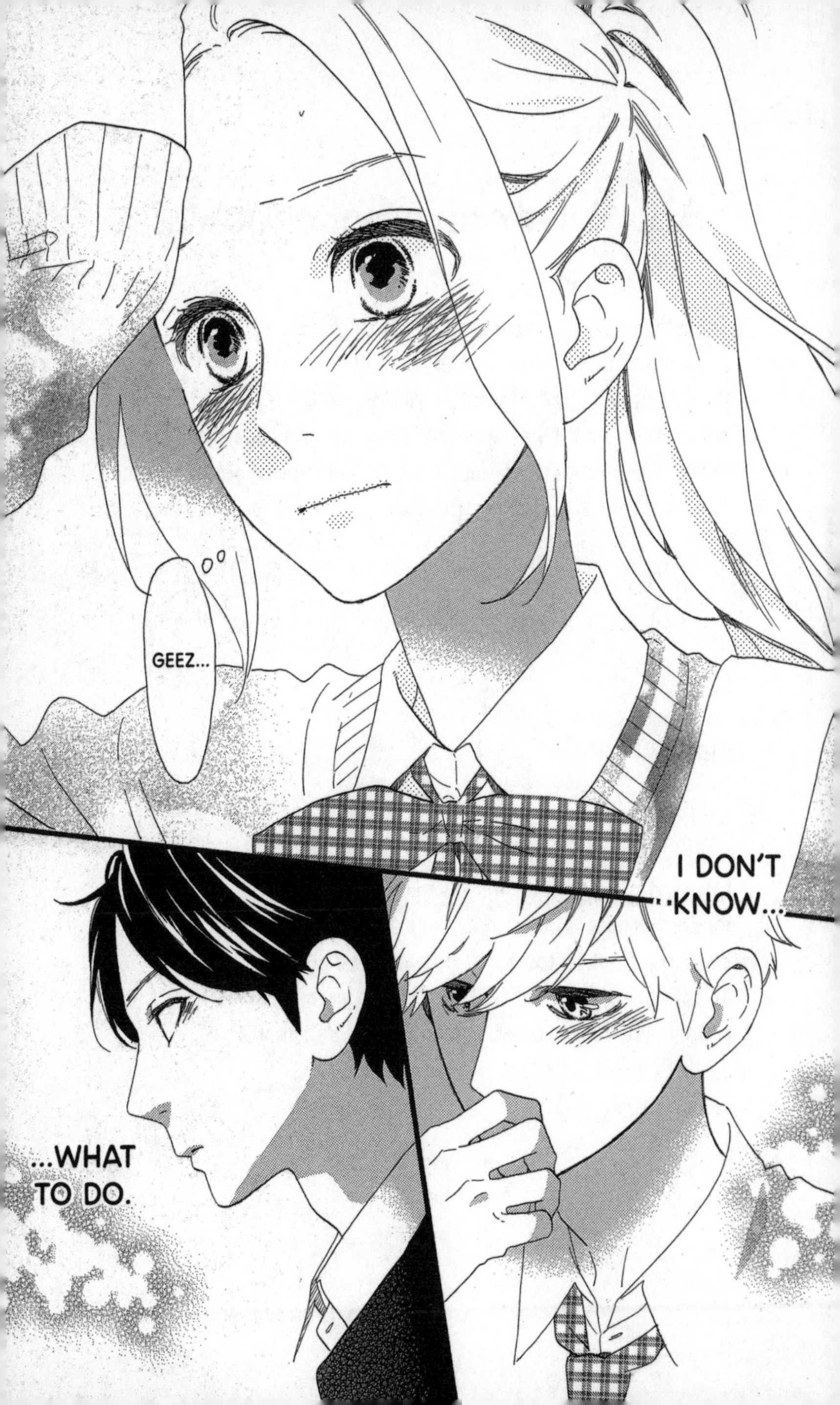
GEEZ...
I DON'T KNOW...
...WHAT TO DO.

About Kentaro Sakaguchi...

The other day, at an event planned by *Margaret*, I got to meet male model Kentaro Sakaguchi!!
He actually inspired Mamura's design, so when I heard about this event, I was stunned. After all, someone I had only seen in magazines was going to suddenly appear before me...as if I were in a shojo manga!

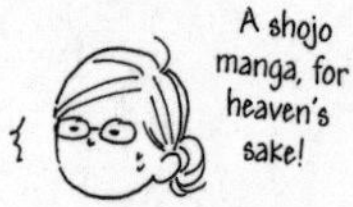
A shojo manga, for heaven's sake!

But that day, I missed my train connection and was very late...!!

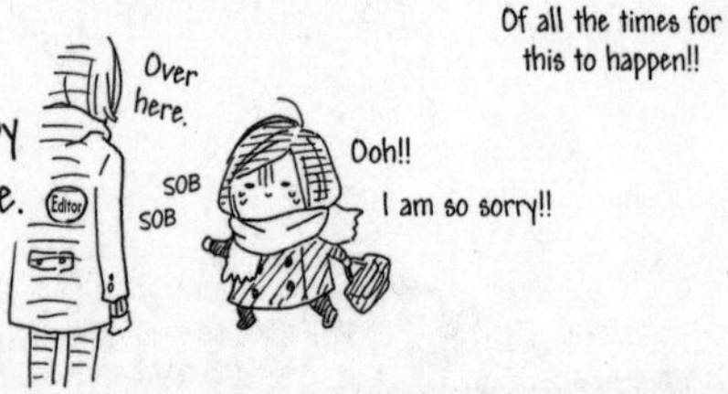
Of all the times for this to happen!!
Over here.
Editor
SOB
SOB
Ooh!!
I am so sorry!!

I was half-crying by the time I got there.

I headed over, despite the overwhelming urge I felt to beg for forgiveness. When I got there, they had already started shooting. I got to see some pictures of Kentaro dressed in a uniform-like outfit!! The pictures were more than enough, so I went to ask if could leave. But then...!

To be continued!!

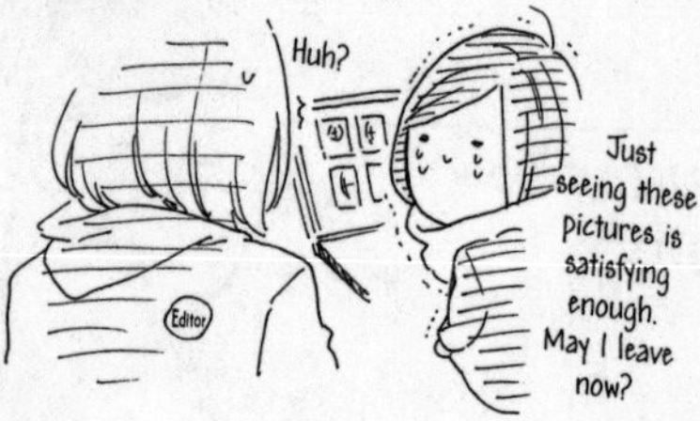
Huh?
Editor
Just seeing these pictures is satisfying enough. May I leave now?

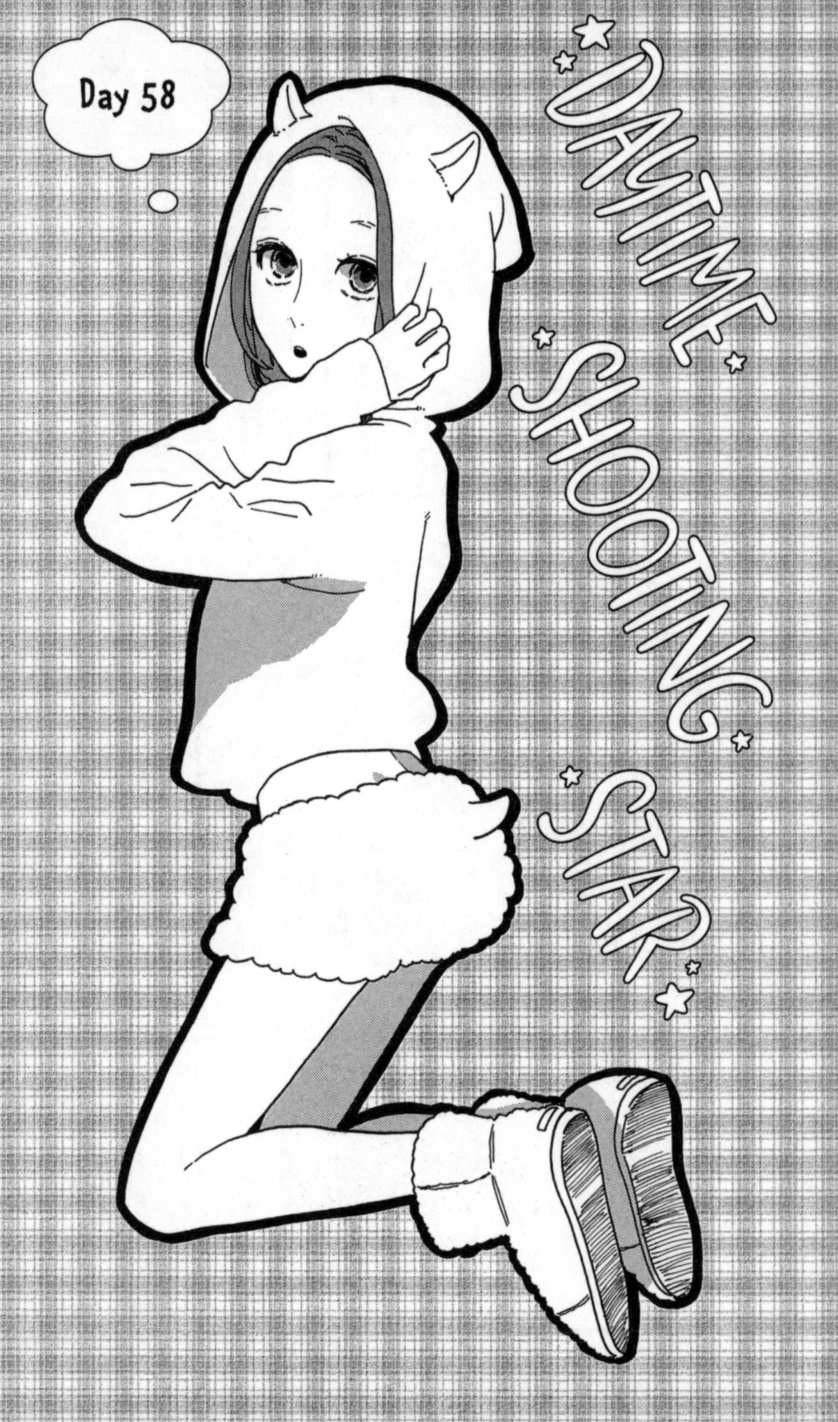
Day 58
DAYTIME SHOOTING STAR

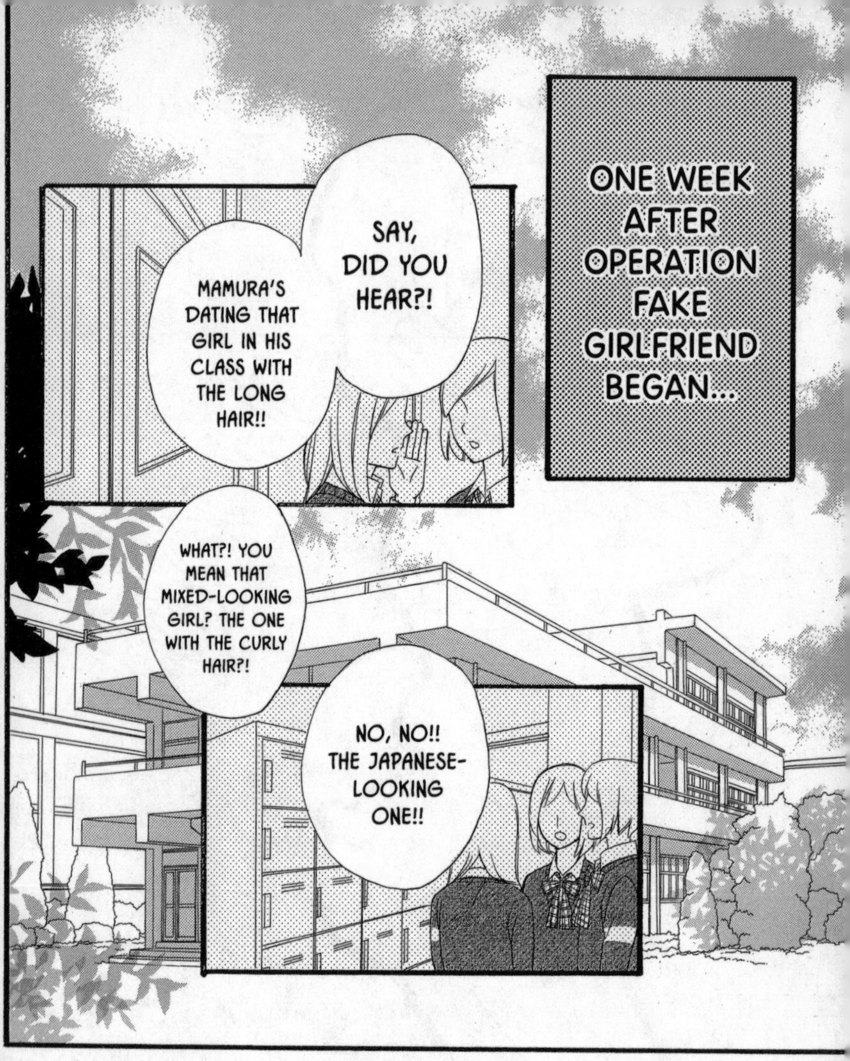
ONE WEEK AFTER OPERATION FAKE GIRLFRIEND BEGAN...
SAY, DID YOU HEAR?!
MAMURA'S DATING THAT GIRL IN HIS CLASS WITH THE LONG HAIR!!
WHAT?! YOU MEAN THAT MIXED-LOOKING GIRL? THE ONE WITH THE CURLY HAIR?!
NO, NO!! THE JAPANESE-LOOKING ONE!!

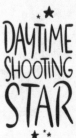

DAYTIME SHOOTING STAR

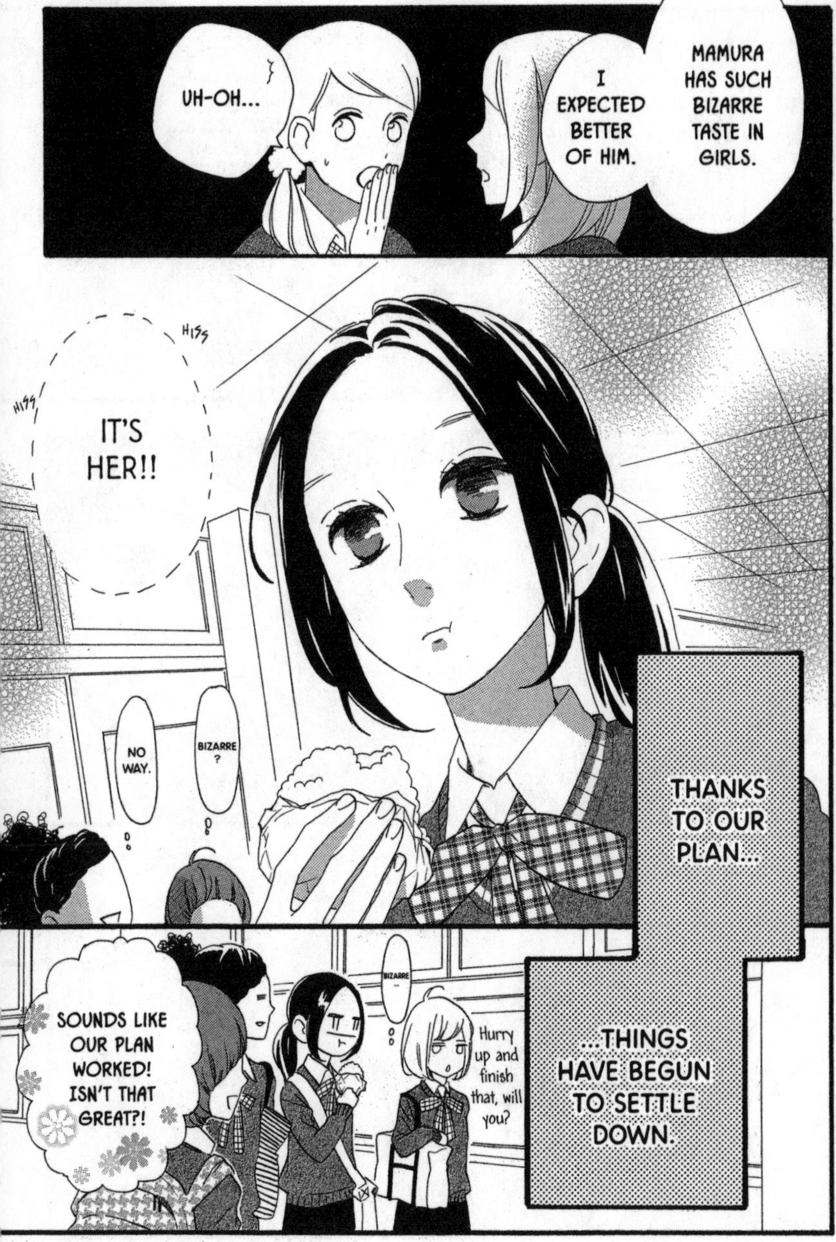
MAMURA HAS SUCH BIZARRE TASTE IN GIRLS.
I EXPECTED BETTER OF HIM.
UH-OH...
HISS
HISS
IT'S HER!!
BIZARRE?
NO WAY.
THANKS TO OUR PLAN...
...THINGS HAVE BEGUN TO SETTLE DOWN.
Hurry up and finish that, will you?
BIZARRE...
SOUNDS LIKE OUR PLAN WORKED! ISN'T THAT GREAT?!

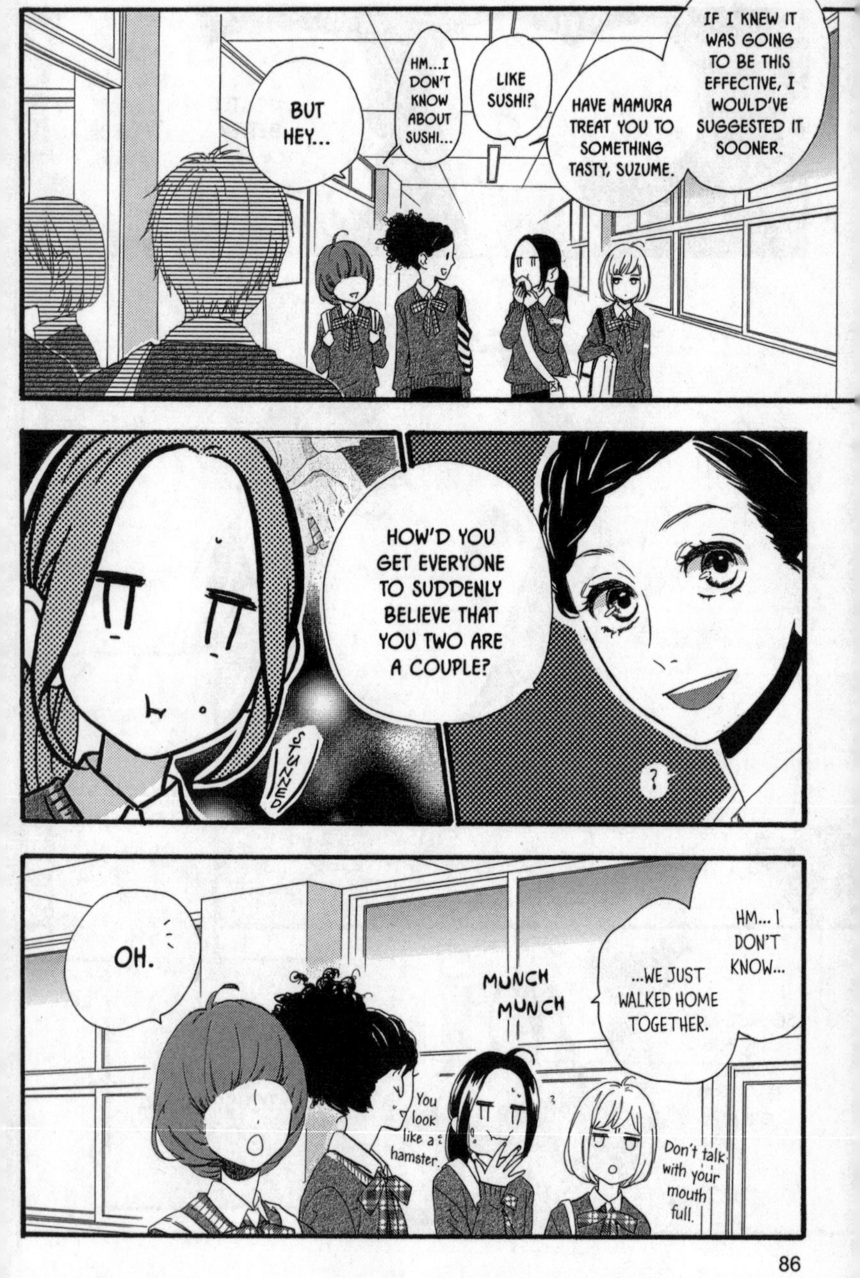
IF I KNEW IT WAS GOING TO BE THIS EFFECTIVE, I WOULD'VE SUGGESTED IT SOONER.
HAVE MAMURA TREAT YOU TO SOMETHING TASTY, SUZUME.
LIKE SUSHI?
HM...I DON'T KNOW ABOUT SUSHI...
BUT HEY...
HOW'D YOU GET EVERYONE TO SUDDENLY BELIEVE THAT YOU TWO ARE A COUPLE?
?
STUNNED
HM... I DON'T KNOW...
...WE JUST WALKED HOME TOGETHER.
MUNCH MUNCH
Don't talk with your mouth full.
You look like a hamster.
OH.

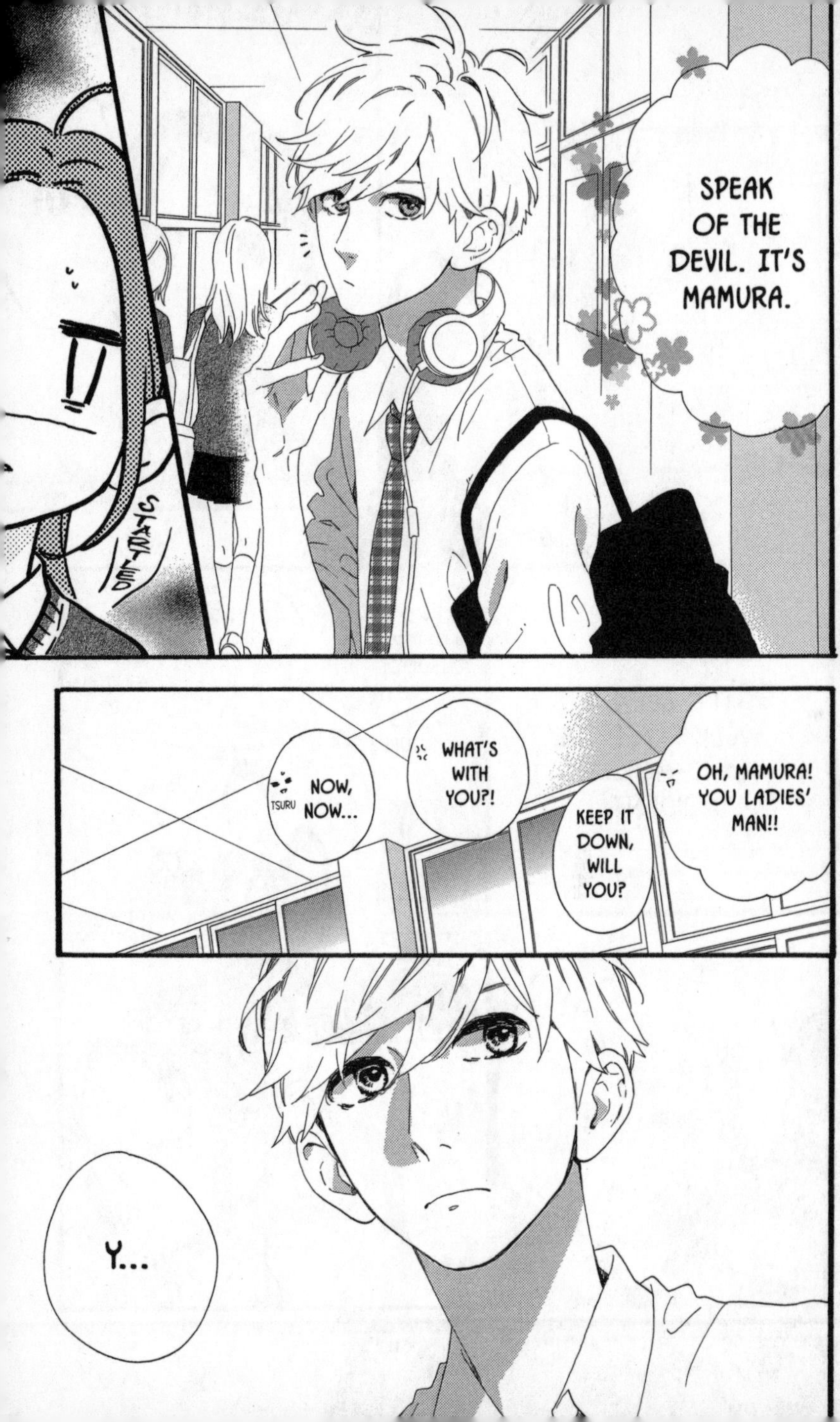
SPEAK OF THE DEVIL. IT'S MAMURA.
STARTLED
OH, MAMURA! YOU LADIES' MAN!!
KEEP IT DOWN, WILL YOU?
WHAT'S WITH YOU?!
TSURU
NOW, NOW...
Y...

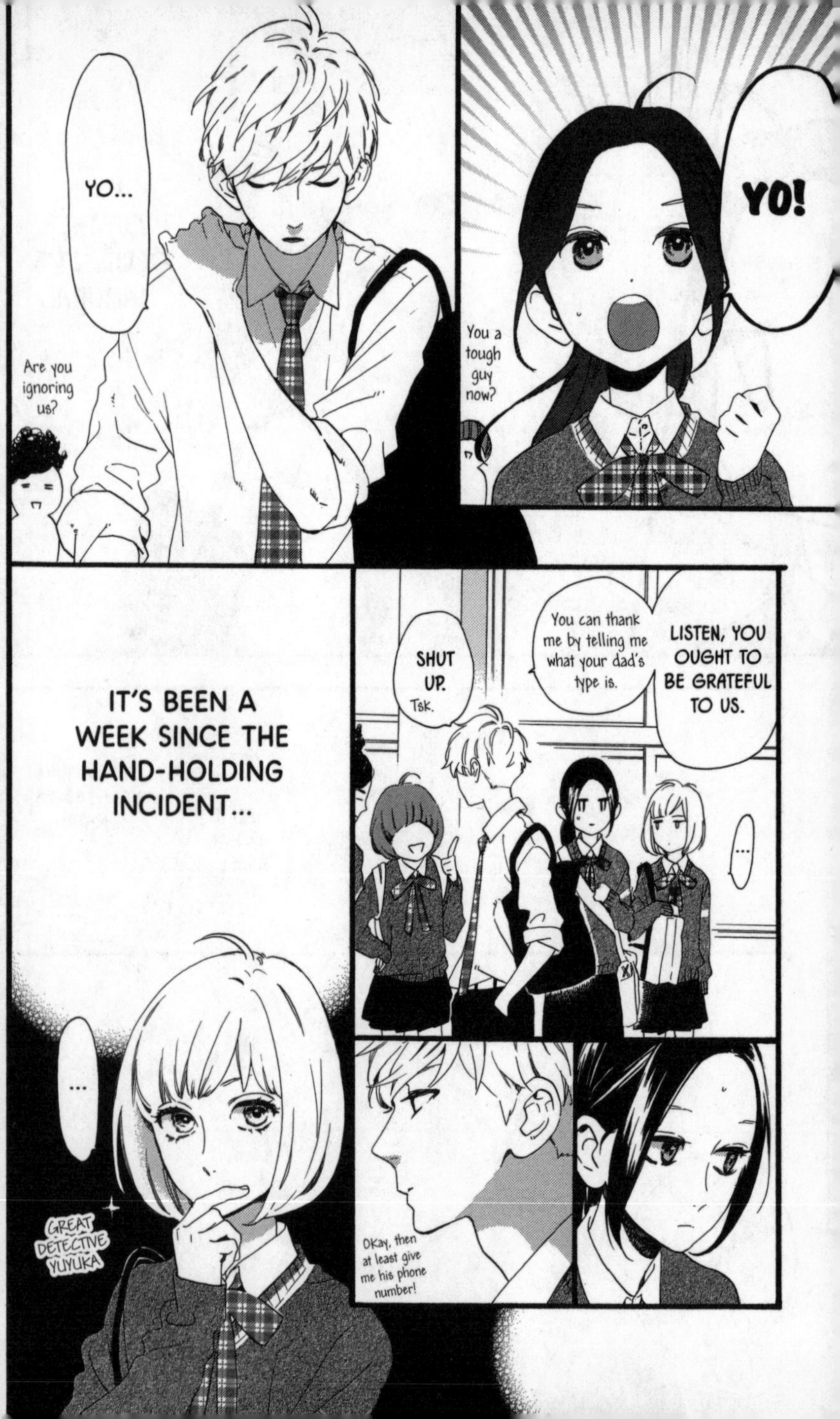
YO!
You a tough guy now?
YO...
Are you ignoring us?
LISTEN, YOU OUGHT TO BE GRATEFUL TO US.
You can thank me by telling me what your dad's type is.
SHUT UP.
Tsk.
...
Okay, then at least give me his phone number!
IT'S BEEN A WEEK SINCE THE HAND-HOLDING INCIDENT...
...
GREAT DETECTIVE YUYUKA

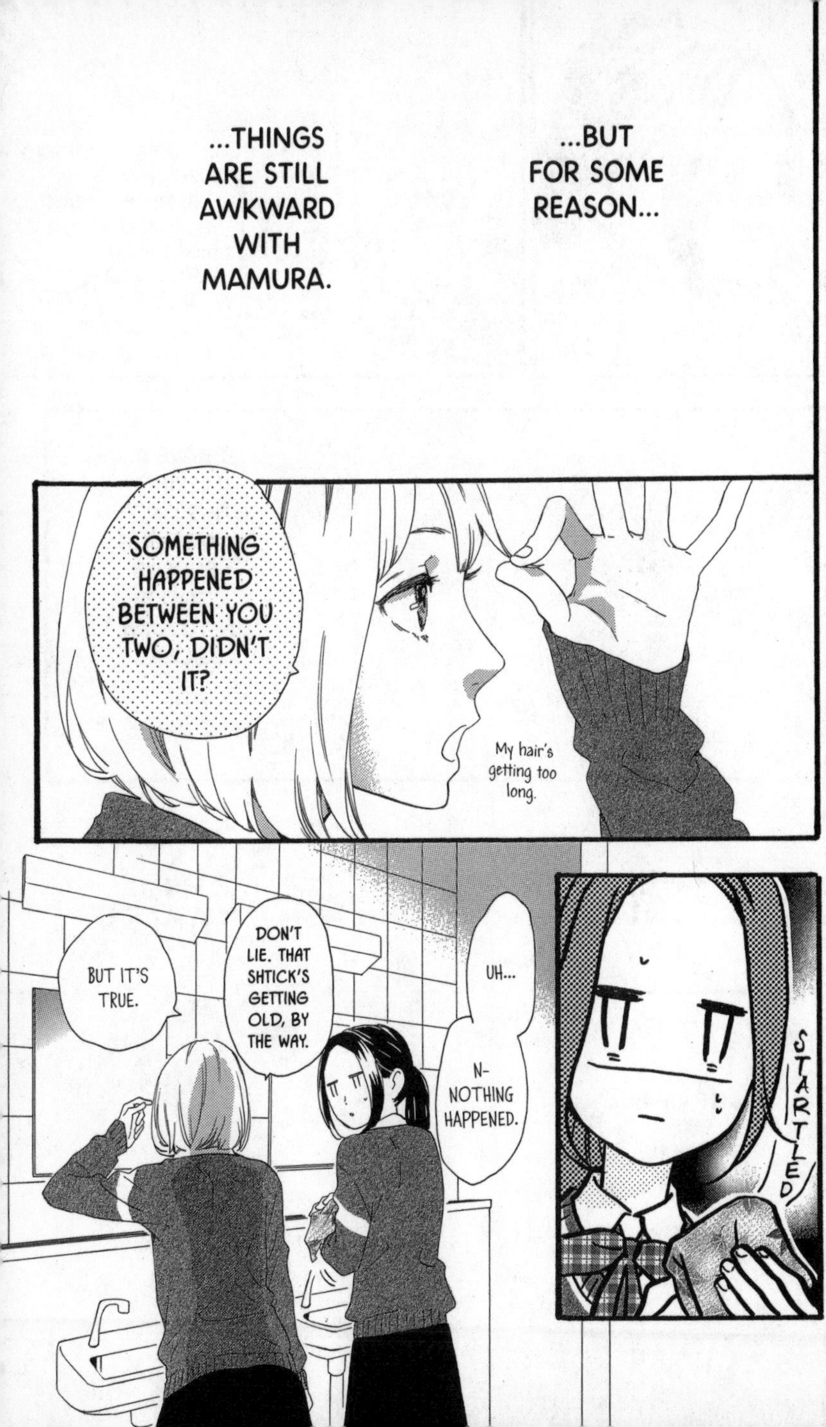
...BUT FOR SOME REASON...
...THINGS ARE STILL AWKWARD WITH MAMURA.
My hair's getting too long.
SOMETHING HAPPENED BETWEEN YOU TWO, DIDN'T IT?
STARTLED
UH...
N-NOTHING HAPPENED.
DON'T LIE. THAT SHTICK'S GETTING OLD, BY THE WAY.
BUT IT'S TRUE.

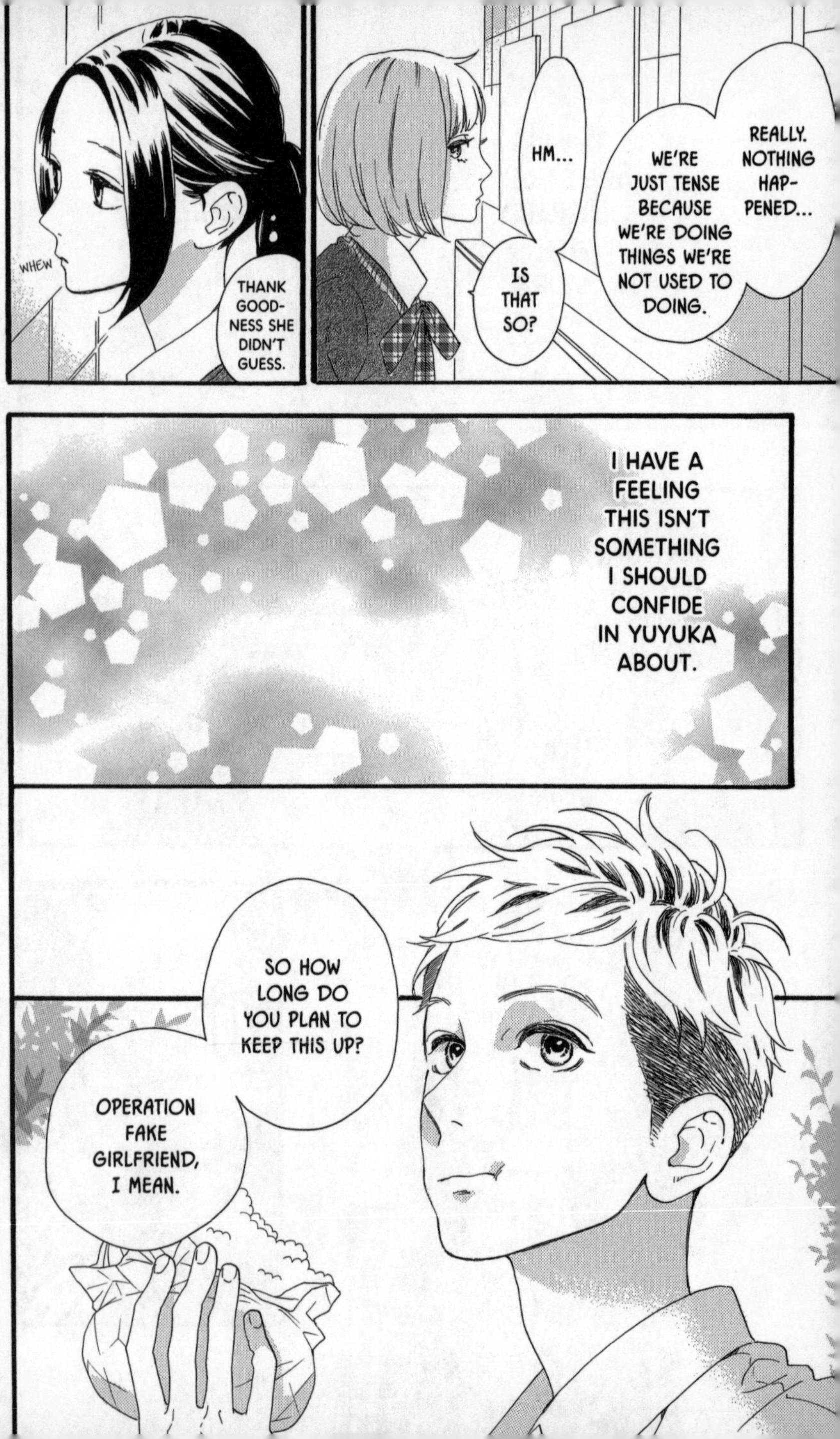
REALLY. NOTHING HAPPENED...
WE'RE JUST TENSE BECAUSE WE'RE DOING THINGS WE'RE NOT USED TO DOING.
HM...
IS THAT SO?
WHEW
THANK GOODNESS SHE DIDN'T GUESS.
I HAVE A FEELING THIS ISN'T SOMETHING I SHOULD CONFIDE IN YUYUKA ABOUT.
SO HOW LONG DO YOU PLAN TO KEEP THIS UP?
OPERATION FAKE GIRLFRIEND, I MEAN.

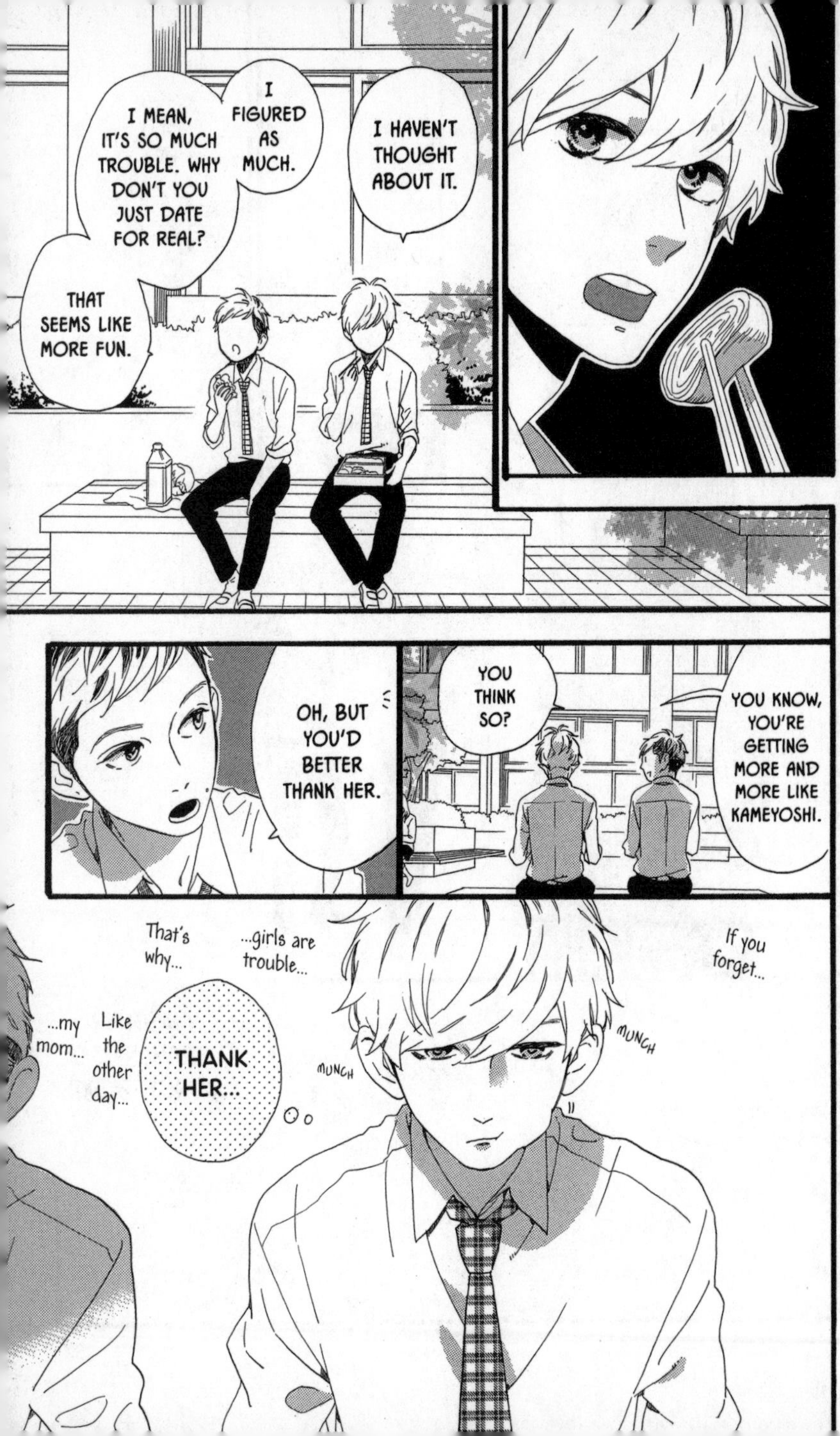
I HAVEN'T THOUGHT ABOUT IT.
I FIGURED AS MUCH.
I MEAN, IT'S SO MUCH TROUBLE. WHY DON'T YOU JUST DATE FOR REAL?
THAT SEEMS LIKE MORE FUN.
YOU KNOW, YOU'RE GETTING MORE AND MORE LIKE KAMEYOSHI.
YOU THINK SO?
OH, BUT YOU'D BETTER THANK HER.
If you forget...
MUNCH
...girls are trouble...
That's why...
MUNCH
THANK HER...
Like the other day...
...my mom...

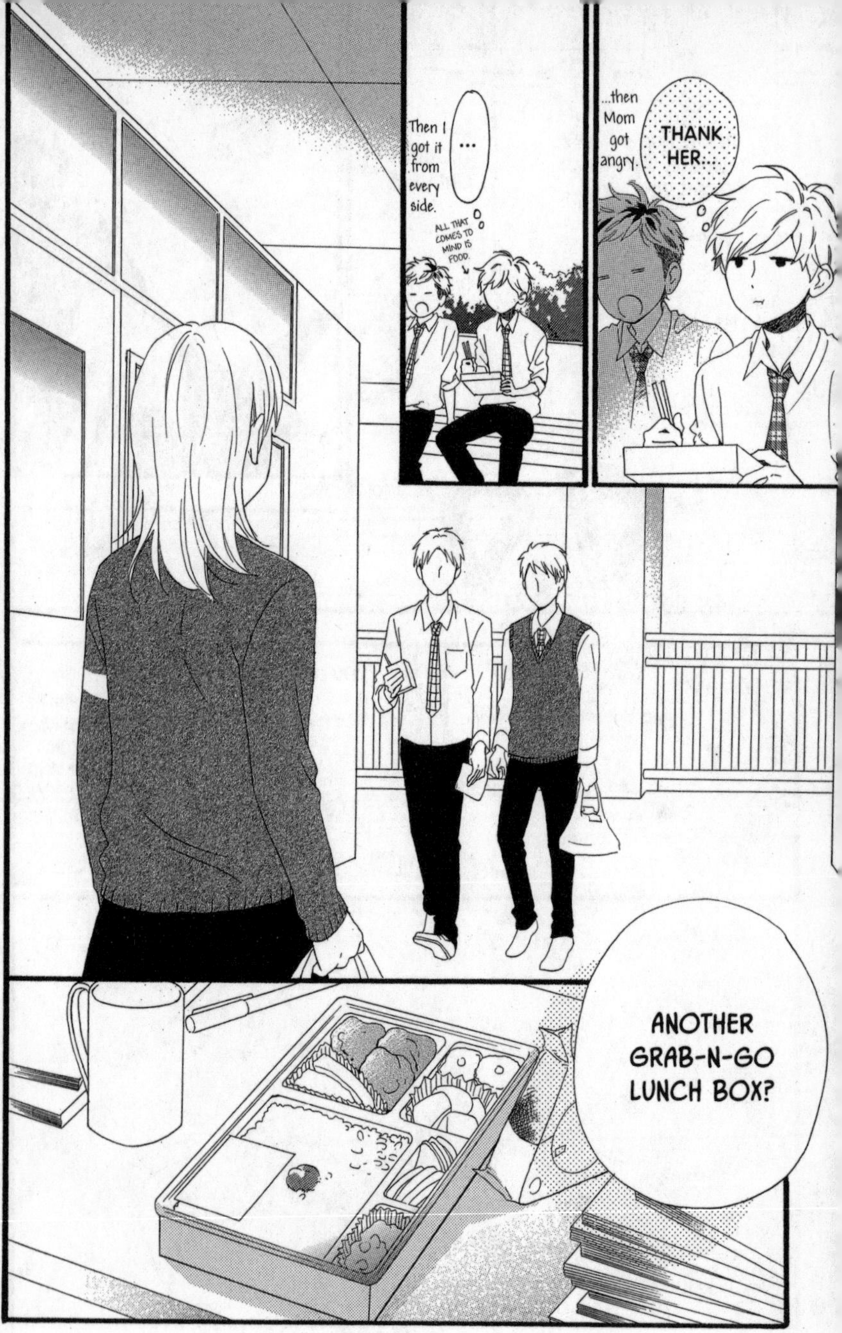
...then Mom got angry.
THANK HER...
Then I got it from every side.
...
ALL THAT COMES TO MIND IS FOOD.
ANOTHER GRAB-N-GO LUNCH BOX?

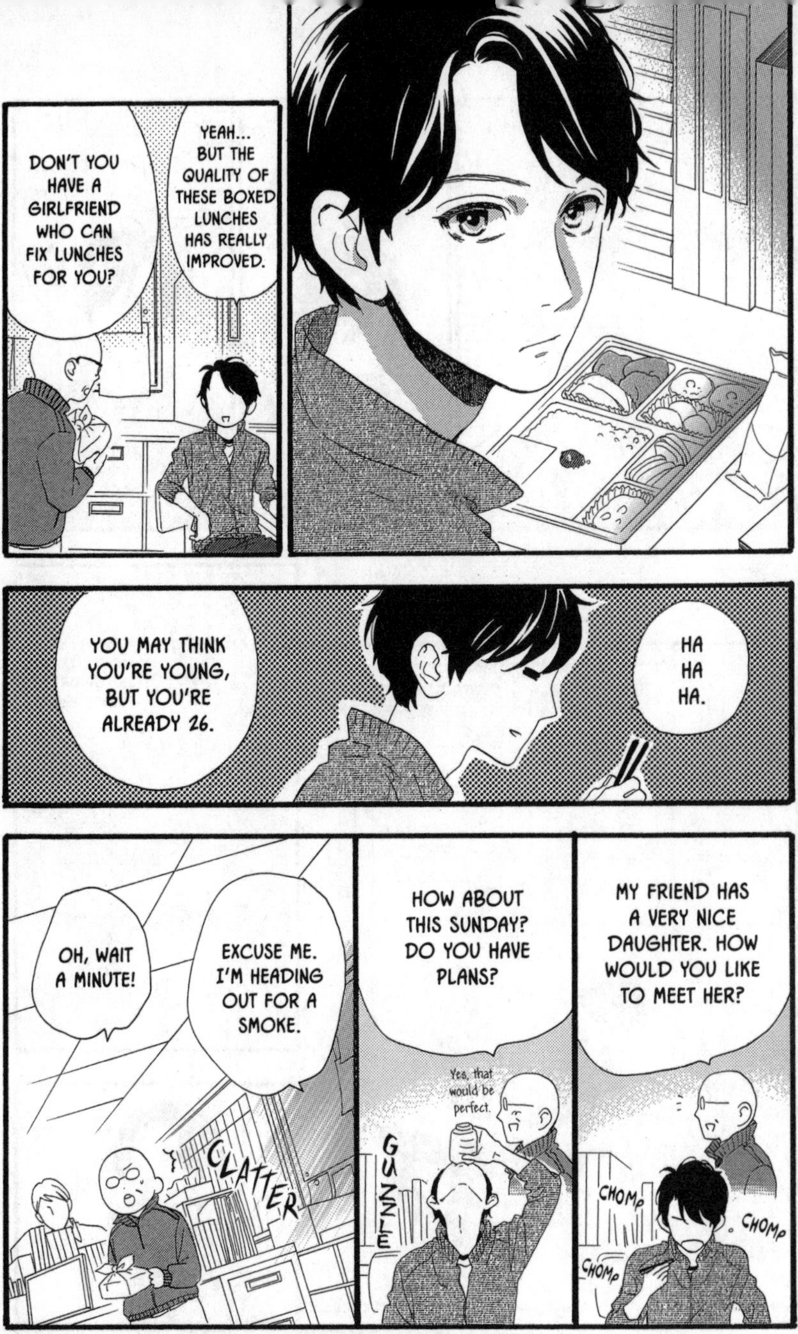
YEAH... BUT THE QUALITY OF THESE BOXED LUNCHES HAS REALLY IMPROVED.
DON'T YOU HAVE A GIRLFRIEND WHO CAN FIX LUNCHES FOR YOU?
HA HA HA.
YOU MAY THINK YOU'RE YOUNG, BUT YOU'RE ALREADY 26.
MY FRIEND HAS A VERY NICE DAUGHTER. HOW WOULD YOU LIKE TO MEET HER?
CHOMP
CHOMP
CHOMP
HOW ABOUT THIS SUNDAY? DO YOU HAVE PLANS?
Yes, that would be perfect.
GUZZLE
EXCUSE ME. I'M HEADING OUT FOR A SMOKE.
OH, WAIT A MINUTE!
CLATTER

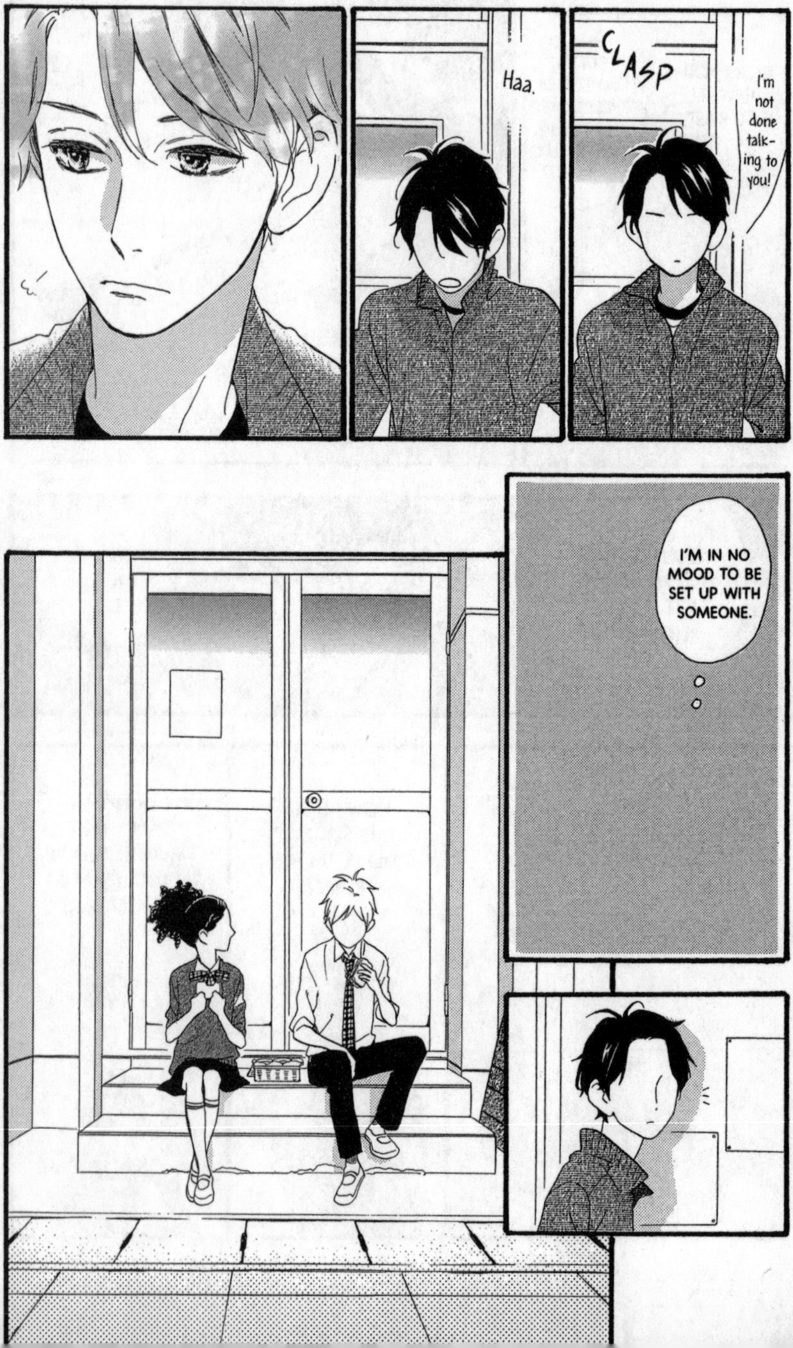

I'm not done talk-ing to you!
CLASP
Haa.
I'M IN NO MOOD TO BE SET UP WITH SOMEONE.

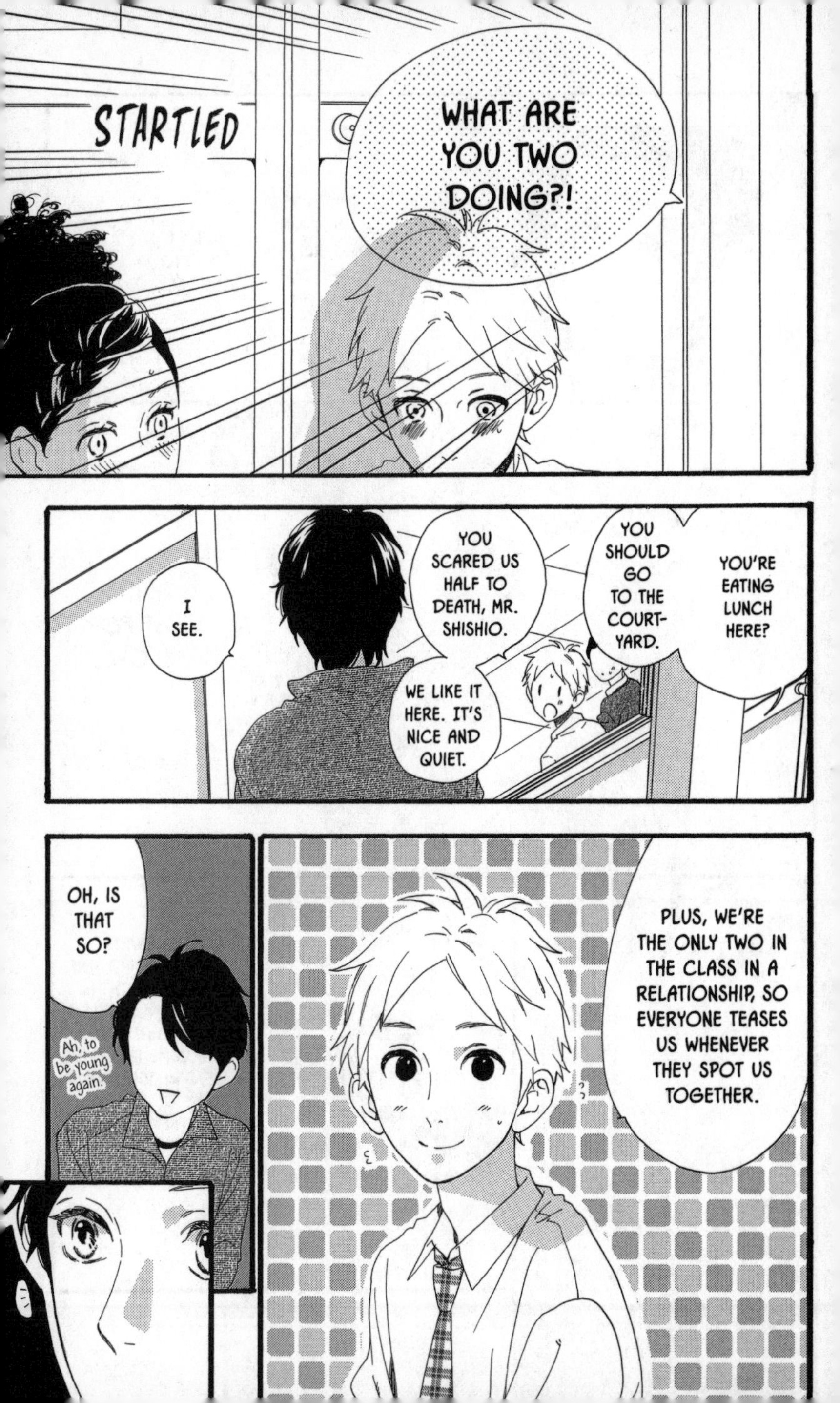

WHAT ARE YOU TWO DOING?!
STARTLED
YOU'RE EATING LUNCH HERE?
YOU SHOULD GO TO THE COURT-YARD.
YOU SCARED US HALF TO DEATH, MR. SHISHIO.
WE LIKE IT HERE. IT'S NICE AND QUIET.
I SEE.
PLUS, WE'RE THE ONLY TWO IN THE CLASS IN A RELATIONSHIP, SO EVERYONE TEASES US WHENEVER THEY SPOT US TOGETHER.
OH, IS THAT SO?
Ah, to be young again.

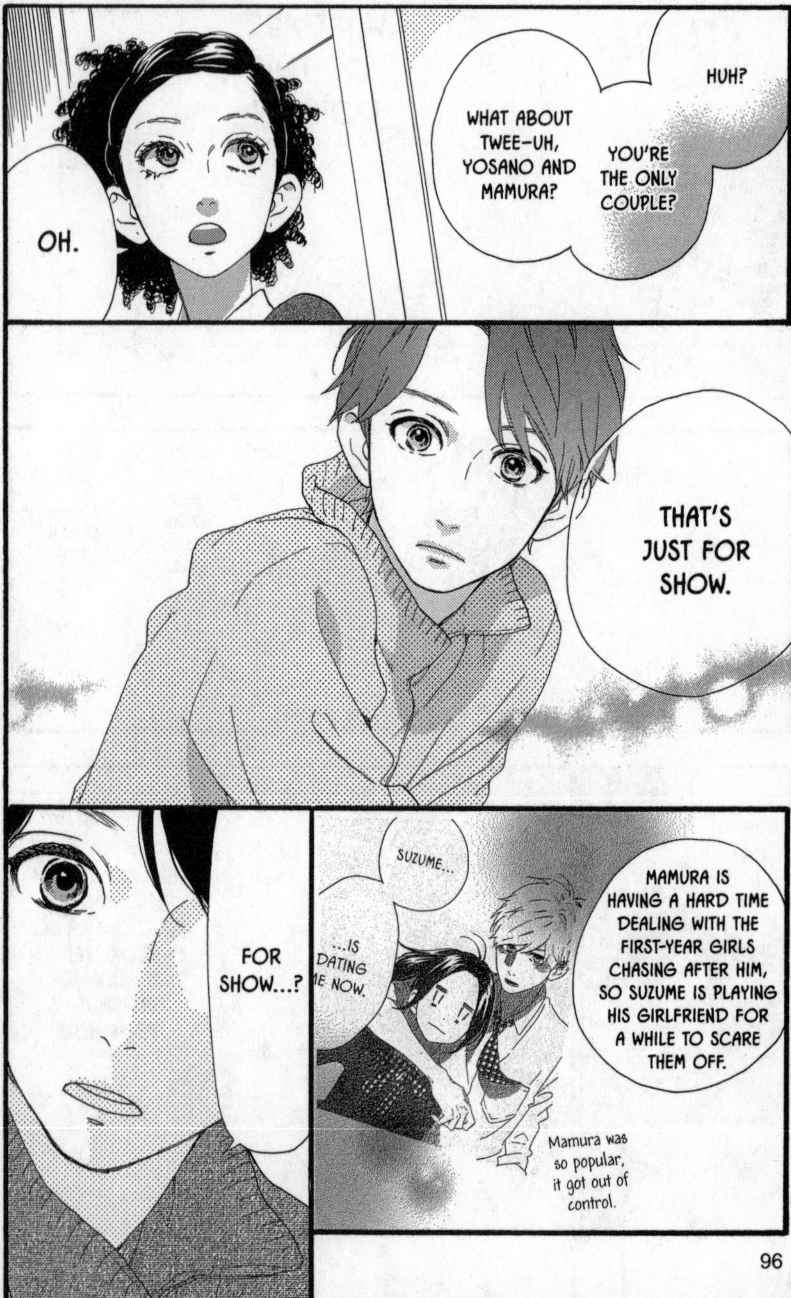
HUH?
WHAT ABOUT TWEE—UH, YOSANO AND MAMURA?
YOU'RE THE ONLY COUPLE?
OH.
THAT'S JUST FOR SHOW.
MAMURA IS HAVING A HARD TIME DEALING WITH THE FIRST-YEAR GIRLS CHASING AFTER HIM, SO SUZUME IS PLAYING HIS GIRLFRIEND FOR A WHILE TO SCARE THEM OFF.
SUZUME...
...IS DATING ME NOW.
Mamura was so popular, it got out of control.
FOR SHOW...?

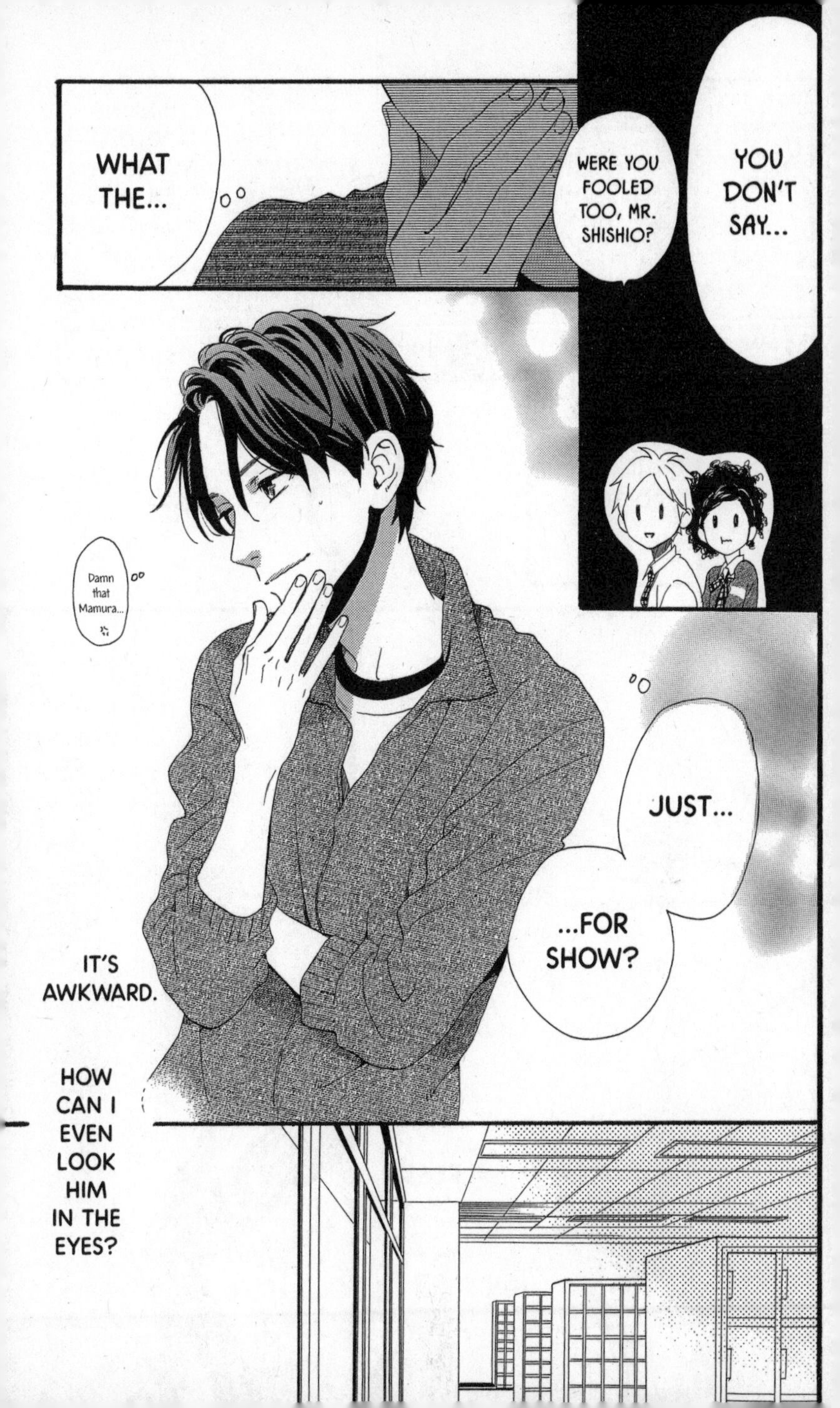
YOU DON'T SAY...
WERE YOU FOOLED TOO, MR. SHISHIO?
WHAT THE...
JUST...
...FOR SHOW?
Damn that Mamura...
IT'S AWKWARD.
HOW CAN I EVEN LOOK HIM IN THE EYES?

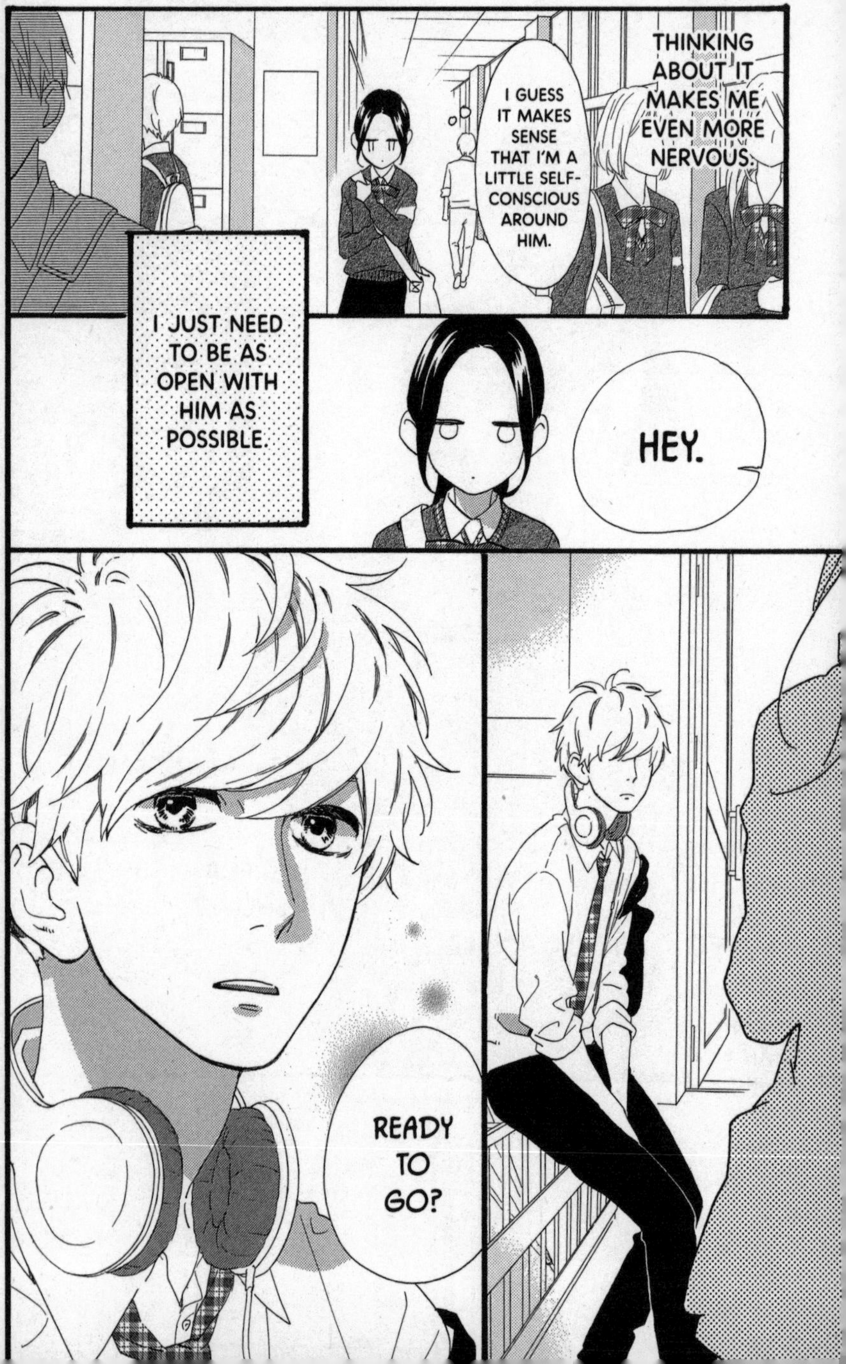
THINKING ABOUT IT MAKES ME EVEN MORE NERVOUS.
I GUESS IT MAKES SENSE THAT I'M A LITTLE SELF-CONSCIOUS AROUND HIM.
I JUST NEED TO BE AS OPEN WITH HIM AS POSSIBLE.
HEY.
READY TO GO?

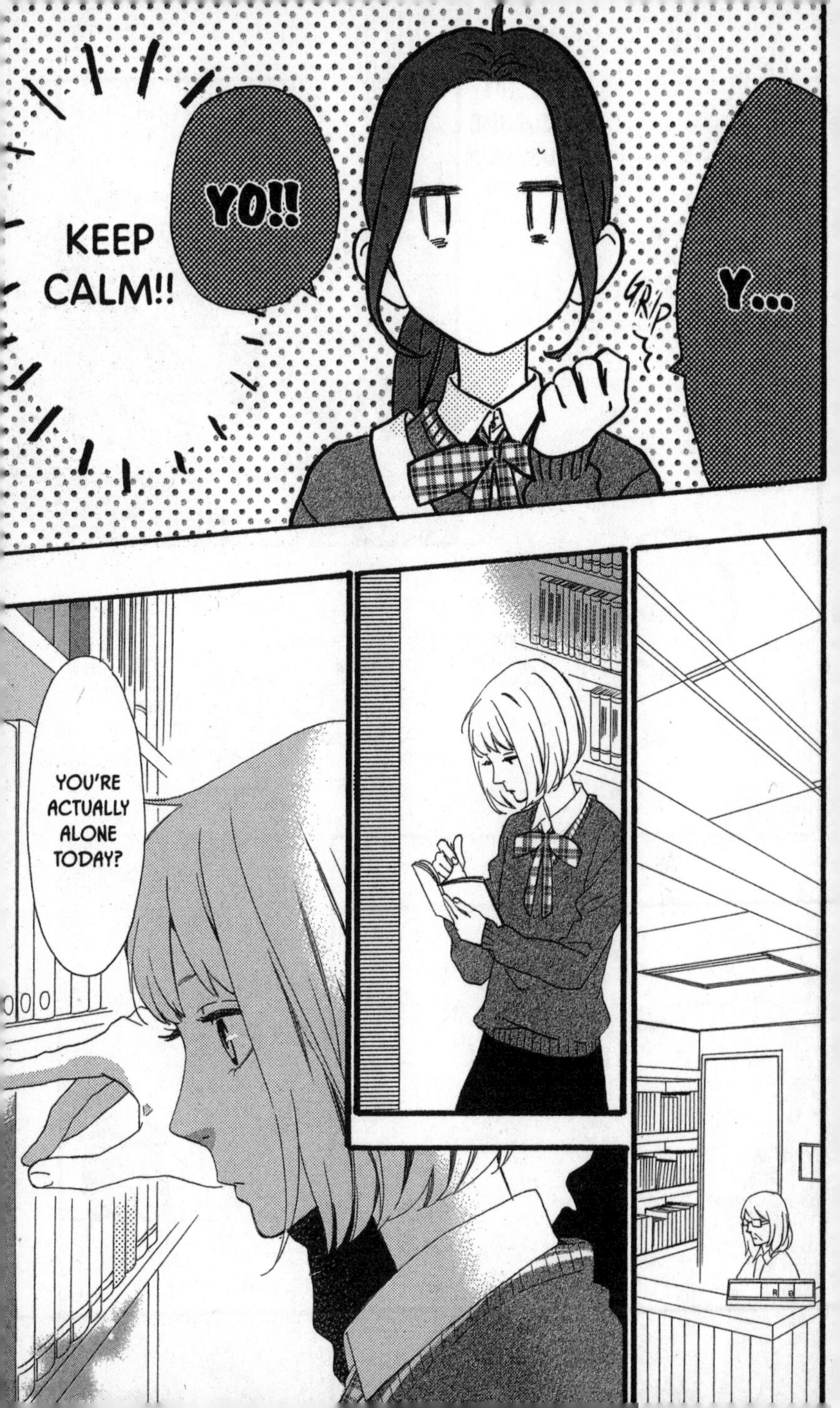
Y...
GRIP
YO!!
KEEP CALM!!
YOU'RE ACTUALLY ALONE TODAY?

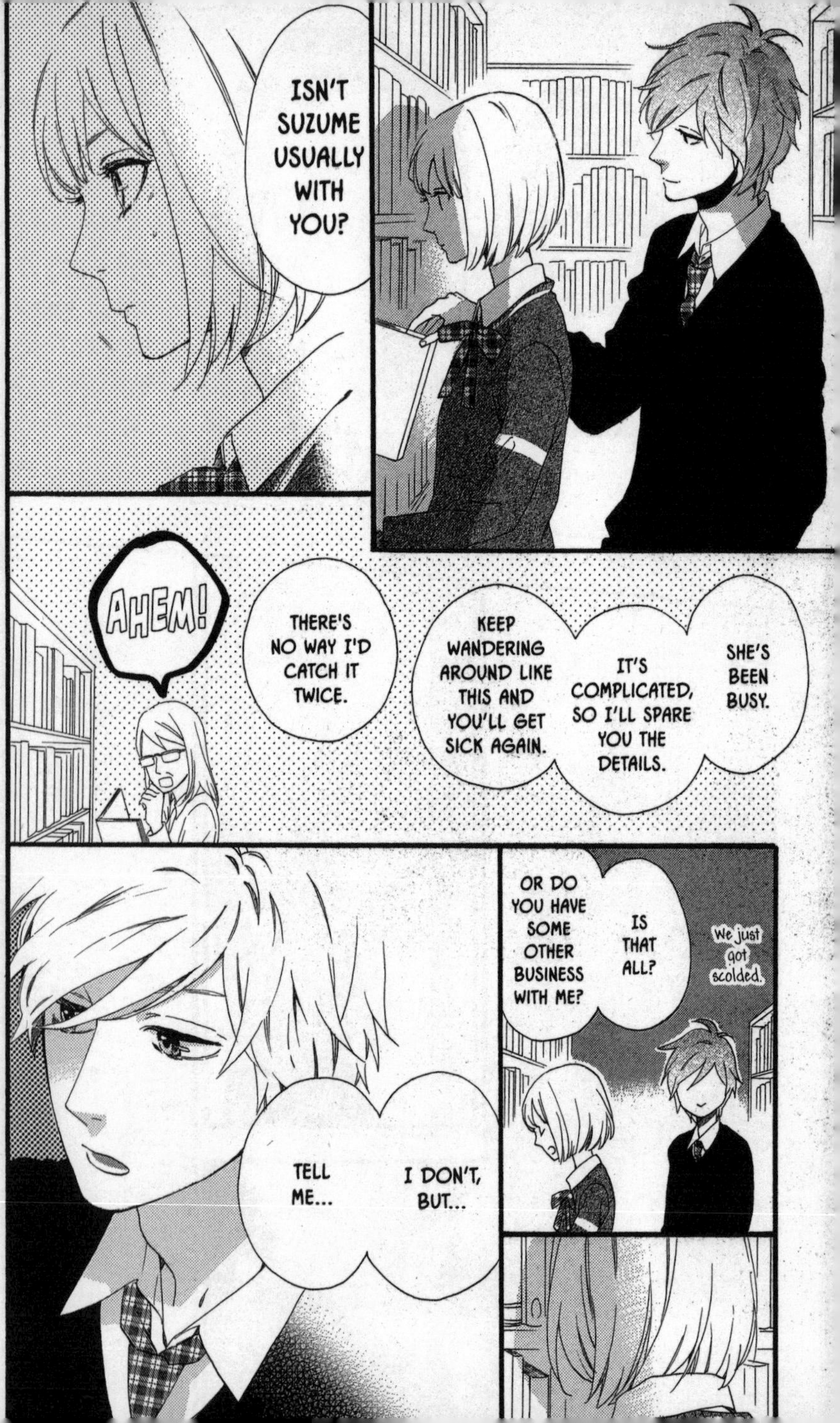
ISN'T SUZUME USUALLY WITH YOU?
SHE'S BEEN BUSY.
IT'S COMPLICATED, SO I'LL SPARE YOU THE DETAILS.
KEEP WANDERING AROUND LIKE THIS AND YOU'LL GET SICK AGAIN.
THERE'S NO WAY I'D CATCH IT TWICE.
AHEM!
IS THAT ALL?
OR DO YOU HAVE SOME OTHER BUSINESS WITH ME?
We just got scolded.
I DON'T, BUT...
TELL ME...

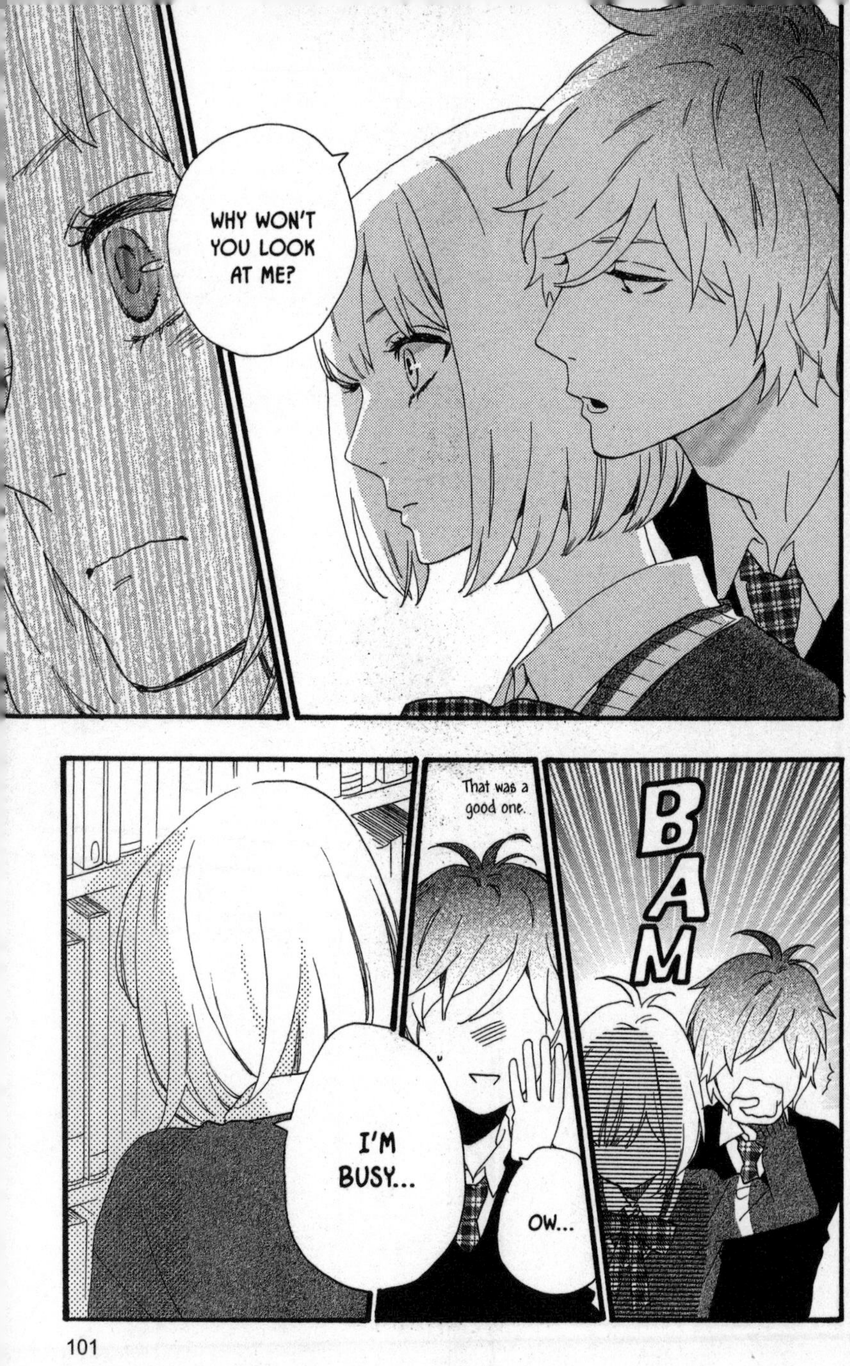
WHY WON'T YOU LOOK AT ME?
BAM
That was a good one.
OW...
I'M BUSY...

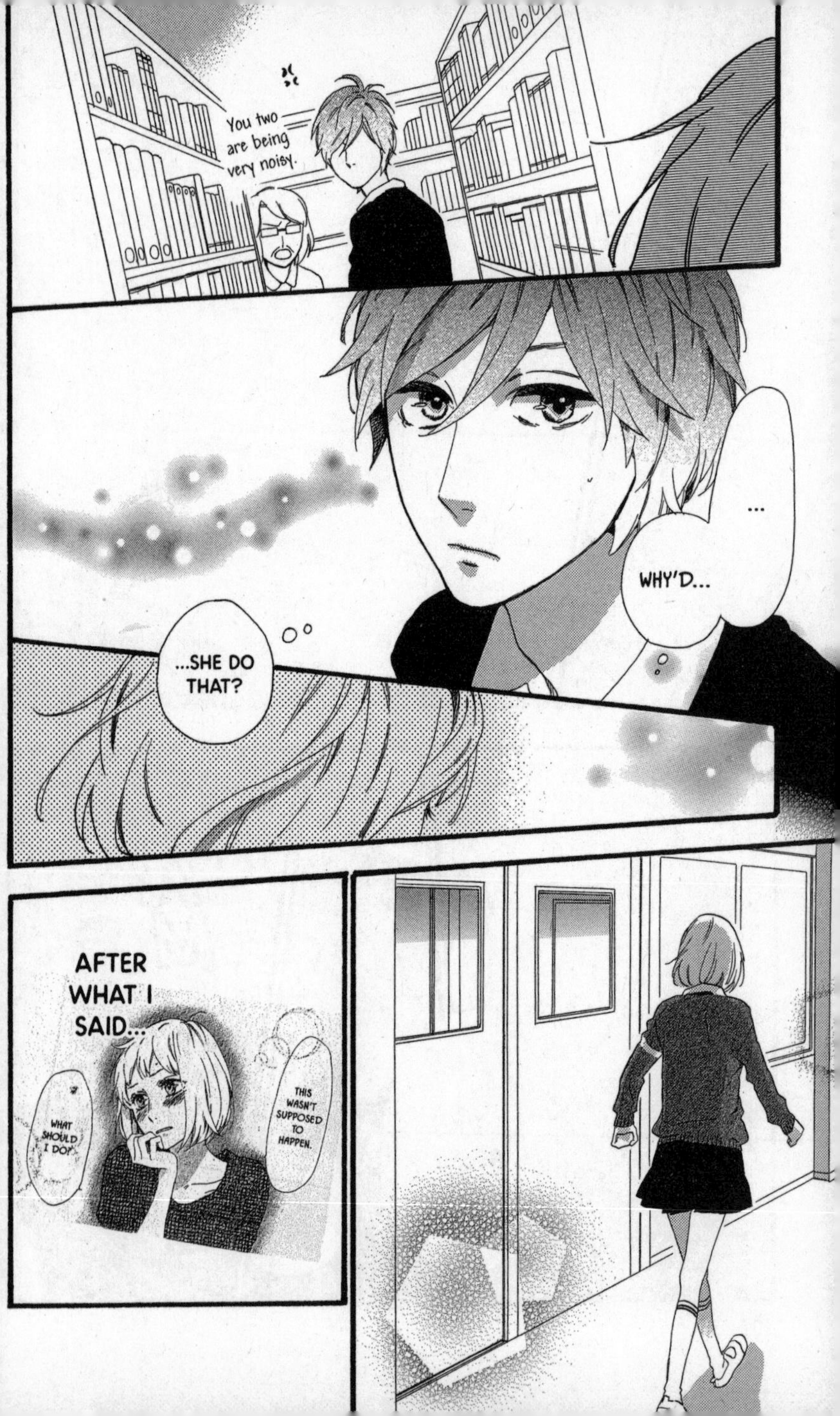
You two are being very noisy.
...
WHY'D...
...SHE DO THAT?
AFTER WHAT I SAID...
THIS WASN'T SUPPOSED TO HAPPEN.
WHAT SHOULD I DO?

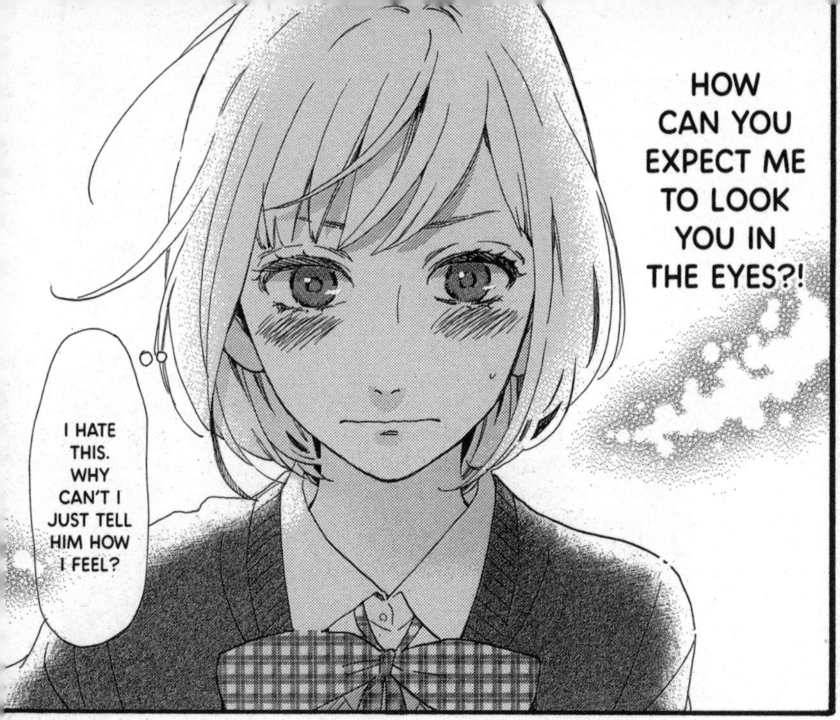
HOW CAN YOU EXPECT ME TO LOOK YOU IN THE EYES?!
I HATE THIS. WHY CAN'T I JUST TELL HIM HOW I FEEL?

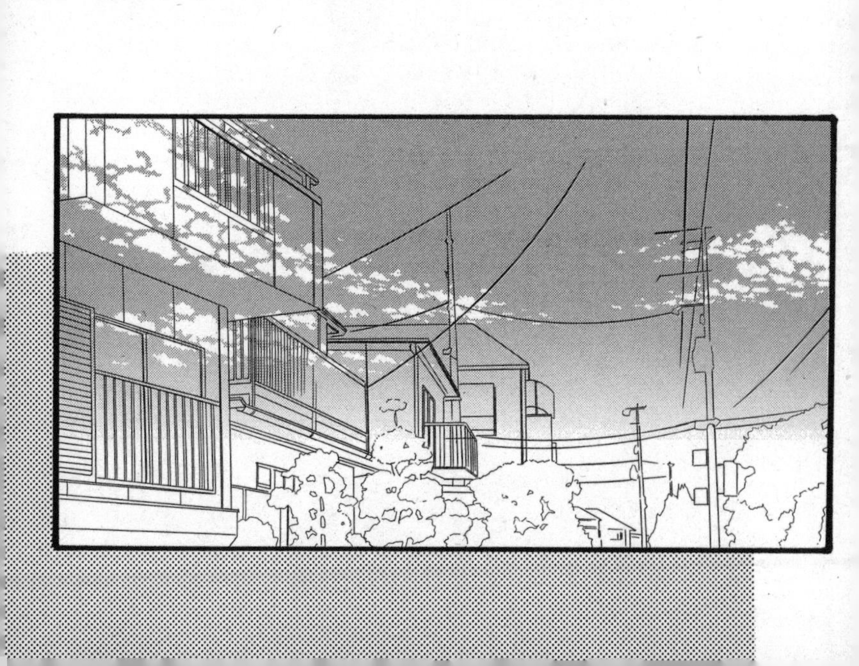

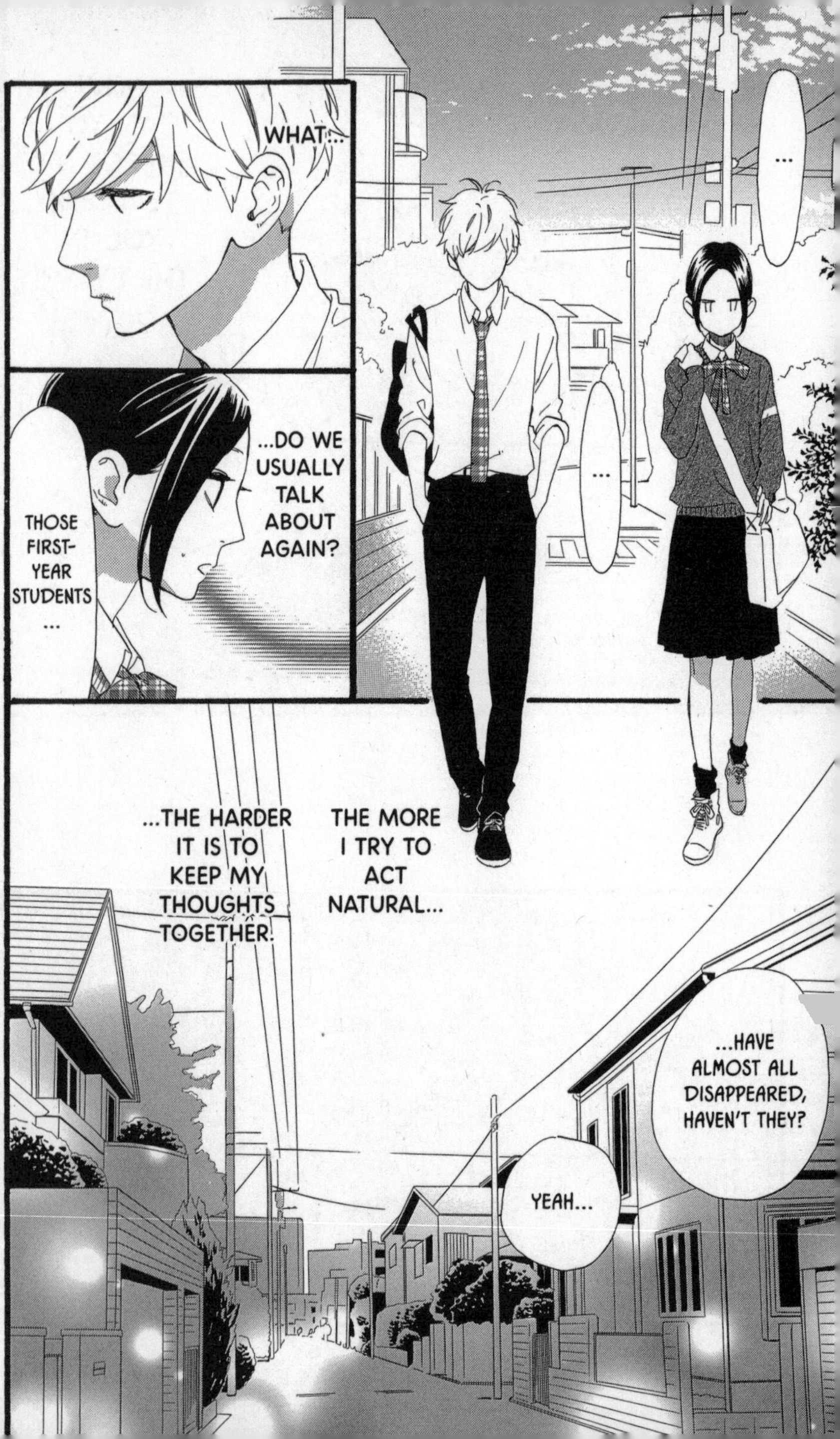
...
...
WHAT...
...DO WE USUALLY TALK ABOUT AGAIN?
THOSE FIRST-YEAR STUDENTS...
THE MORE I TRY TO ACT NATURAL...
...THE HARDER IT IS TO KEEP MY THOUGHTS TOGETHER.
...HAVE ALMOST ALL DISAPPEARED, HAVEN'T THEY?
YEAH...

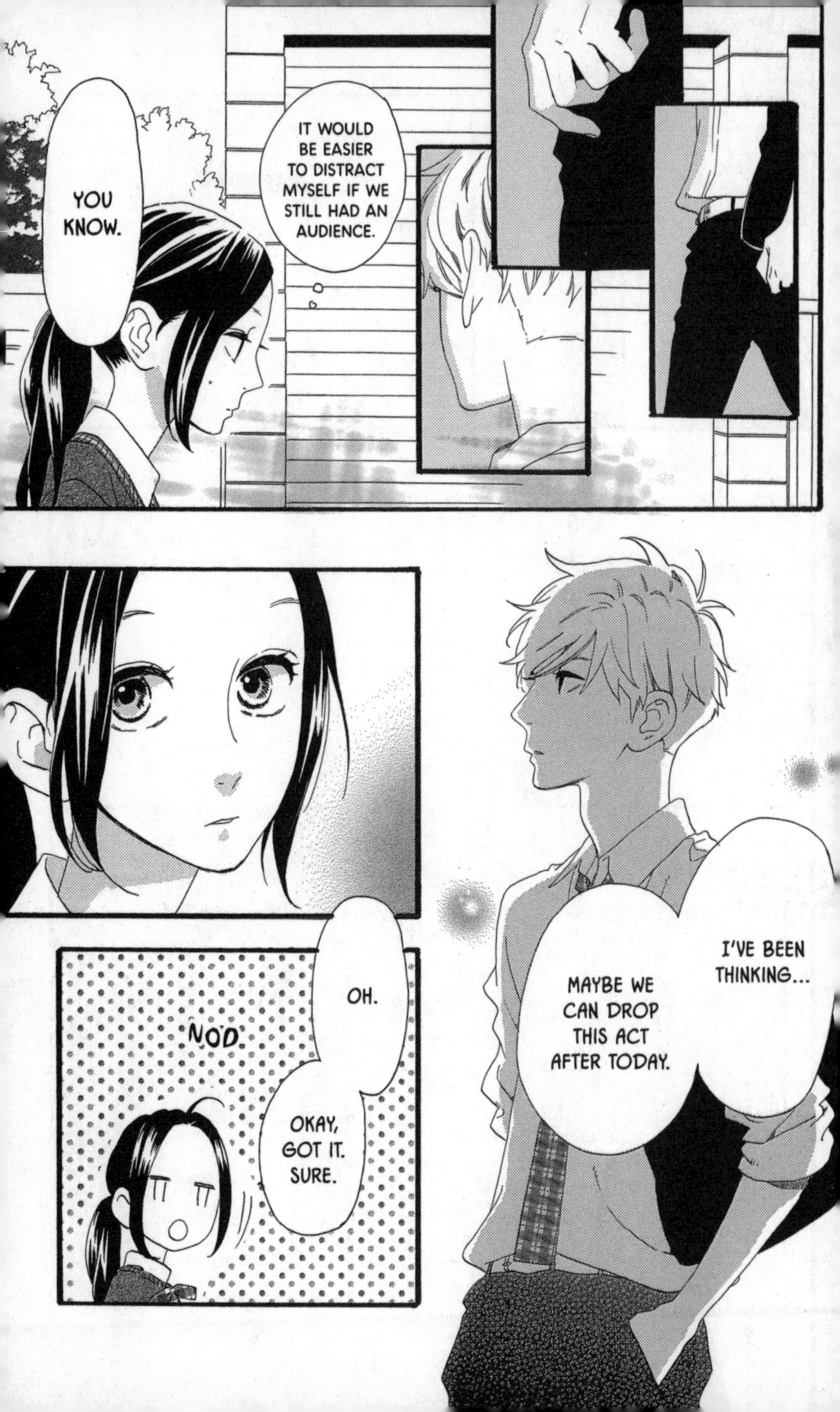
IT WOULD BE EASIER TO DISTRACT MYSELF IF WE STILL HAD AN AUDIENCE.
YOU KNOW.
I'VE BEEN THINKING...
MAYBE WE CAN DROP THIS ACT AFTER TODAY.
OH.
NOD
OKAY, GOT IT. SURE.

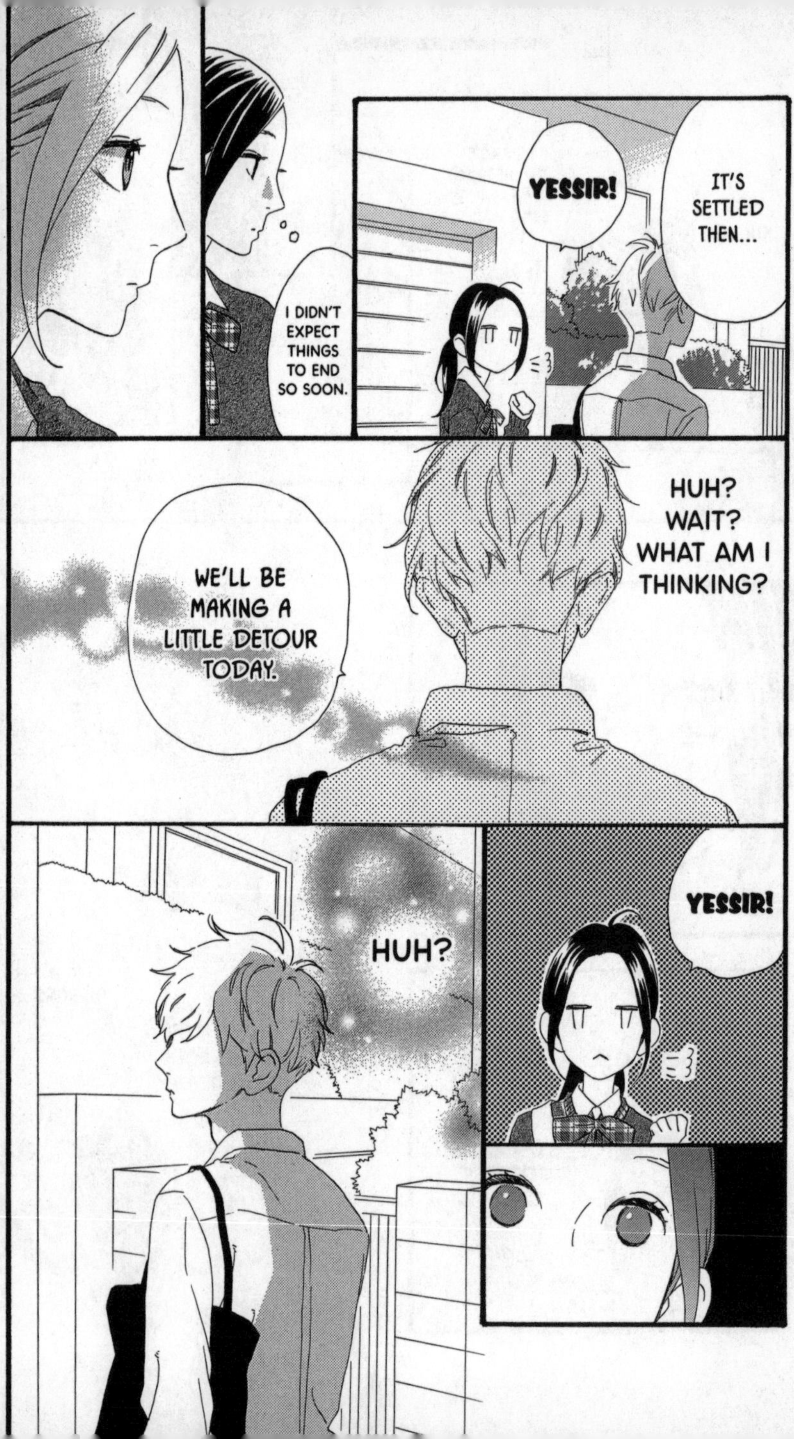
IT'S SETTLED THEN...
YESSIR!
I DIDN'T EXPECT THINGS TO END SO SOON.
HUH? WAIT? WHAT AM I THINKING?
WE'LL BE MAKING A LITTLE DETOUR TODAY.
YESSIR!
HUH?

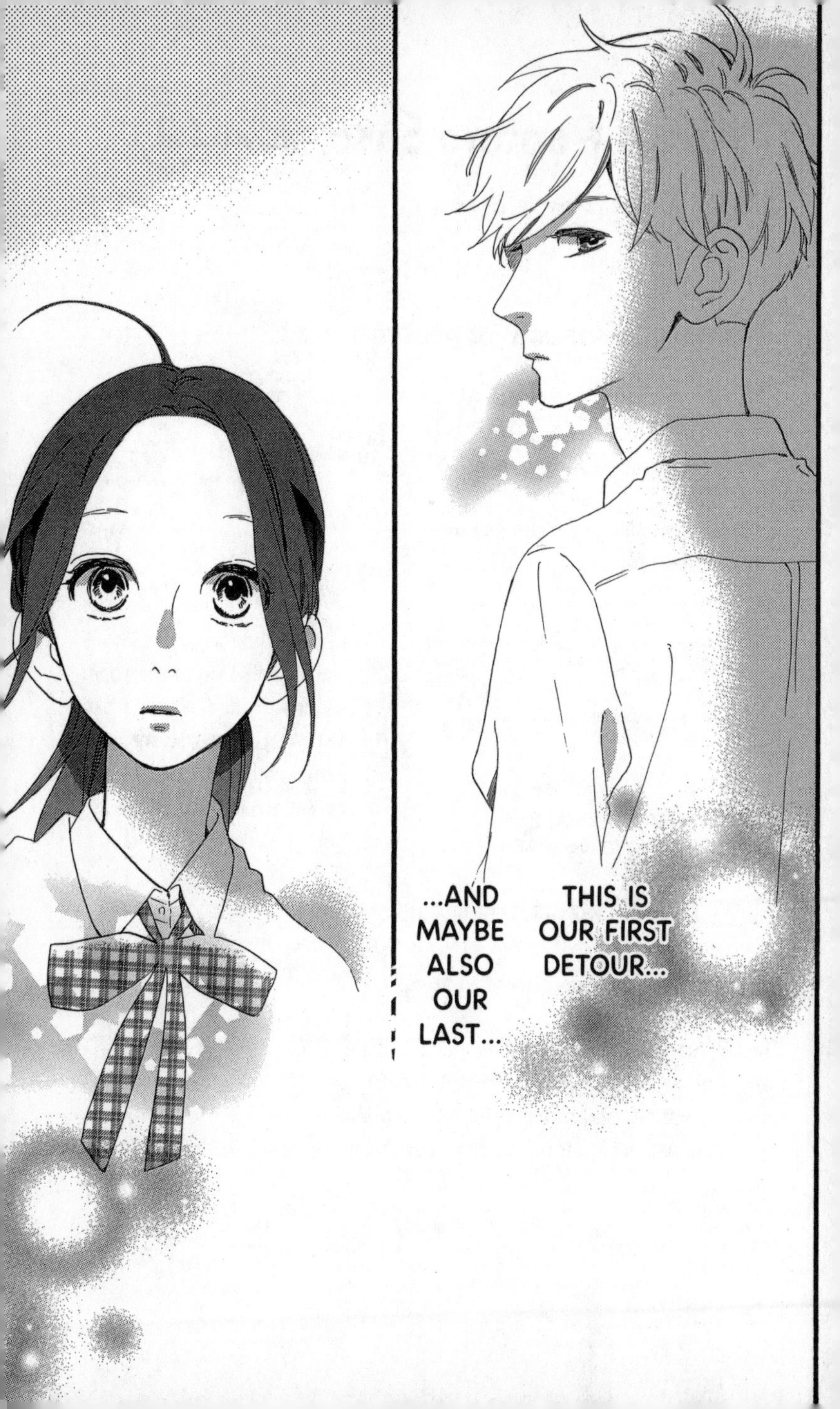
THIS IS OUR FIRST DETOUR...
...AND MAYBE ALSO OUR LAST...

About Kentaro Sakaguchi ②

Picking up where we left off... But then...

Kentaro Sakaguchi appeared!!

I froze.
(I even forgot my own name.)

WHAT IT LOOKED LIKE IN MY BRAIN.

I was so nervous that I couldn't look him in the eyes.

MESMERIZING!!

How do you do?

*My drawing skills aren't doing his good lucks justice.

Miss Yamamori, don't you want to get a better look at him?

STYLIST

SAKAGUCHI

PEEKING

UNABLE TO MAKE DIRECT EYE CONTACT.

Listen! When a person who is usually holed up in her room suddenly comes across a handsome guy, of course she would freeze up!! All I could manage to do was sneak quick peeks at him. Am I a stalker, or what?!

I was awestruck!! I had only seen him in magazines up till then, but there he was before me, talking and moving... It was amazing!! Like a dream!!
And Kentaro was so beautiful, how could I have any regrets? As that thought flashed through my mind toward the end of the shoot, I had no idea my editor had yet another surprise in store for me...!!

SAKAGUCHI

SNEAKING PEEKS

I'm so grateful!

MOVED

To be continued!!

By the way, Ms. Yamamori...

SANRIO FACE

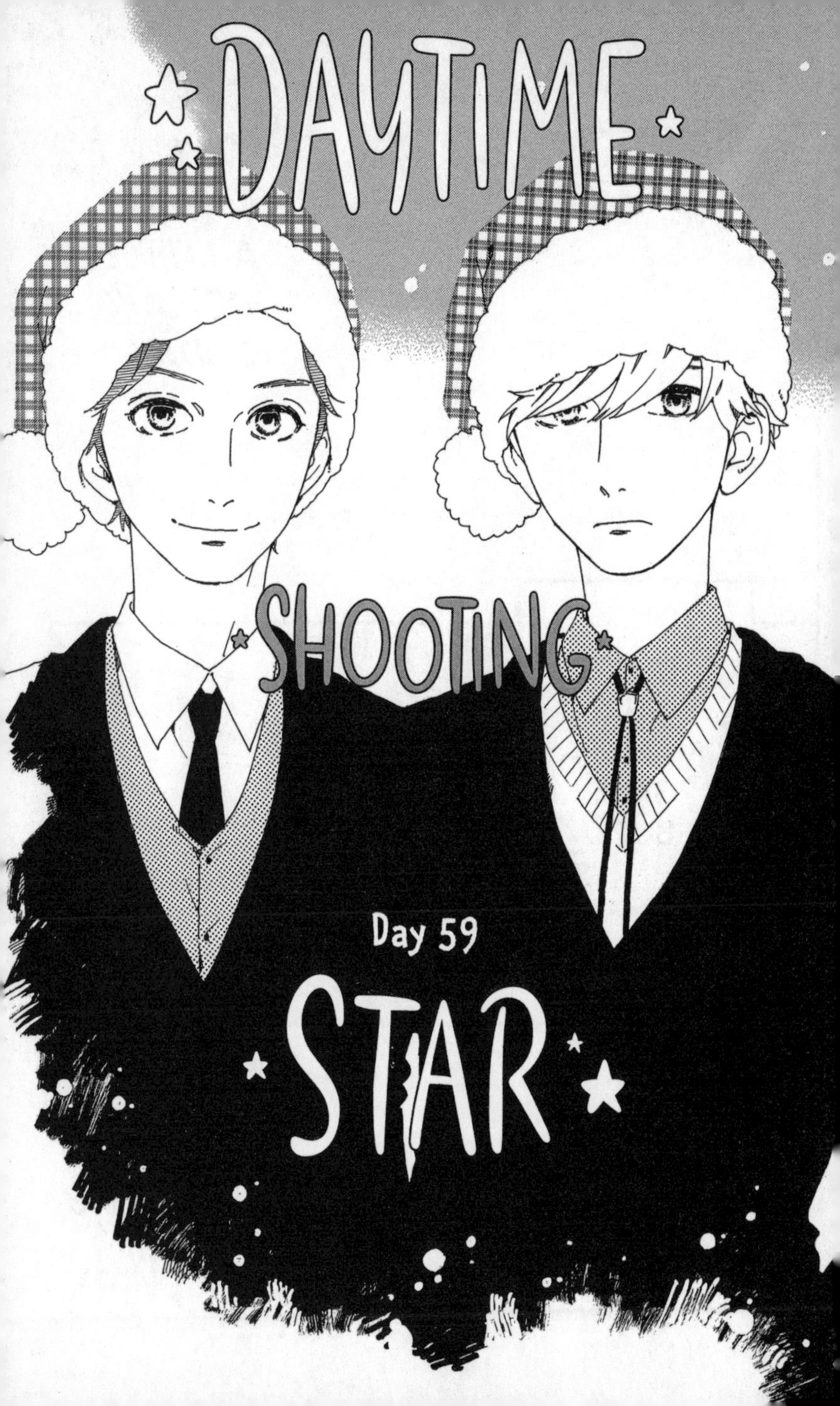
DAYTIME
SHOOTING
Day 59
STAR

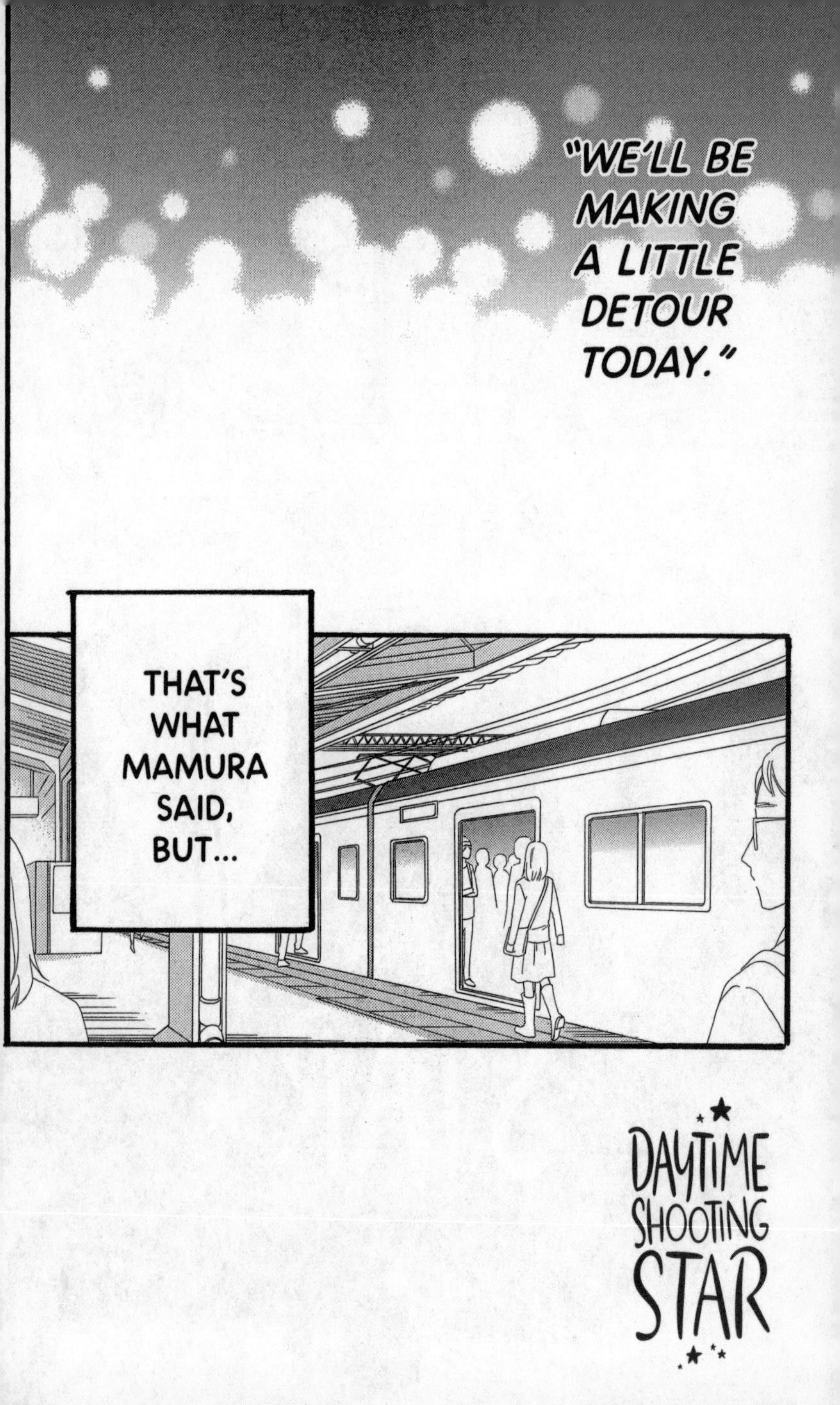
"WE'LL BE MAKING A LITTLE DETOUR TODAY."
THAT'S WHAT MAMURA SAID, BUT...
DAYTIME SHOOTING STAR

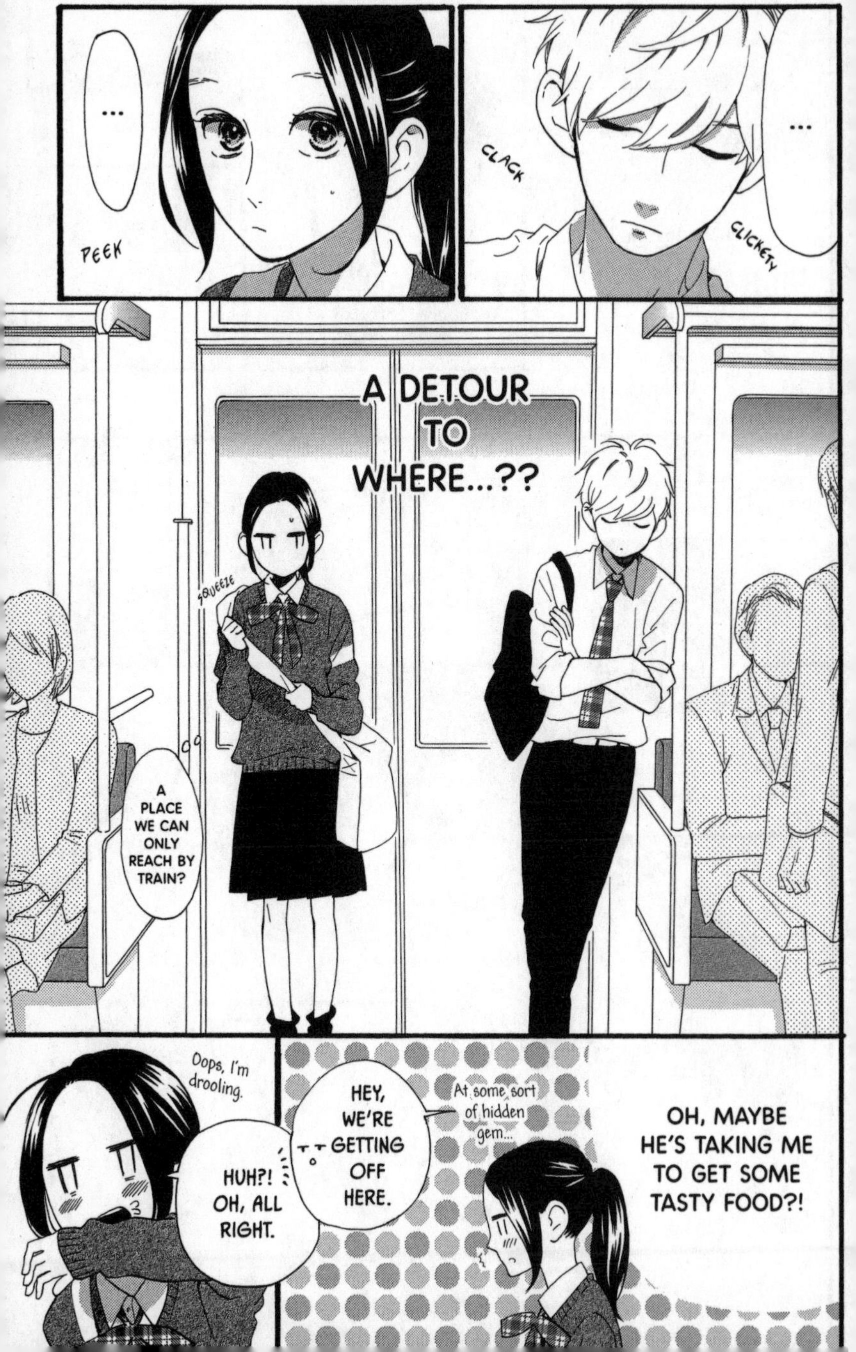
...
CLACK
CLICKETY
...
PEEK
A DETOUR TO WHERE...??
SQUEEZE
A PLACE WE CAN ONLY REACH BY TRAIN?
OH, MAYBE HE'S TAKING ME TO GET SOME TASTY FOOD?!
At some sort of hidden gem...
HEY, WE'RE GETTING OFF HERE.
HUH?! OH, ALL RIGHT.
Oops, I'm drooling.

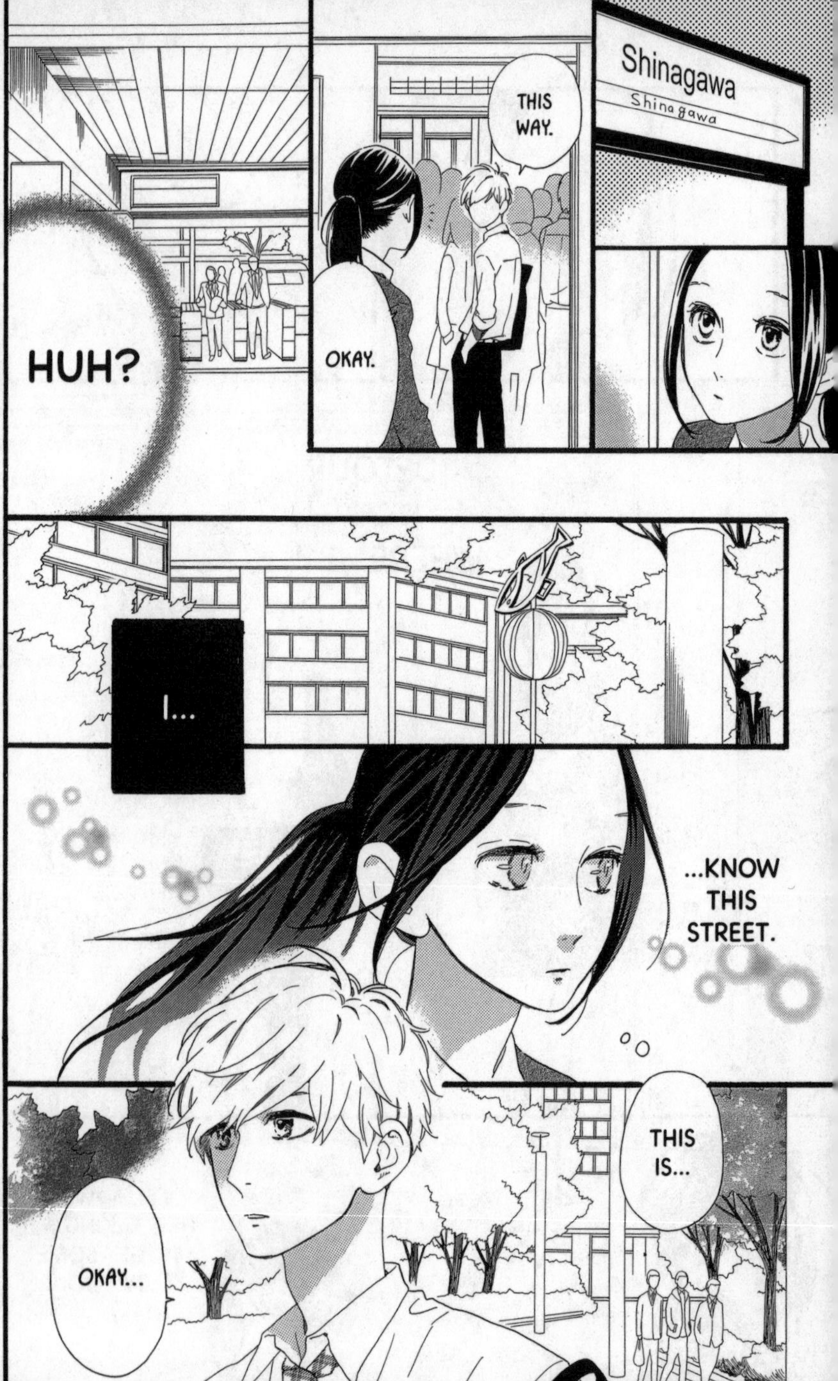
Shinagawa
Shinagawa
THIS WAY.
OKAY.
HUH?
I...
...KNOW THIS STREET.
THIS IS...
OKAY...

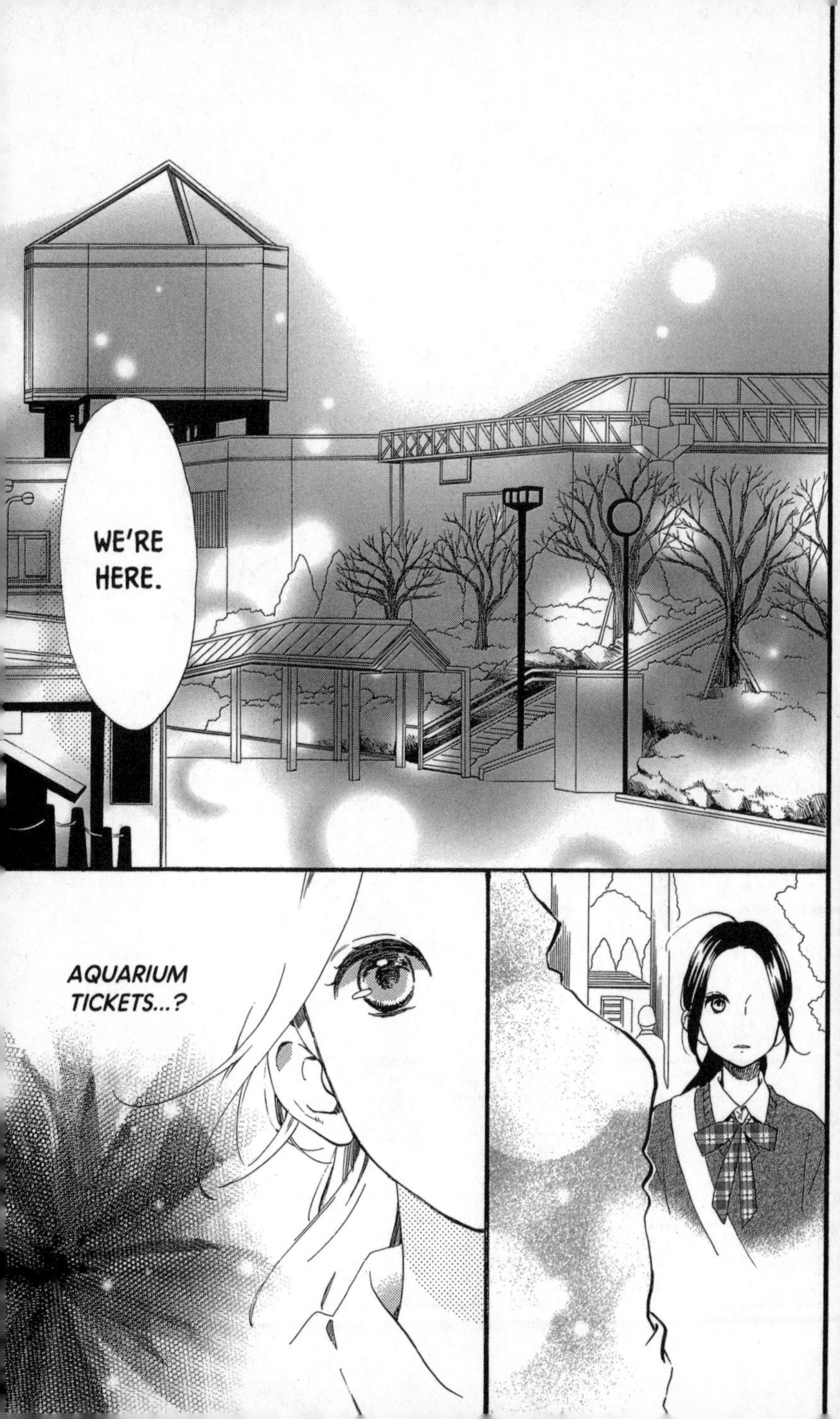
WE'RE HERE.
AQUARIUM TICKETS...?

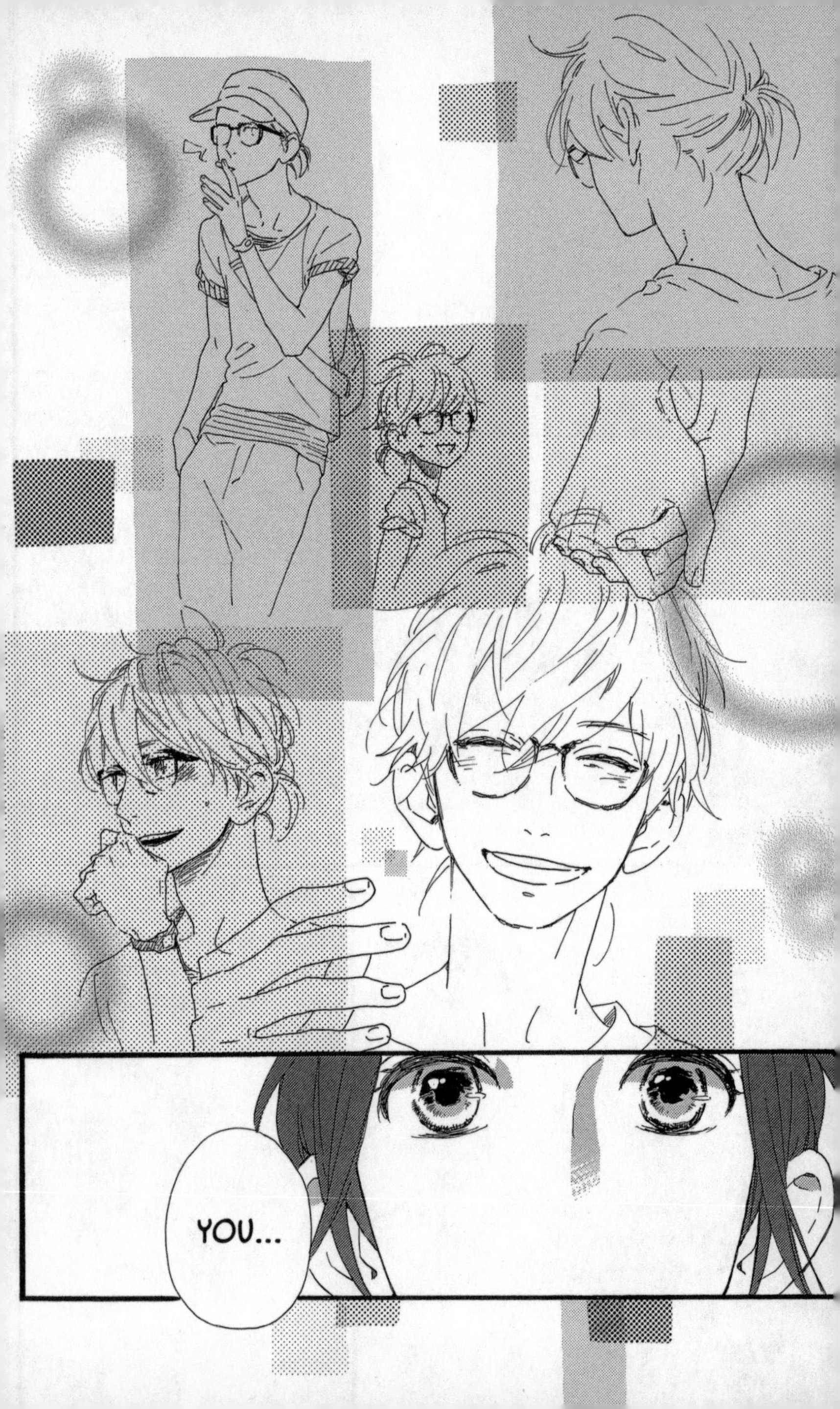
YOU...

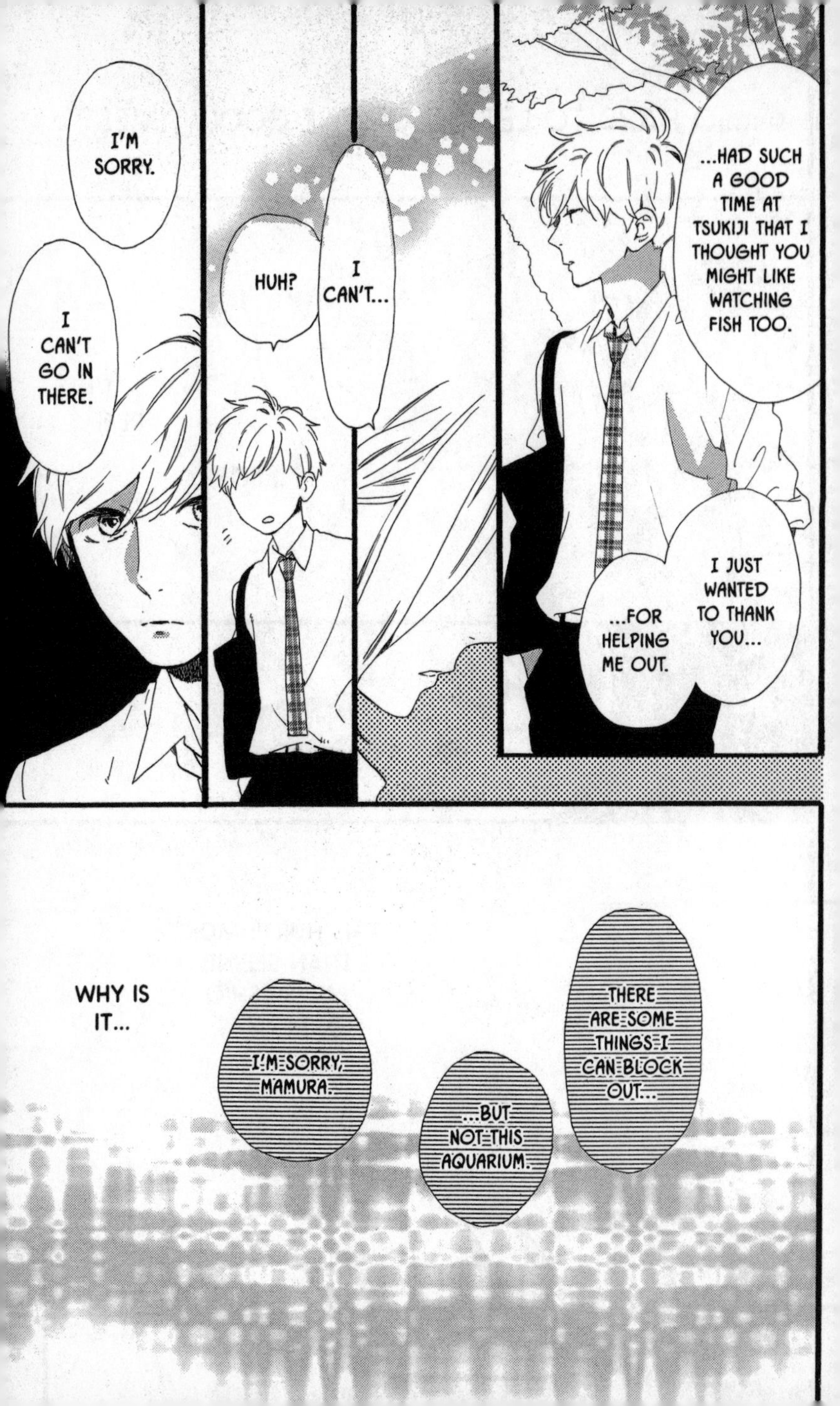
...HAD SUCH A GOOD TIME AT TSUKIJI THAT I THOUGHT YOU MIGHT LIKE WATCHING FISH TOO.
I JUST WANTED TO THANK YOU...
...FOR HELPING ME OUT.
I CAN'T...
HUH?
I'M SORRY.
I CAN'T GO IN THERE.
THERE ARE SOME THINGS I CAN BLOCK OUT...
...BUT NOT THIS AQUARIUM.
I'M SORRY, MAMURA.
WHY IS IT...

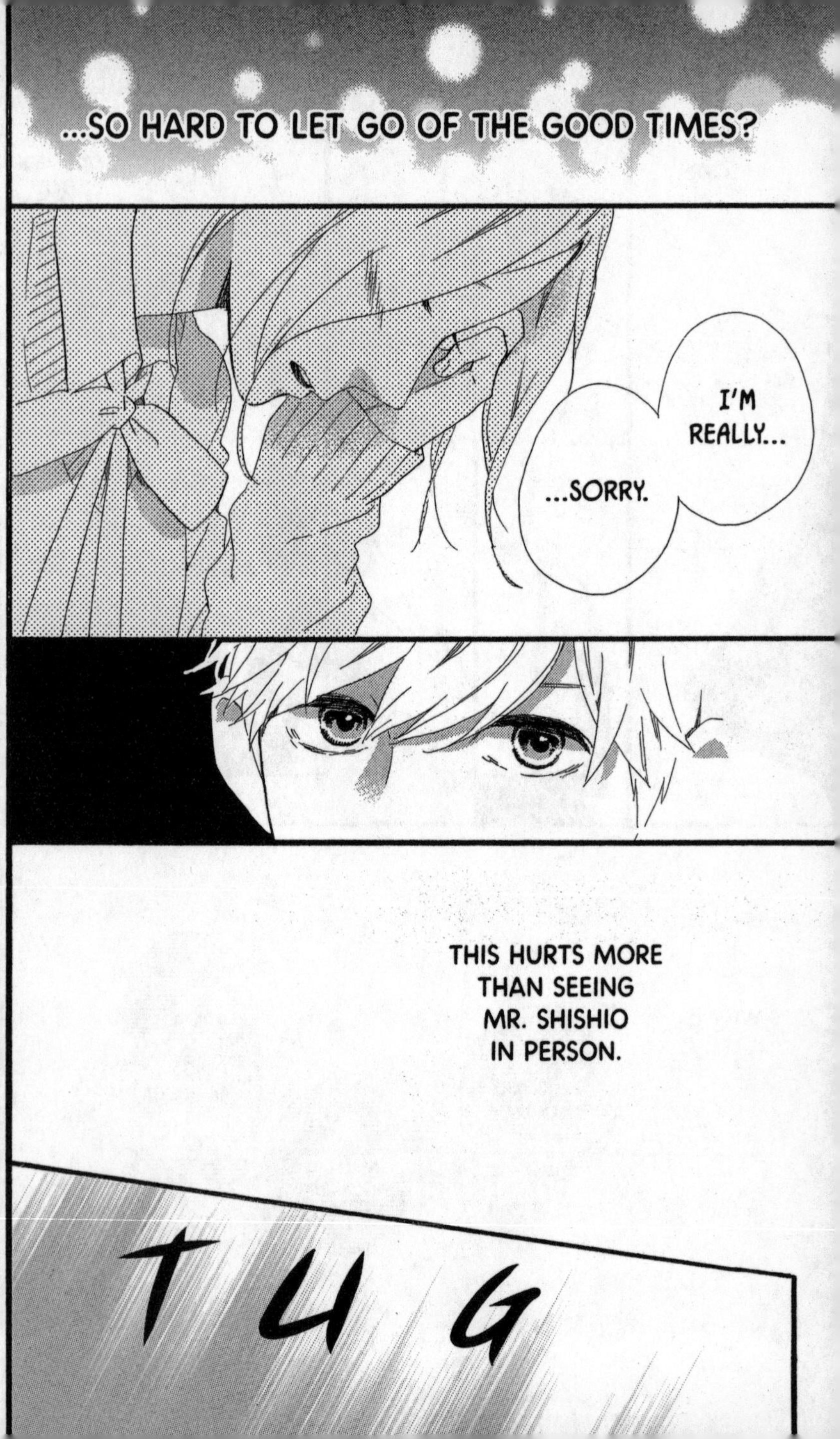
...SO HARD TO LET GO OF THE GOOD TIMES?
I'M REALLY...
...SORRY.
THIS HURTS MORE THAN SEEING MR. SHISHIO IN PERSON.
TUG

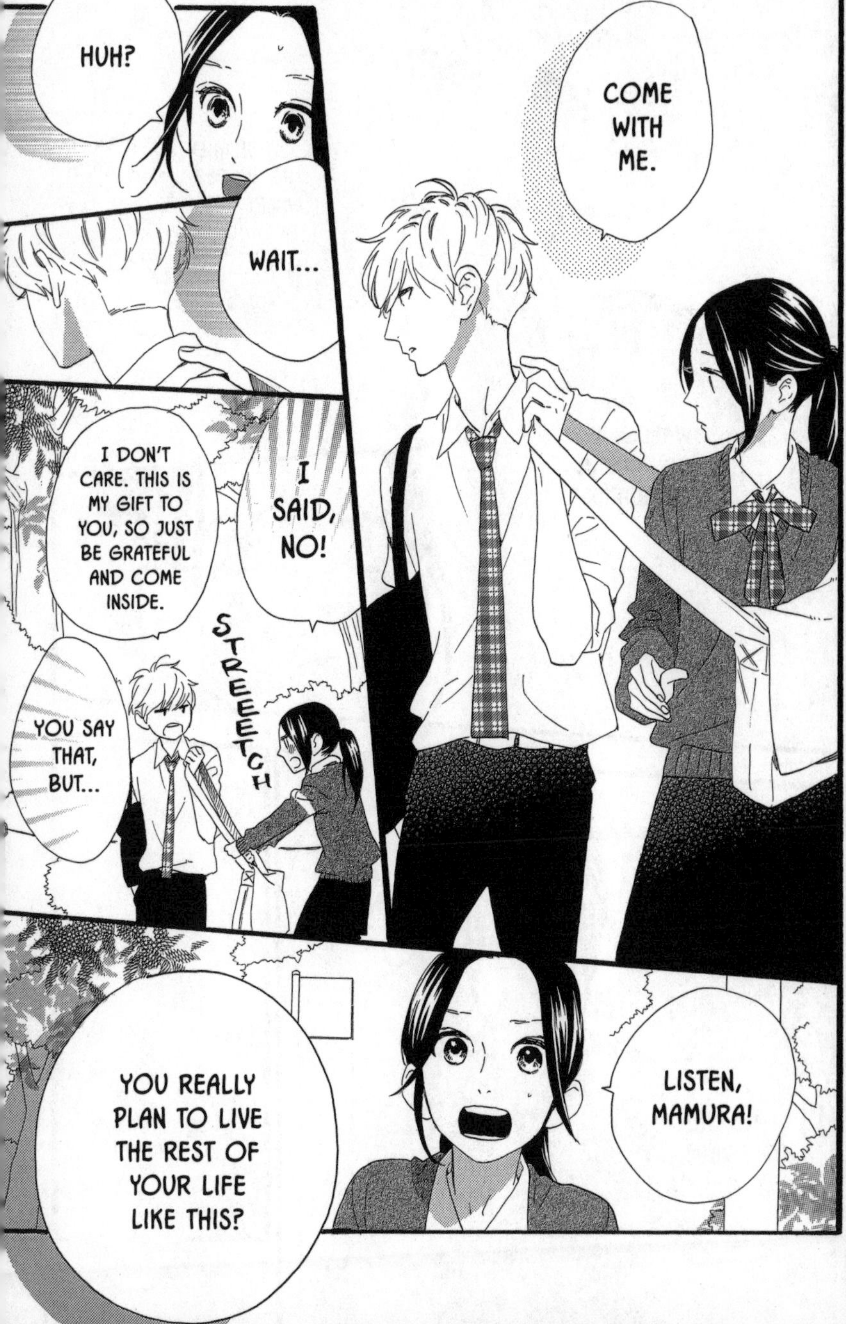
COME WITH ME.
HUH?
WAIT...
I SAID, NO!
I DON'T CARE. THIS IS MY GIFT TO YOU, SO JUST BE GRATEFUL AND COME INSIDE.
STREEETCH
YOU SAY THAT, BUT...
LISTEN, MAMURA!
YOU REALLY PLAN TO LIVE THE REST OF YOUR LIFE LIKE THIS?

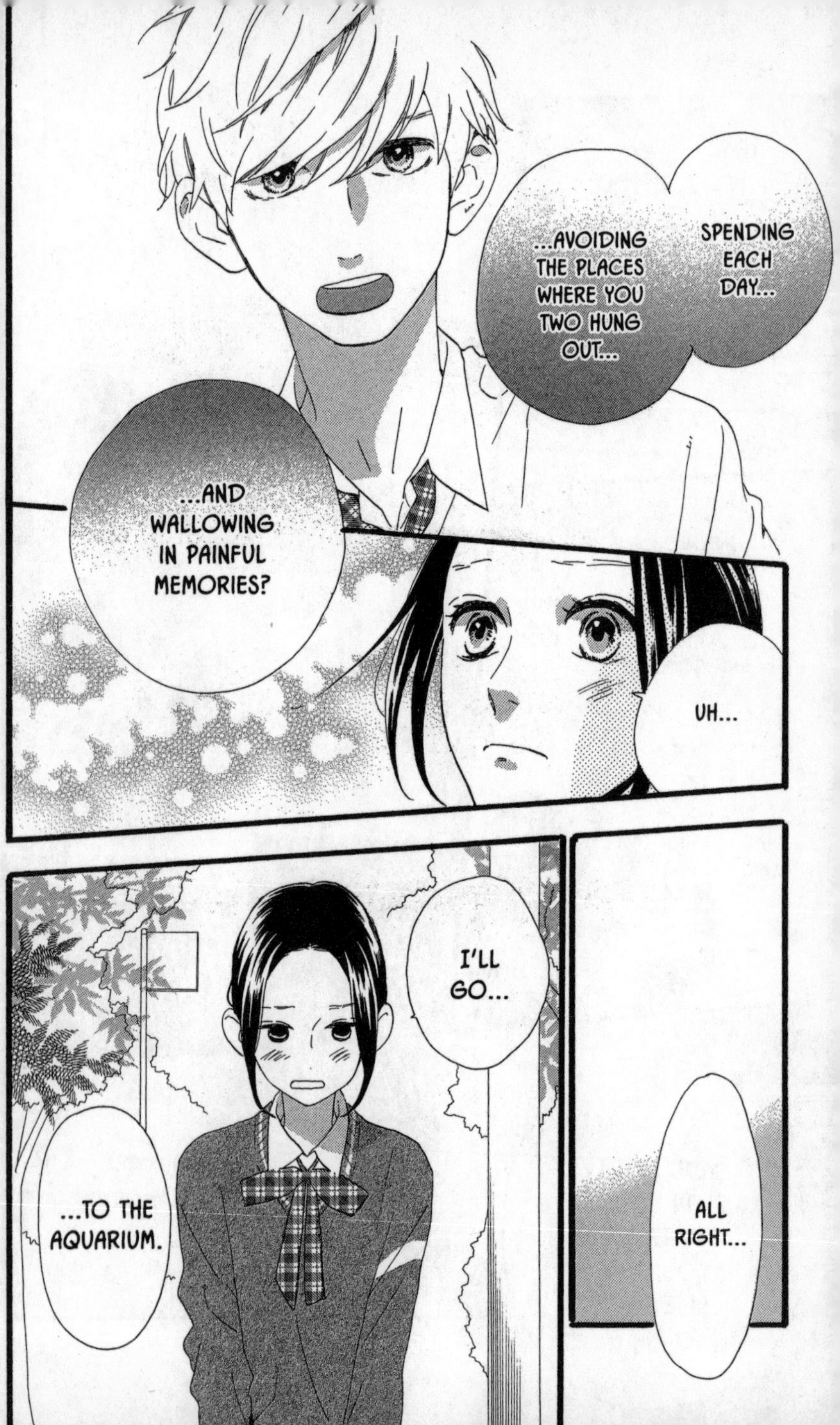
SPENDING EACH DAY...
...AVOIDING THE PLACES WHERE YOU TWO HUNG OUT...
...AND WALLOWING IN PAINFUL MEMORIES?
UH...
ALL RIGHT...
I'LL GO...
...TO THE AQUARIUM.

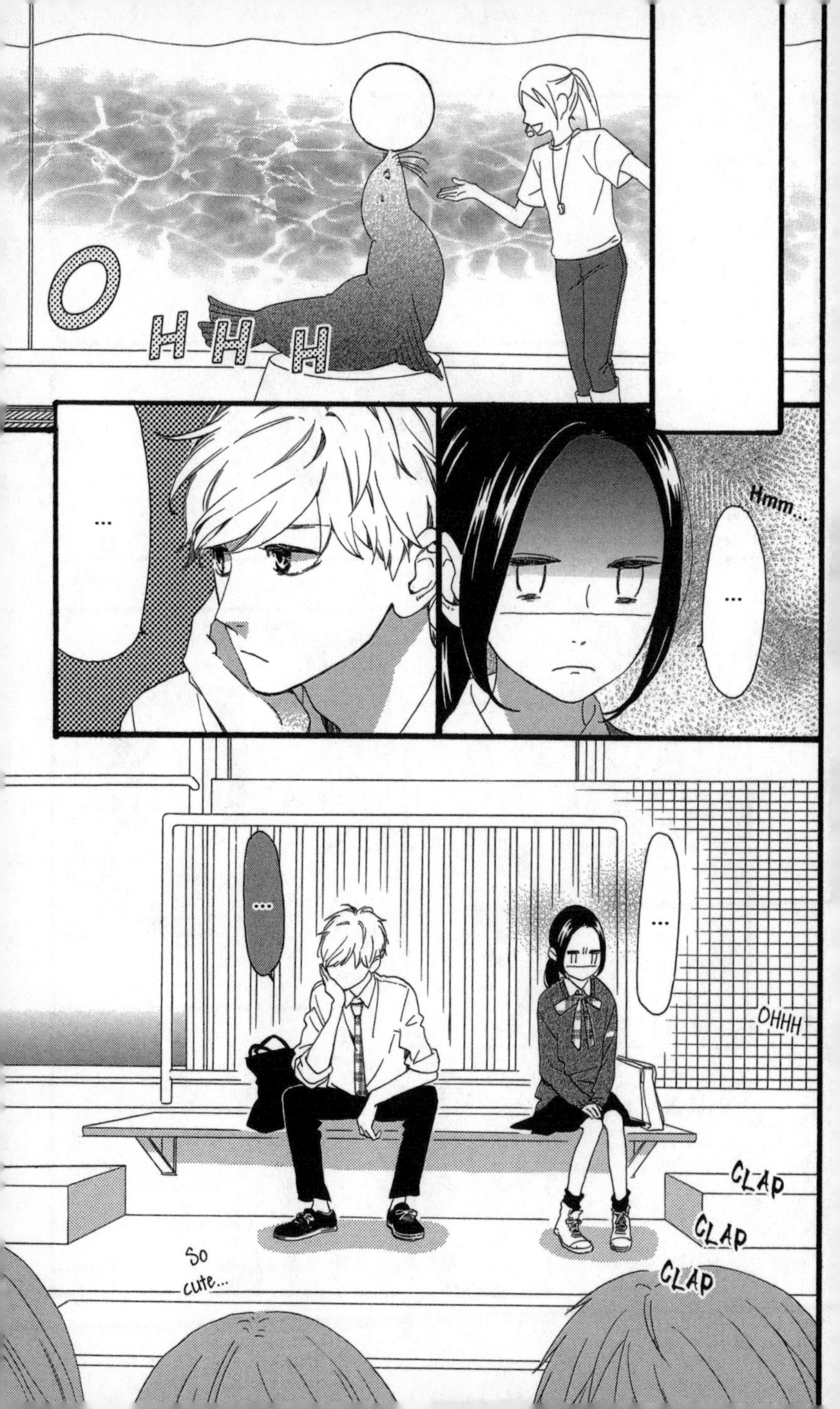
OHHH
Hmm...
...
...
...
OHHH
CLAP
CLAP
CLAP
...
So cute...

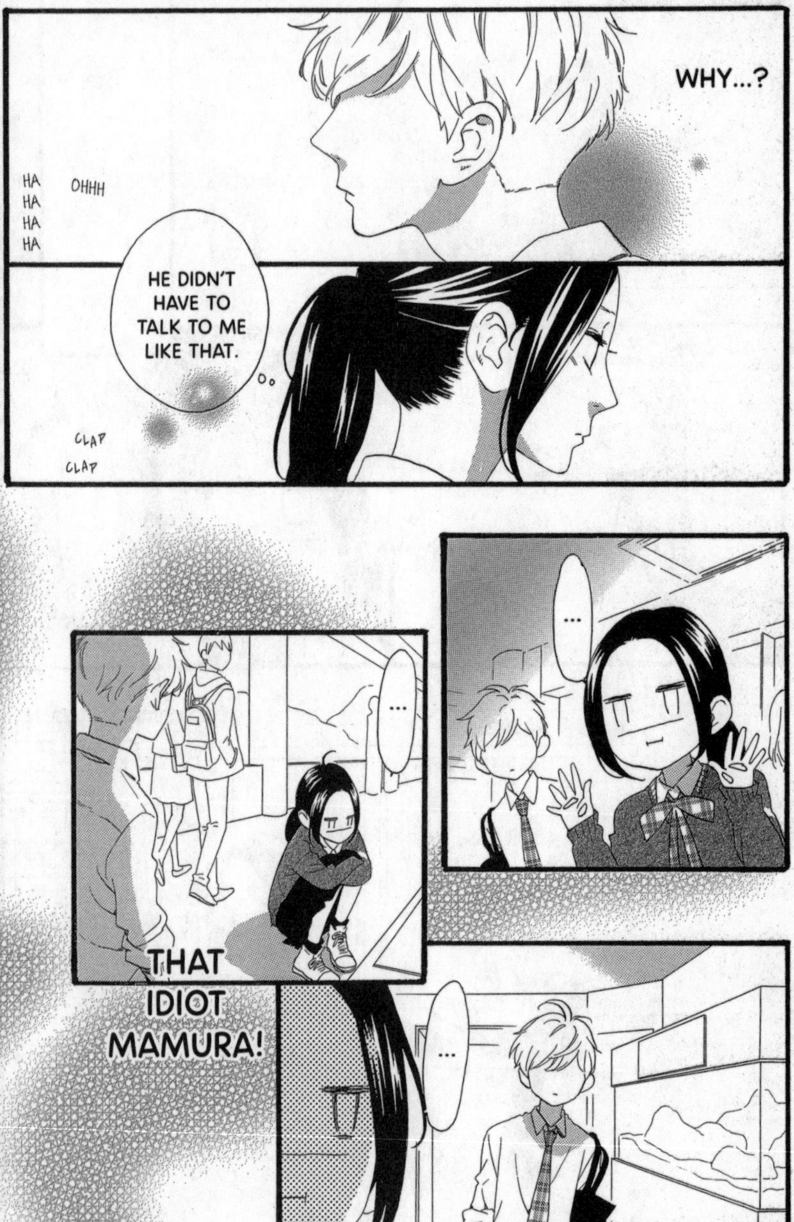
WHY...?
HA HA HA HA
OHHH
HE DIDN'T HAVE TO TALK TO ME LIKE THAT.
CLAP CLAP
...
...
THAT IDIOT MAMURA!
...

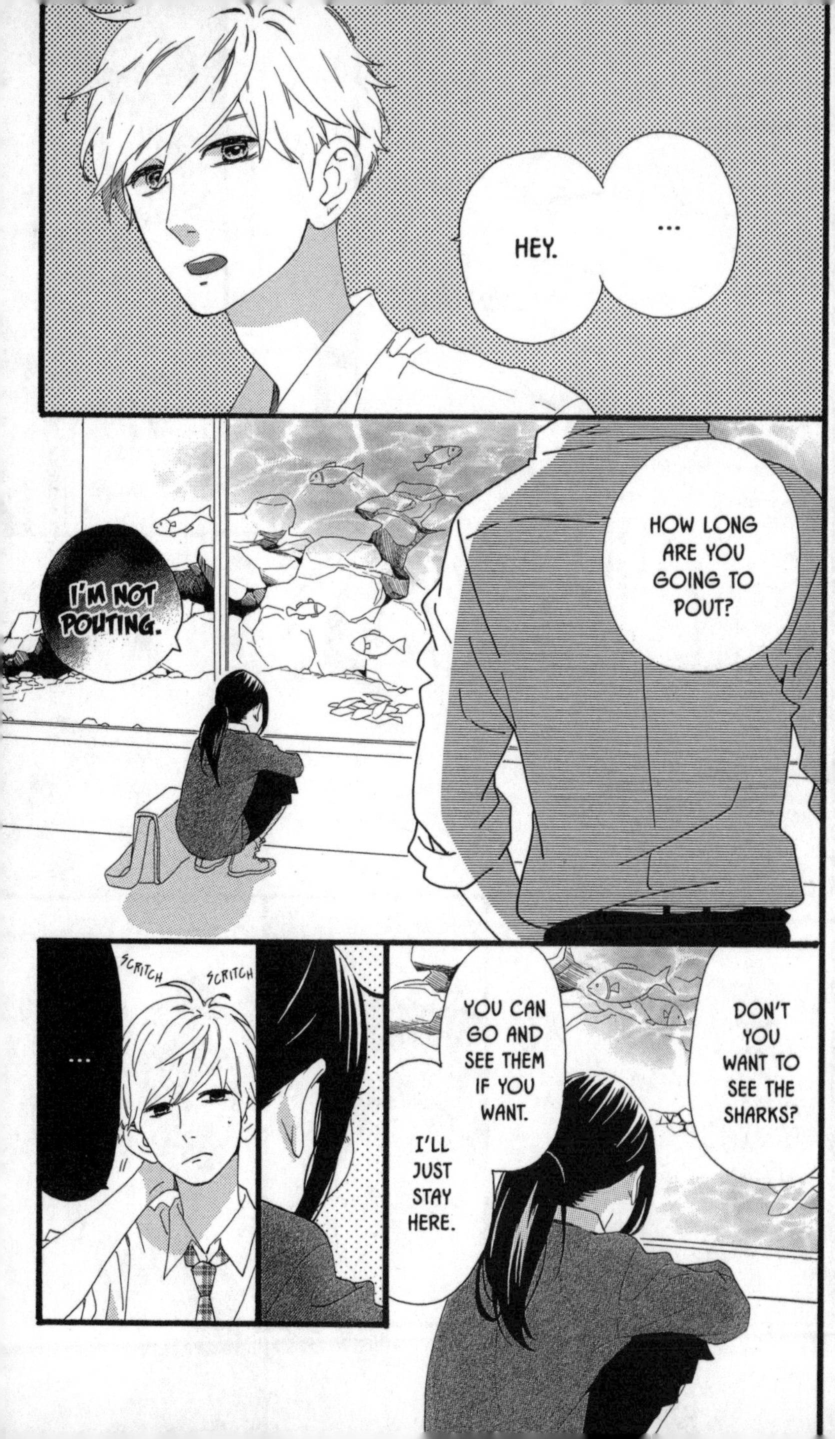
...
HEY.
HOW LONG ARE YOU GOING TO POUT?
I'M NOT POUTING.
DON'T YOU WANT TO SEE THE SHARKS?
YOU CAN GO AND SEE THEM IF YOU WANT.
I'LL JUST STAY HERE.
SCRITCH
SCRITCH
...

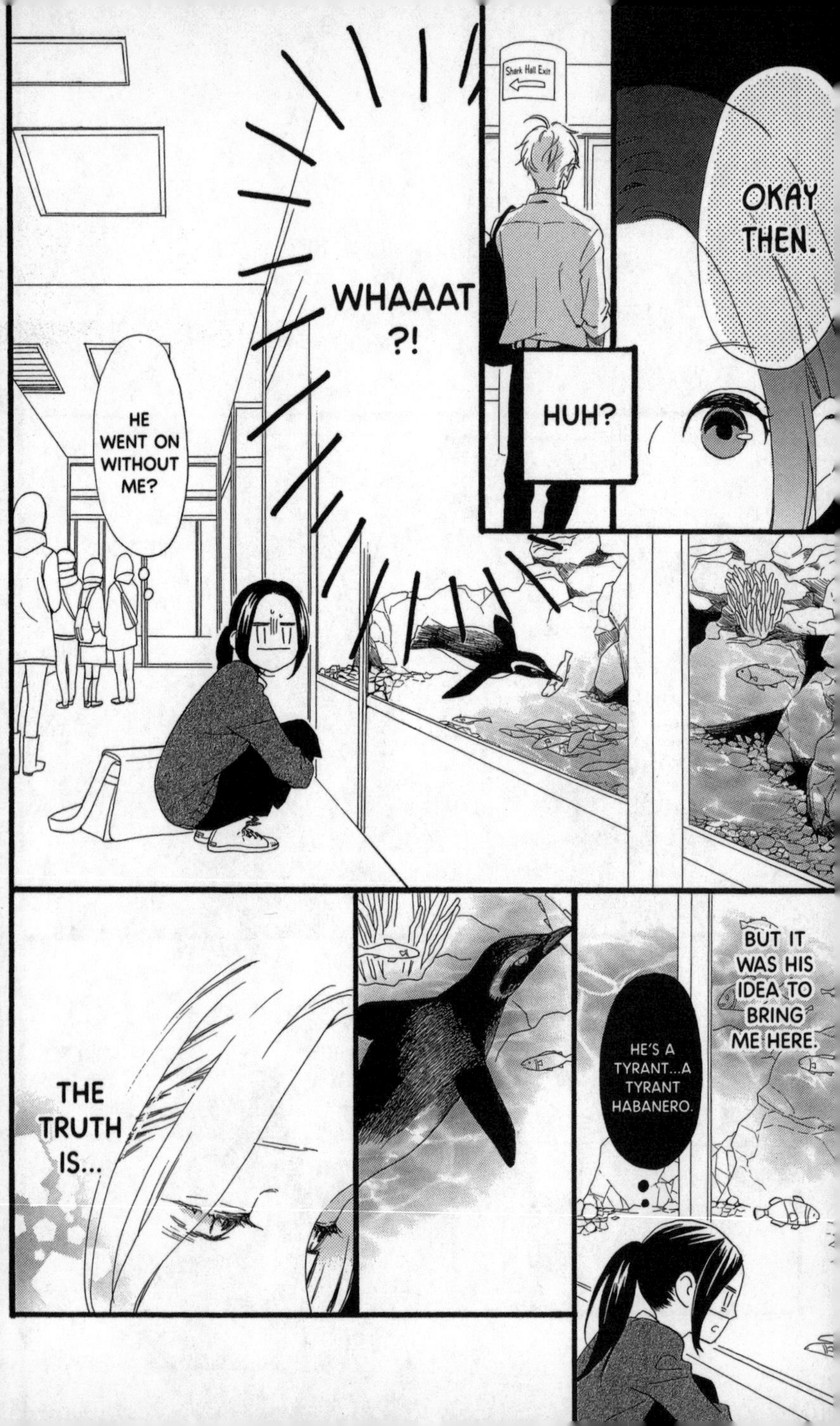
OKAY THEN.
Shark Hall Exit
HUH?
WHAAAT?!
HE WENT ON WITHOUT ME?
BUT IT WAS HIS IDEA TO BRING ME HERE.
HE'S A TYRANT...A TYRANT HABANERO.
THE TRUTH IS...

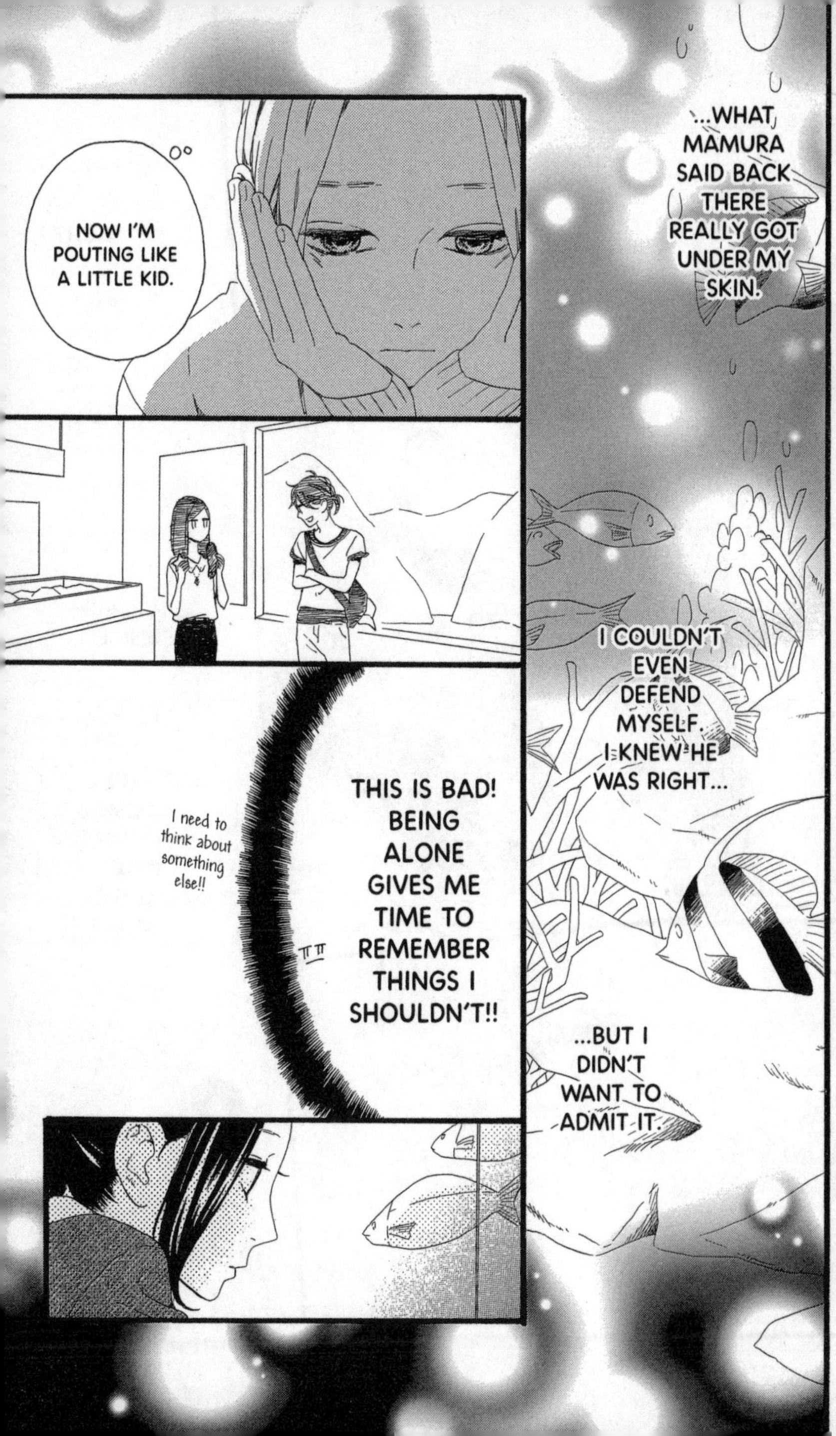
...WHAT MAMURA SAID BACK THERE REALLY GOT UNDER MY SKIN.
I COULDN'T EVEN DEFEND MYSELF. I KNEW HE WAS RIGHT...
...BUT I DIDN'T WANT TO ADMIT IT.
NOW I'M POUTING LIKE A LITTLE KID.
THIS IS BAD! BEING ALONE GIVES ME TIME TO REMEMBER THINGS I SHOULDN'T!!
I need to think about something else!!

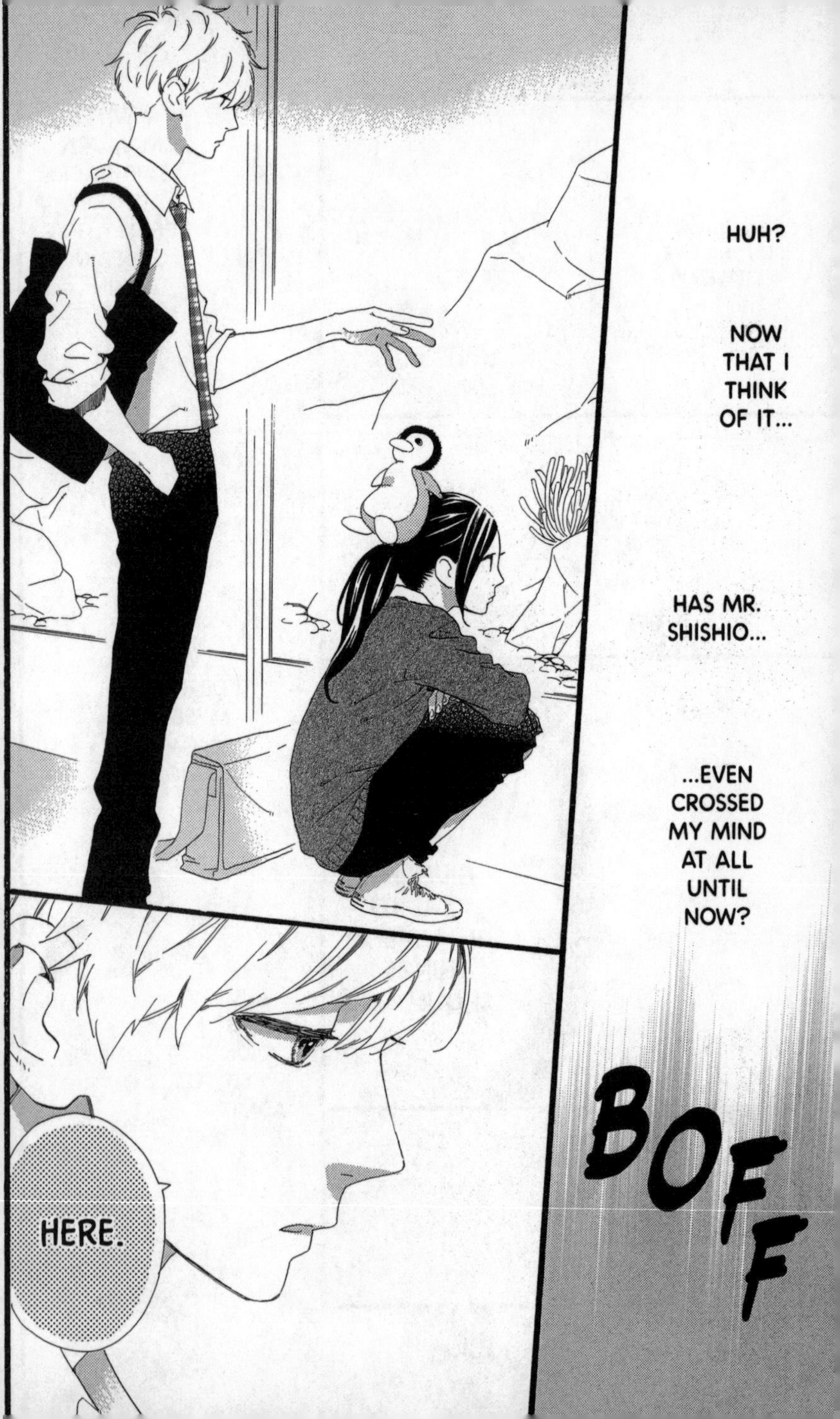
HUH?
NOW THAT I THINK OF IT...
HAS MR. SHISHIO...
...EVEN CROSSED MY MIND AT ALL UNTIL NOW?
BOFF
HERE.

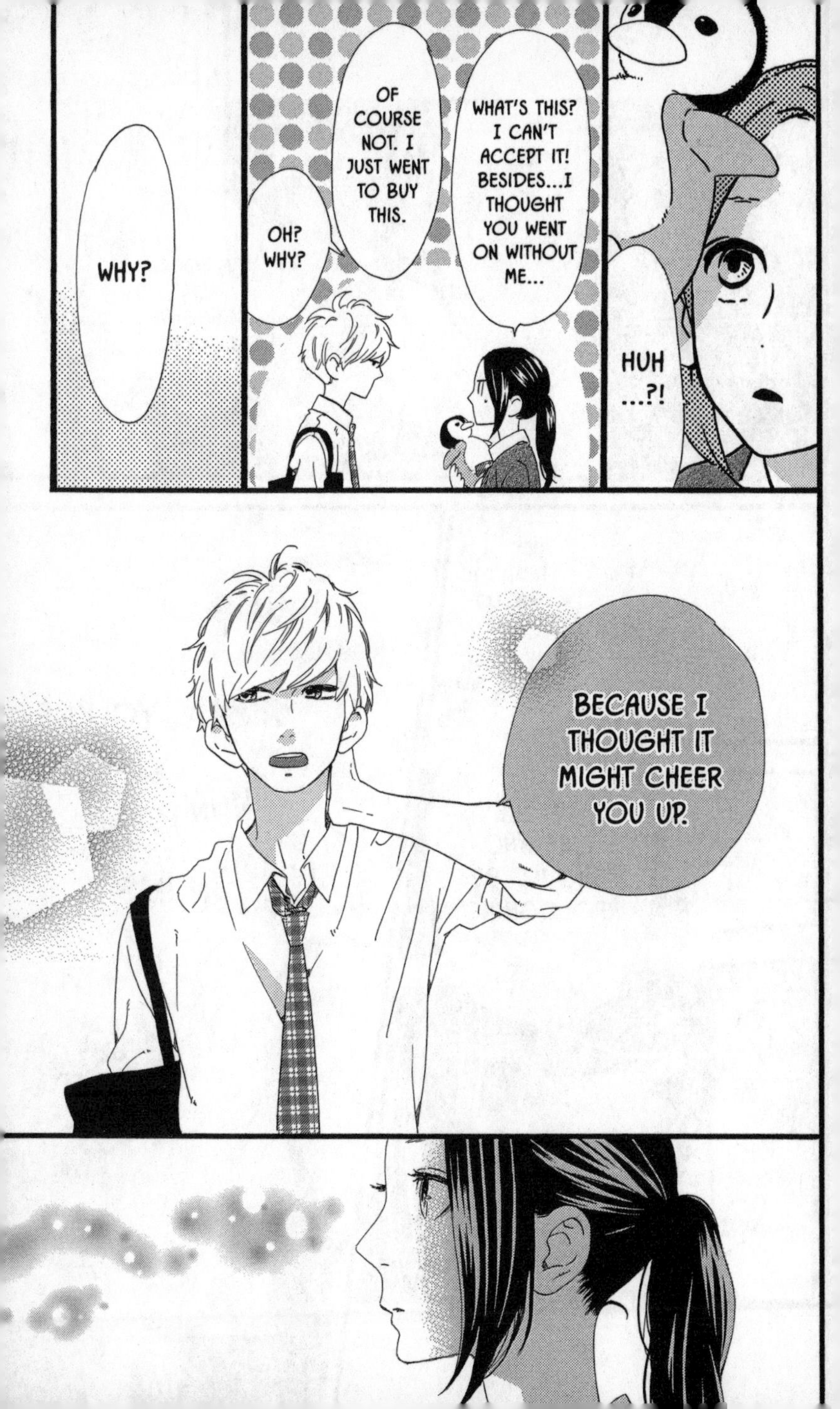
HUH ...?!
WHAT'S THIS? I CAN'T ACCEPT IT! BESIDES...I THOUGHT YOU WENT ON WITHOUT ME...
OF COURSE NOT. I JUST WENT TO BUY THIS.
OH? WHY?
WHY?
BECAUSE I THOUGHT IT MIGHT CHEER YOU UP.

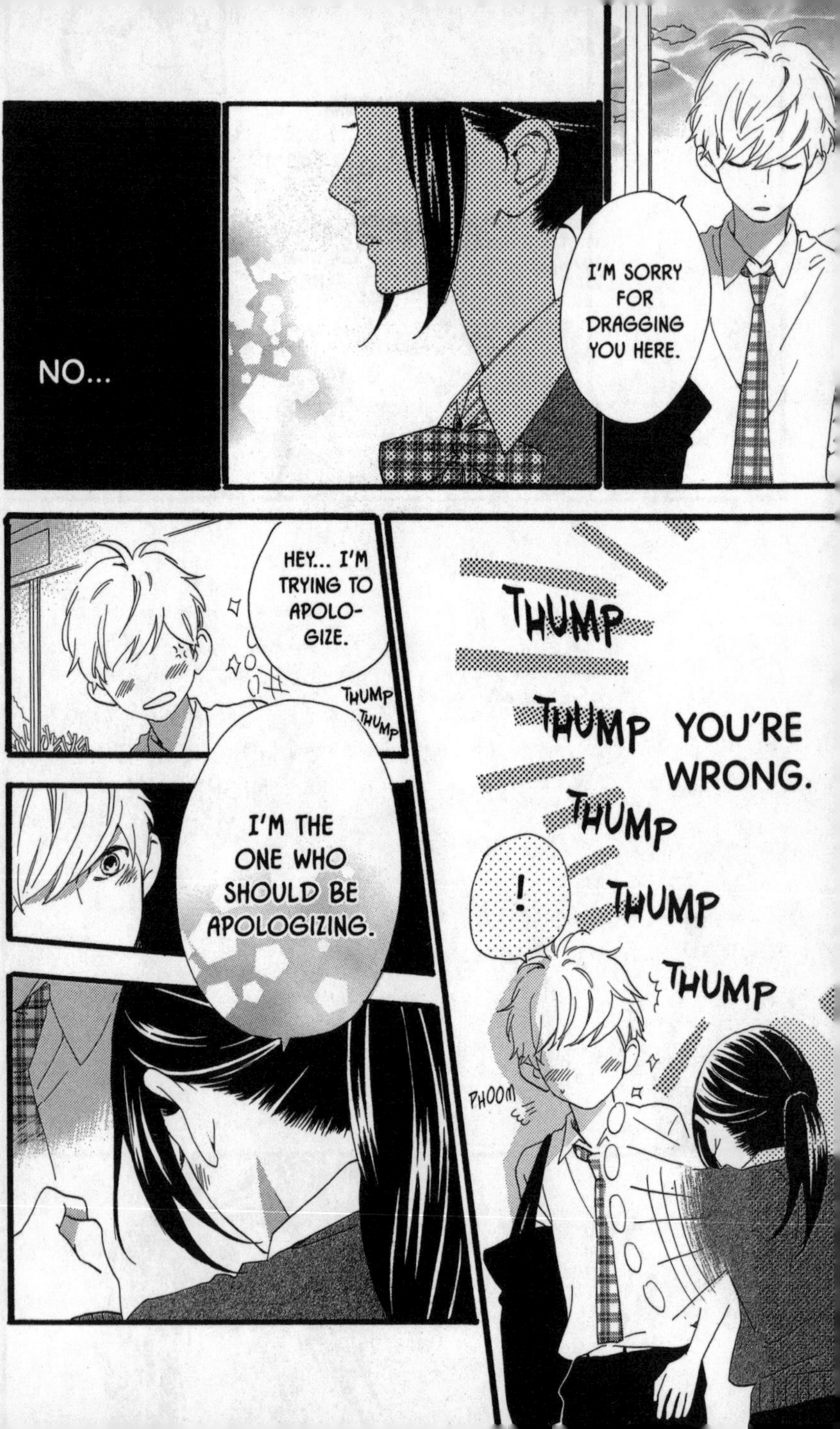
I'M SORRY FOR DRAGGING YOU HERE.
NO...
THUMP
THUMP
YOU'RE WRONG.
THUMP
!
THUMP
THUMP
PHOOM
HEY... I'M TRYING TO APOLO-GIZE.
THUMP THUMP
I'M THE ONE WHO SHOULD BE APOLOGIZING.

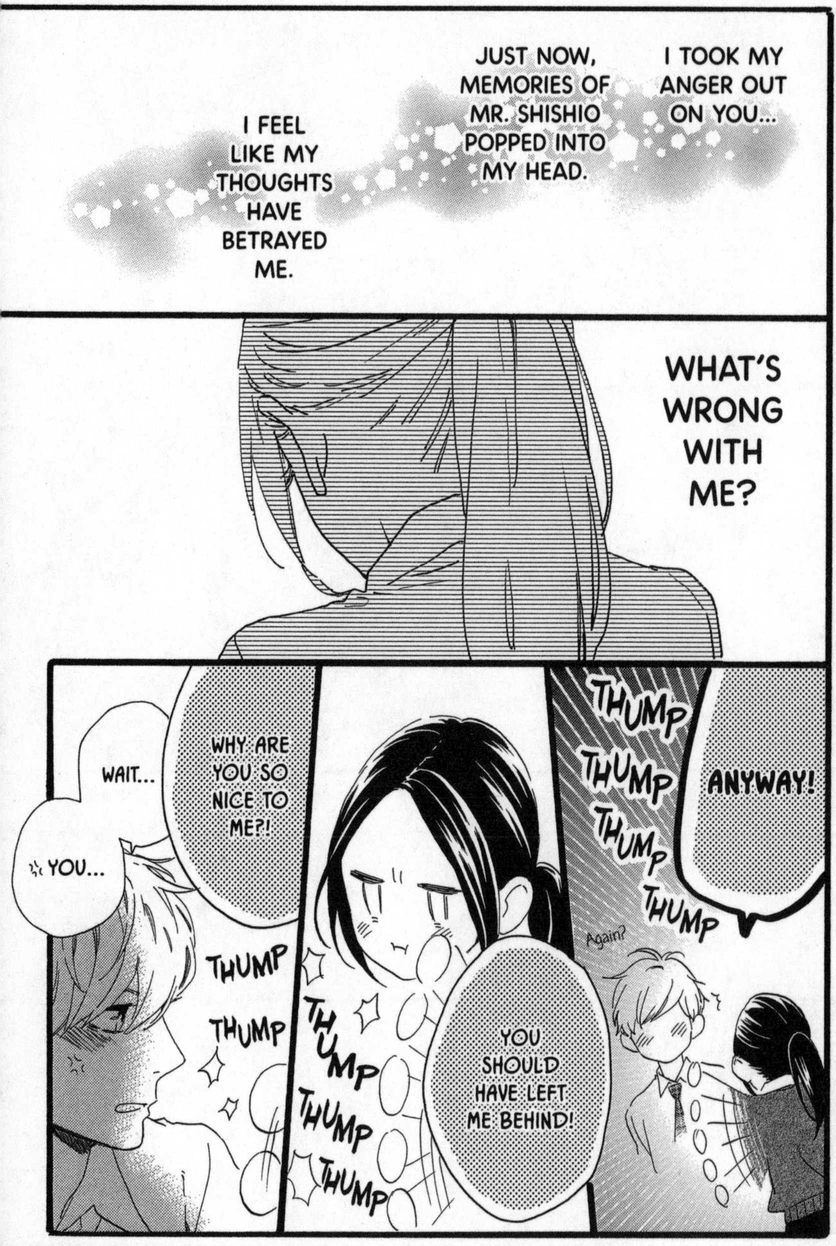
I TOOK MY ANGER OUT ON YOU...
JUST NOW, MEMORIES OF MR. SHISHIO POPPED INTO MY HEAD.
I FEEL LIKE MY THOUGHTS HAVE BETRAYED ME.
WHAT'S WRONG WITH ME?
ANYWAY!
THUMP
THUMP
THUMP
THUMP
Again?
YOU SHOULD HAVE LEFT ME BEHIND!
THUMP
THUMP
THUMP
WHY ARE YOU SO NICE TO ME?!
WAIT...
YOU...
THUMP
THUMP

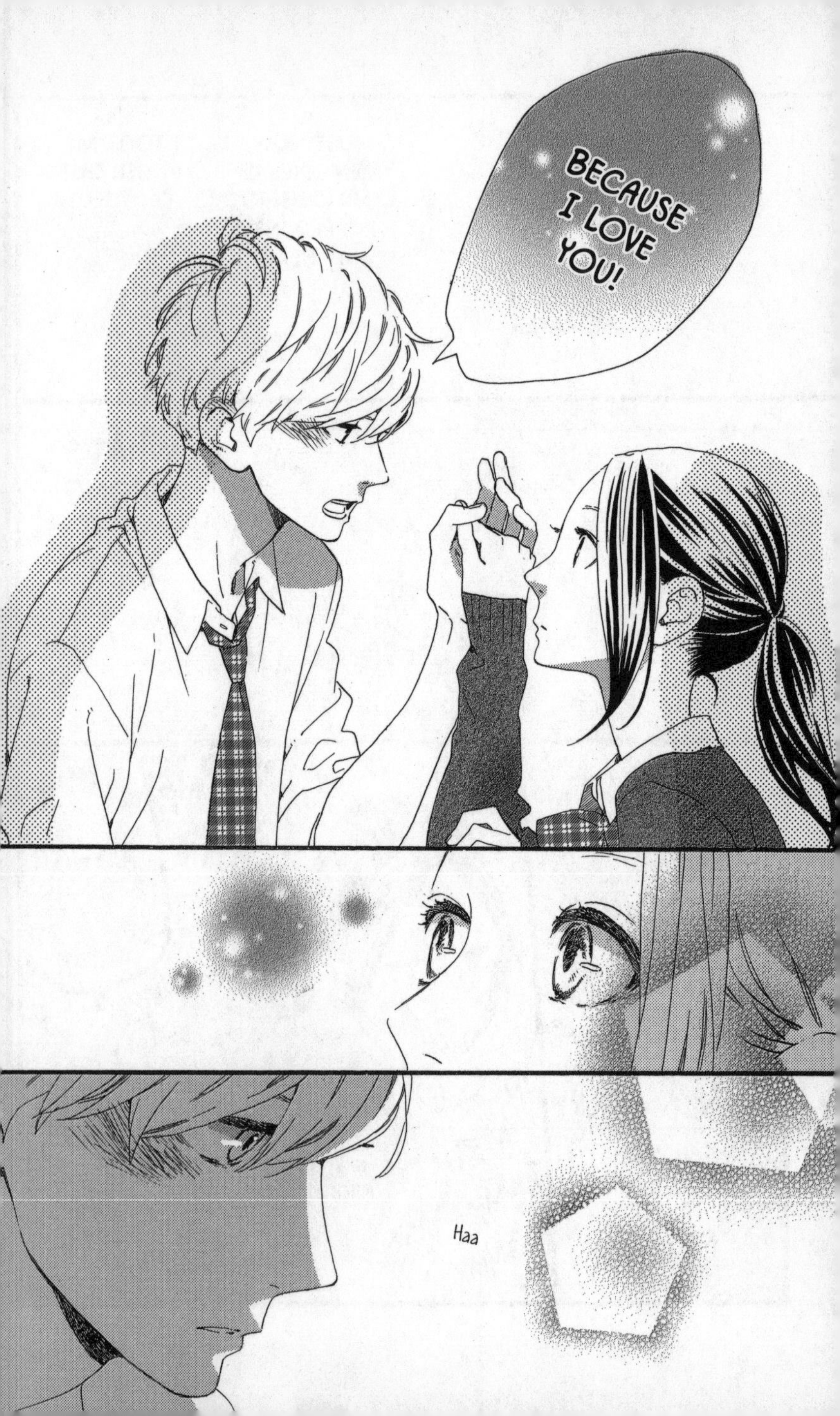
BECAUSE I LOVE YOU!
Haa

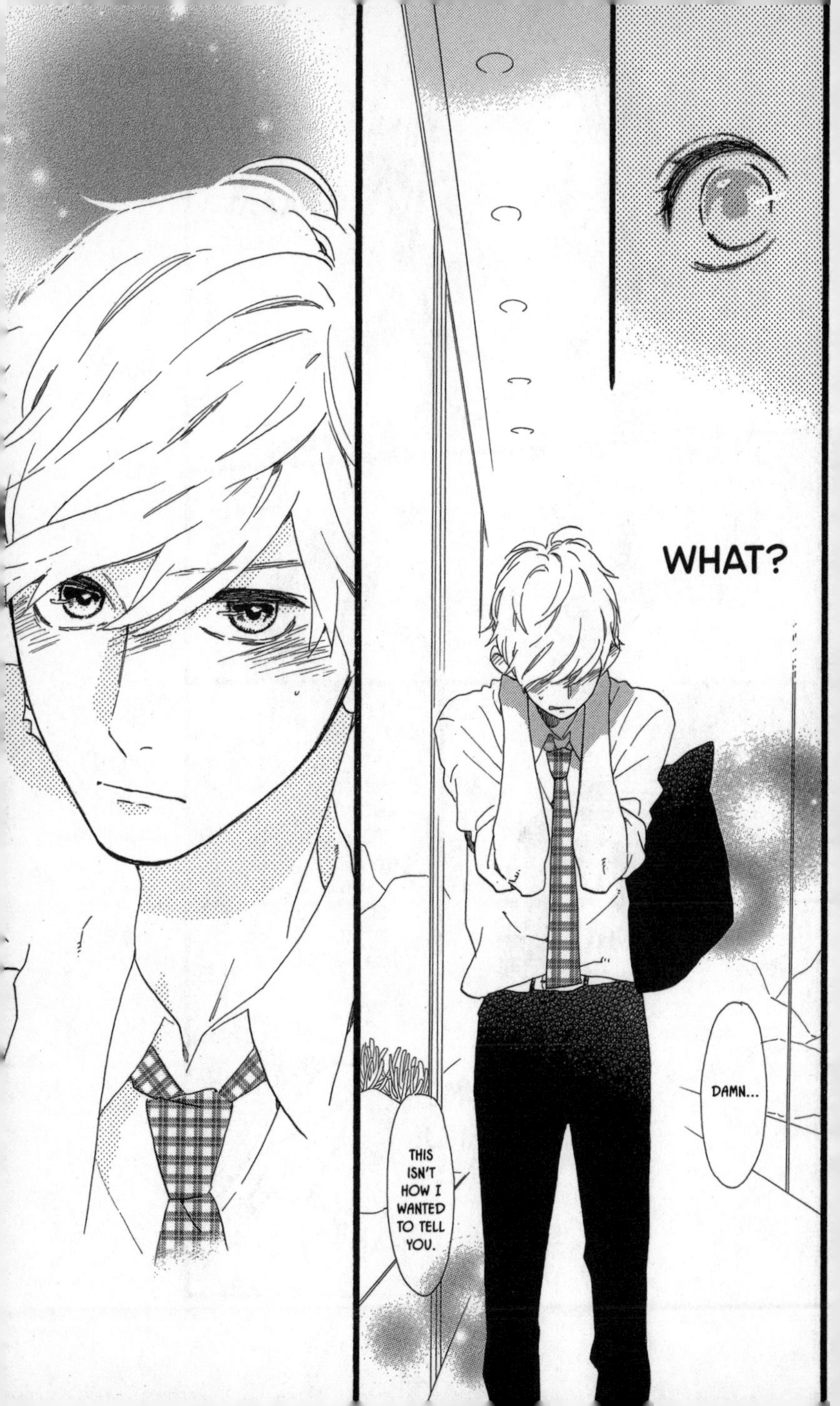
WHAT?
DAMN...
THIS ISN'T HOW I WANTED TO TELL YOU.

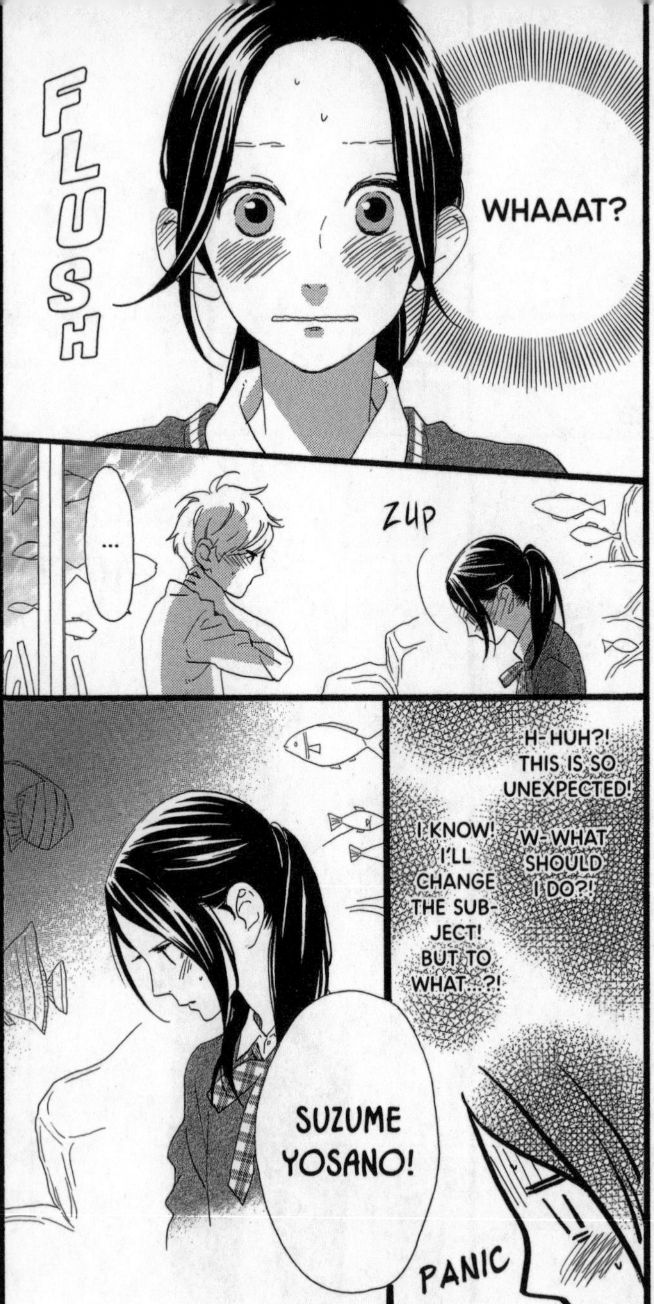
WHAT?
WHAAAT?
FLUSH
HUH?
ZUP
...
DID HE...?
H-HUH?! THIS IS SO UNEXPECTED!
W-WHAT SHOULD I DO?!
I KNOW! I'LL CHANGE THE SUB-JECT! BUT TO WHAT...?!
PANIC
SUZUME YOSANO!

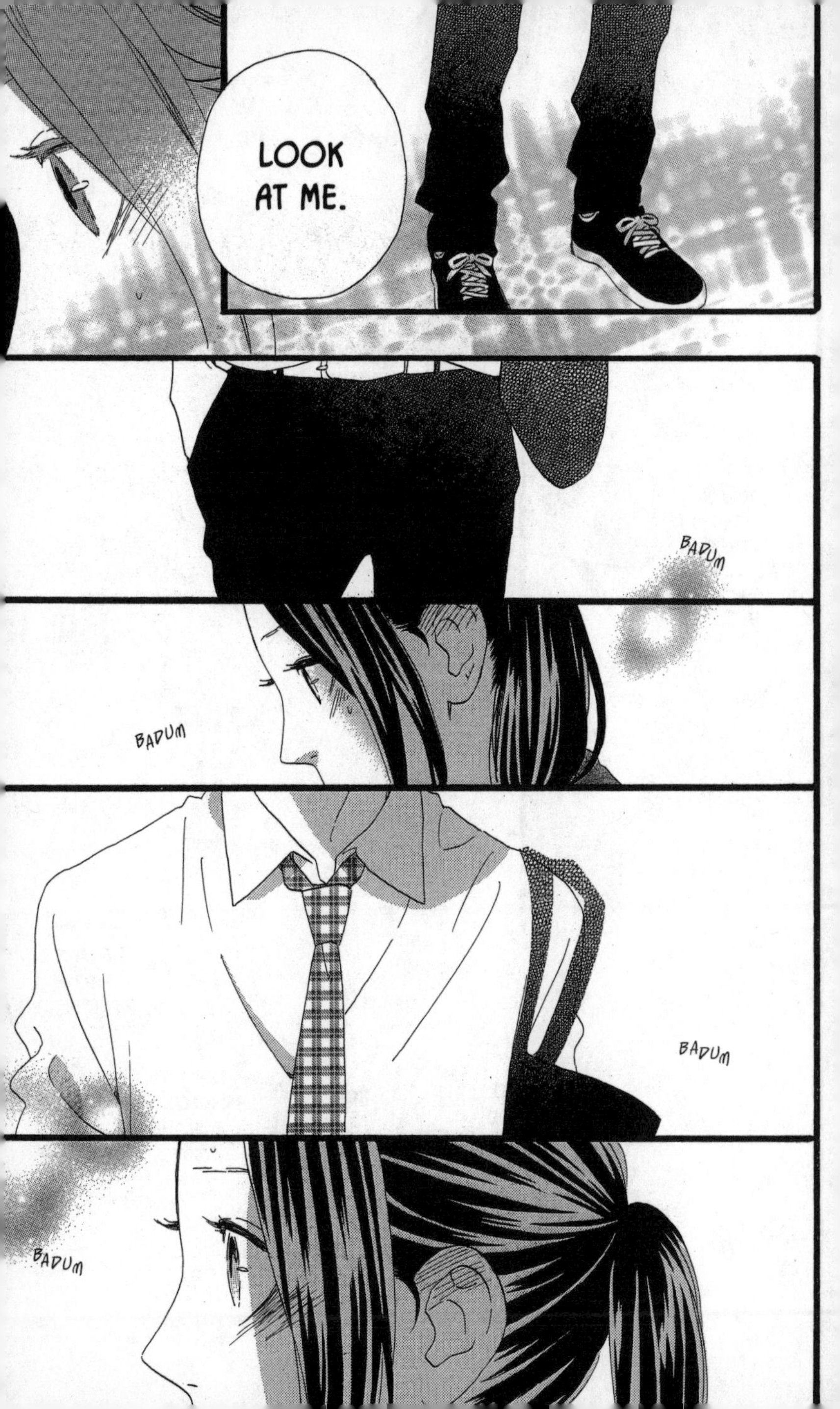
LOOK AT ME.
BADUM
BADUM
BADUM
BADUM

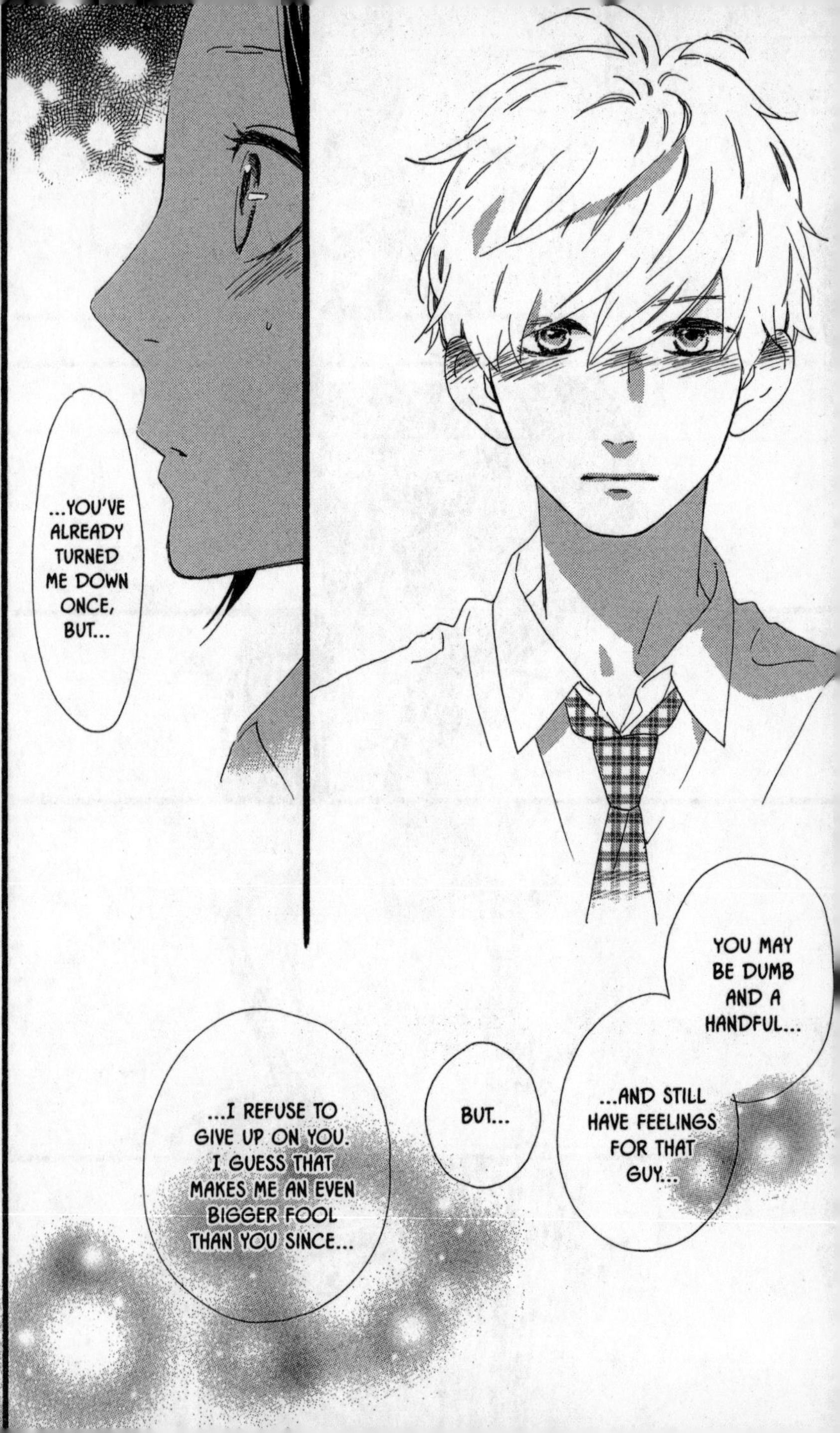
YOU MAY BE DUMB AND A HANDFUL...
...AND STILL HAVE FEELINGS FOR THAT GUY...
BUT...
...I REFUSE TO GIVE UP ON YOU. I GUESS THAT MAKES ME AN EVEN BIGGER FOOL THAN YOU SINCE...
...YOU'VE ALREADY TURNED ME DOWN ONCE, BUT...

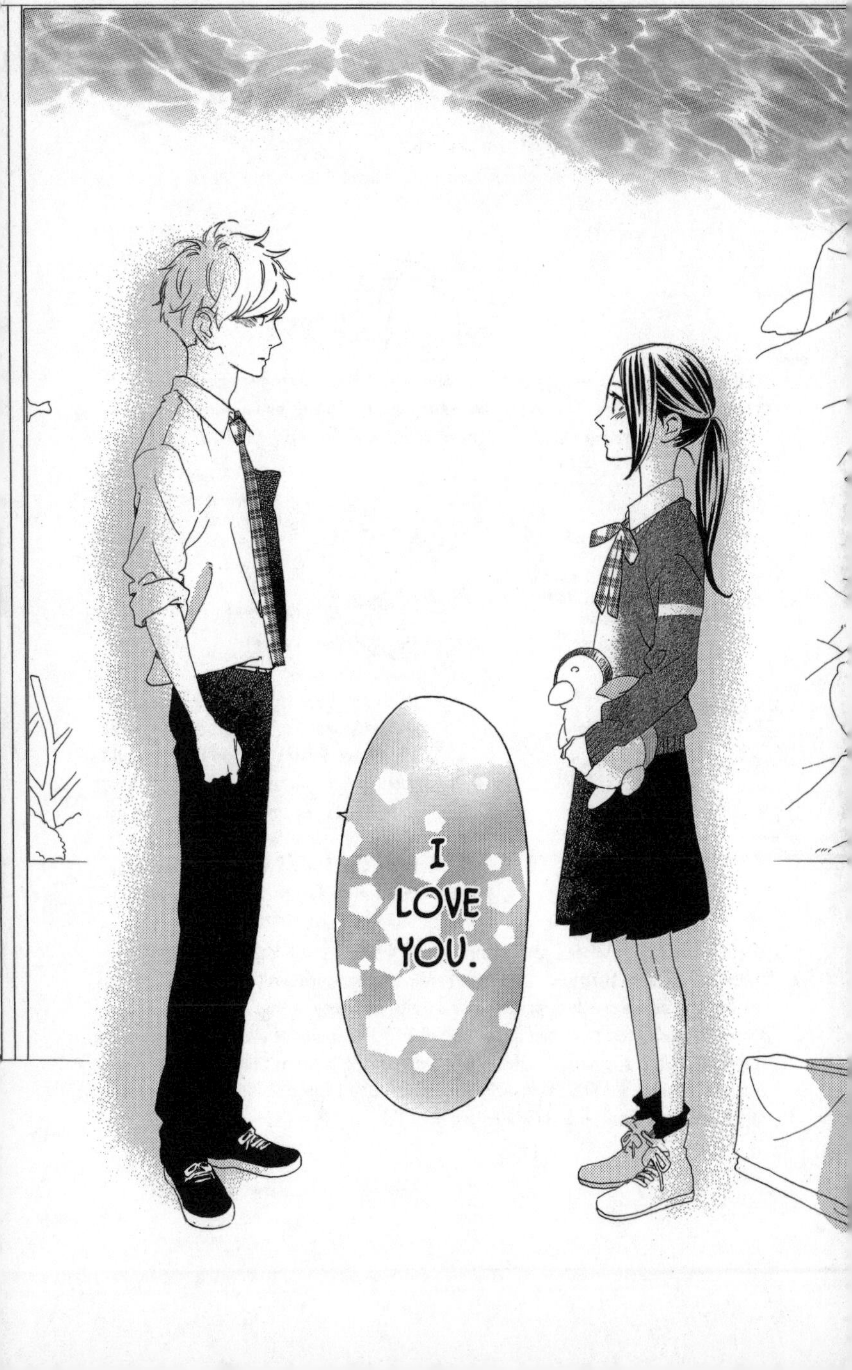
I LOVE YOU.

About Kentaro Sakaguchi ③

Picking up where we left off... Editor: After this, we'll interview Kentaro over lunch together.
What...?! Lunch...?!

Pardon?!

IMAGE IN MY BRAIN

Huh? Wait. Did you just say that we're all going to have lunch together? You realize that's a big deal, right? Can I be excused? I can't even look him in the eye. I'd be even worse over lunch. I might never recover. So, may I go home? Please?

I was surprised by how well my editor conducted herself. I guess stuff like this doesn't faze people with healthy social lives.
Sob!!

The pizza is very good here.

I had these thoughts while on my way to lunch...

ON THE CHARTERED BUS WITH EVERYONE.

THE SAKAGUCHI ZONE

But I insist... Please...

KENTARO SAT BY HIMSELF.

No, please. I won't be able to eat a thing!!

Eventually, we had the photographer sit next to him.

Of course, I was tense the whole time! Both the stylist and the hair and makeup artist offered me the seat next to Kentaro, but I shouted, "No, please. I won't be able to eat a thing!!" I'm so sorry... It would have been too big an honor to take the seat next to him—plus I would've been blinded by his beauty. (If I said that out loud, it would have sounded weird, I'm sure.)

But it didn't matter where I sat. I couldn't taste the food at all. Please forgive my rudeness!! Kentaro Sakaguchi was just an ordinary handsome guy!! He was quiet, refined, calm and loved sweets. He was like a character from a shojo manga. It's hard to believe there are really people like him in the world!! To this day, that photo shoot still feels like something out of a dream. I really need to stop stealing peeks at people when I'm nervous. Kentaro and staff, thank you very much!! Oh!! I ended up writing more about my nervousness than I did about Kentaro...

Three pages just isn't enough to cover how wonderful he is. I have enough words to fill a book!!

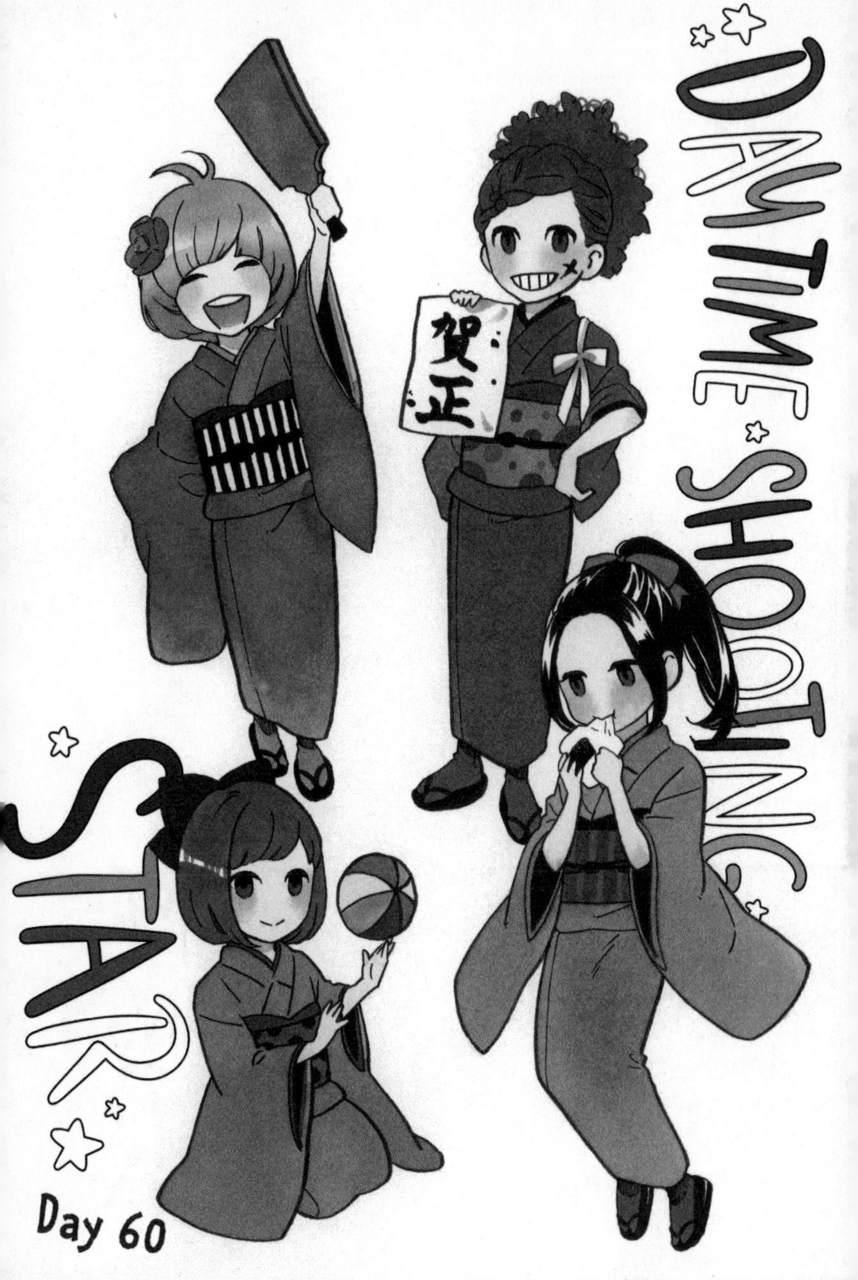
DAYTIME SHOOTING STAR
賀正
Day 60

DAYTIME SHOOTING STAR

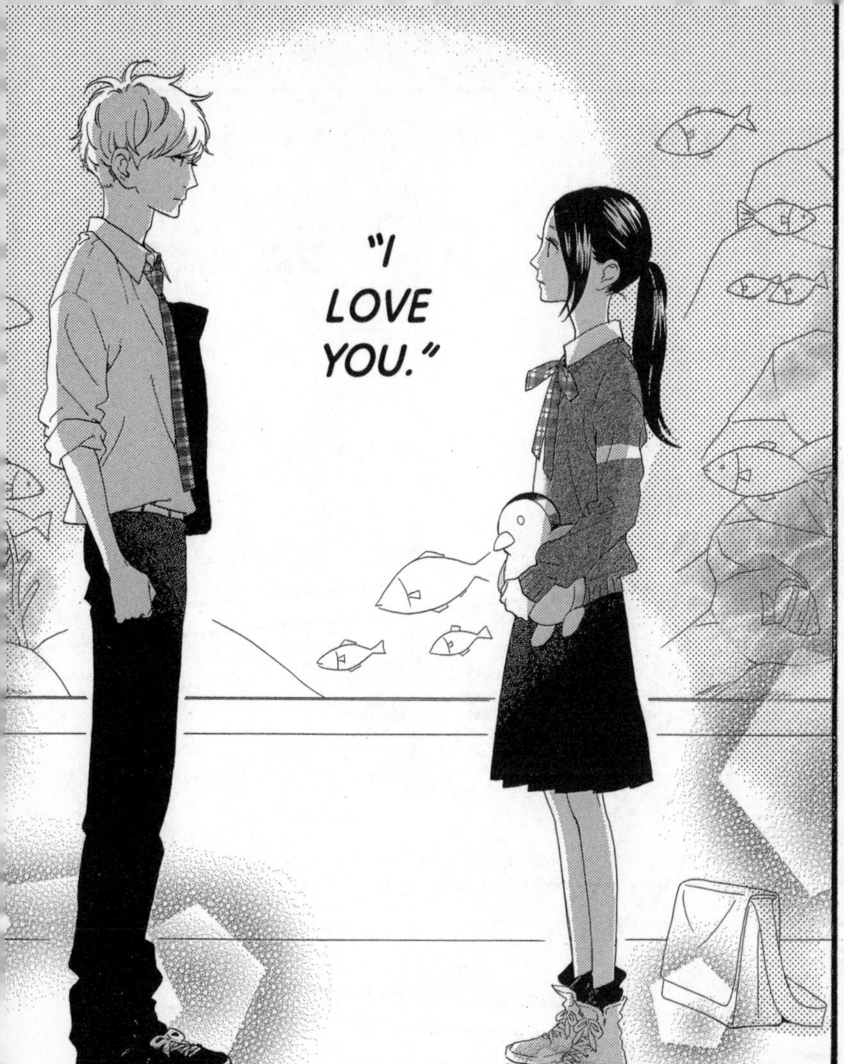
"I LOVE YOU."

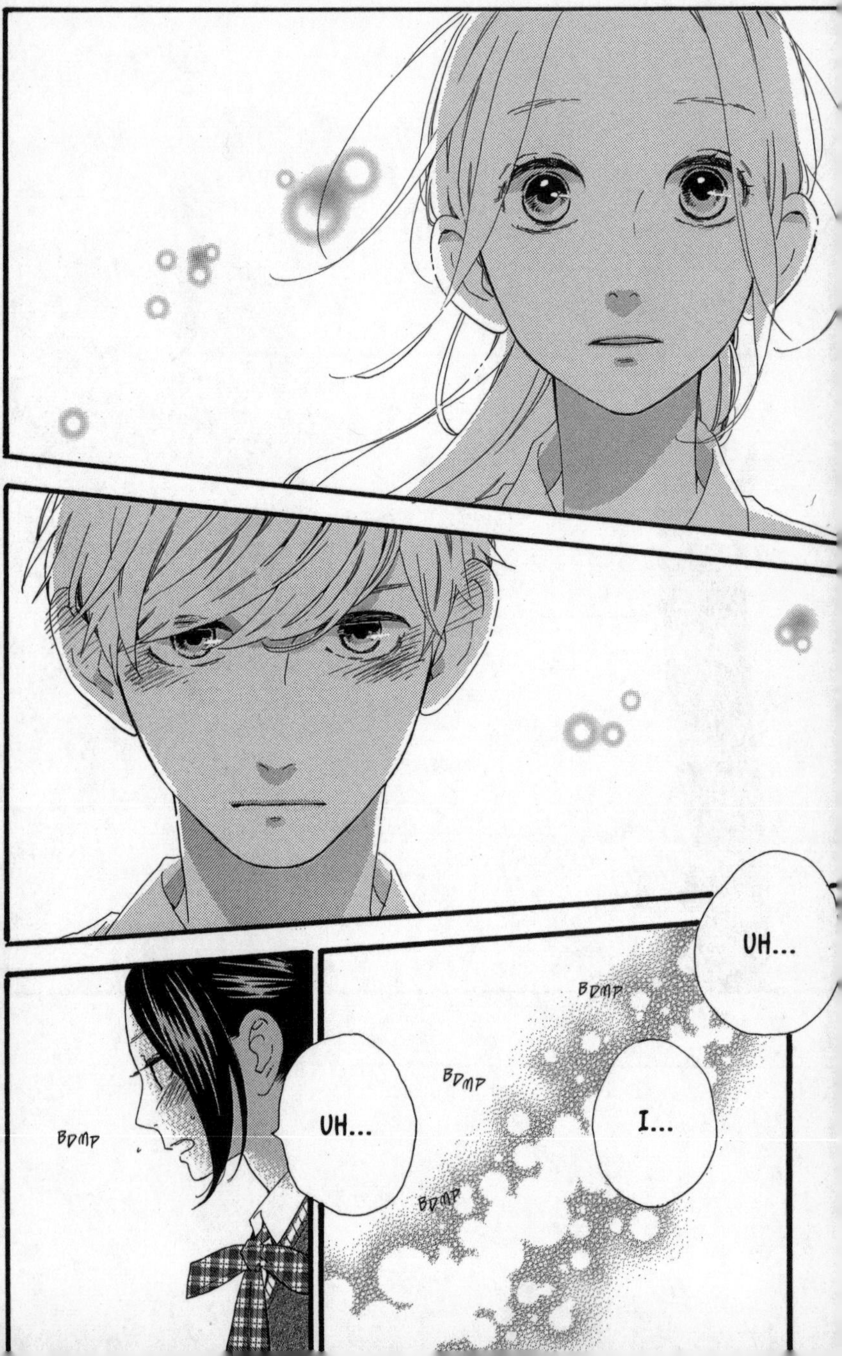
UH...
BDMP
BDMP
I...
BDMP
UH...
BDMP

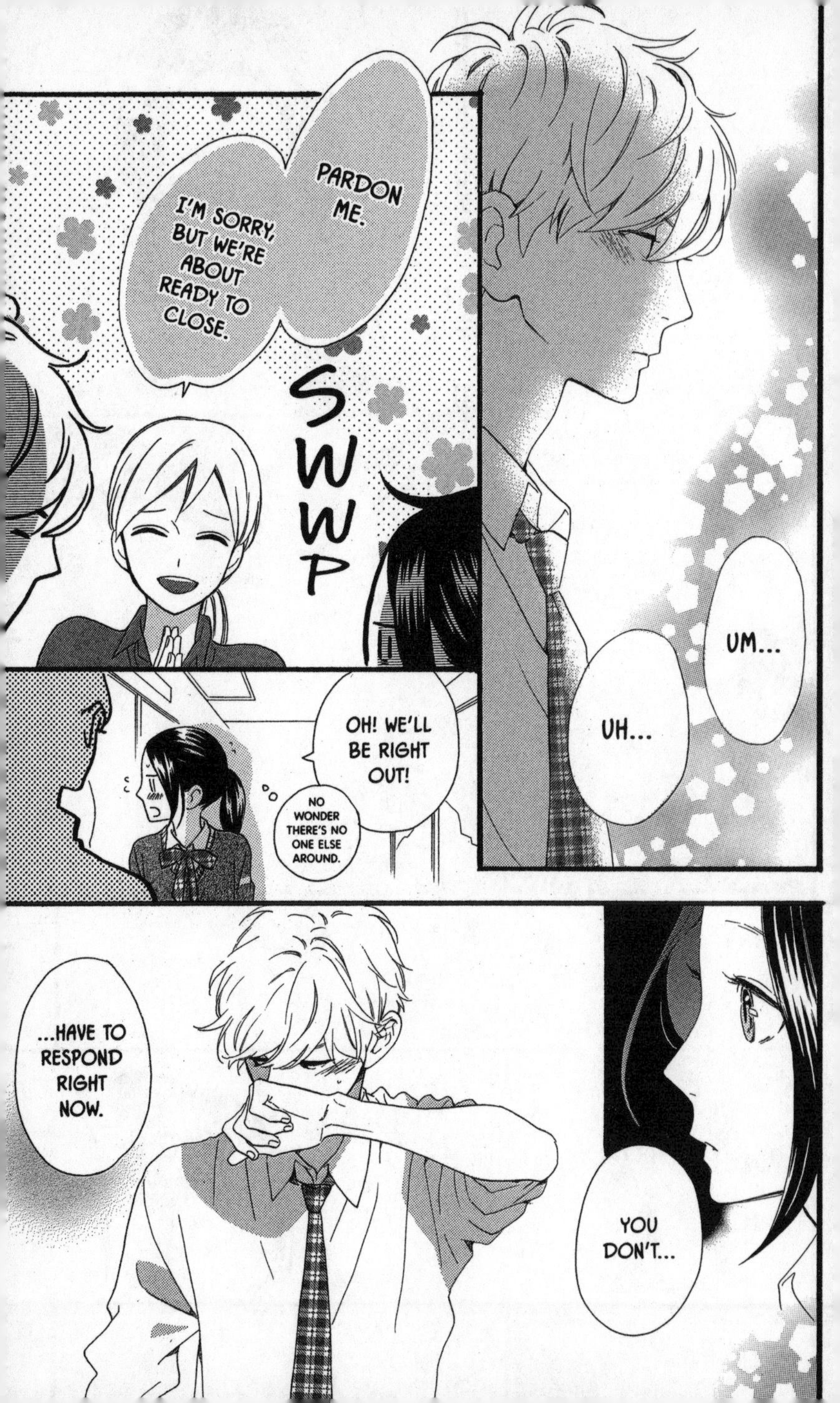
UM...
UH...
PARDON ME.
I'M SORRY, BUT WE'RE ABOUT READY TO CLOSE.
SWWP
OH! WE'LL BE RIGHT OUT!
NO WONDER THERE'S NO ONE ELSE AROUND.
YOU DON'T...
...HAVE TO RESPOND RIGHT NOW.

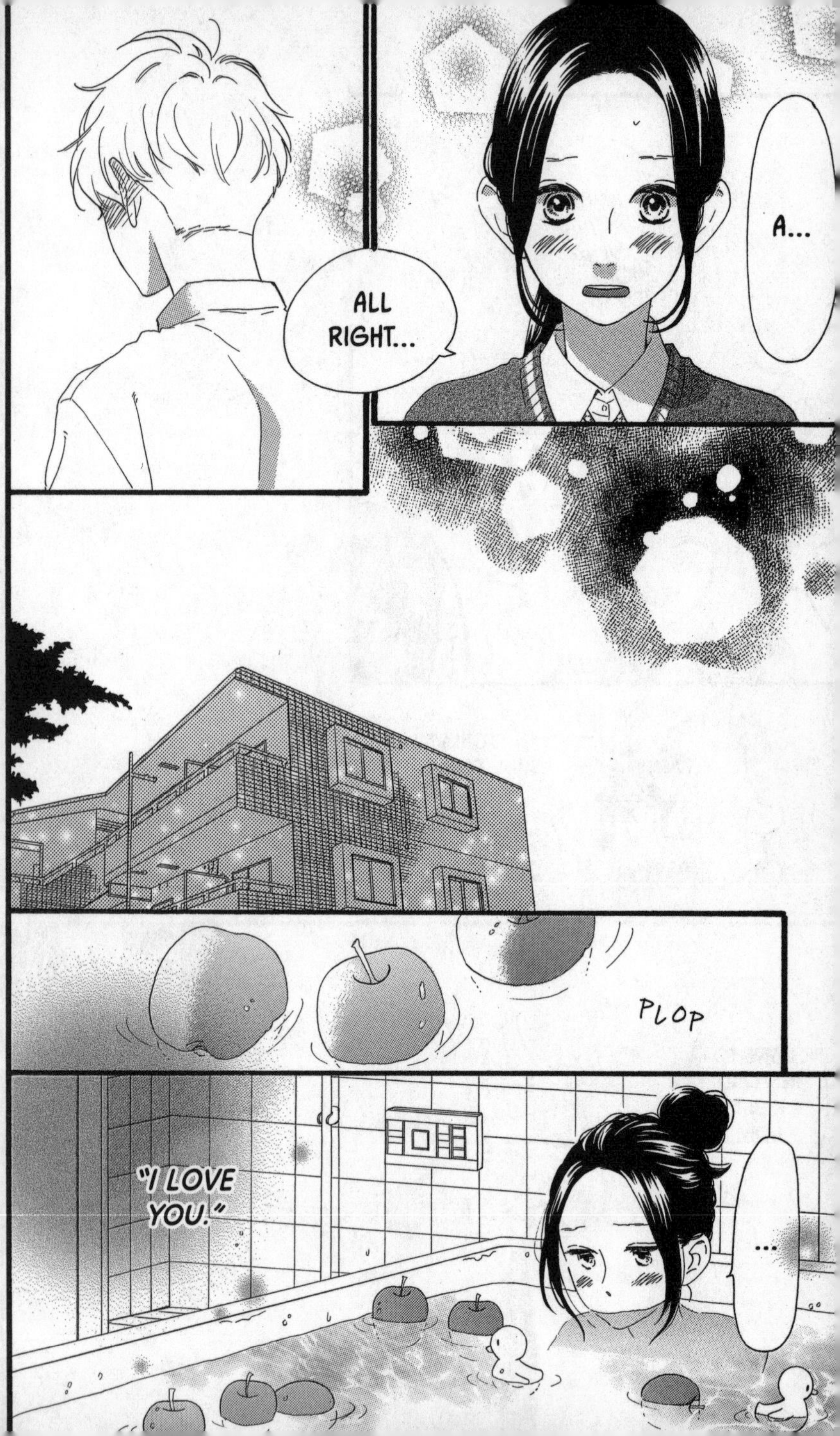
A...
ALL RIGHT...
PLOP
"I LOVE YOU."
...

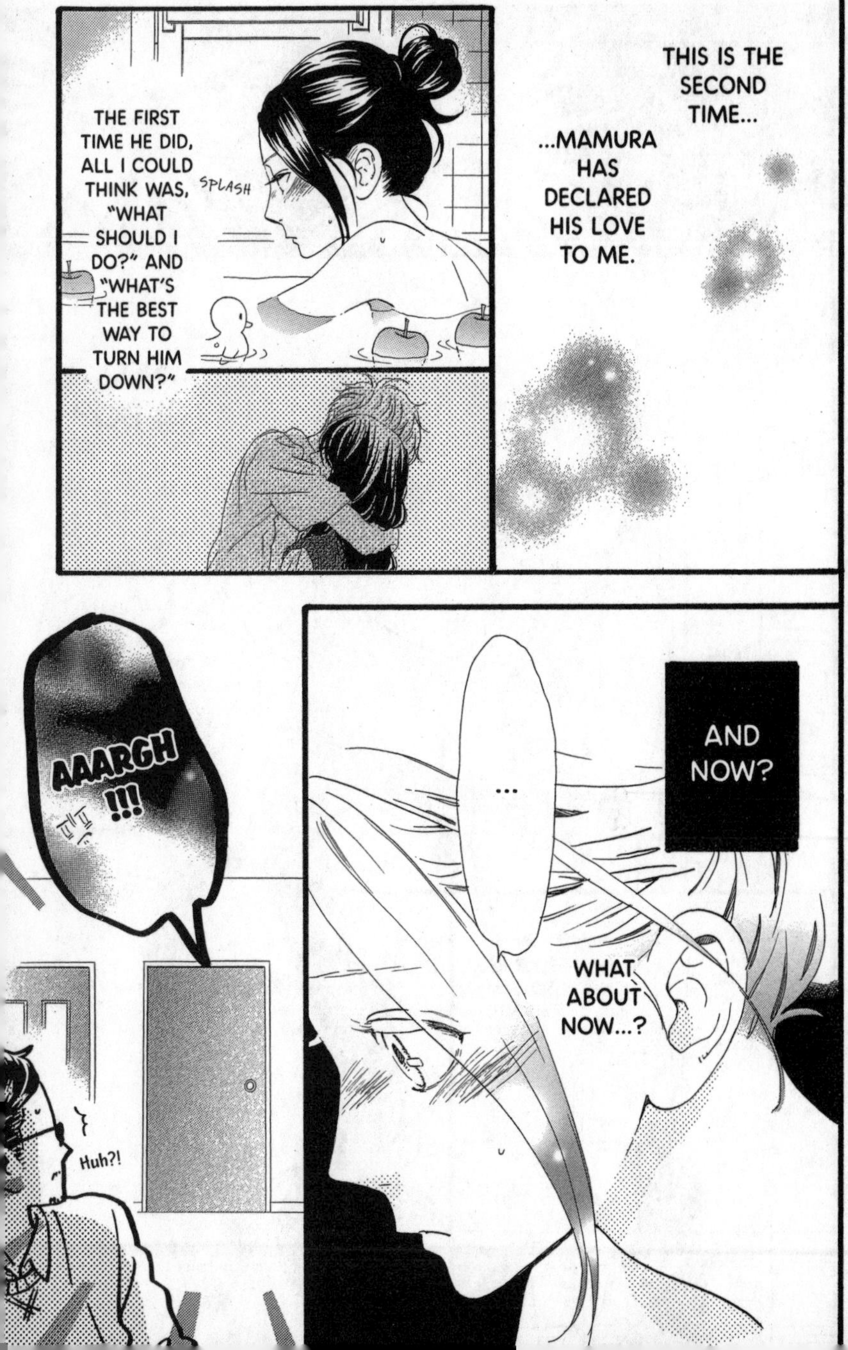
THIS IS THE SECOND TIME...
...MAMURA HAS DECLARED HIS LOVE TO ME.
THE FIRST TIME HE DID, ALL I COULD THINK WAS, "WHAT SHOULD I DO?" AND "WHAT'S THE BEST WAY TO TURN HIM DOWN?"
SPLASH
AND NOW?
...
WHAT ABOUT NOW...?
AAARGH!!!
Huh?!

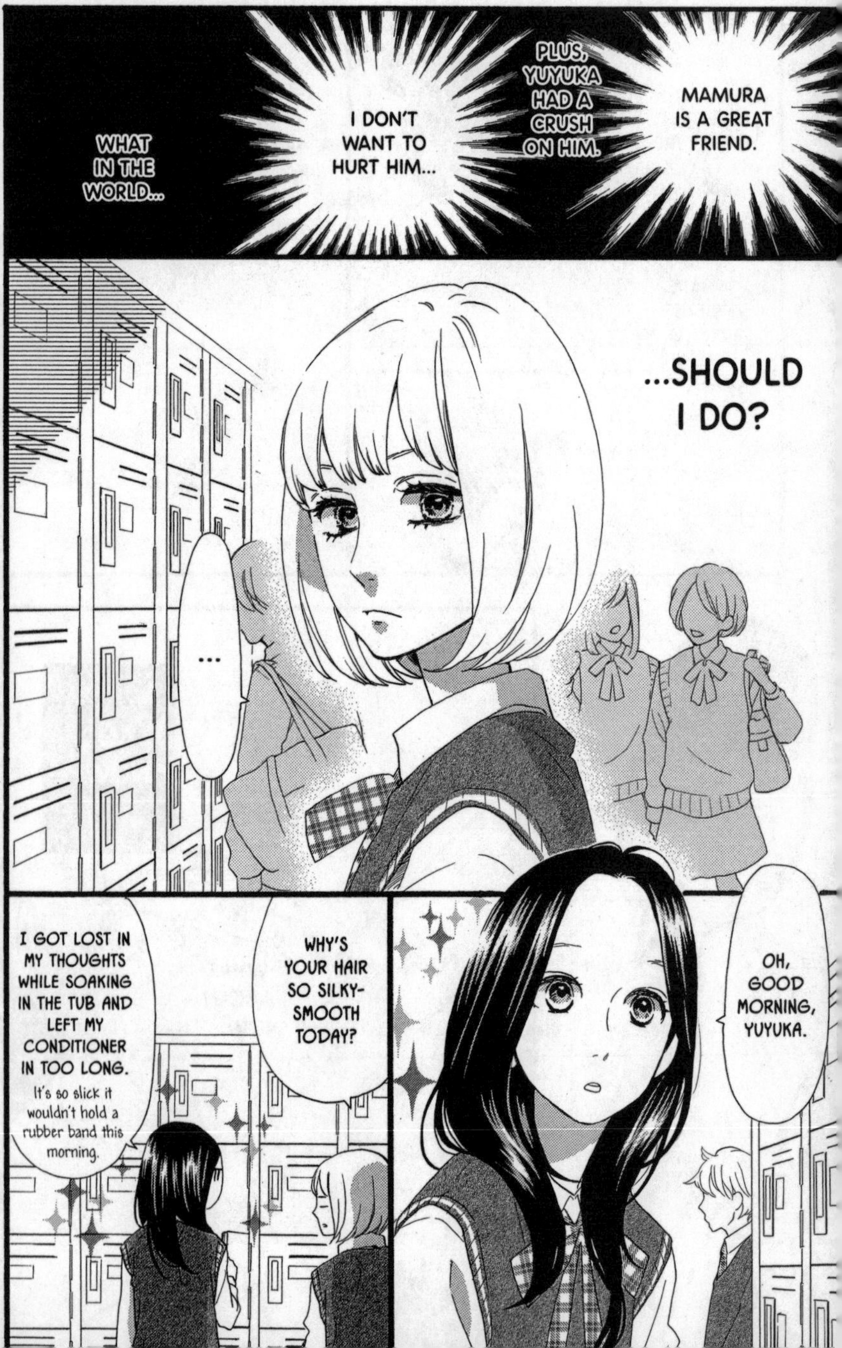
MAMURA IS A GREAT FRIEND.
PLUS, YUYUKA HAD A CRUSH ON HIM.
I DON'T WANT TO HURT HIM...
WHAT IN THE WORLD...
...SHOULD I DO?
...
OH, GOOD MORNING, YUYUKA.
WHY'S YOUR HAIR SO SILKY-SMOOTH TODAY?
I GOT LOST IN MY THOUGHTS WHILE SOAKING IN THE TUB AND LEFT MY CONDITIONER IN TOO LONG.
It's so slick it wouldn't hold a rubber band this morning.

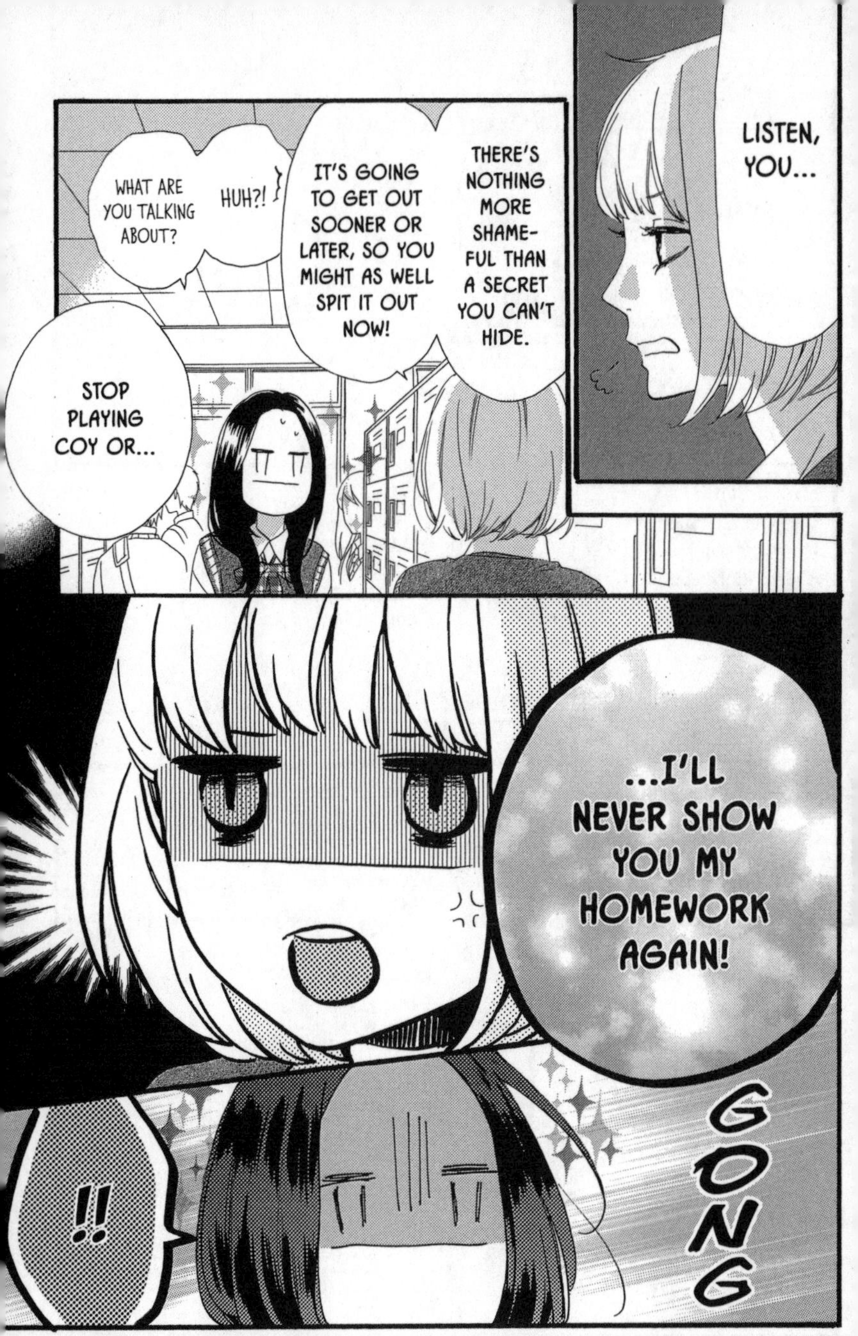
LISTEN, YOU...
THERE'S NOTHING MORE SHAME-FUL THAN A SECRET YOU CAN'T HIDE.
IT'S GOING TO GET OUT SOONER OR LATER, SO YOU MIGHT AS WELL SPIT IT OUT NOW!
HUH?!
WHAT ARE YOU TALKING ABOUT?
STOP PLAYING COY OR...
...I'LL NEVER SHOW YOU MY HOMEWORK AGAIN!
GONG
!!

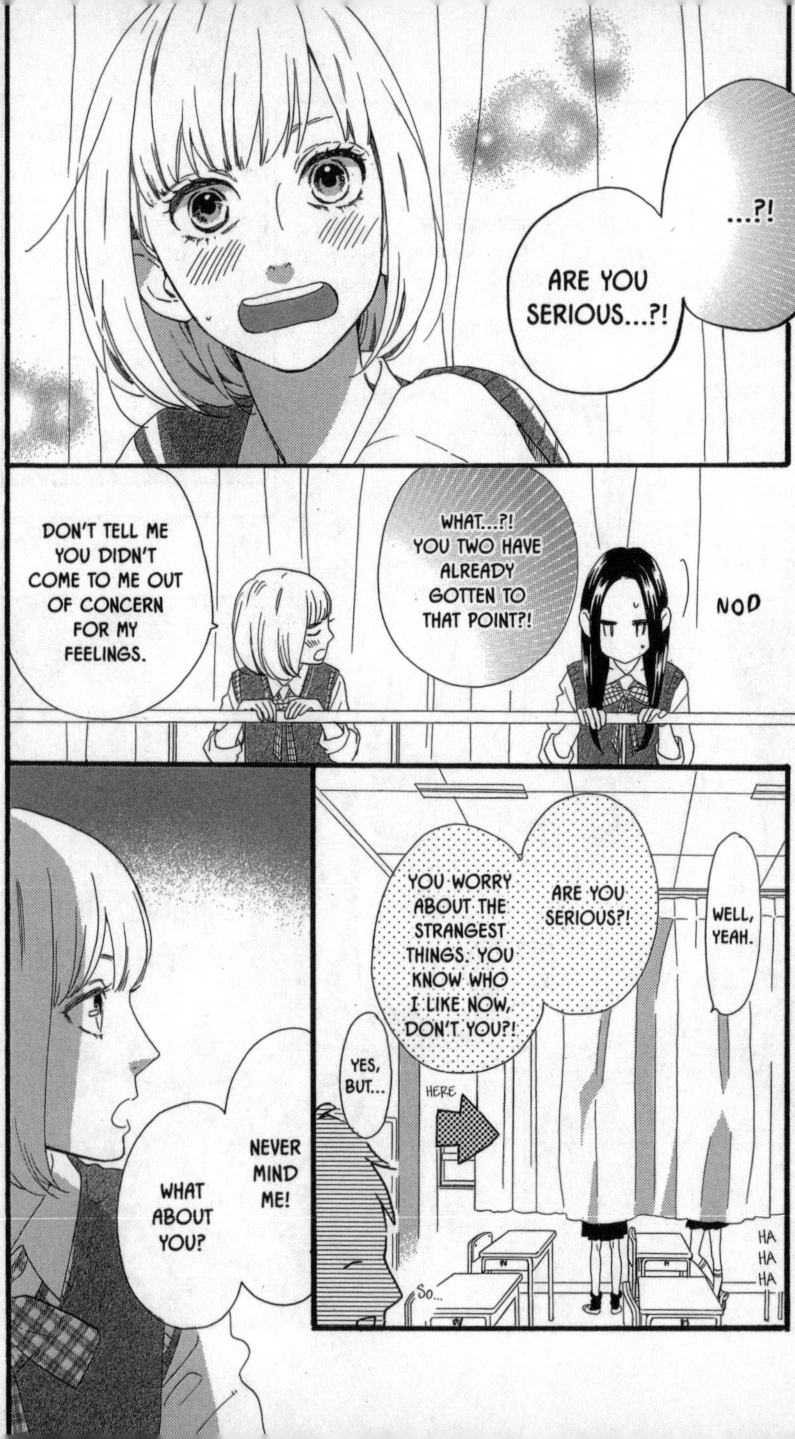
...?!
ARE YOU SERIOUS...?!
NOD
WHAT...?! YOU TWO HAVE ALREADY GOTTEN TO THAT POINT?!
DON'T TELL ME YOU DIDN'T COME TO ME OUT OF CONCERN FOR MY FEELINGS.
WELL, YEAH.
HA HA HA
ARE YOU SERIOUS?!
YOU WORRY ABOUT THE STRANGEST THINGS. YOU KNOW WHO I LIKE NOW, DON'T YOU?!
YES, BUT...
HERE
So...
NEVER MIND ME!
WHAT ABOUT YOU?

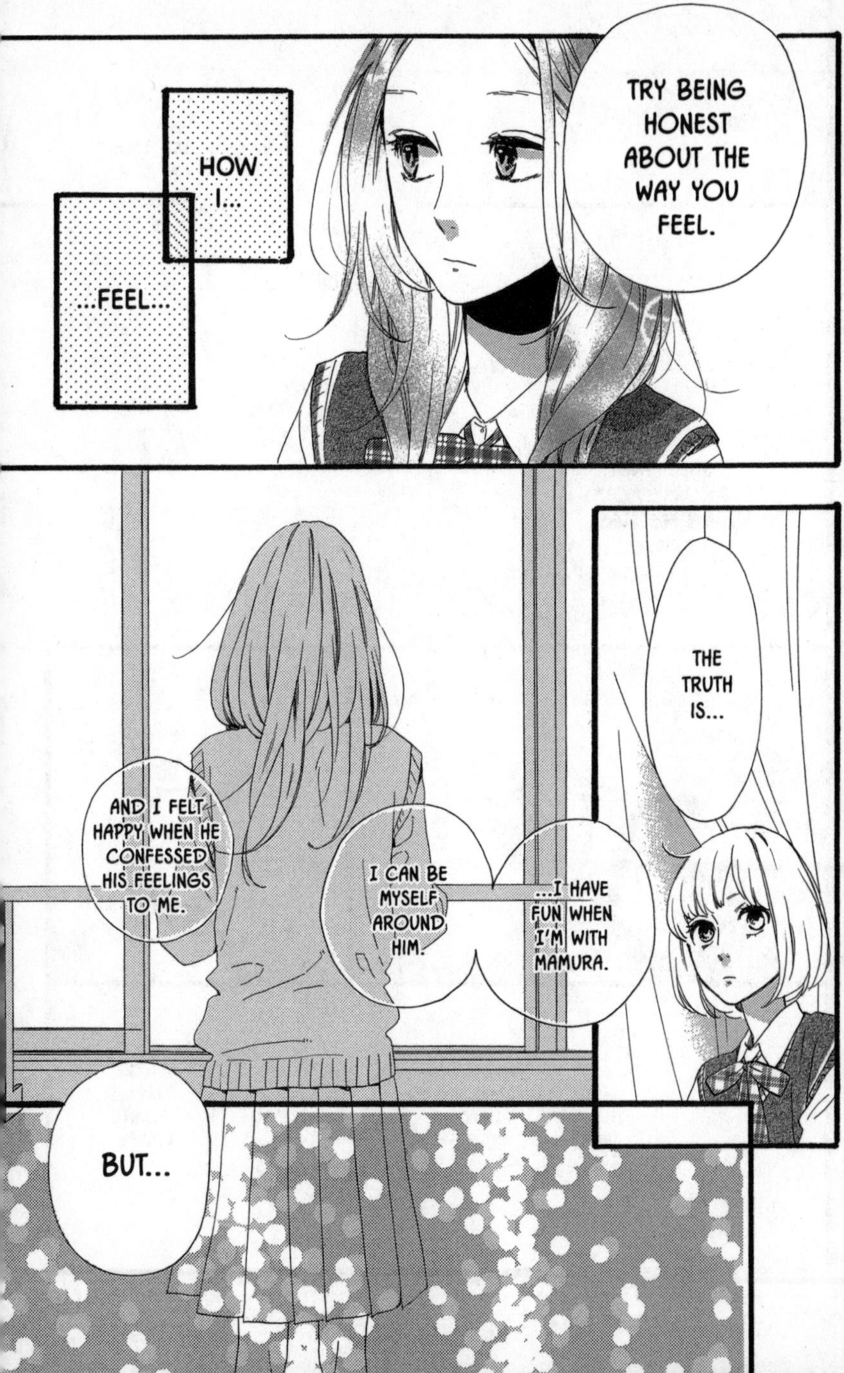
TRY BEING HONEST ABOUT THE WAY YOU FEEL.
HOW I...
...FEEL...
THE TRUTH IS...
...I HAVE FUN WHEN I'M WITH MAMURA.
I CAN BE MYSELF AROUND HIM.
AND I FELT HAPPY WHEN HE CONFESSED HIS FEELINGS TO ME.
BUT...

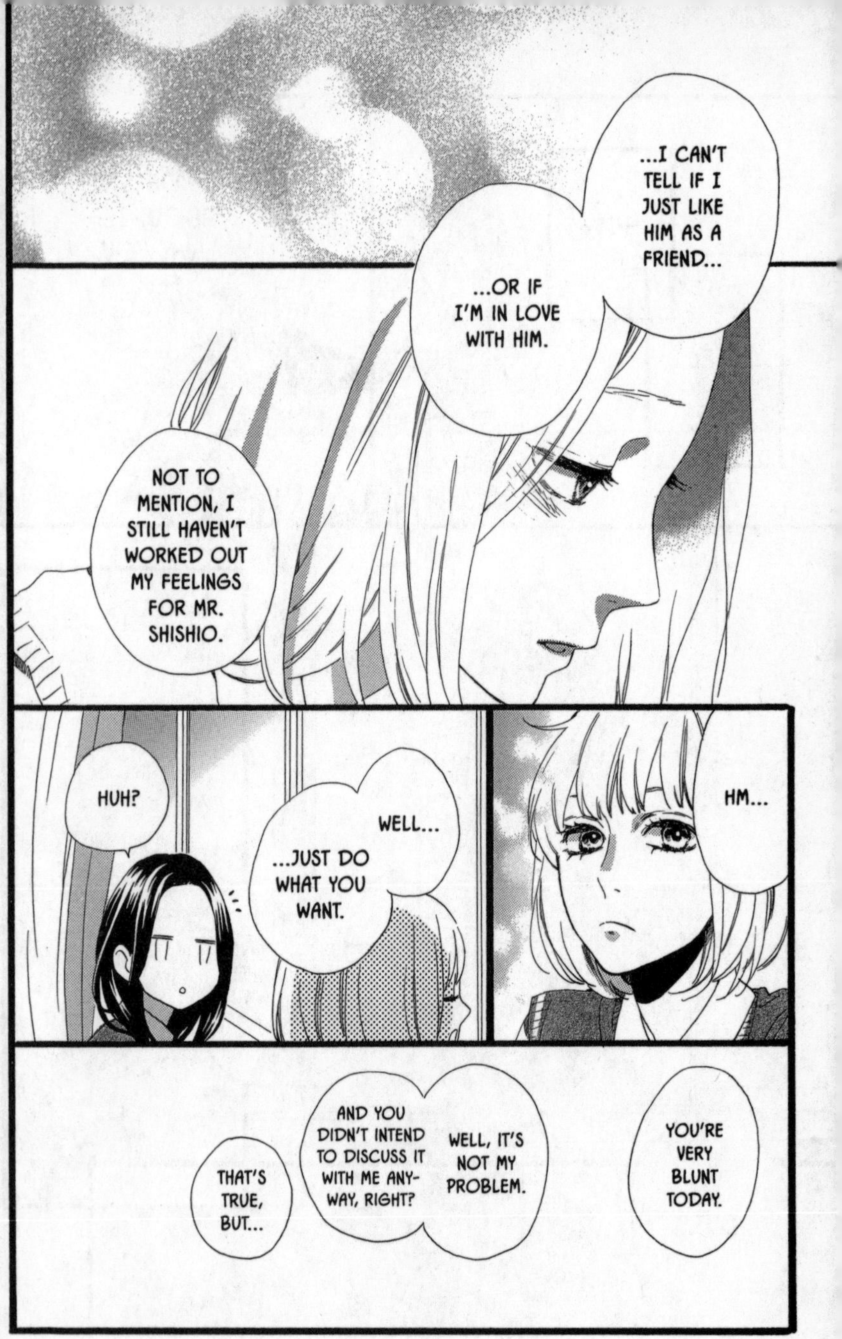
...I CAN'T TELL IF I JUST LIKE HIM AS A FRIEND...
...OR IF I'M IN LOVE WITH HIM.
NOT TO MENTION, I STILL HAVEN'T WORKED OUT MY FEELINGS FOR MR. SHISHIO.
HM...
WELL...
...JUST DO WHAT YOU WANT.
HUH?
YOU'RE VERY BLUNT TODAY.
WELL, IT'S NOT MY PROBLEM.
AND YOU DIDN'T INTEND TO DISCUSS IT WITH ME ANY-WAY, RIGHT?
THAT'S TRUE, BUT...

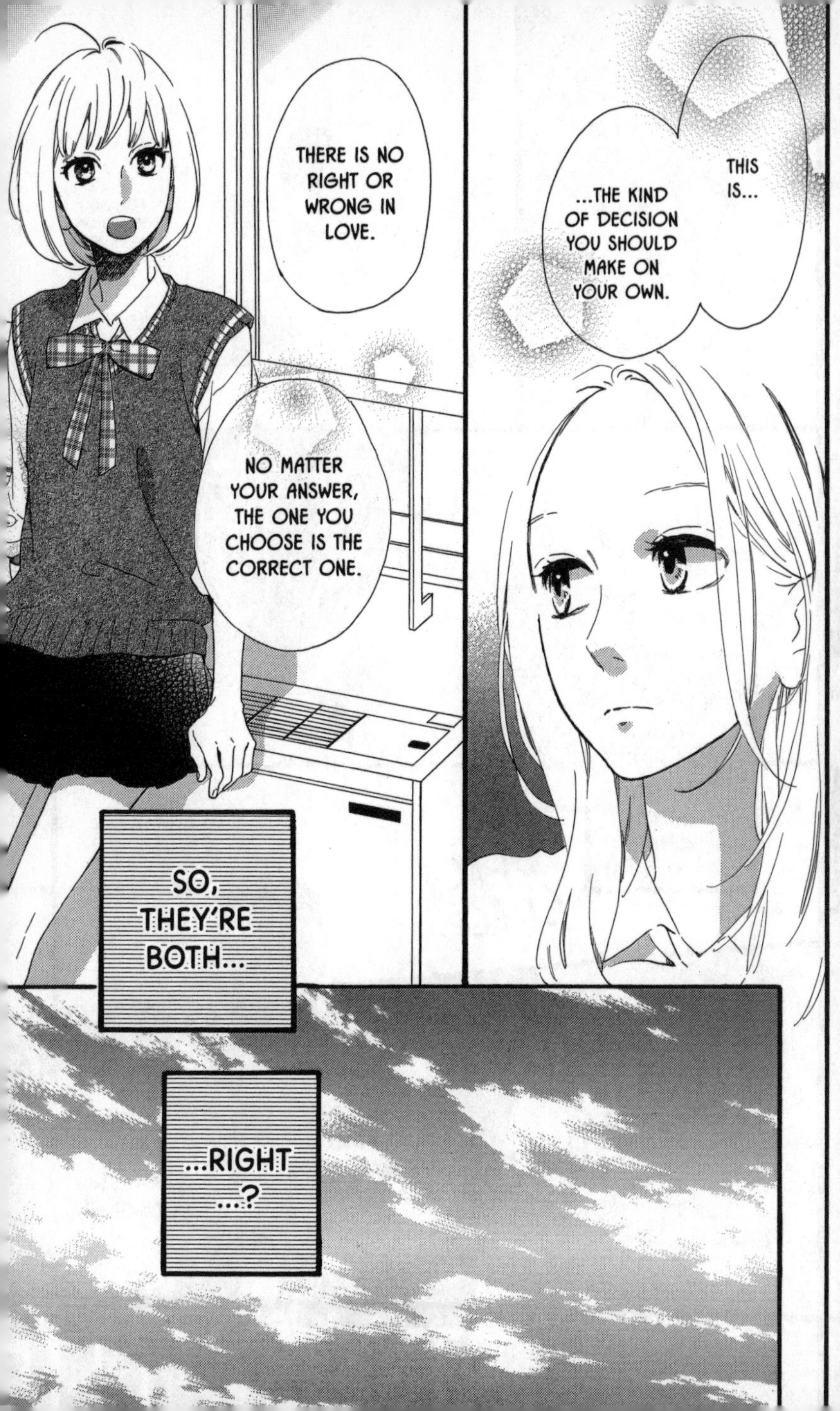
THIS IS...
...THE KIND OF DECISION YOU SHOULD MAKE ON YOUR OWN.
THERE IS NO RIGHT OR WRONG IN LOVE.
NO MATTER YOUR ANSWER, THE ONE YOU CHOOSE IS THE CORRECT ONE.
SO, THEY'RE BOTH...
...RIGHT ...?

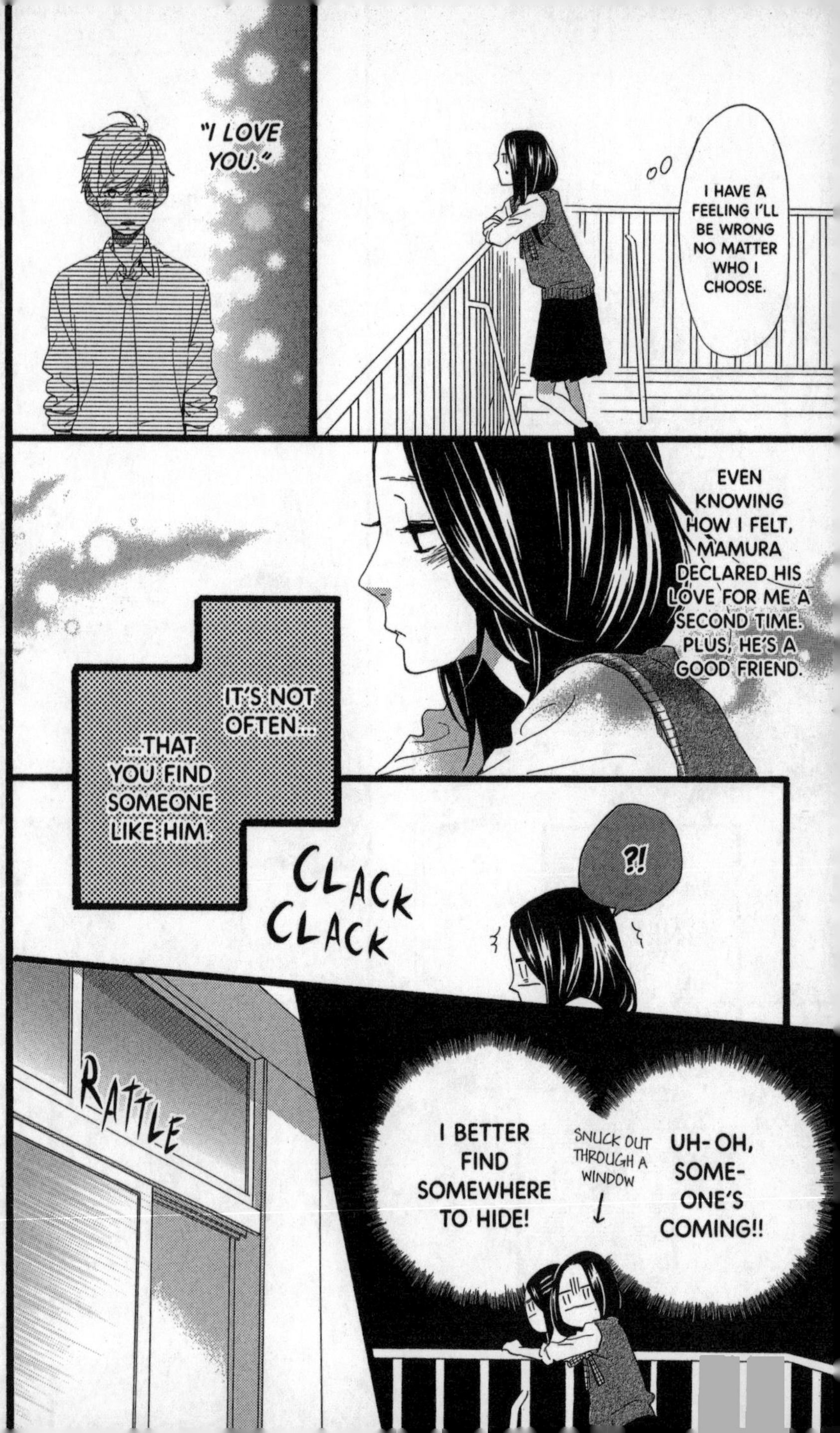
I HAVE A FEELING I'LL BE WRONG NO MATTER WHO I CHOOSE.
"I LOVE YOU."
EVEN KNOWING HOW I FELT, MAMURA DECLARED HIS LOVE FOR ME A SECOND TIME. PLUS, HE'S A GOOD FRIEND.
IT'S NOT OFTEN...
...THAT YOU FIND SOMEONE LIKE HIM.
?!
CLACK CLACK
UH-OH, SOME-ONE'S COMING!!
SNUCK OUT THROUGH A WINDOW
I BETTER FIND SOMEWHERE TO HIDE!
RATTLE

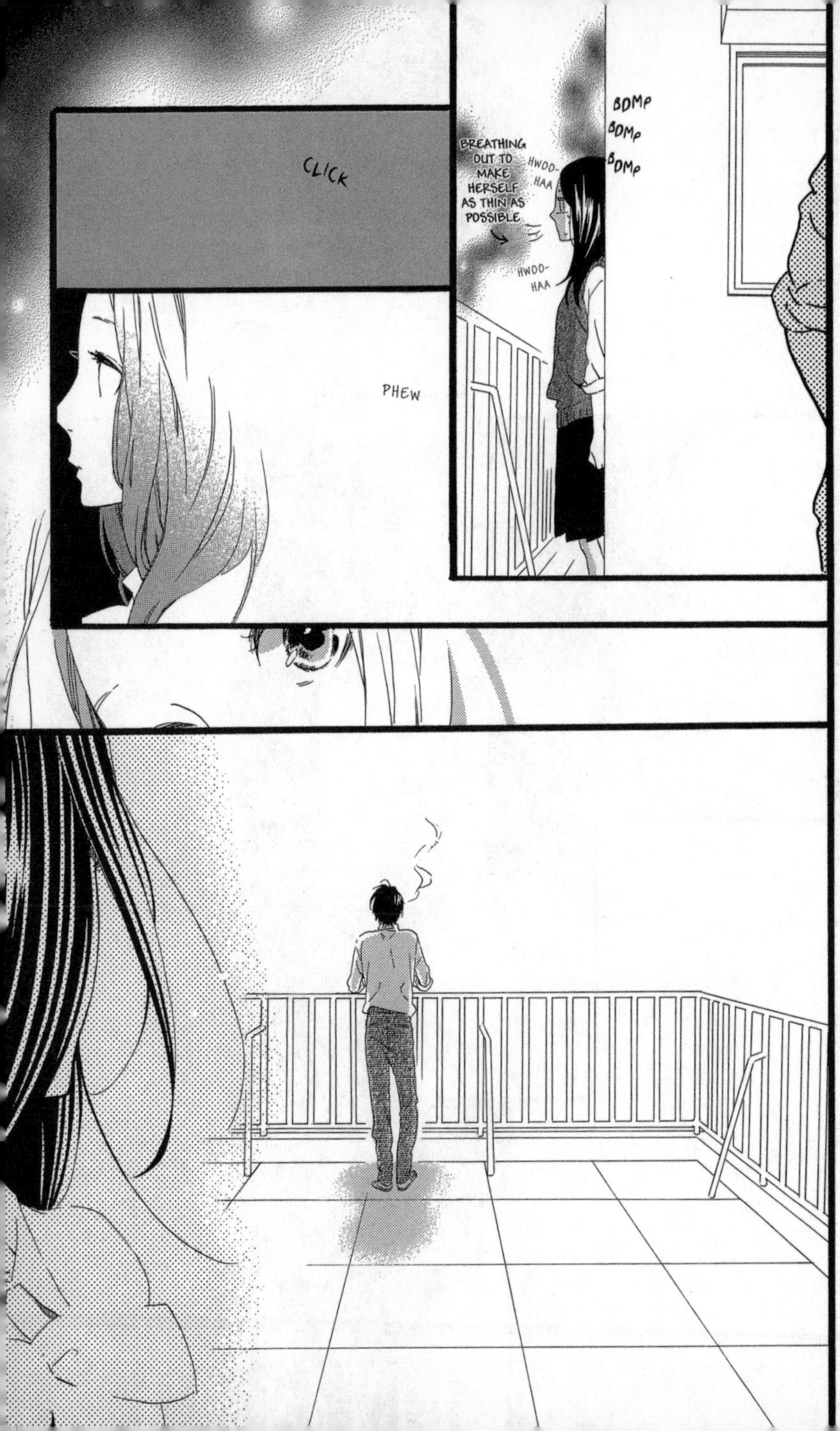
BDMP
BDMP
BDMP
HWOO-HAA
BREATHING OUT TO MAKE HERSELF AS THIN AS POSSIBLE
HWOO-HAA
CLICK
PHEW

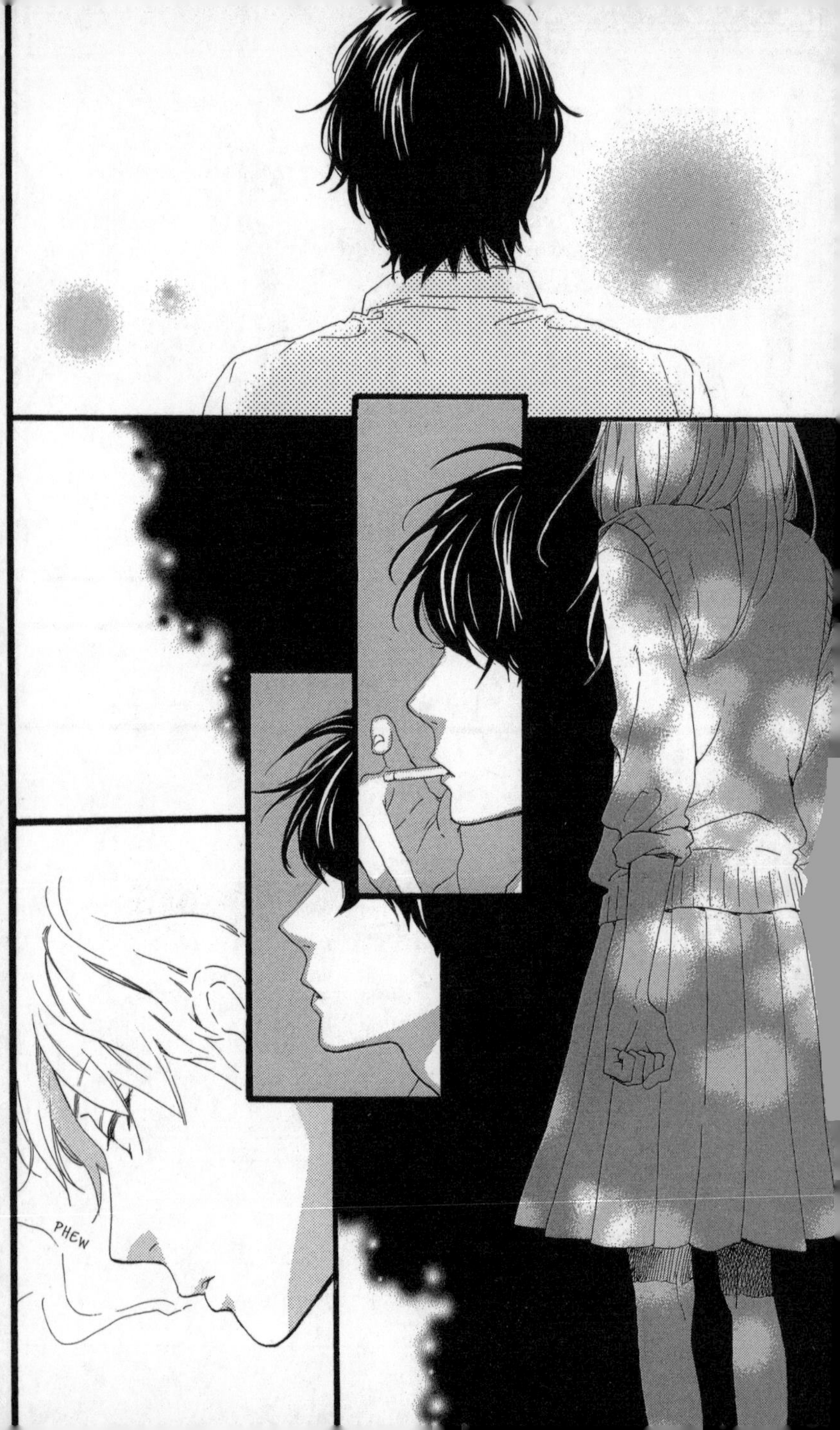
PHEW

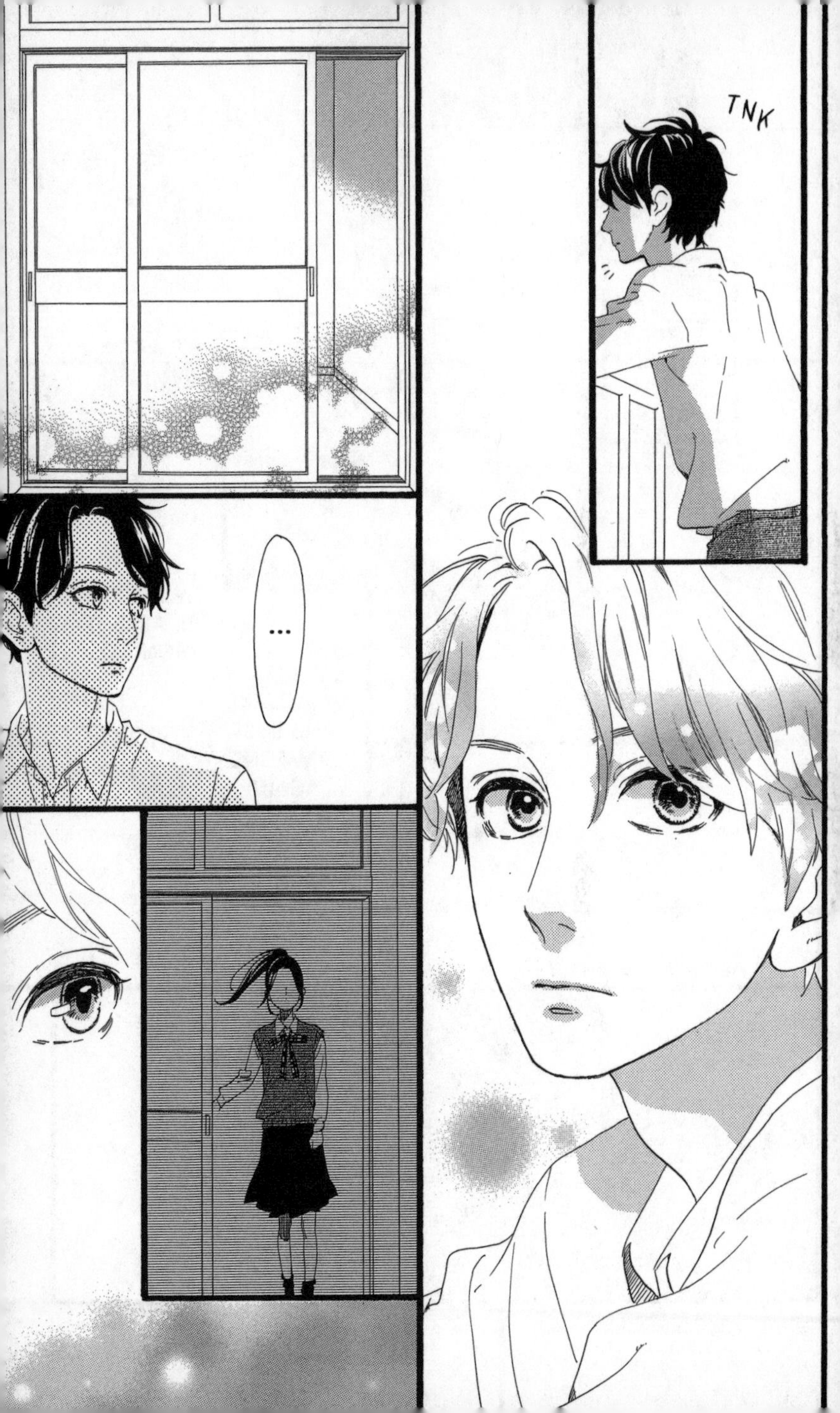
TNK
...

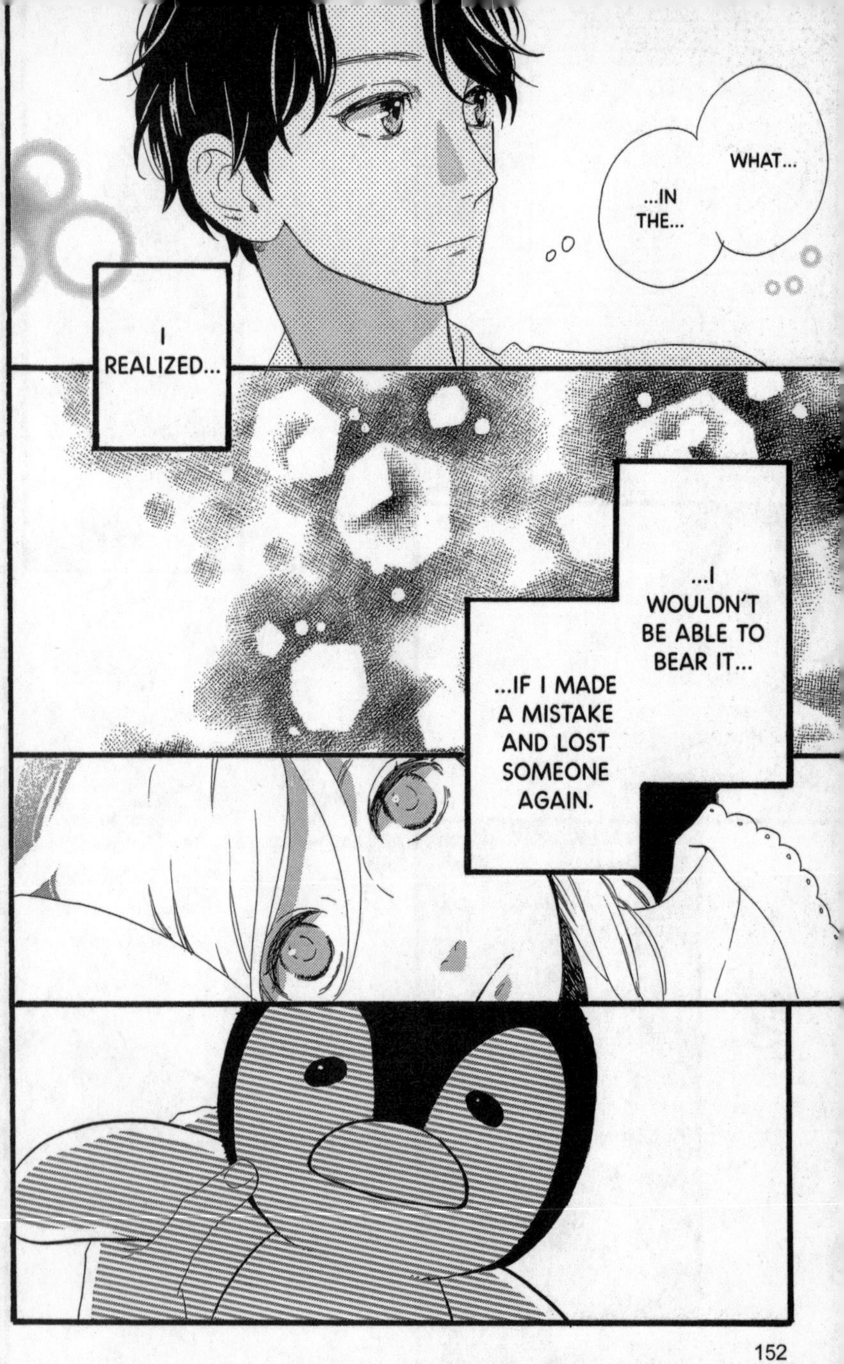
WHAT... ...IN THE...
I REALIZED...
...I WOULDN'T BE ABLE TO BEAR IT...
...IF I MADE A MISTAKE AND LOST SOMEONE AGAIN.

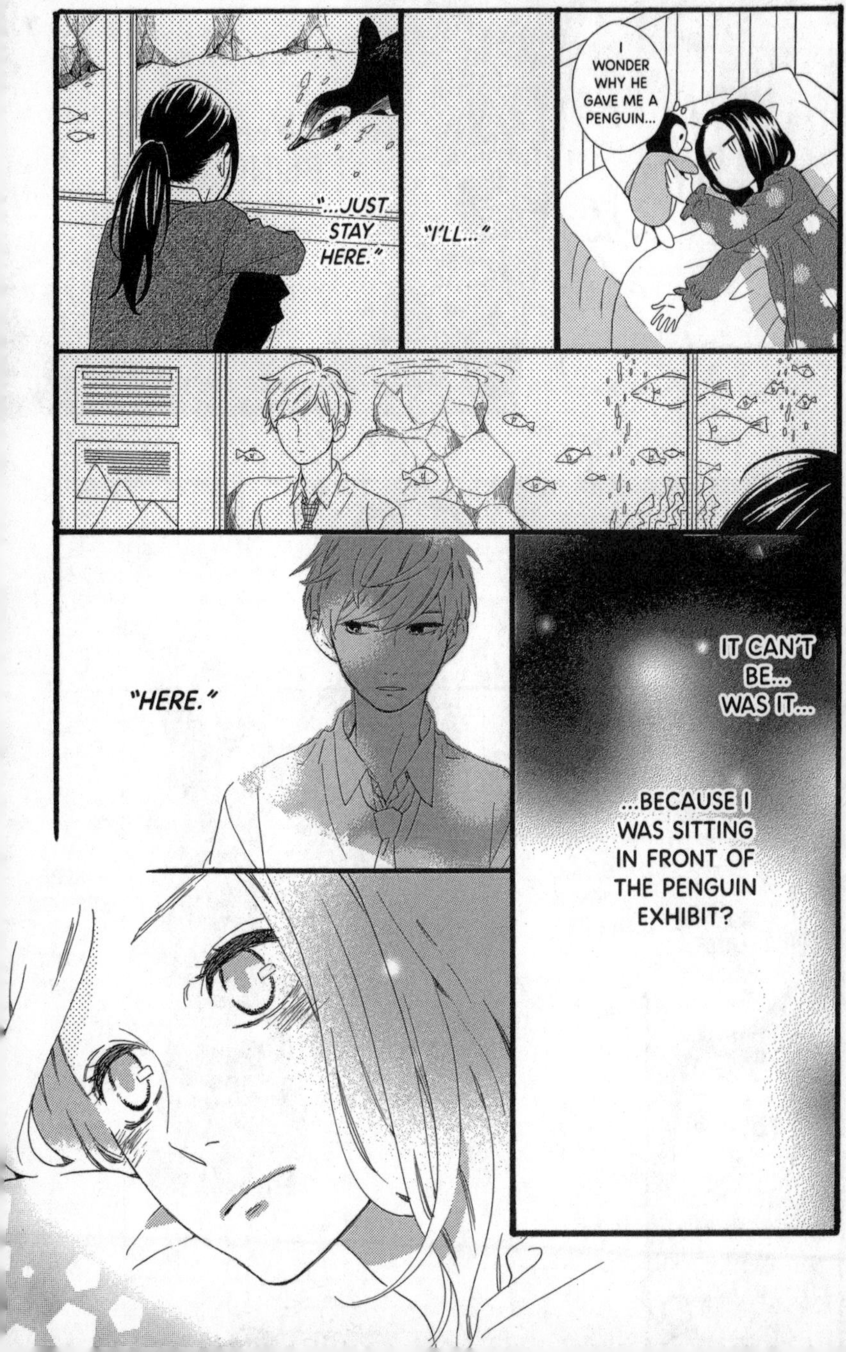
I WONDER WHY HE GAVE ME A PENGUIN...
"I'LL..."
"...JUST STAY HERE."
IT CAN'T BE... WAS IT...
...BECAUSE I WAS SITTING IN FRONT OF THE PENGUIN EXHIBIT?
"HERE."

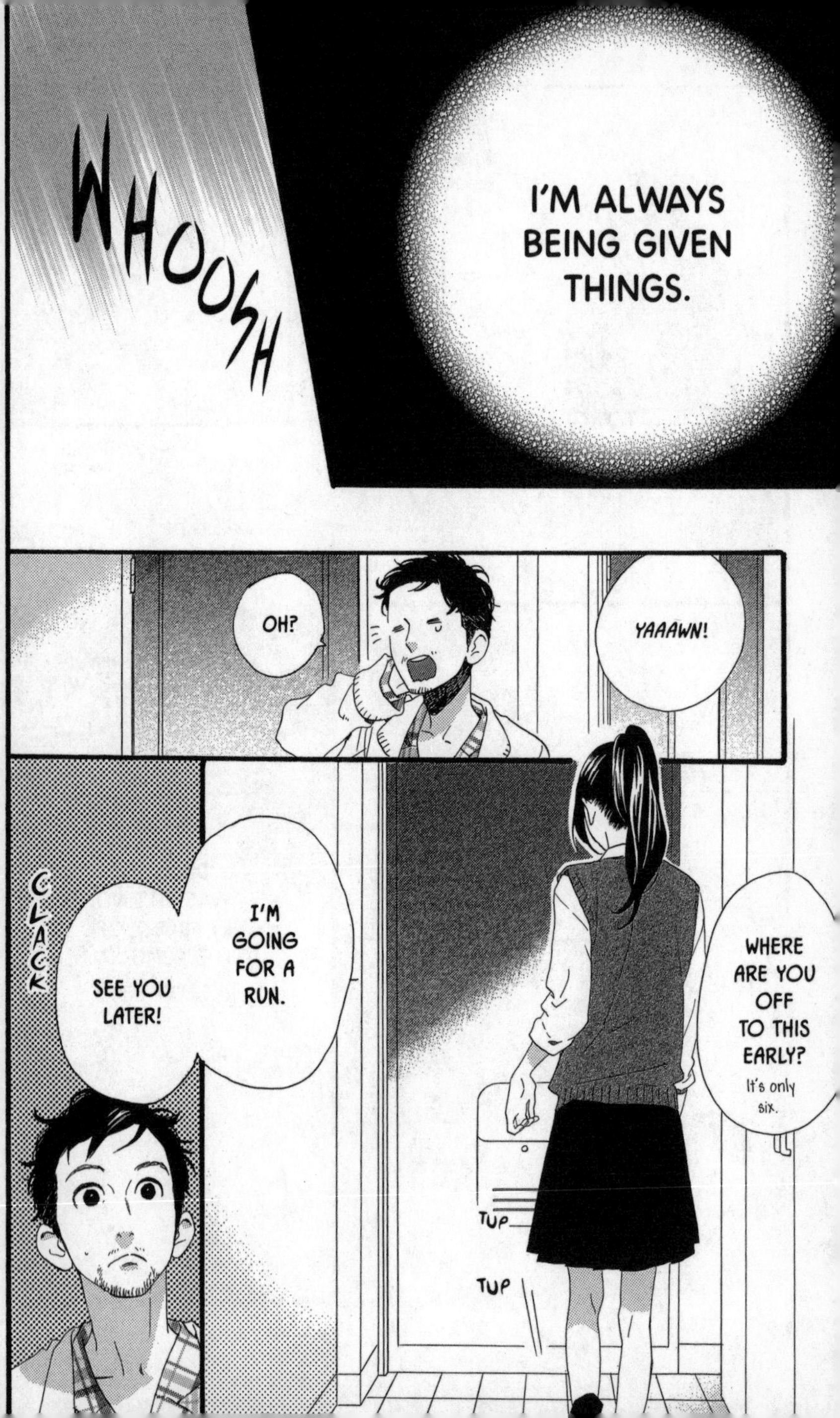

I'M ALWAYS BEING GIVEN THINGS.
WHOOSH
YAAAWN!
OH?
WHERE ARE YOU OFF TO THIS EARLY?
It's only six.
TUP
TUP
I'M GOING FOR A RUN.
SEE YOU LATER!
CLACK

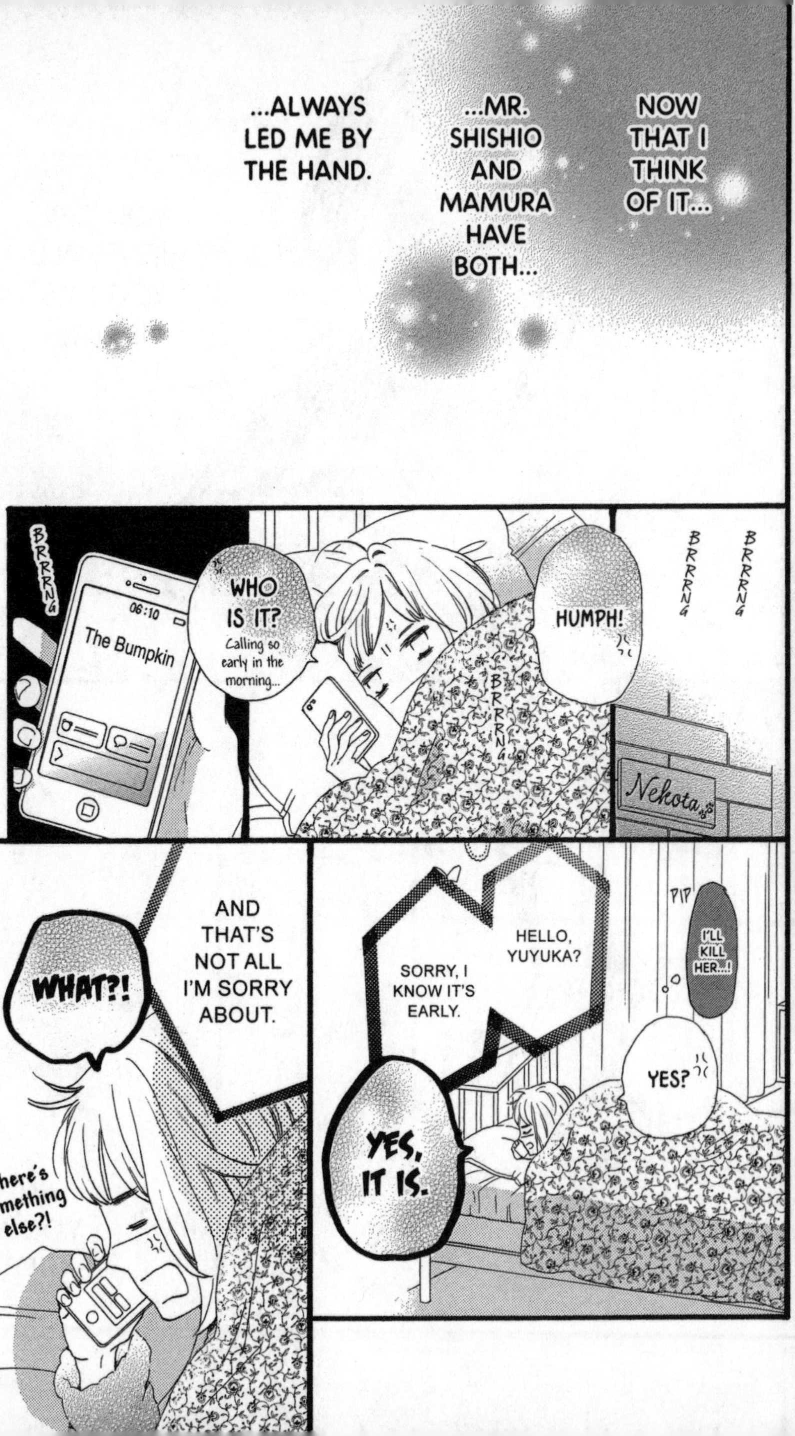
NOW THAT I THINK OF IT...
...MR. SHISHIO AND MAMURA HAVE BOTH...
...ALWAYS LED ME BY THE HAND.
BRRRNG
BRRRNG
Nekota
HUMPH!
BRRRNG
WHO IS IT? Calling so early in the morning...
BRRRNG
06:10
The Bumpkin
PIP
I'LL KILL HER...!
YES?
HELLO, YUYUKA?
SORRY, I KNOW IT'S EARLY.
YES, IT IS.
AND THAT'S NOT ALL I'M SORRY ABOUT.
WHAT?!
There's something else?!

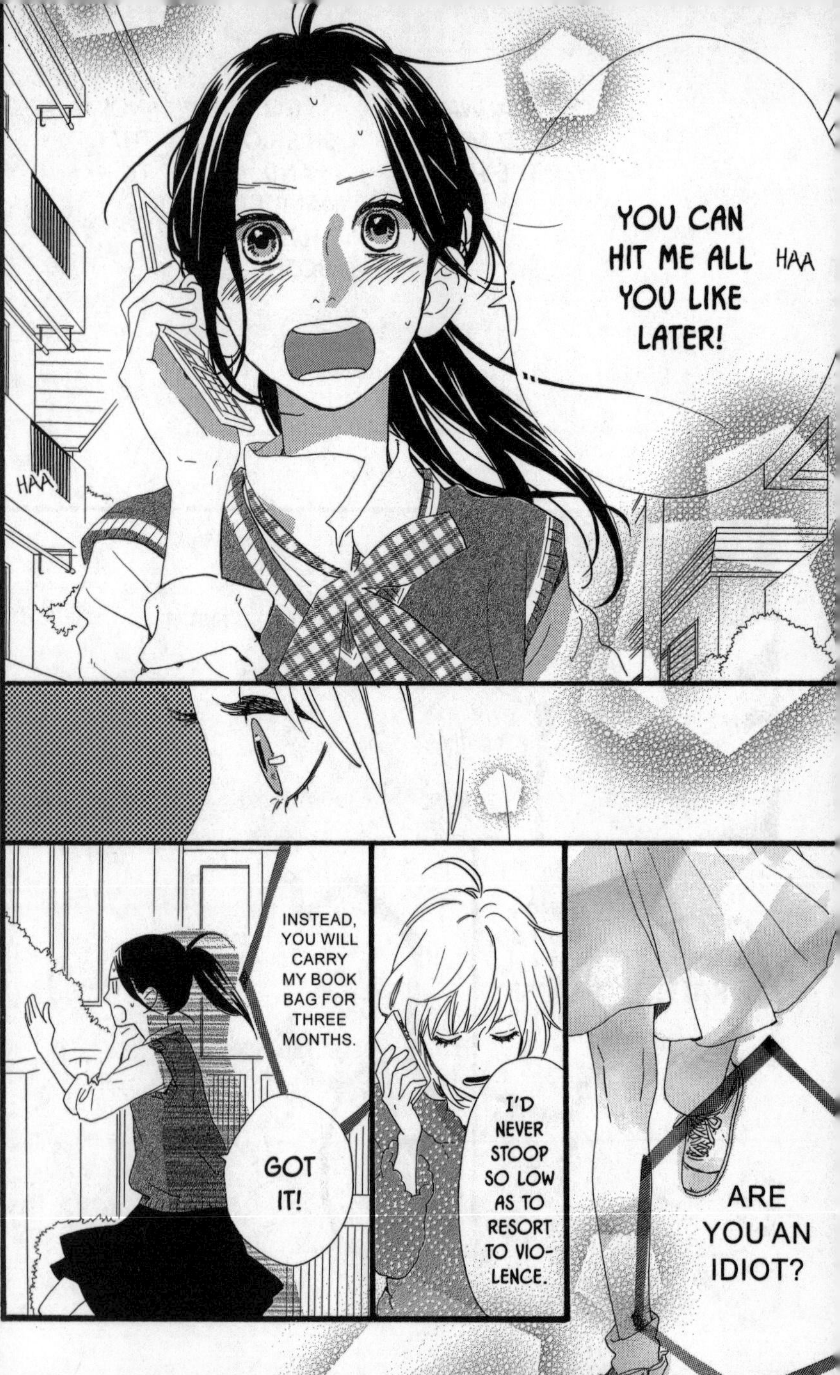
YOU CAN HIT ME ALL YOU LIKE LATER!
HAA
HAA
ARE YOU AN IDIOT?
I'D NEVER STOOP SO LOW AS TO RESORT TO VIO- LENCE.
INSTEAD, YOU WILL CARRY MY BOOK BAG FOR THREE MONTHS.
GOT IT!

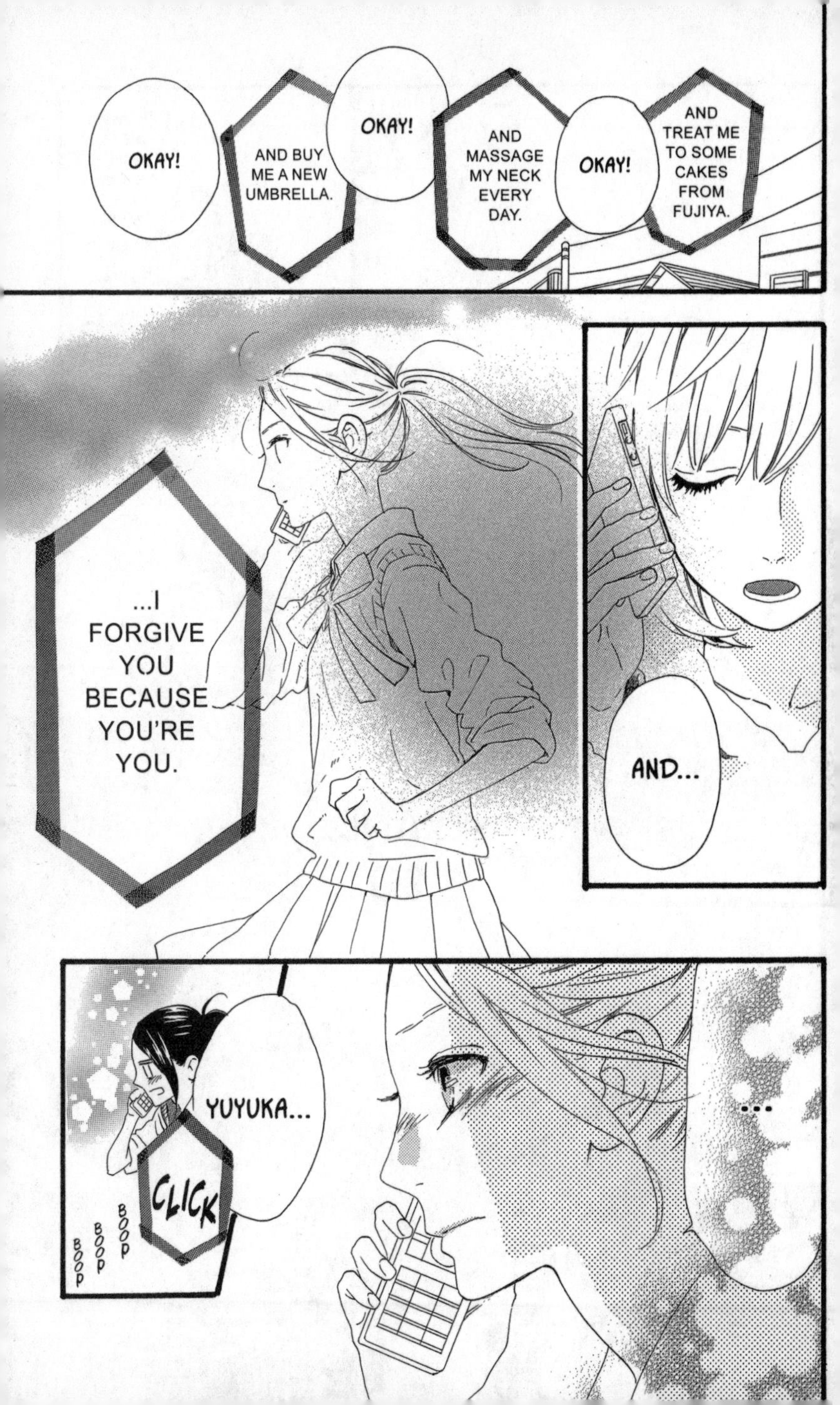
AND TREAT ME TO SOME CAKES FROM FUJIYA.
OKAY!
AND MASSAGE MY NECK EVERY DAY.
OKAY!
AND BUY ME A NEW UMBRELLA.
OKAY!
AND...
...I FORGIVE YOU BECAUSE YOU'RE YOU.
...
YUYUKA...
CLICK
BOOP
BOOP
BOOP

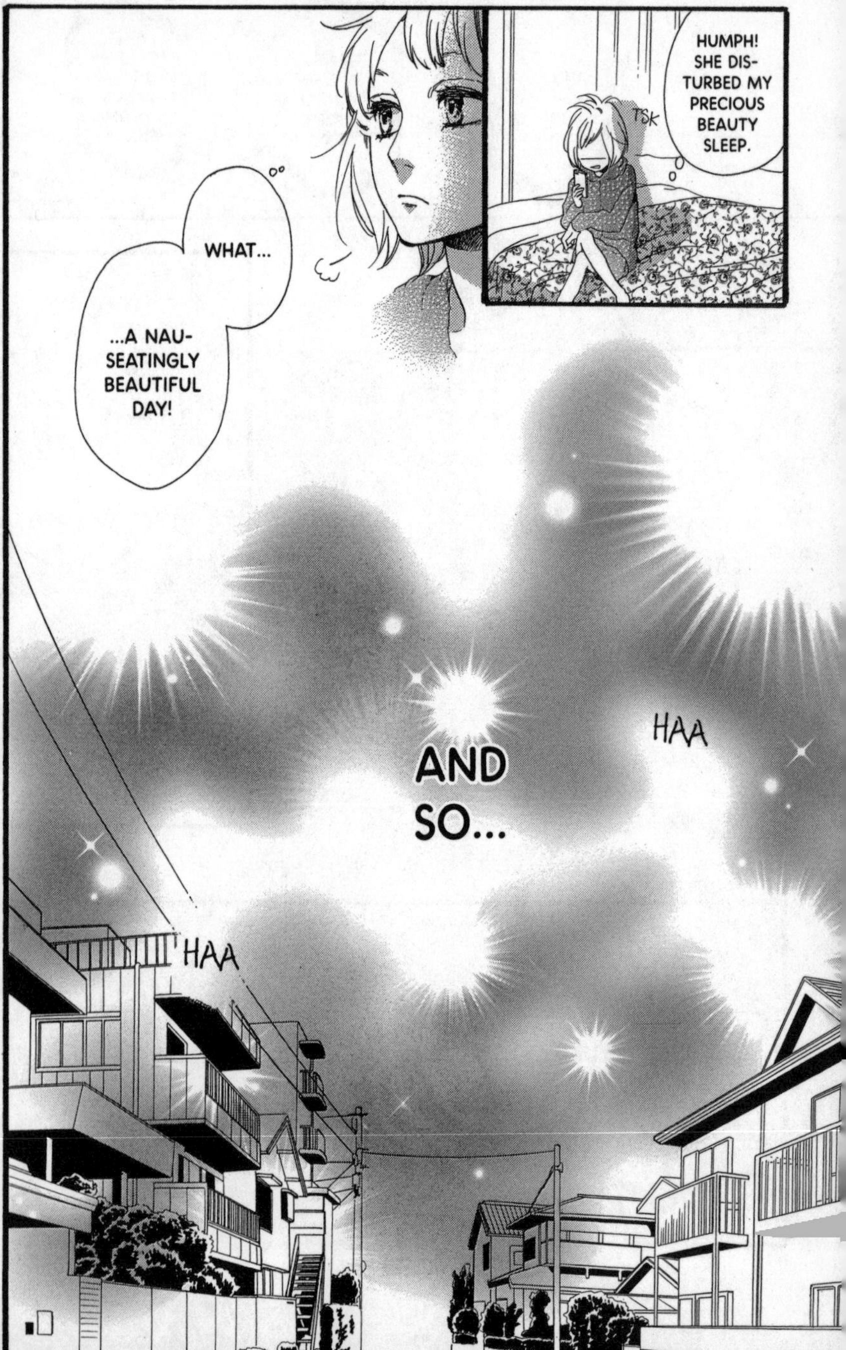

HUMPH! SHE DISTURBED MY PRECIOUS BEAUTY SLEEP.
TSK
WHAT...
...A NAUSEATINGLY BEAUTIFUL DAY!
HAA
AND SO...
HAA

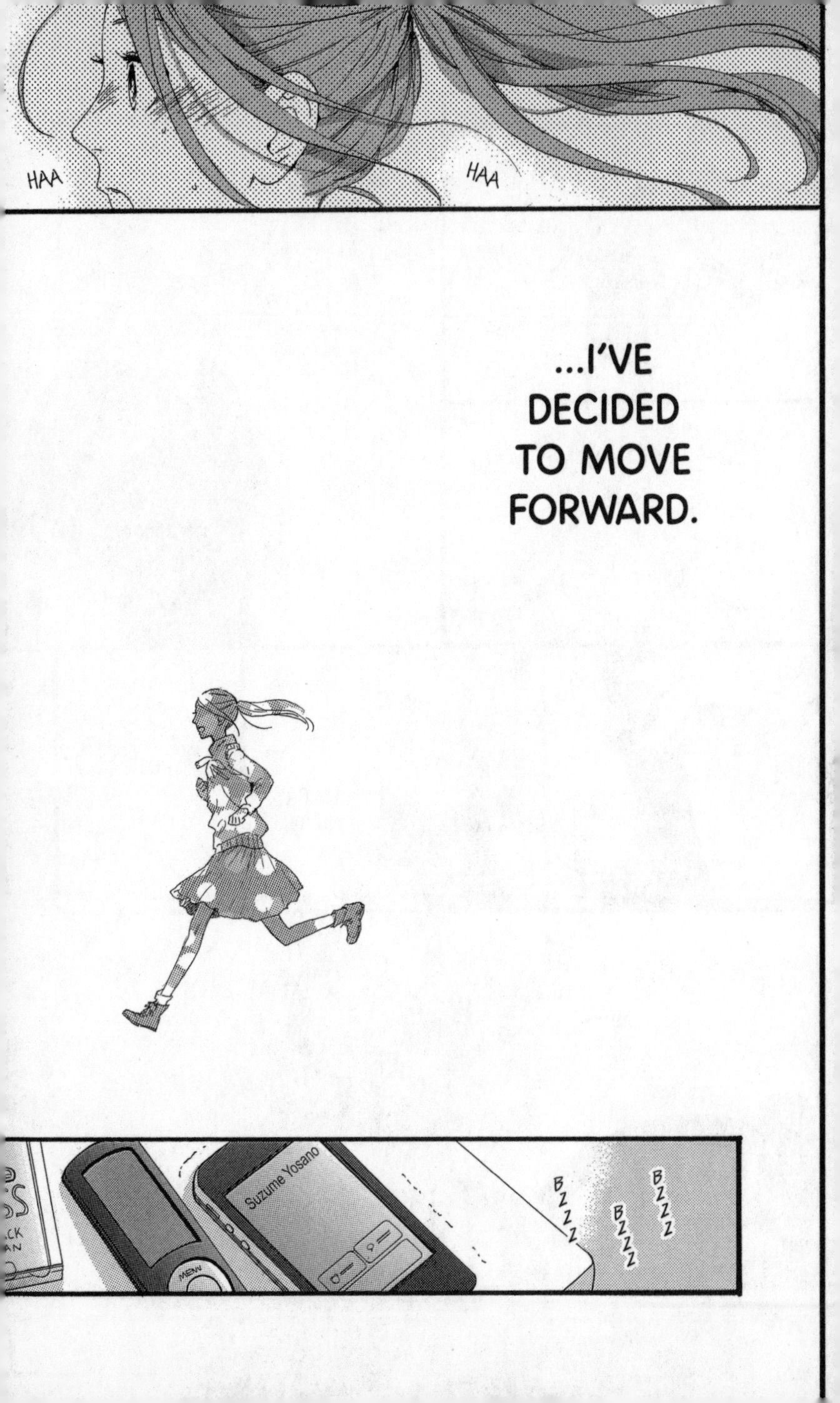
HAA
HAA
...I'VE DECIDED TO MOVE FORWARD.
BZZZ
BZZZ
BZZZ
Suzume Yosano

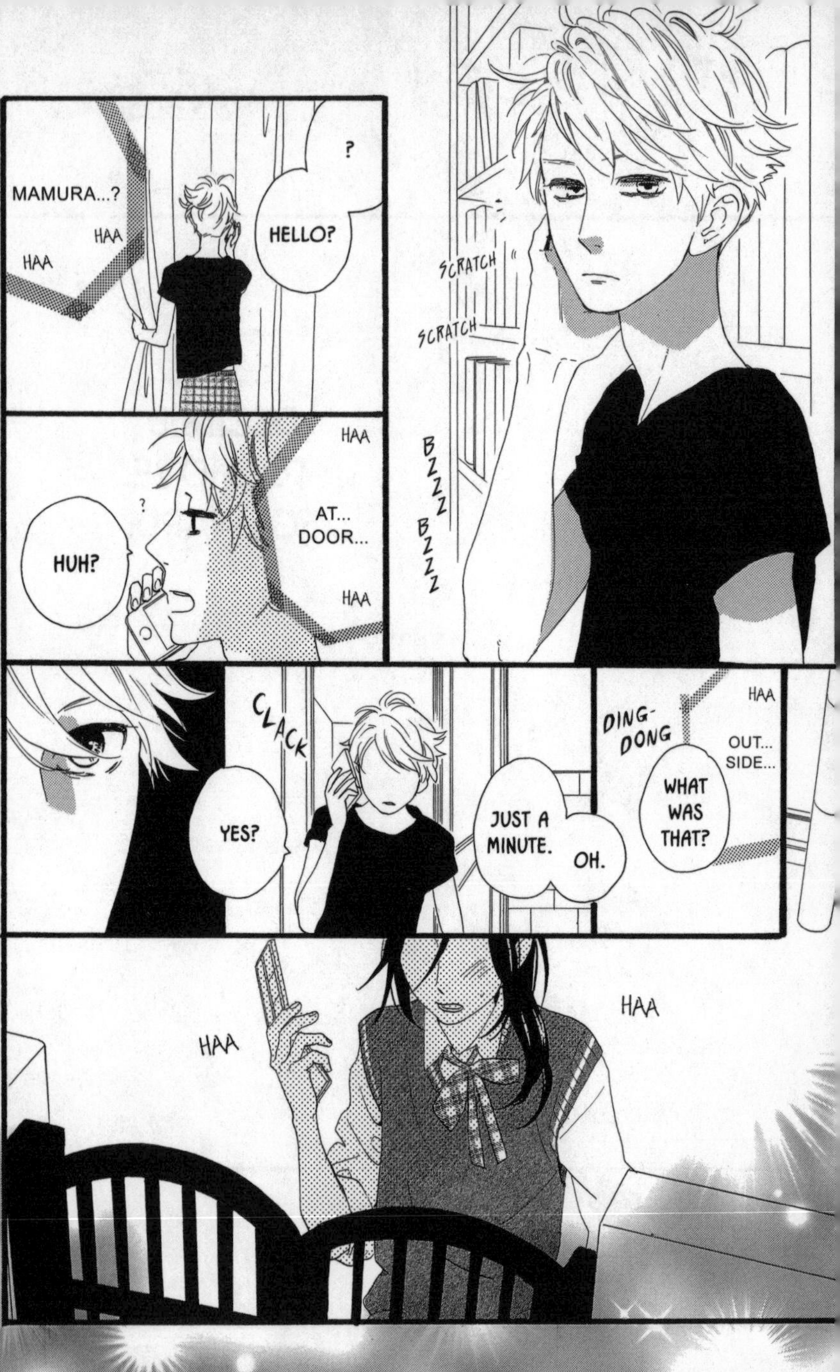
SCRATCH
SCRATCH
BZZZ
BZZZ
?
HELLO?
MAMURA...?
HAA
HAA
HAA
AT... DOOR...
HAA
HUH?
HAA
DING-DONG
OUT... SIDE...
WHAT WAS THAT?
OH.
JUST A MINUTE.
CLACK
YES?
HAA
HAA

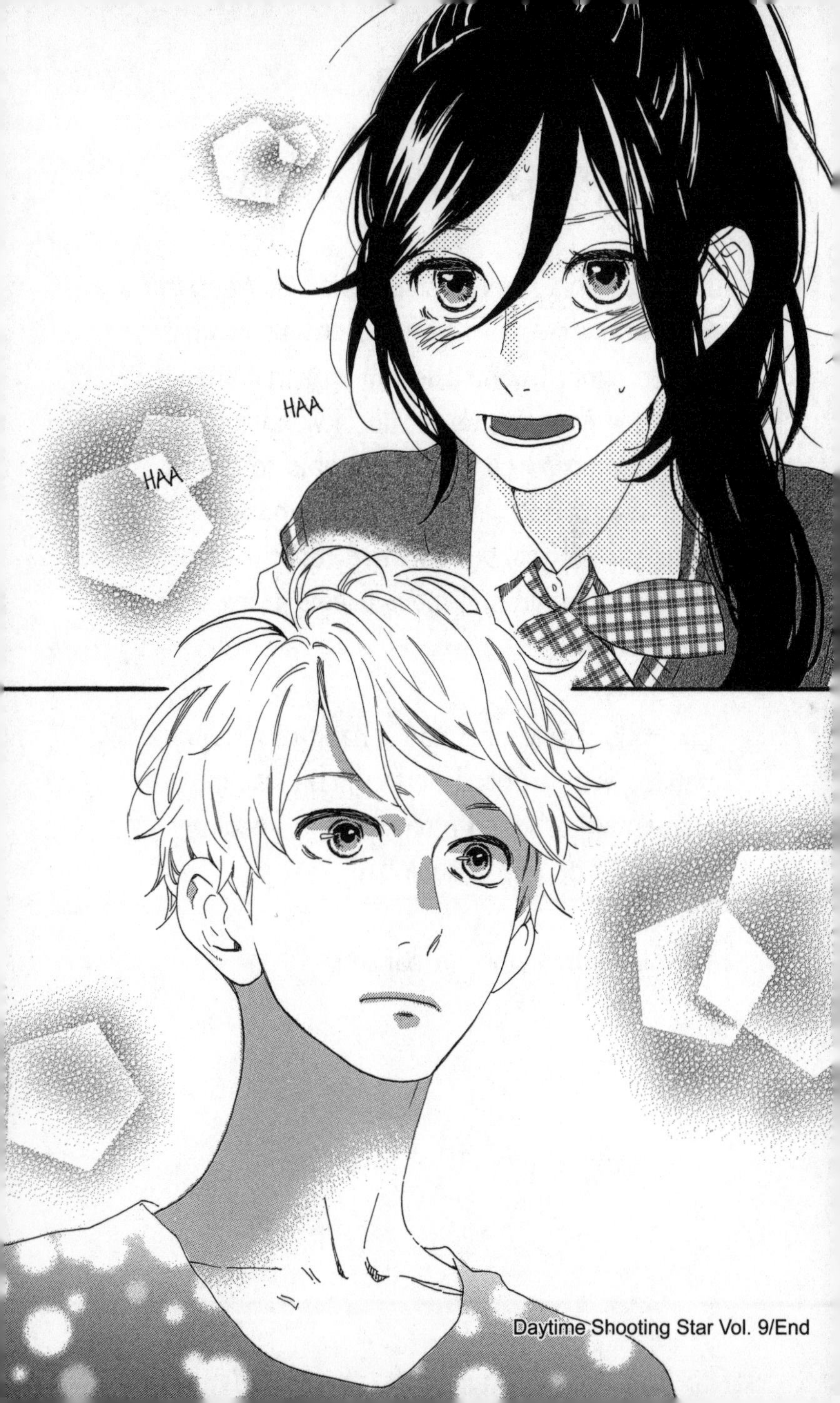
HAA
HAA
Daytime Shooting Star Vol. 9/End

About "More Than Words."

I created this story in celebration of *Margaret*'s 50th anniversary. At first, I didn't know what kind of story I wanted to tell, but that changed when my mother said to me, "I wonder if 50 years from now people will be able to choose their own gender." I'm not very good at writing futuristic stories, but I wanted to write something that would still move people years down the line.

Like this character, I had a habit of always walking with my head down when I was in elementary school. I often used to imagine myself walking on a huge ball.

I dedicate this story to Sakami.

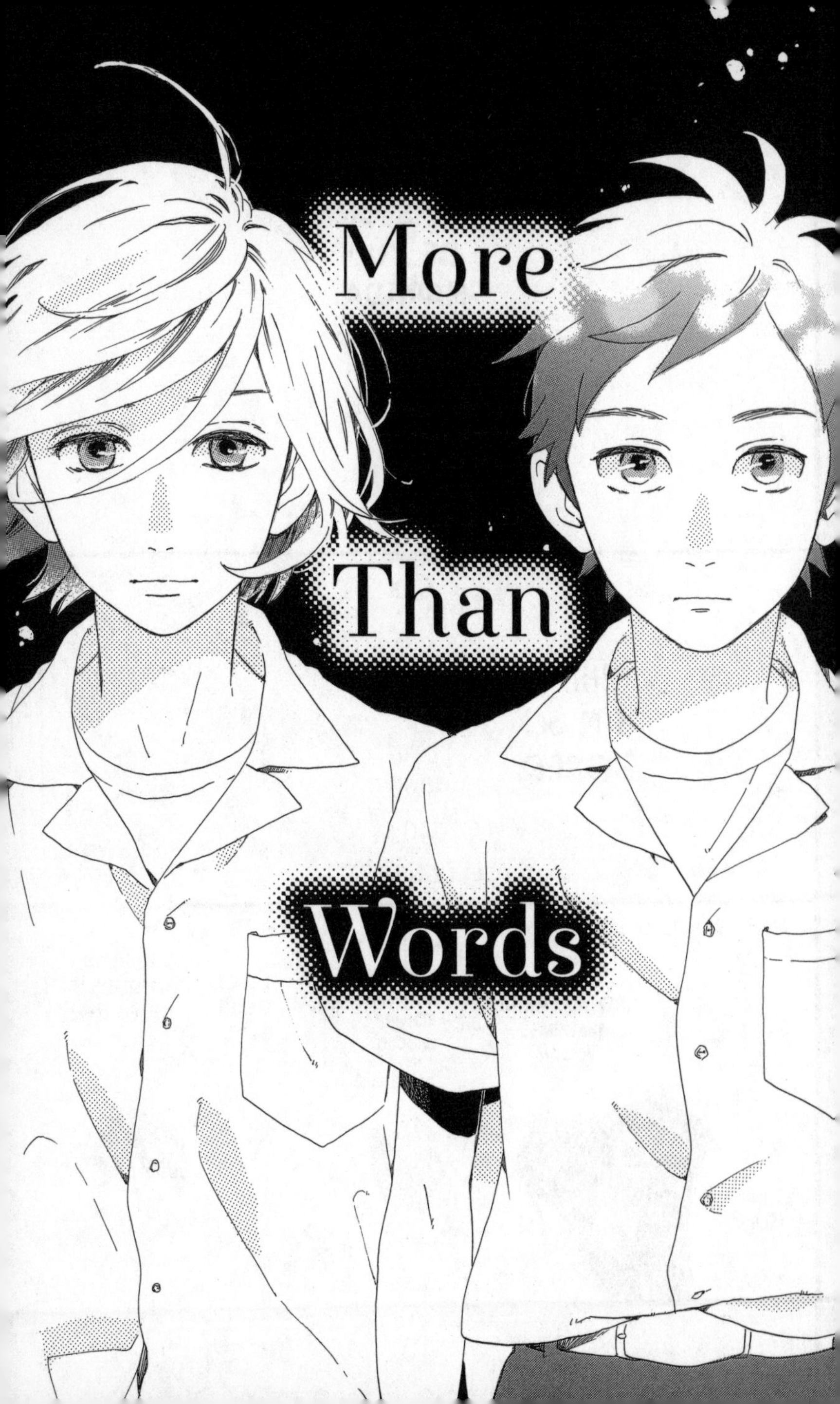
More
Than
Words

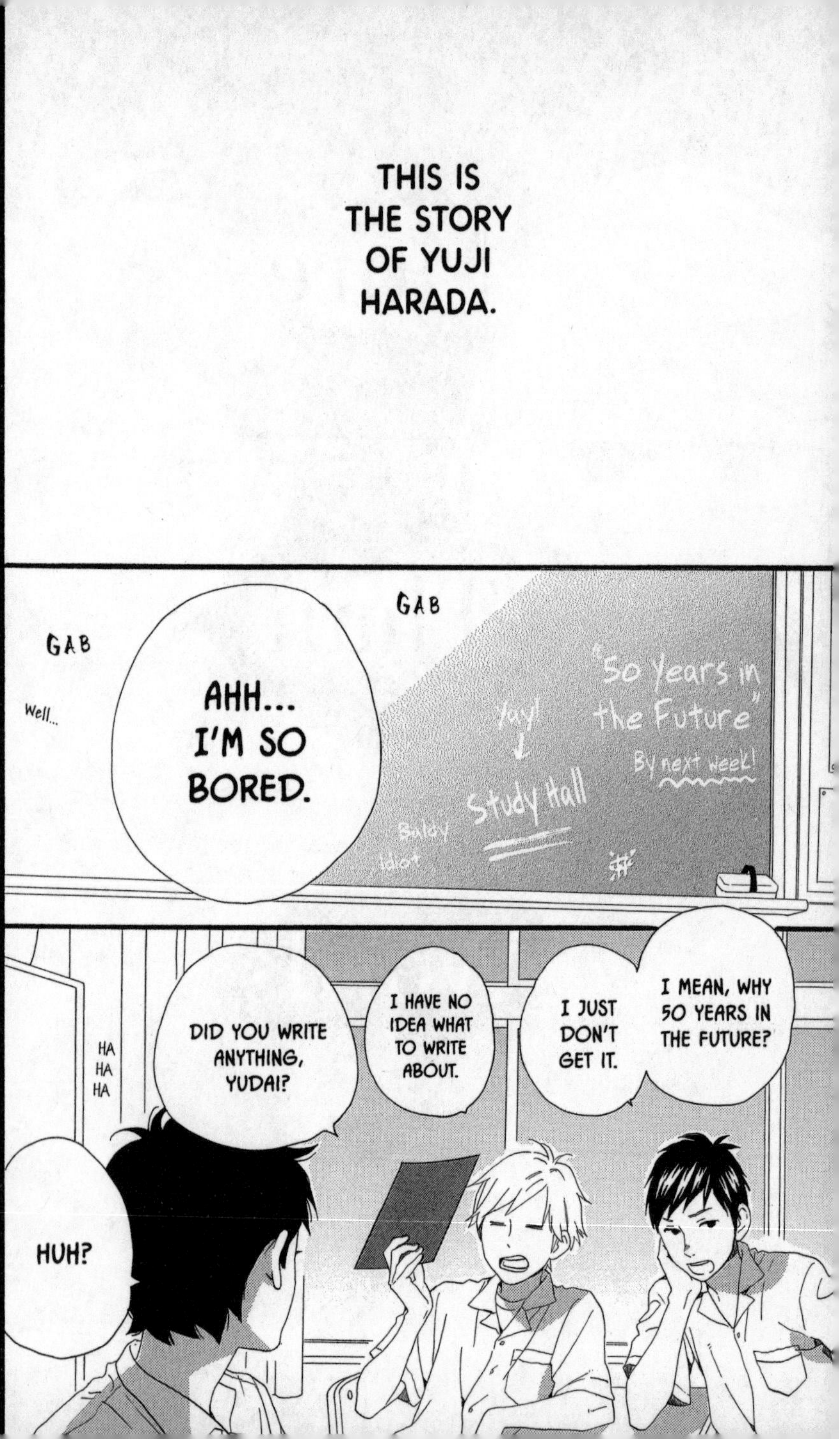
THIS IS THE STORY OF YUJI HARADA.
"50 Years in the Future"
By next week!
Yay!
Study Hall
Baldy
Idiot
GAB
AHH... I'M SO BORED.
GAB
Well...
I MEAN, WHY 50 YEARS IN THE FUTURE?
I JUST DON'T GET IT.
I HAVE NO IDEA WHAT TO WRITE ABOUT.
DID YOU WRITE ANYTHING, YUDAI?
HA HA HA
HUH?

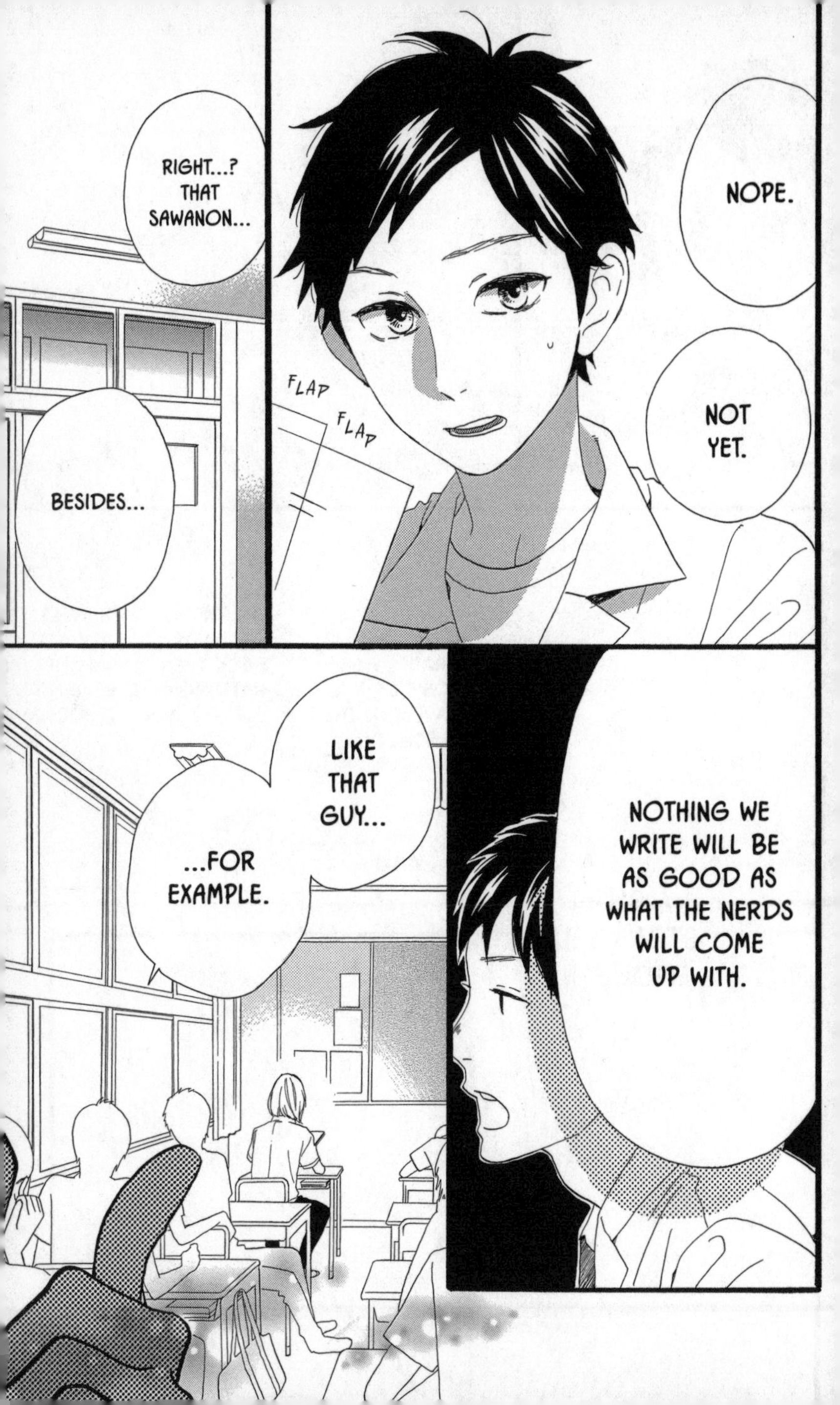
NOPE.
NOT YET.
FLAP
FLAP
RIGHT...? THAT SAWANON...
BESIDES...
NOTHING WE WRITE WILL BE AS GOOD AS WHAT THE NERDS WILL COME UP WITH.
LIKE THAT GUY...
...FOR EXAMPLE.

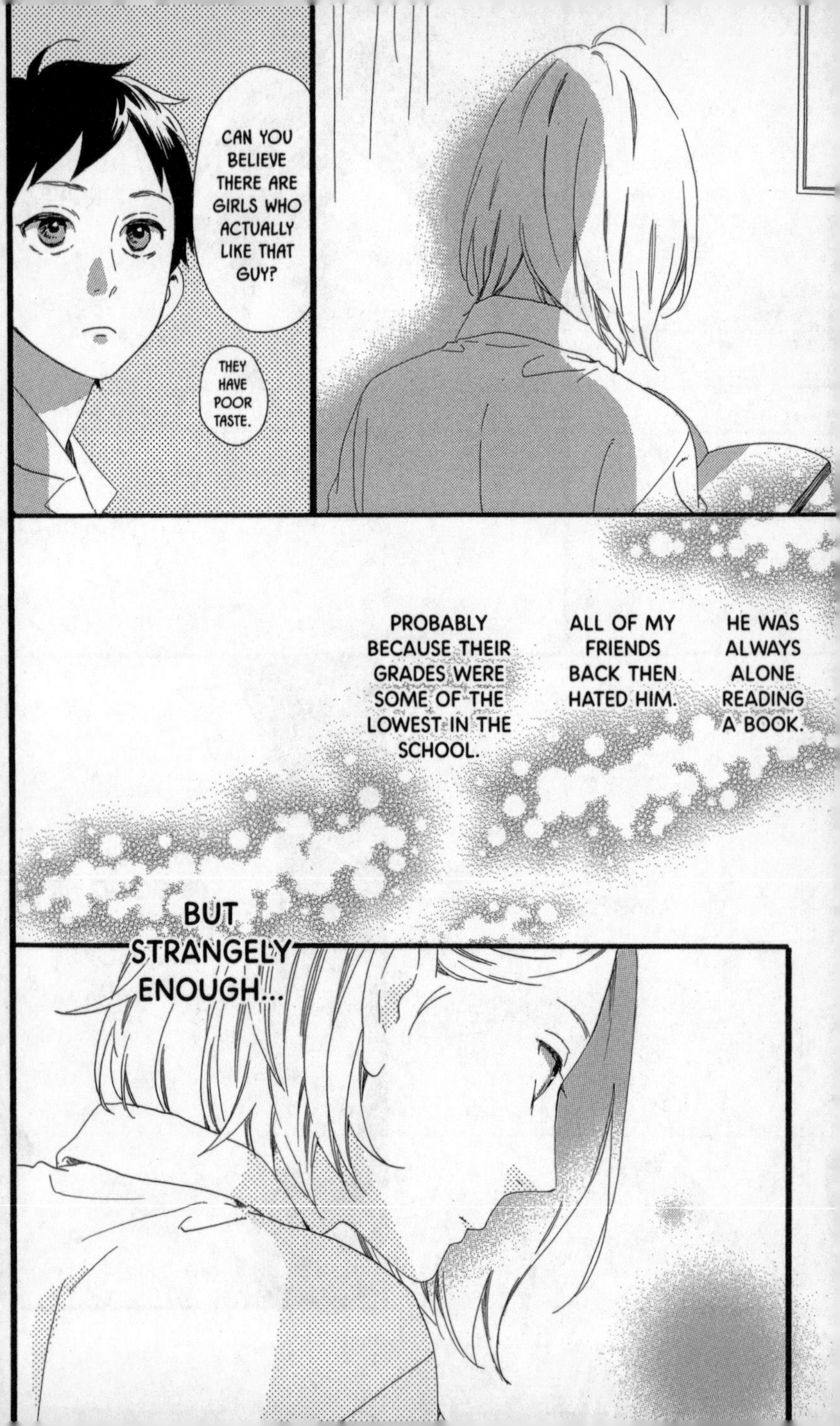
CAN YOU BELIEVE THERE ARE GIRLS WHO ACTUALLY LIKE THAT GUY?
THEY HAVE POOR TASTE.
HE WAS ALWAYS ALONE READING A BOOK.
ALL OF MY FRIENDS BACK THEN HATED HIM.
PROBABLY BECAUSE THEIR GRADES WERE SOME OF THE LOWEST IN THE SCHOOL.
BUT STRANGELY ENOUGH...

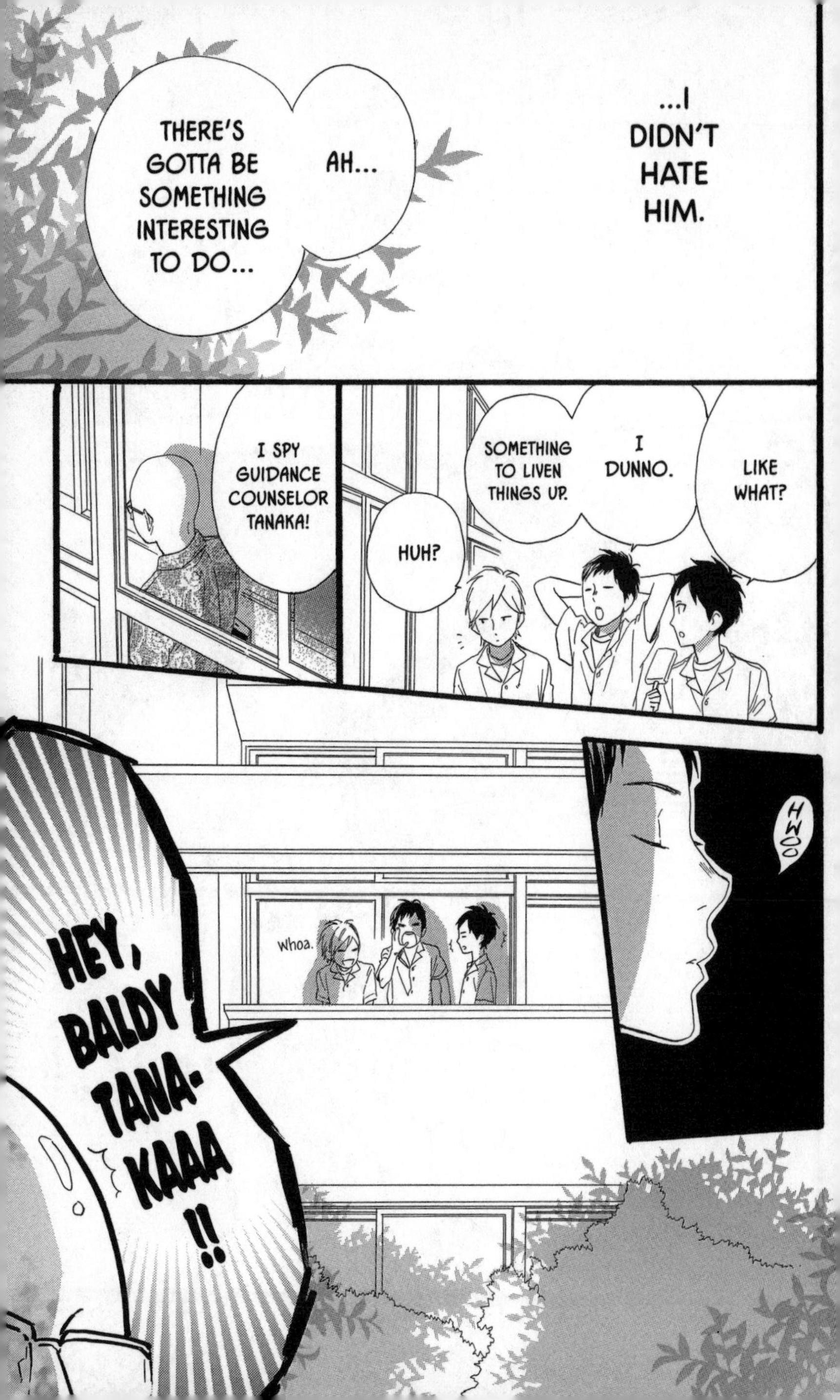
...I DIDN'T HATE HIM.
AH...
THERE'S GOTTA BE SOMETHING INTERESTING TO DO...
LIKE WHAT?
I DUNNO.
SOMETHING TO LIVEN THINGS UP.
HUH?
I SPY GUIDANCE COUNSELOR TANAKA!
HWOO
Whoa.
HEY, BALDY TANA-KAAA!!

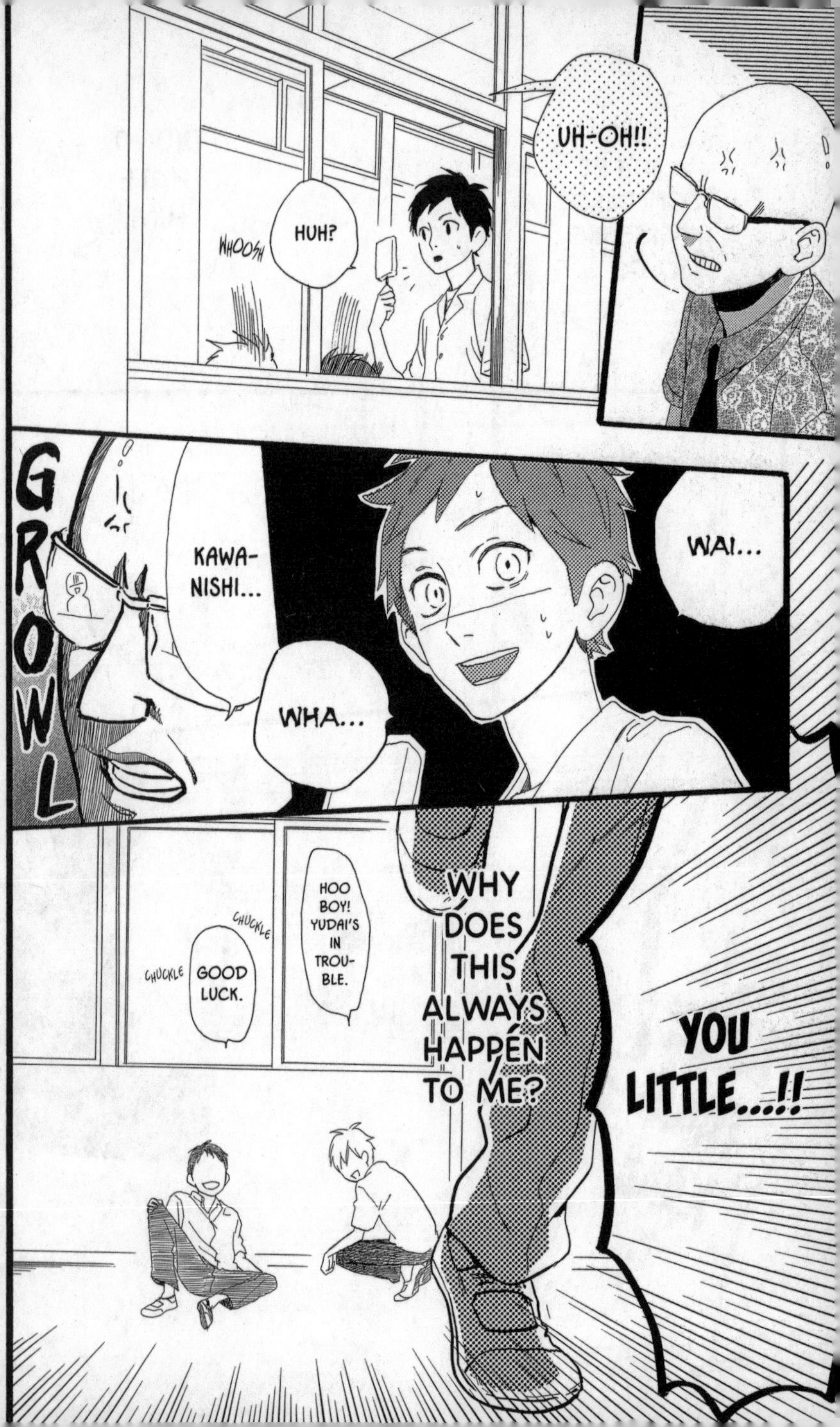
UH-OH!!
HUH?
WHOOSH
WAI...
KAWA-NISHI...
WHA...
GROWL
YOU LITTLE...!!
WHY DOES THIS ALWAYS HAPPEN TO ME?
HOO BOY! YUDAI'S IN TROUBLE.
CHUCKLE
GOOD LUCK.
CHUCKLE

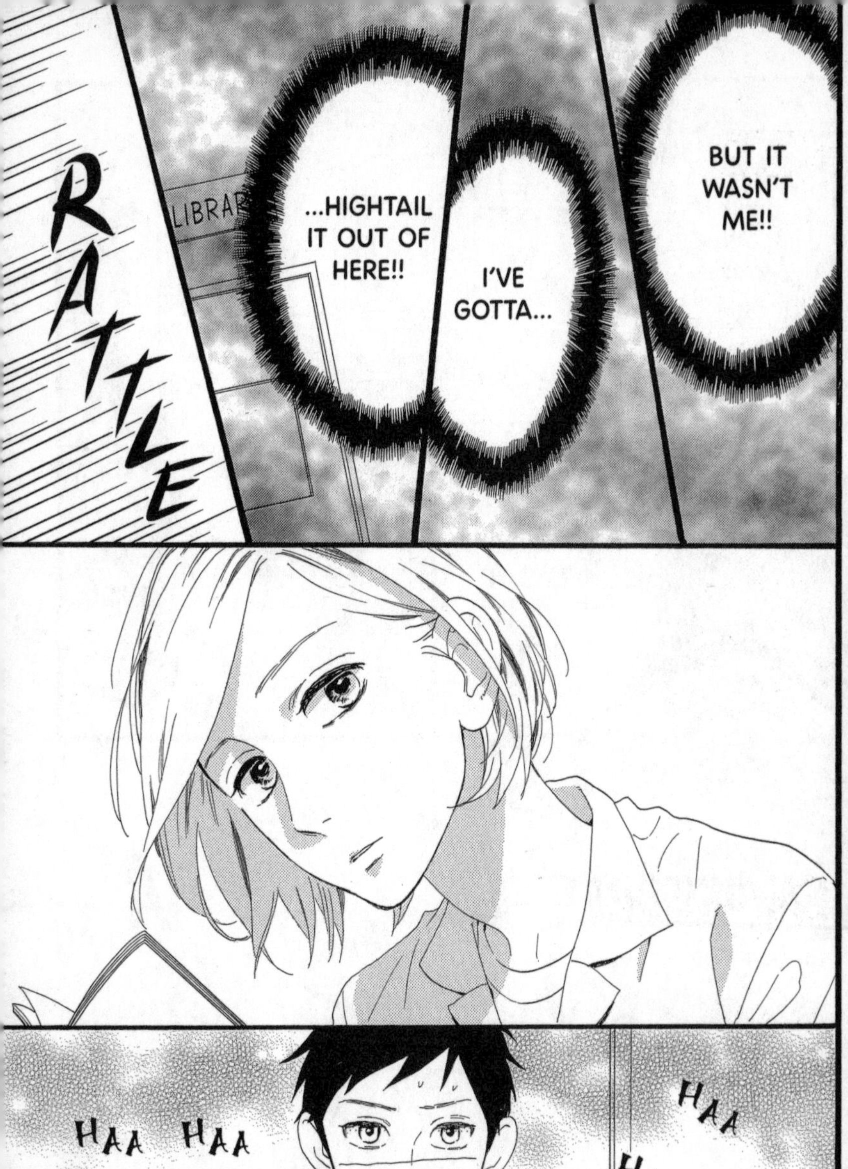
BUT IT WASN'T ME!!
I'VE GOTTA...
...HIGHTAIL IT OUT OF HERE!!
LIBRAR
RATTLE
HAA
HAA
HAA HAA

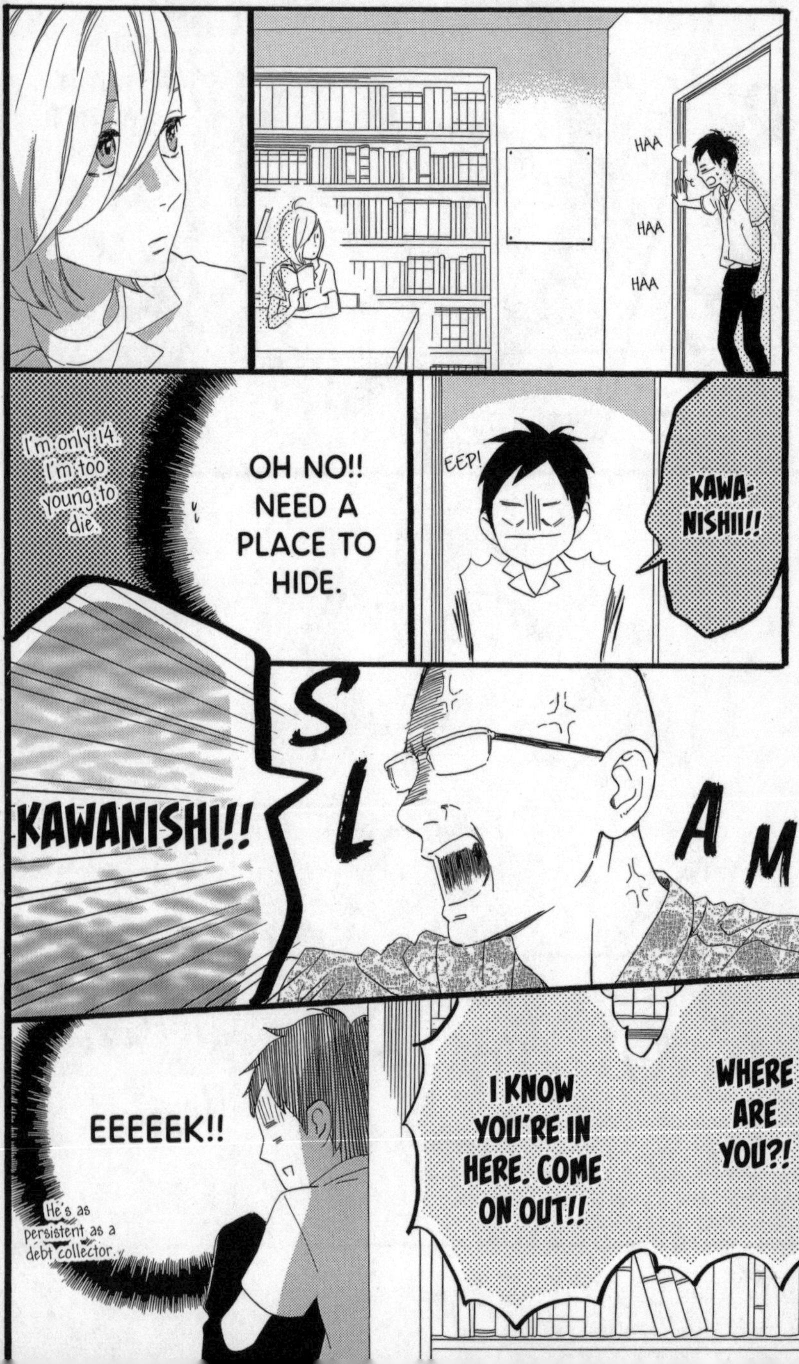
HAA
HAA
HAA
KAWA-NISHII!!
EEP!
OH NO!! NEED A PLACE TO HIDE.
I'm only 14. I'm too young to die.
S L A M
KAWANISHI!!
WHERE ARE YOU?!
I KNOW YOU'RE IN HERE. COME ON OUT!!
EEEEEK!!
He's as persistent as a debt collector.

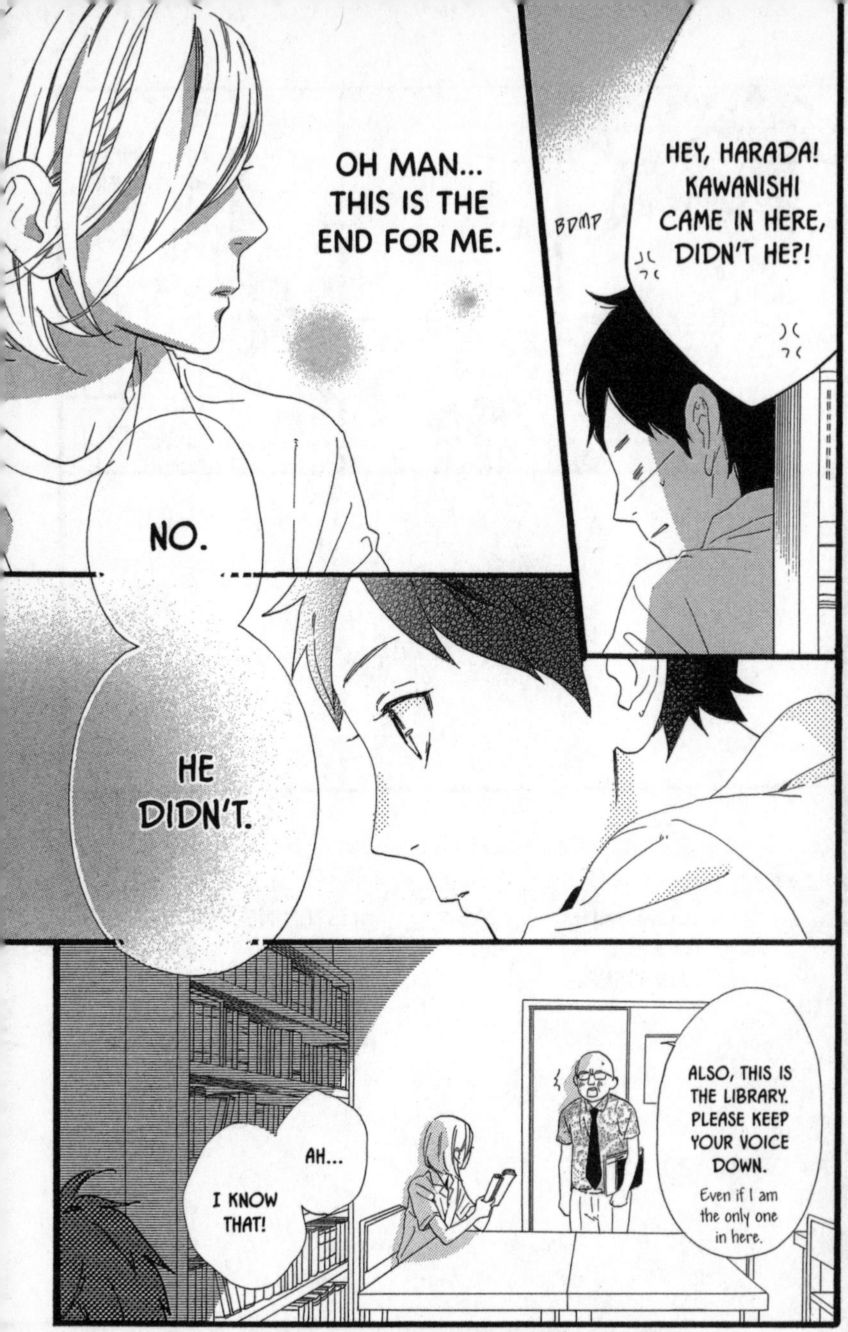

HEY, HARADA! KAWANISHI CAME IN HERE, DIDN'T HE?!
BDMP
OH MAN... THIS IS THE END FOR ME.
NO.
HE DIDN'T.
ALSO, THIS IS THE LIBRARY. PLEASE KEEP YOUR VOICE DOWN.
Even if I am the only one in here.
AH...
I KNOW THAT!

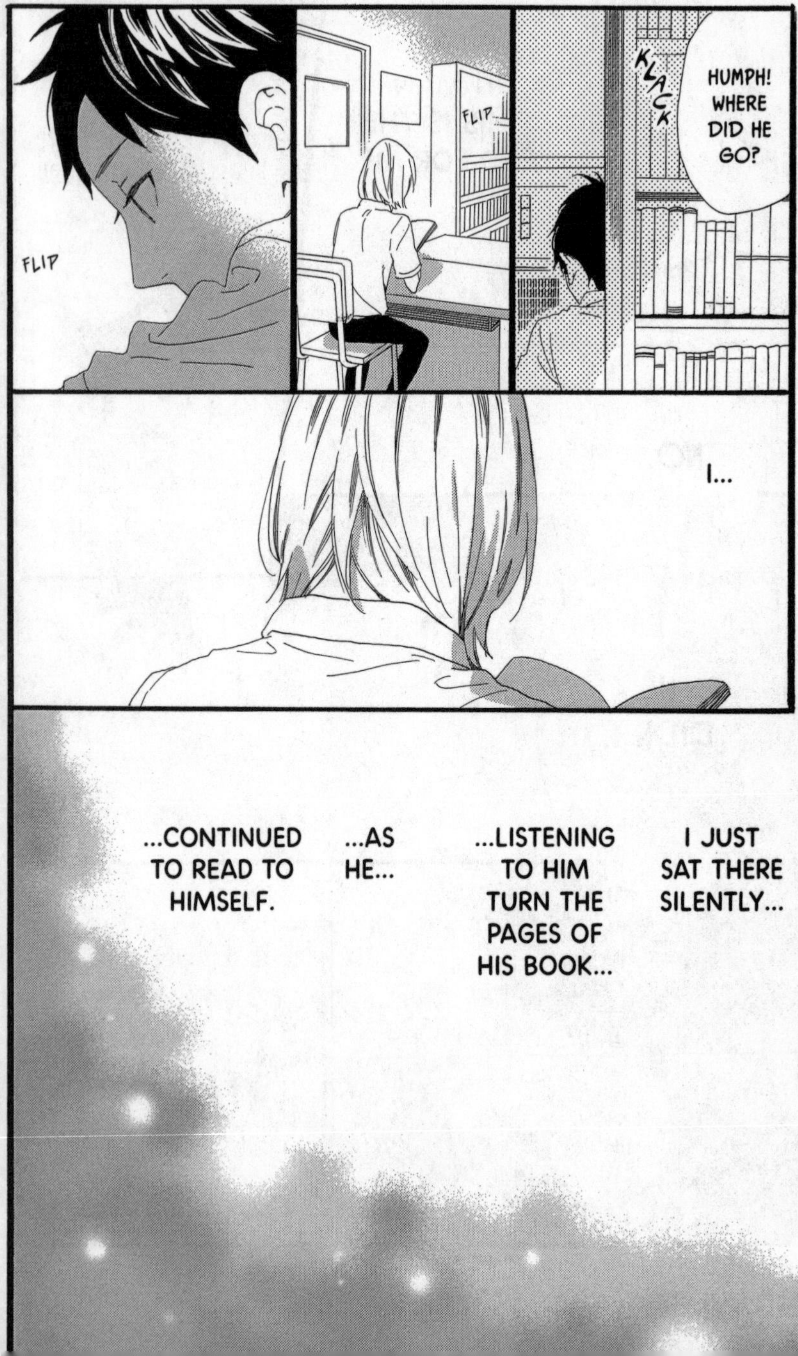
KLACK
HUMPH! WHERE DID HE GO?
FLIP
FLIP
I...
I JUST SAT THERE SILENTLY...
...LISTENING TO HIM TURN THE PAGES OF HIS BOOK...
...AS HE...
...CONTINUED TO READ TO HIMSELF.

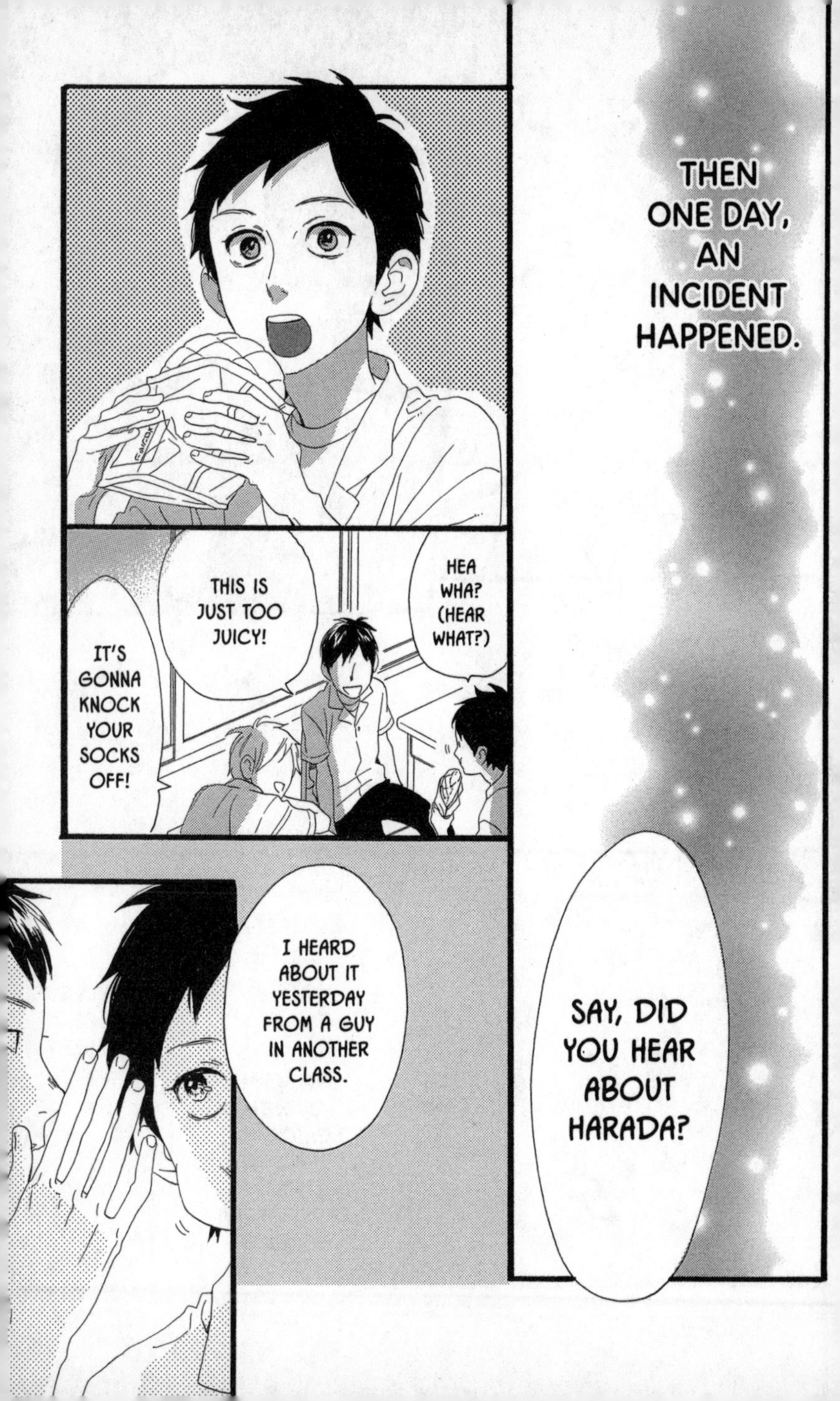

THEN ONE DAY, AN INCIDENT HAPPENED.
SAY, DID YOU HEAR ABOUT HARADA?
HEA WHA? (HEAR WHAT?)
THIS IS JUST TOO JUICY!
IT'S GONNA KNOCK YOUR SOCKS OFF!
I HEARD ABOUT IT YESTERDAY FROM A GUY IN ANOTHER CLASS.

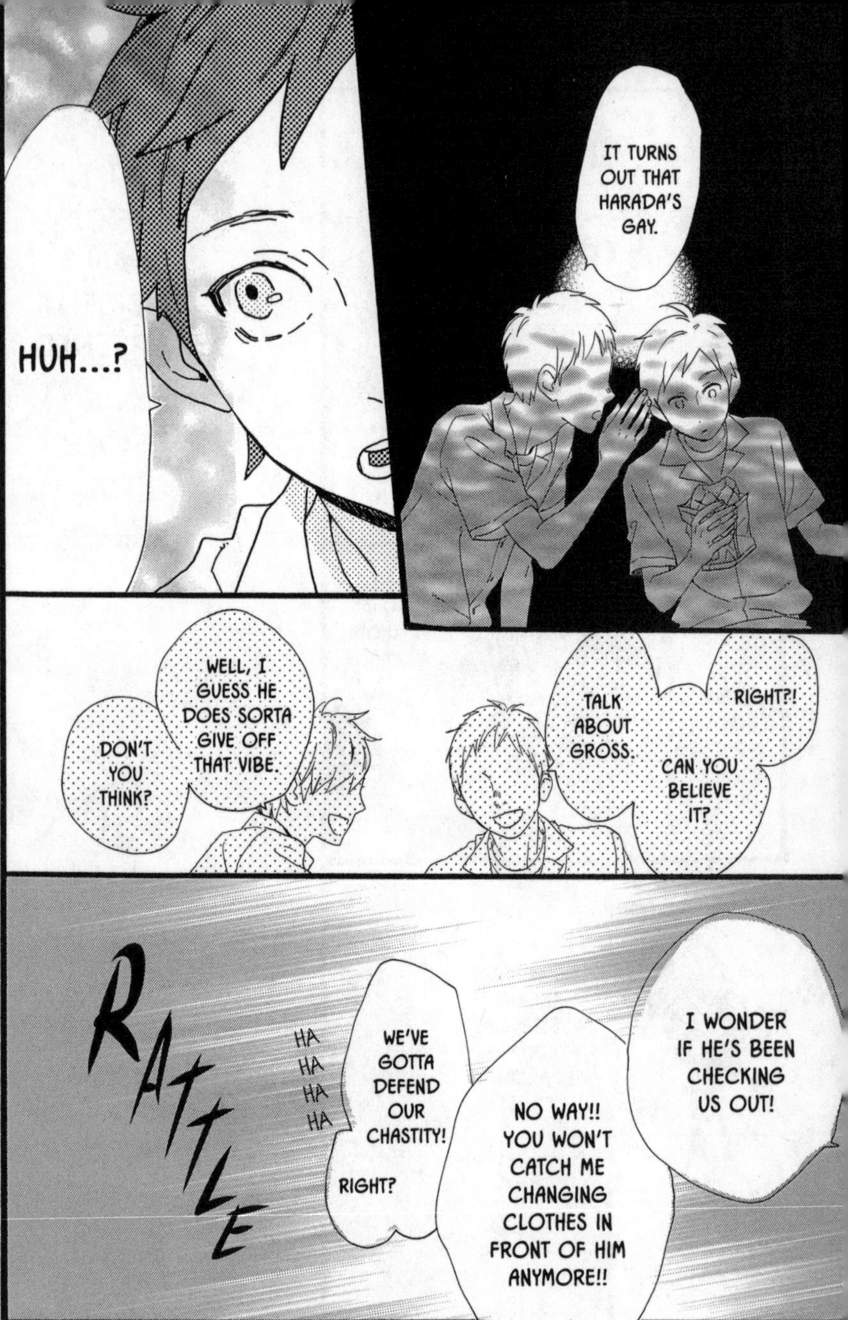
IT TURNS OUT THAT HARADA'S GAY.
HUH...?
RIGHT?!
TALK ABOUT GROSS.
CAN YOU BELIEVE IT?
WELL, I GUESS HE DOES SORTA GIVE OFF THAT VIBE.
DON'T YOU THINK?
I WONDER IF HE'S BEEN CHECKING US OUT!
NO WAY!! YOU WON'T CATCH ME CHANGING CLOTHES IN FRONT OF HIM ANYMORE!!
WE'VE GOTTA DEFEND OUR CHASTITY!
RIGHT?
HA HA HA HA
RATTLE

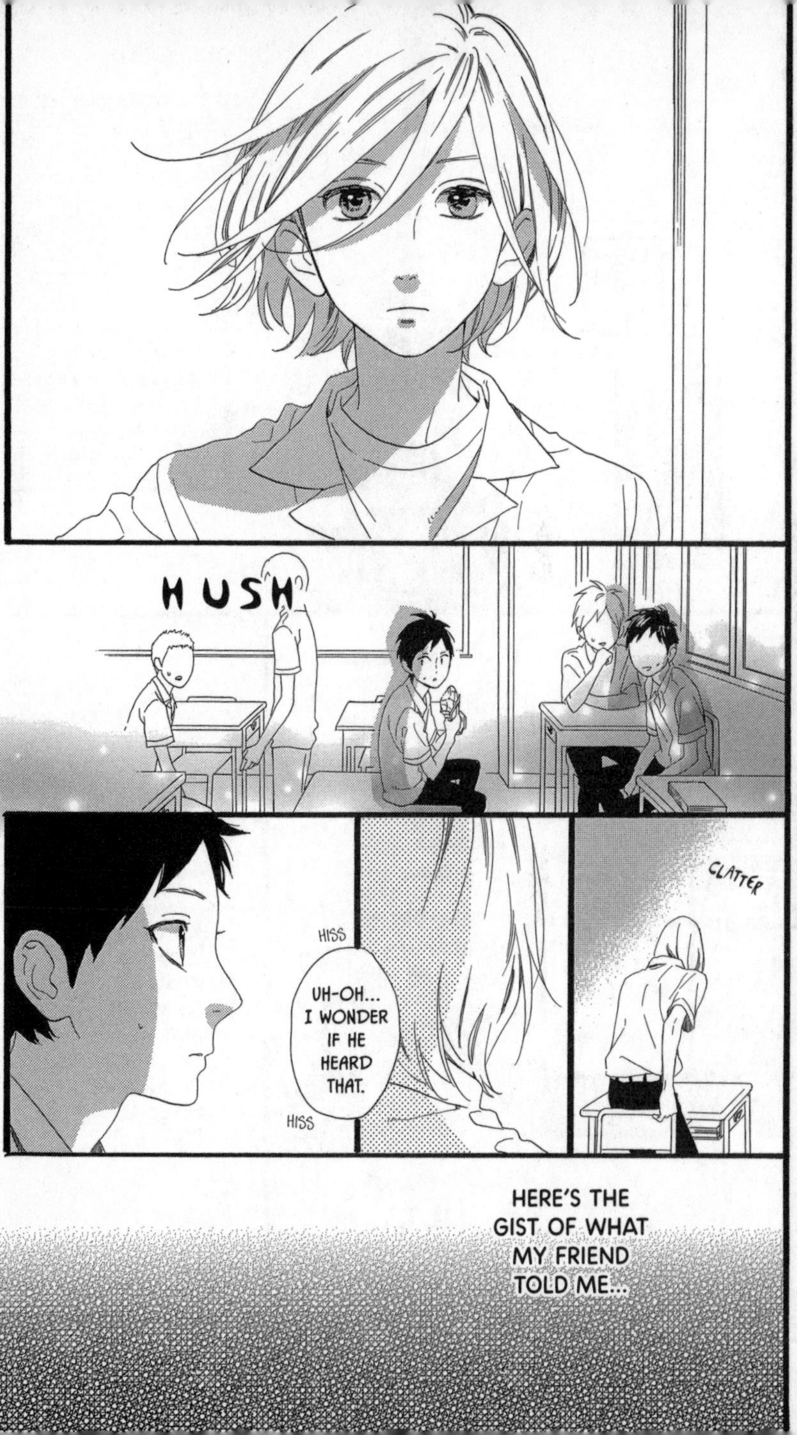
HUSH
CLATTER
HISS
UH-OH... I WONDER IF HE HEARD THAT.
HISS
HERE'S THE GIST OF WHAT MY FRIEND TOLD ME...

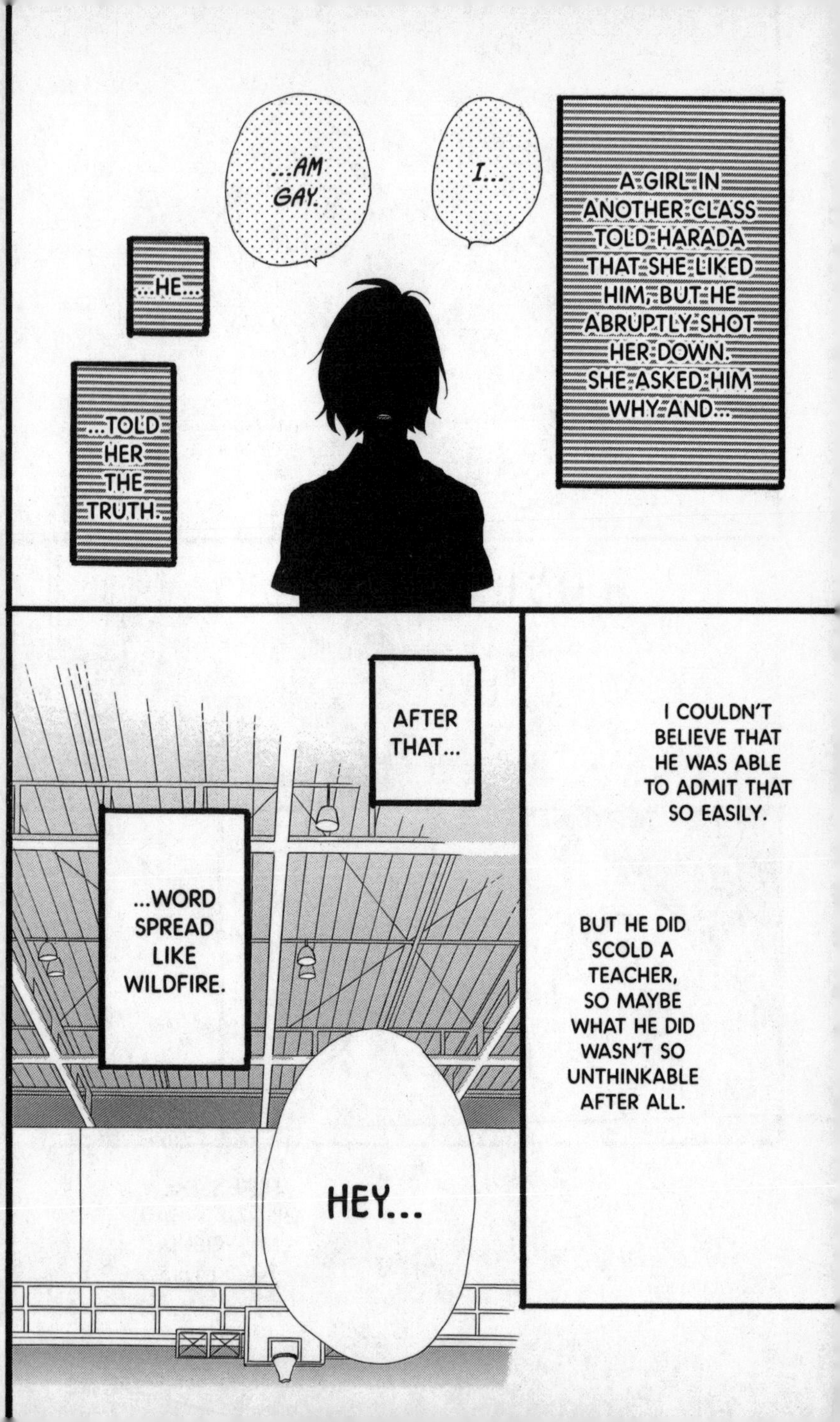
A GIRL IN ANOTHER CLASS TOLD HARADA THAT SHE LIKED HIM, BUT HE ABRUPTLY SHOT HER DOWN. SHE ASKED HIM WHY AND...
I...
...AM GAY.
...HE...
...TOLD HER THE TRUTH.
I COULDN'T BELIEVE THAT HE WAS ABLE TO ADMIT THAT SO EASILY.
BUT HE DID SCOLD A TEACHER, SO MAYBE WHAT HE DID WASN'T SO UNTHINKABLE AFTER ALL.
AFTER THAT...
...WORD SPREAD LIKE WILDFIRE.
HEY...

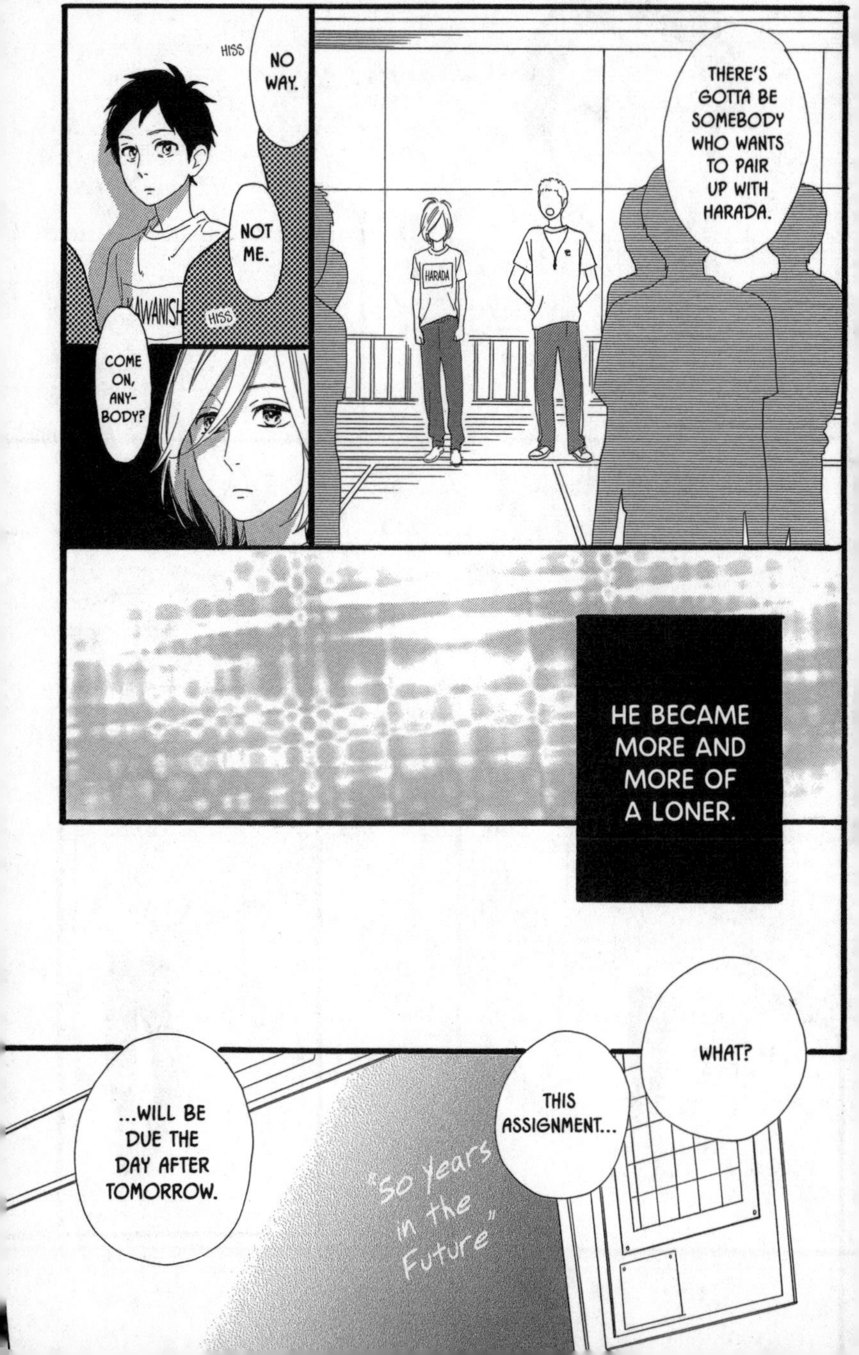
THERE'S GOTTA BE SOMEBODY WHO WANTS TO PAIR UP WITH HARADA.
HARADA
HISS
NO WAY.
NOT ME.
KAWANISH
HISS
COME ON, ANY-BODY?
HE BECAME MORE AND MORE OF A LONER.
WHAT?
THIS ASSIGNMENT...
...WILL BE DUE THE DAY AFTER TOMORROW.
"50 Years in the Future"

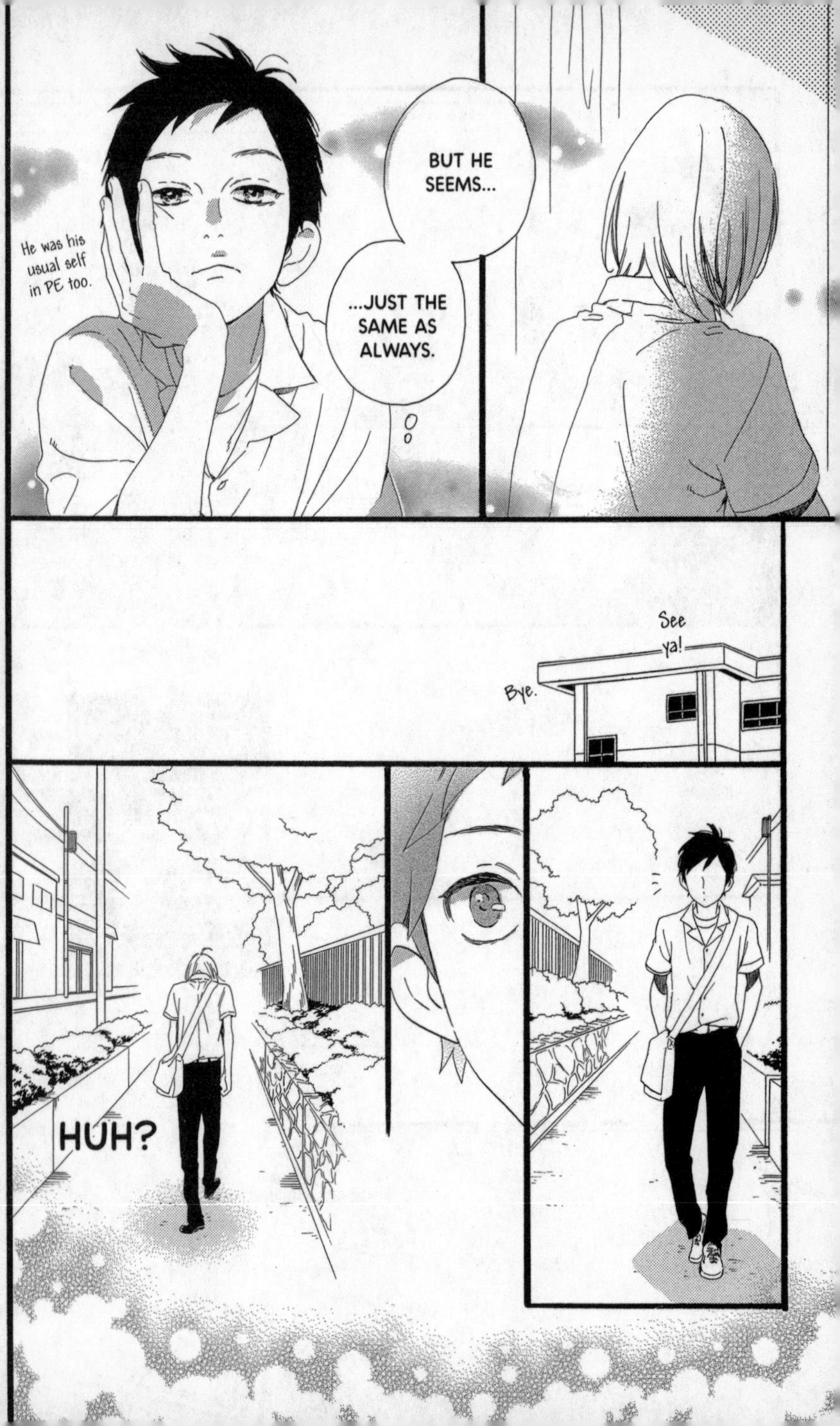
BUT HE SEEMS...
...JUST THE SAME AS ALWAYS.
He was his usual self in PE too.
See ya!
Bye.
HUH?

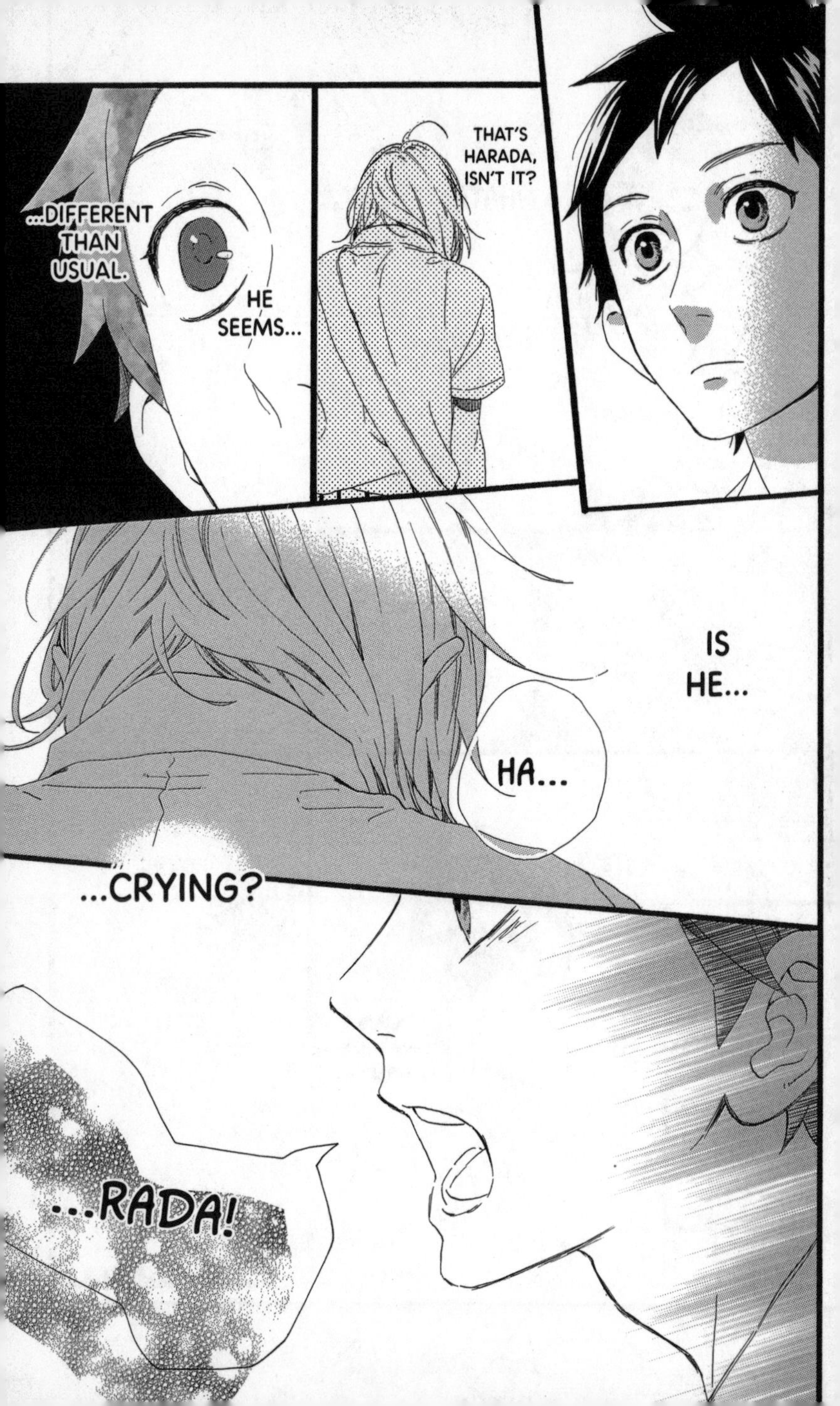
THAT'S HARADA, ISN'T IT?
HE SEEMS...
...DIFFERENT THAN USUAL.
IS HE...
HA...
...CRYING?
...RADA!

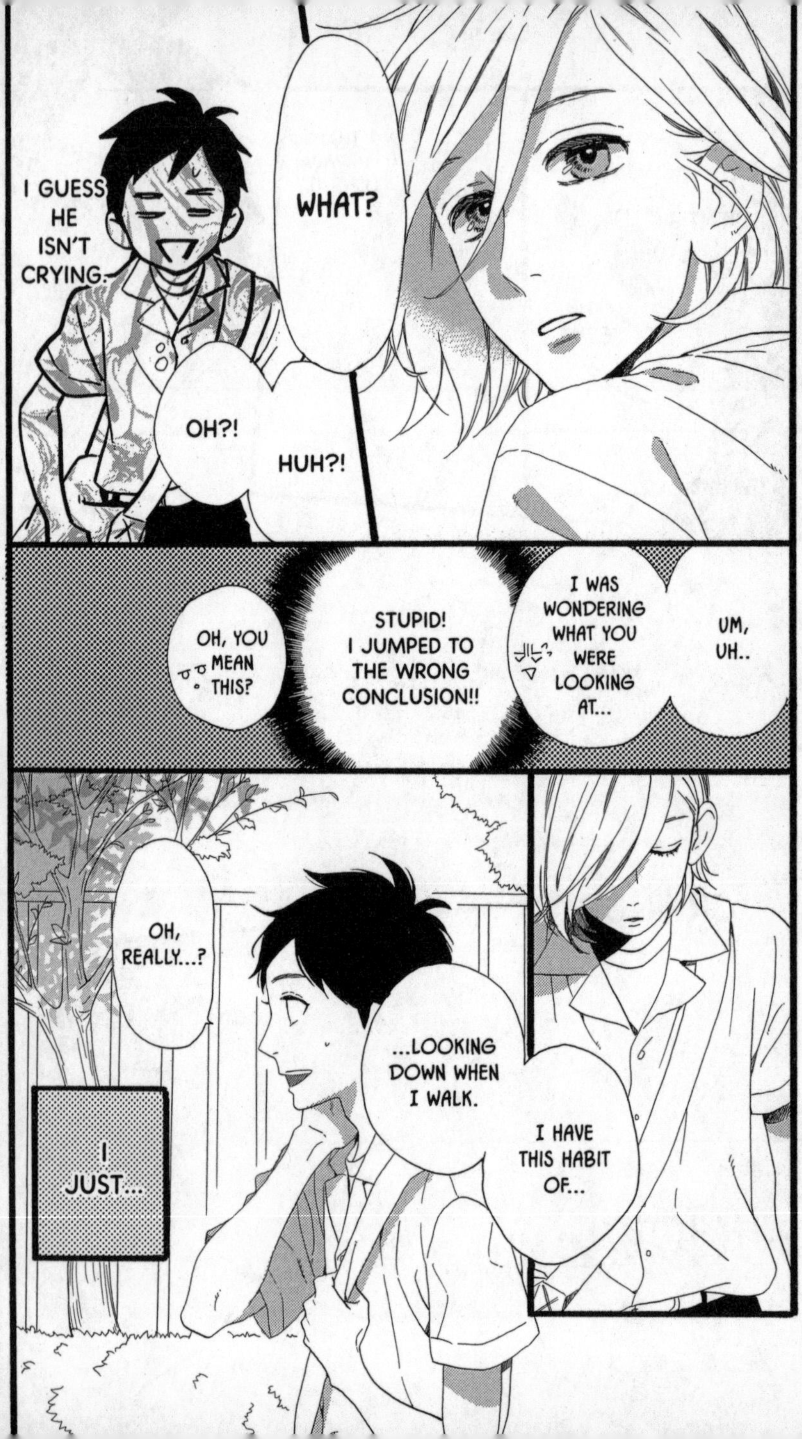
WHAT?
I GUESS HE ISN'T CRYING.
OH?!
HUH?!
UM, UH..
I WAS WONDERING WHAT YOU WERE LOOKING AT...
STUPID! I JUMPED TO THE WRONG CONCLUSION!!
OH, YOU MEAN THIS?
I HAVE THIS HABIT OF...
...LOOKING DOWN WHEN I WALK.
OH, REALLY...?
I JUST...

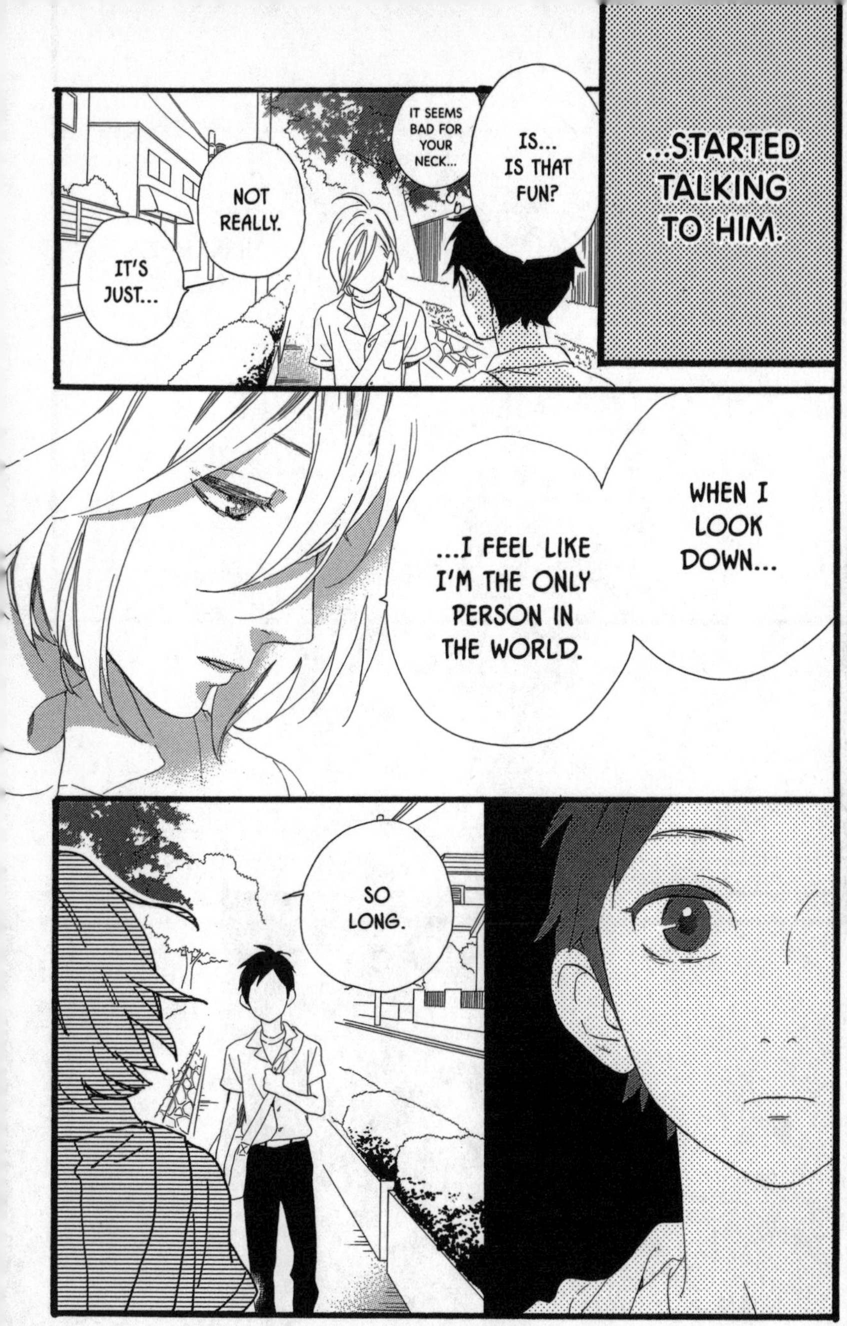
...STARTED TALKING TO HIM.
IS... IS THAT FUN?
IT SEEMS BAD FOR YOUR NECK...
NOT REALLY.
IT'S JUST...
WHEN I LOOK DOWN...
...I FEEL LIKE I'M THE ONLY PERSON IN THE WORLD.
SO LONG.

THANKS FOR TALKING TO ME.

WHEN HE THANKED ME...

...FOR THE FIRST AND ONLY TIME IN MY LIFE...

...I GOT CHOKED UP.

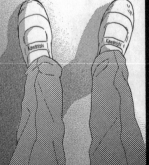

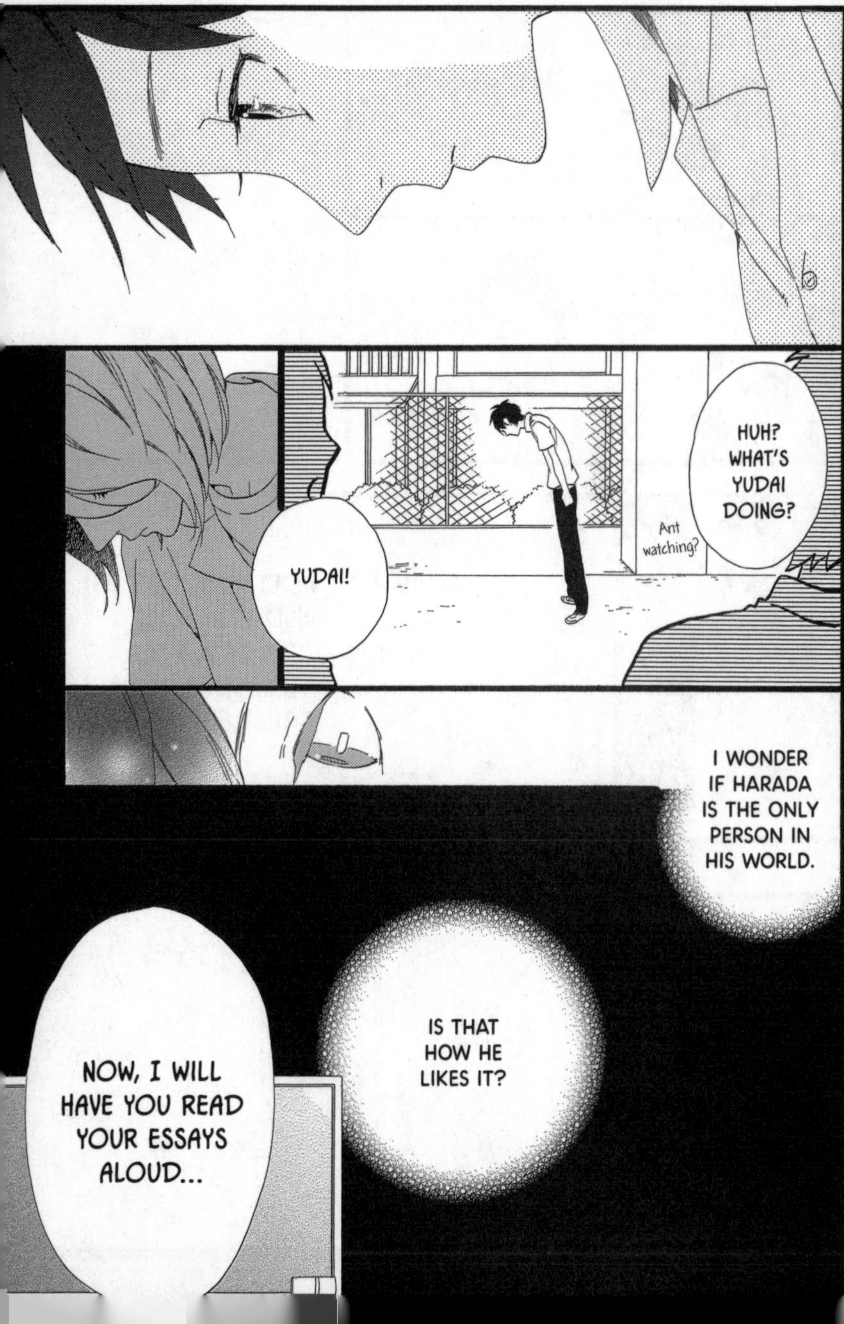
HUH? WHAT'S YUDAI DOING?
Ant watching?
YUDAI!
I WONDER IF HARADA IS THE ONLY PERSON IN HIS WORLD.
IS THAT HOW HE LIKES IT?
NOW, I WILL HAVE YOU READ YOUR ESSAYS ALOUD...

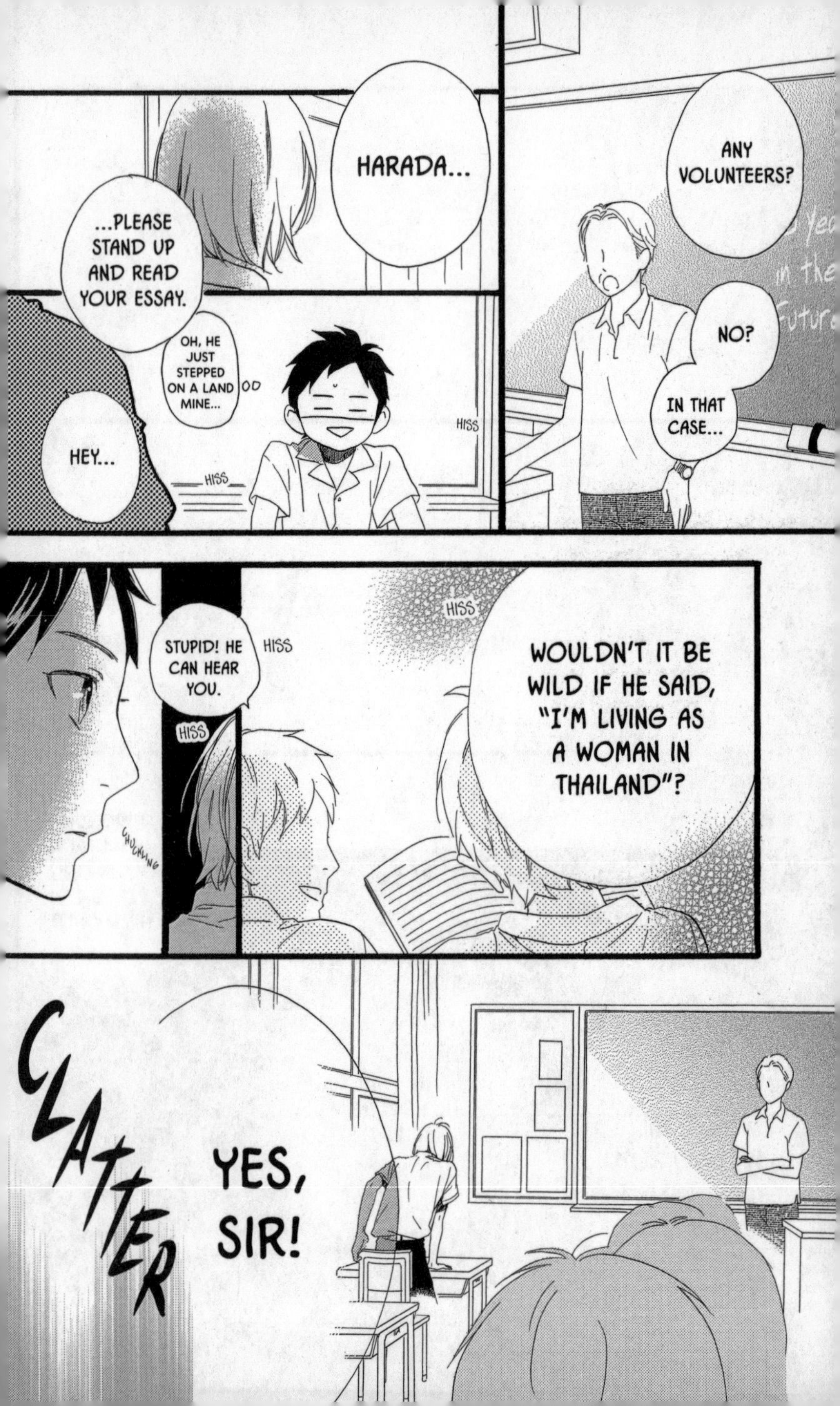
ANY VOLUNTEERS?
NO?
IN THAT CASE...
HARADA...
...PLEASE STAND UP AND READ YOUR ESSAY.
OH, HE JUST STEPPED ON A LAND MINE...
HISS
HEY...
HISS
HISS
WOULDN'T IT BE WILD IF HE SAID, "I'M LIVING AS A WOMAN IN THAILAND"?
HISS
STUPID! HE CAN HEAR YOU.
HISS
CHUCKLING
YES, SIR!
CLATTER

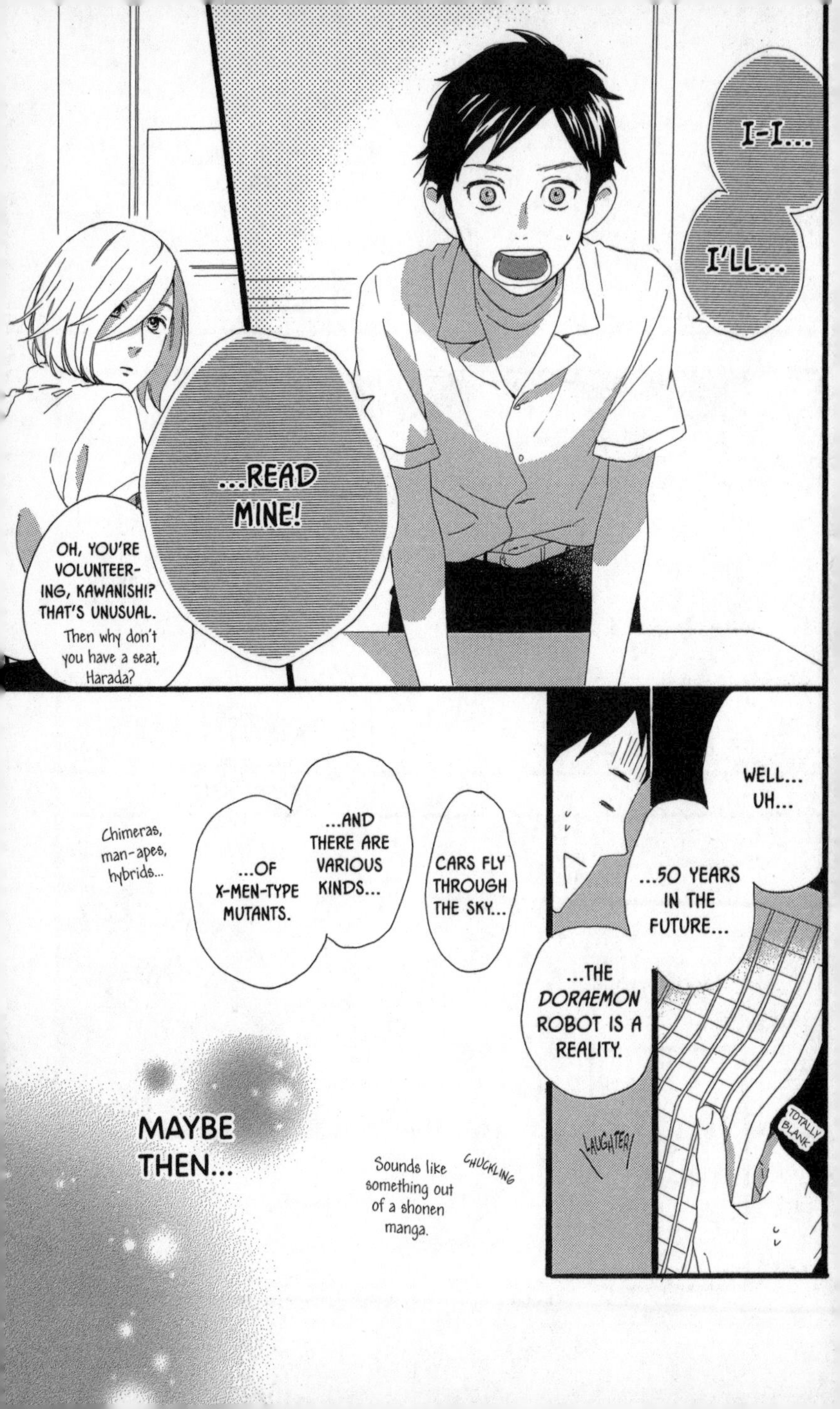
I-I...
I'LL...
...READ MINE!
OH, YOU'RE VOLUNTEERING, KAWANISHI? THAT'S UNUSUAL.
Then why don't you have a seat, Harada?
WELL... UH...
...50 YEARS IN THE FUTURE...
...THE *DORAEMON* ROBOT IS A REALITY.
TOTALLY BLANK
LAUGHTER!
CARS FLY THROUGH THE SKY...
...AND THERE ARE VARIOUS KINDS...
...OF X-MEN-TYPE MUTANTS.
Chimeras, man-apes, hybrids...
CHUCKLING
Sounds like something out of a shonen manga.
MAYBE THEN...

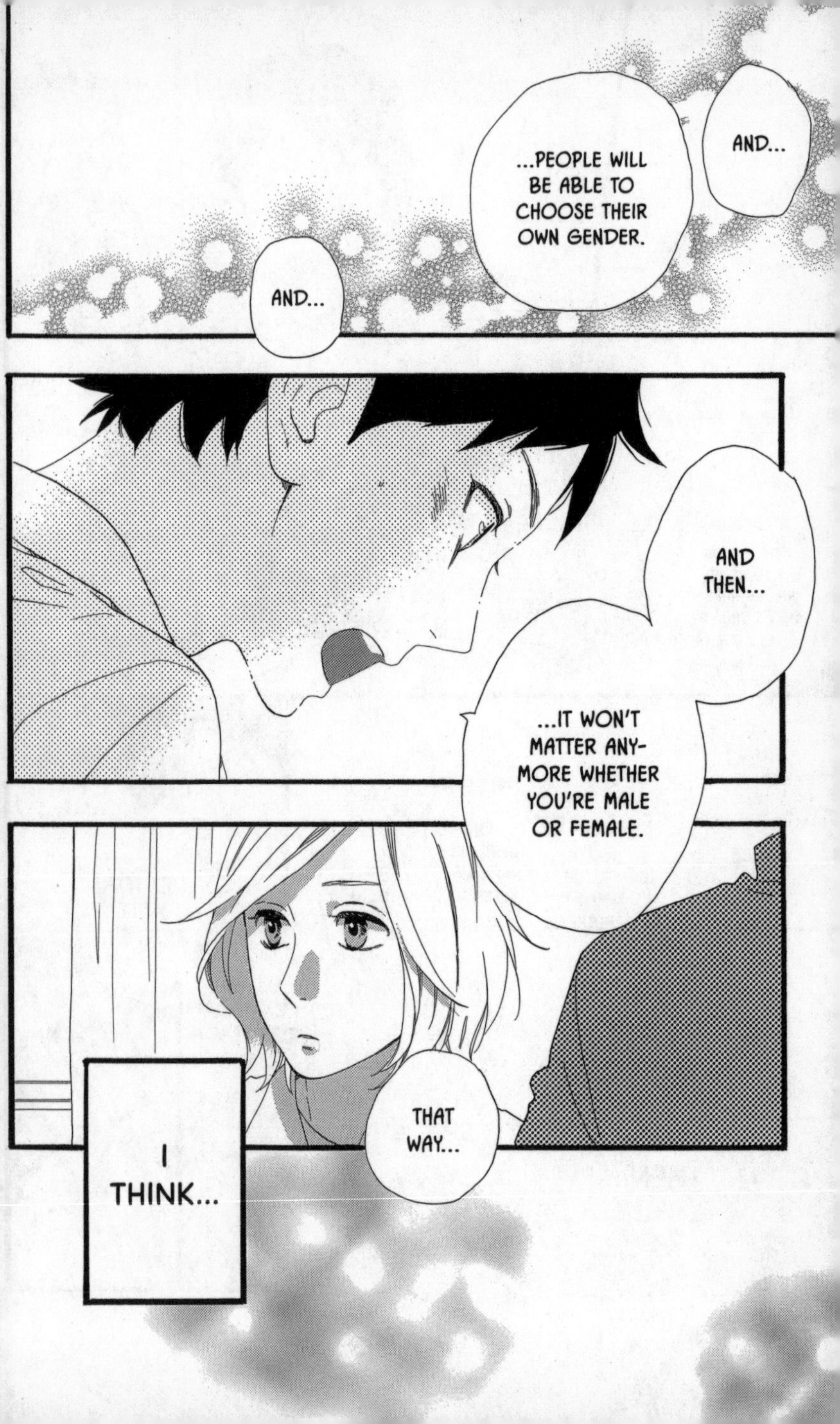
AND...
...PEOPLE WILL BE ABLE TO CHOOSE THEIR OWN GENDER.
AND...
AND THEN...
...IT WON'T MATTER ANY-MORE WHETHER YOU'RE MALE OR FEMALE.
THAT WAY...
I THINK...

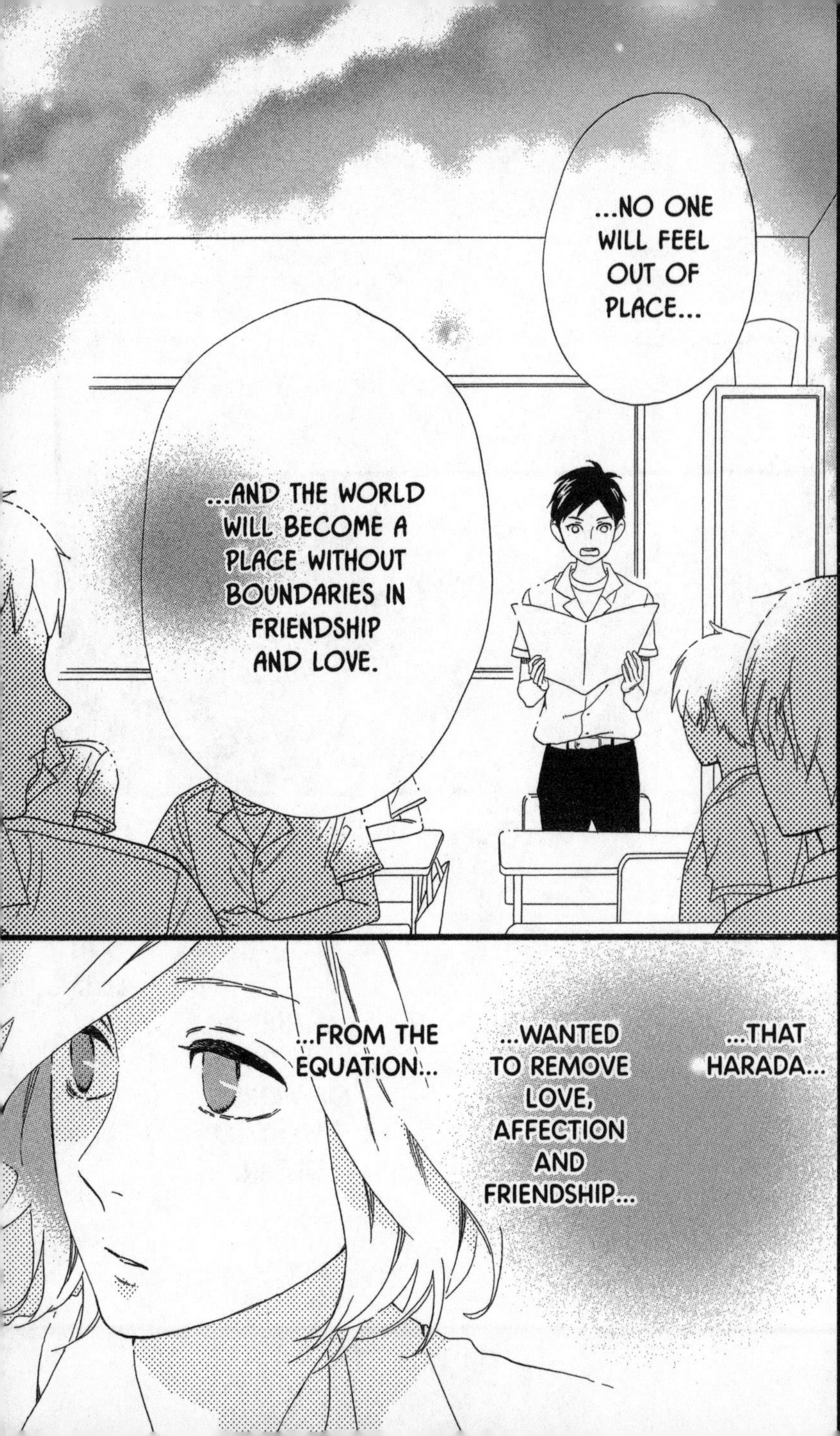
...NO ONE WILL FEEL OUT OF PLACE...
...AND THE WORLD WILL BECOME A PLACE WITHOUT BOUNDARIES IN FRIENDSHIP AND LOVE.
...THAT HARADA...
...WANTED TO REMOVE LOVE, AFFECTION AND FRIENDSHIP...
...FROM THE EQUATION...

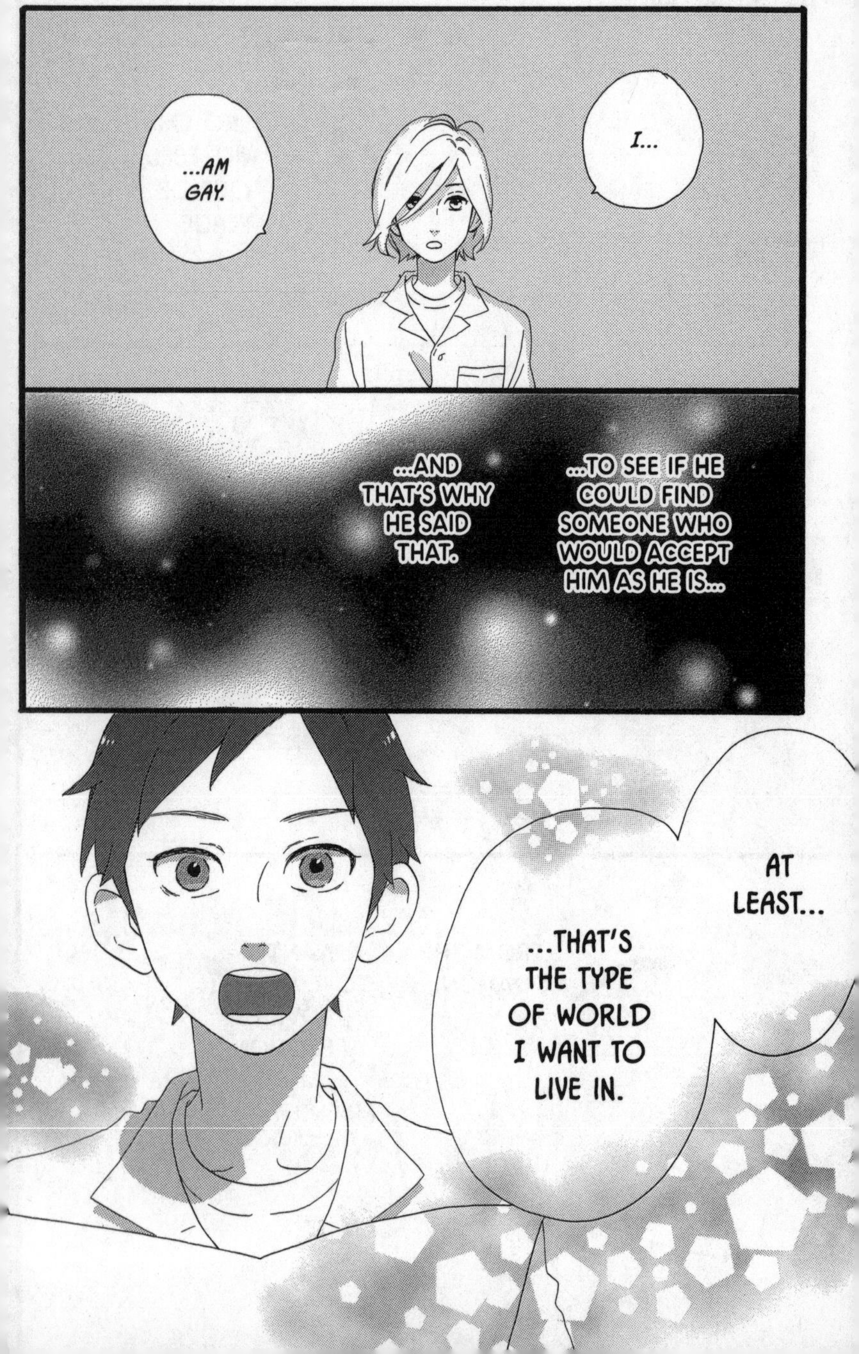
I...
...AM GAY.
...TO SEE IF HE COULD FIND SOMEONE WHO WOULD ACCEPT HIM AS HE IS...
...AND THAT'S WHY HE SAID THAT.
AT LEAST...
...THAT'S THE TYPE OF WORLD I WANT TO LIVE IN.

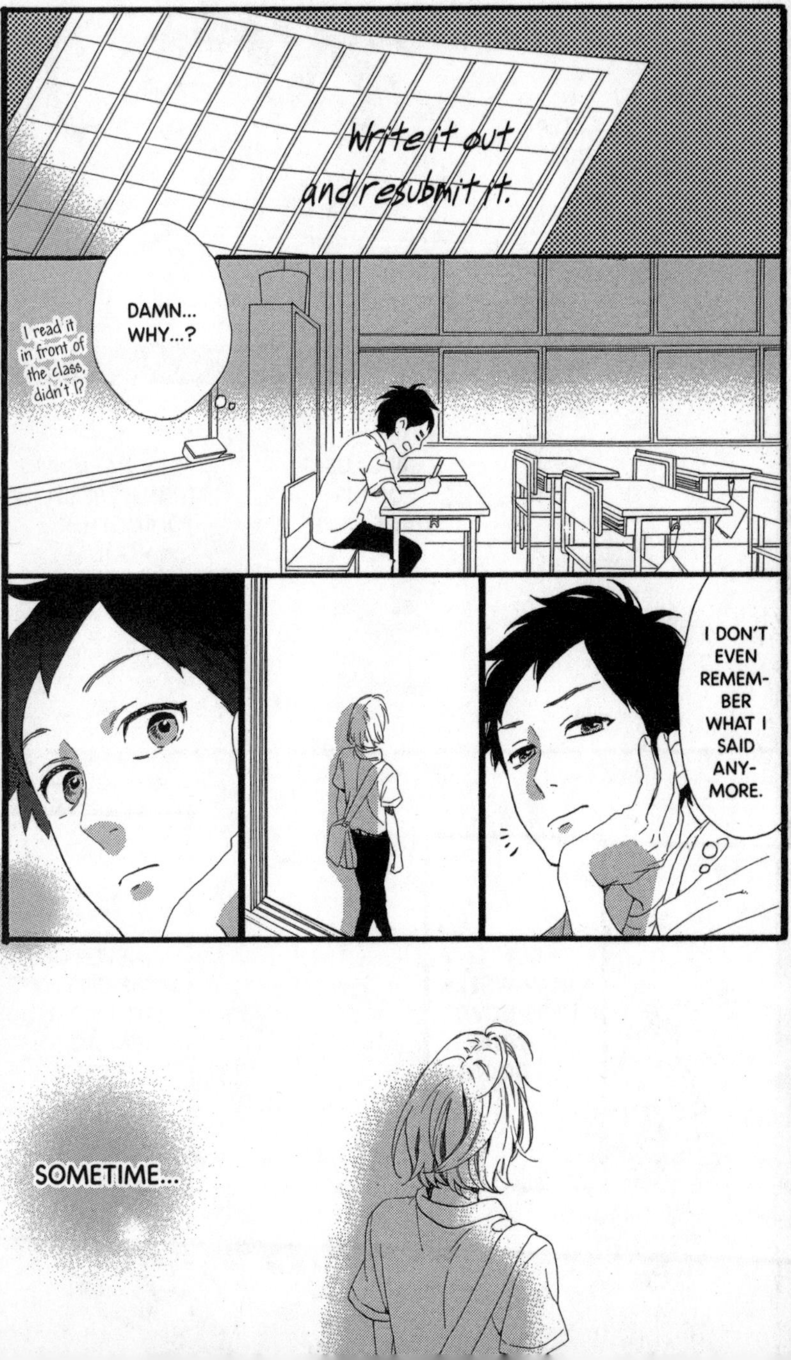
Write it out and resubmit it.
DAMN... WHY...?
I read it in front of the class, didn't I?
I DON'T EVEN REMEMBER WHAT I SAID ANYMORE.
SOMETIME...

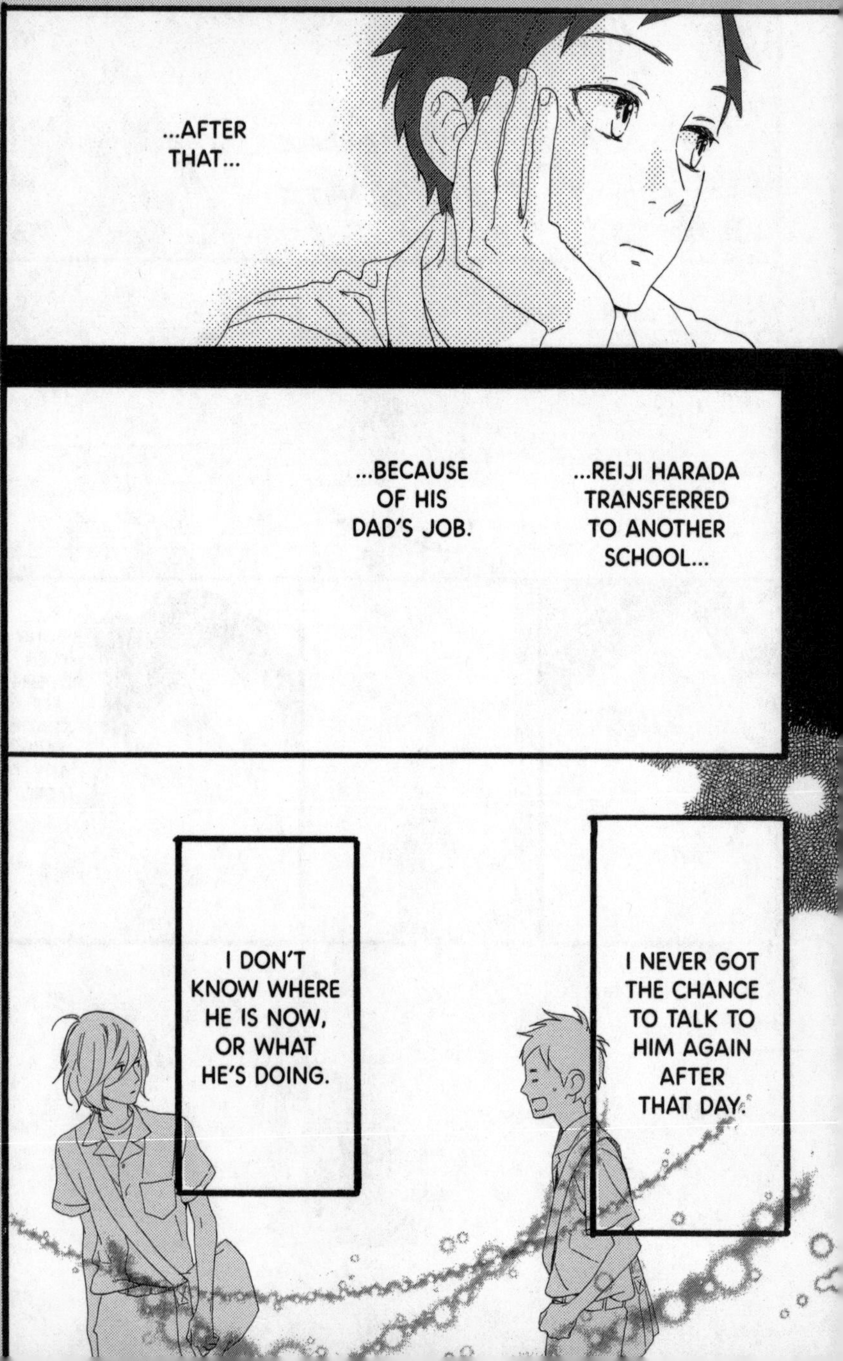
...AFTER THAT...
...REIJI HARADA TRANSFERRED TO ANOTHER SCHOOL...
...BECAUSE OF HIS DAD'S JOB.
I NEVER GOT THE CHANCE TO TALK TO HIM AGAIN AFTER THAT DAY.
I DON'T KNOW WHERE HE IS NOW, OR WHAT HE'S DOING.

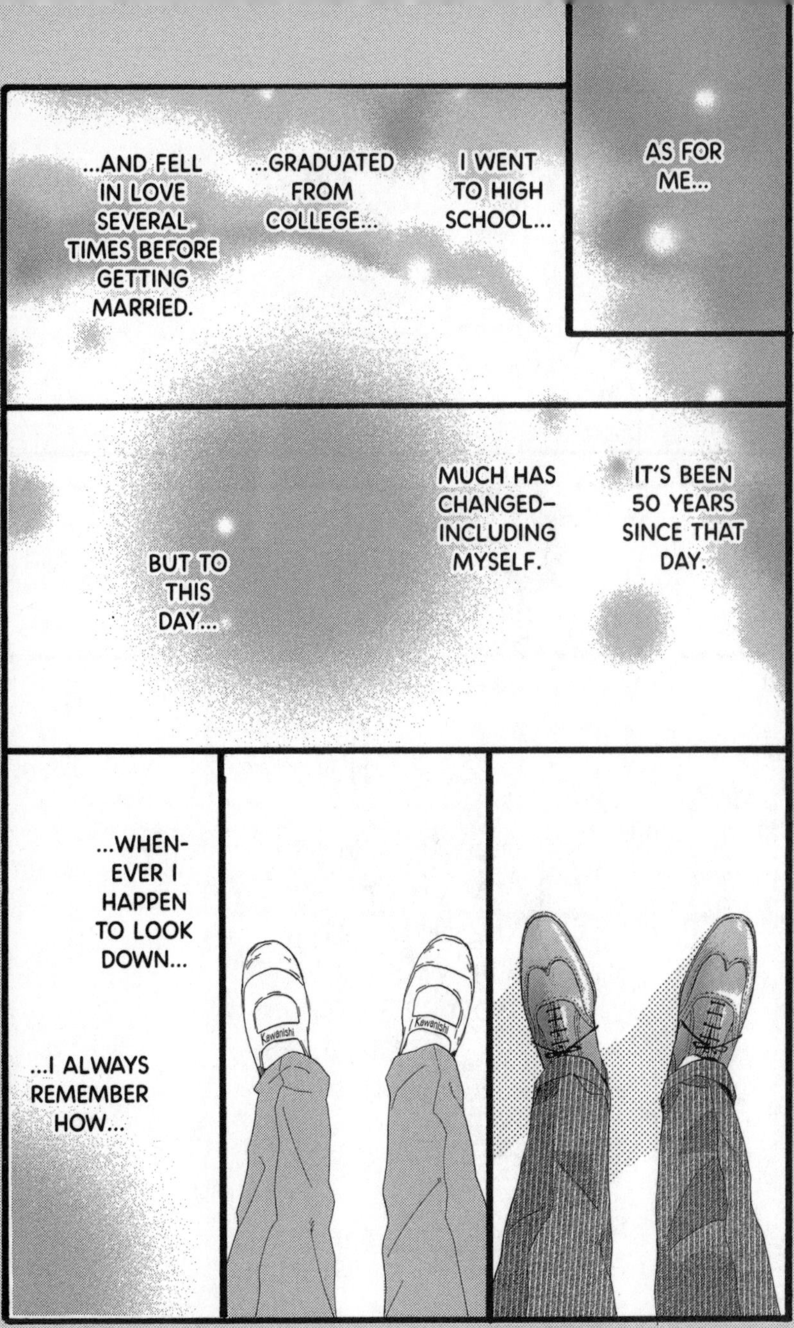
AS FOR ME...
I WENT TO HIGH SCHOOL...
...GRADUATED FROM COLLEGE...
...AND FELL IN LOVE SEVERAL TIMES BEFORE GETTING MARRIED.
IT'S BEEN 50 YEARS SINCE THAT DAY.
MUCH HAS CHANGED—INCLUDING MYSELF.
BUT TO THIS DAY...
Kawanishi
Kawanishi
...WHEN-EVER I HAPPEN TO LOOK DOWN...
...I ALWAYS REMEMBER HOW...

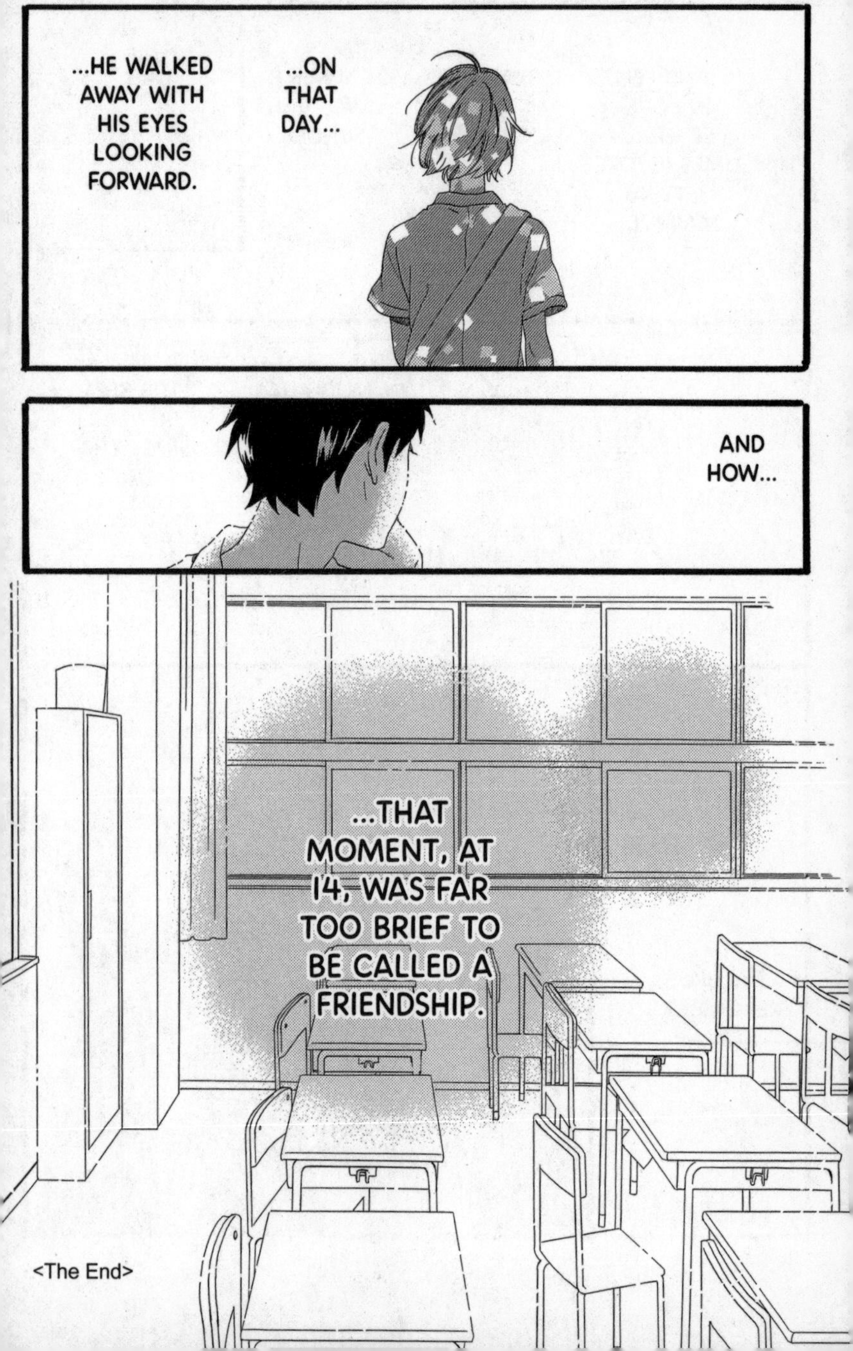
...ON THAT DAY...
...HE WALKED AWAY WITH HIS EYES LOOKING FORWARD.
AND HOW...
...THAT MOMENT, AT 14, WAS FAR TOO BRIEF TO BE CALLED A FRIENDSHIP.
<The End>

Mika Satonaka, known as Naka-yan to me...

...drew an illustration for *Daytime Shooting Star*! Thank you very much!!
Naka-yan and I used to have the same editor. When she was reassigned to someone else, we were both pretty sad about it. (LOL)
As you can tell from her drawing, Naka-yan is a very good person. *Marin to Yuurei* and *Kage Hinata* (original work by Fumika Takeuchi) are chicken soup for my soul. For some reason when I read her manga, I feel inspired to try even harder. If I were to compare her to a confection, I'd say she's like a marshmallow cookie.
And so, I hope you will read *Marin to Yuurei* and *Kage Hinata*. ♫

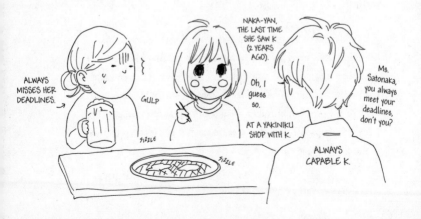

Ms. Satonaka, you always meet your deadlines, don't you?
ALWAYS CAPABLE K.
NAKA-YAN, THE LAST TIME SHE SAW K (2 YEARS AGO).
Oh, I guess so.
AT A YAKINIKU SHOP WITH K.
SIZZLE
SIZZLE
GULP
ALWAYS MISSES HER DEADLINES.

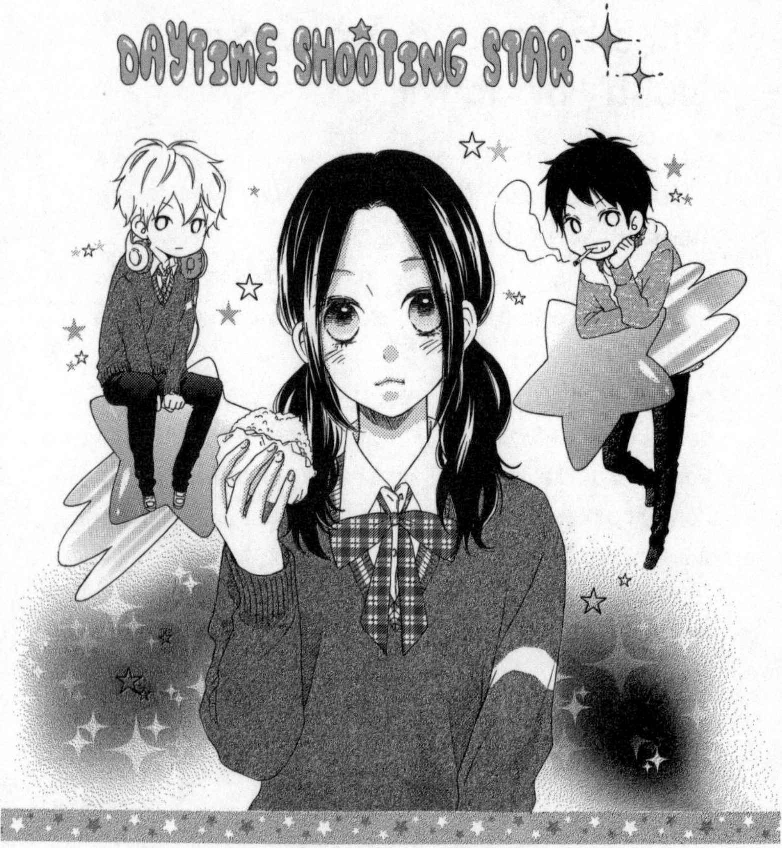
DAYTIME SHOOTING STAR

Hello! I'm sorry for taking up precious space here!! I'm nervous.˜ I initially only intended to draw Suzume. Forgive me, Mori-rin!! *Daytime Shooting Star* is so fantastic that it leaves me in constant agony like Suzume. You want me to choose between Mamura or Shishio...? Why can't I choose them both?! I love them equally!! Mori-rin's pictures are always well done. She has my respect. I will always be a huge fan of her work.✧

Mika Satonaka

And so...

How was it? I hope you enjoyed this volume. I'll see you again in three months!!

☆ Special Thanx ☆

Sanae Kameyama
Sachie Noborio
Nils Machimura
The Print Shop staff
All My Readers!!

Editor U
Designer Kawatani
Members of the Editorial Staff

Send your cards and letters here!
↓↓   ↓↓

Shueisha Margaret Editorial Staff
2-5-10 Hitotsubashi, Chiyoda-ku,
Tokyo 101-8050
Attention: Mika Yamamori

Until next time!

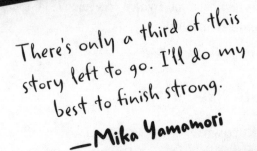

There's only a third of this story left to go. I'll do my best to finish strong.

—Mika Yamamori

Mika Yamamori is from Ishikawa Prefecture in Japan. She began her professional manga career in 2006 with "Kimi no Kuchibiru kara Mahou" (The Magic from Your Lips) in *The Margaret* magazine. Her other works include *Sugars* and *Tsubaki Cho Lonely Planet*.

★DAYTIME★SHOOTING★STAR★ ★9

SHOJO BEAT EDITION

Story & Art by
Mika Yamamori

Translation ★ **JN Productions**
Touch-Up Art & Lettering ★ **Inori Fukuda Trant**
Design ★ **Alice Lewis**
Editor ★ **Karla Clark**

HIRUNAKA NO RYUSEI © 2011 by Mika Yamamori
All rights reserved.
First published in Japan in 2011 by SHUEISHA Inc., Tokyo.
English translation rights arranged by SHUEISHA Inc.

Printed in the U.S.A.

Published by VIZ Media, LLC
P.O. Box 77010
San Francisco, CA 94107

10 9 8 7 6 5 4 3 2 1
First printing, November 2020

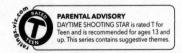

viz.com   shojobeat.com

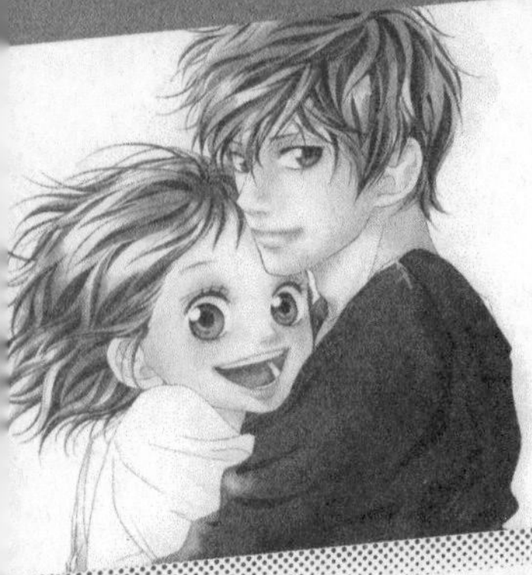

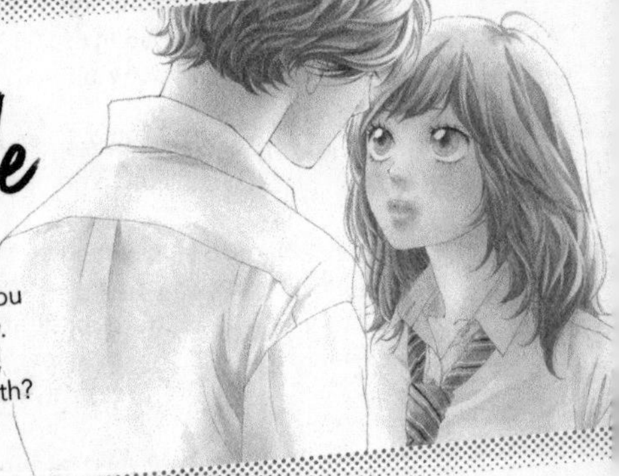

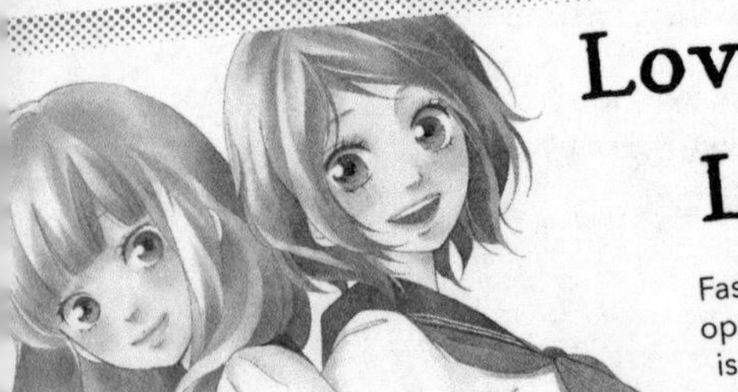

Honey
So Sweet

Story and Art by *Amu Meguro*

Little did Nao Kogure realize back in middle school that when she left an umbrella and a box of bandages in the rain for injured delinquent Taiga Onise that she would meet him again in high school. Nao wants nothing to do with the gruff and frightening Taiga, but he suddenly presents her with a huge bouquet of flowers and asks her to date him—with marriage in mind! Is Taiga really so scary, or is he a sweetheart in disguise?

viz me
viz.com

RATED
T
FOR
TEEN
ratings.viz.com

SHORTCAKE CAKE

STORY AND ART BY
suu Morishita

An unflappable girl and a cast of lovable roommates at a boardinghouse create bonds of friendship and romance!

When Ten moves out of her parents' home in the mountains to live in a boardinghouse, she finds herself becoming fast friends with her male roommates. But can love and romance be far behind?

SHORTCAKE CAKE
1

RATED
T
TEEN